THE UNITED STATES AND CHINA IN THE ERA OF GLOBAL TRANSFORMATIONS

Geographies of Rivalry

Edited by
Salvador Santino F. Regilme Jr

First published in Great Britain in 2025 by

Bristol University Press
University of Bristol
1-9 Old Park Hill
Bristol
BS2 8BB
UK
t: +44 (0)117 374 6645
e: bup-info@bristol.ac.uk

Details of international sales and distribution partners are available at bristoluniversitypress.co.uk

© Bristol University Press 2025

British Library Cataloguing in Publication Data
A catalogue record for this book is available from the British Library

ISBN 978-1-5292-2844-1 hardcover
ISBN 978-1-5292-2845-8 paperback
ISBN 978-1-5292-2846-5 ePub
ISBN 978-1-5292-2847-2 ePdf

The right of Salvador Santino F. Regilme Jr to be identified as editor of this work has been asserted by him in accordance with the Copyright, Designs and Patents Act 1988.

All rights reserved: no part of this publication may be reproduced, stored in a retrieval system, or transmitted in any form or by any means, electronic, mechanical, photocopying, recording, or otherwise without the prior permission of Bristol University Press.

Every reasonable effort has been made to obtain permission to reproduce copyrighted material. If, however, anyone knows of an oversight, please contact the publisher.

The statements and opinions contained within this publication are solely those of the editor and contributors and not of the University of Bristol or Bristol University Press. The University of Bristol and Bristol University Press disclaim responsibility for any injury to persons or property resulting from any material published in this publication.

Bristol University Press works to counter discrimination on grounds of gender, race, disability, age and sexuality.

Cover design: Hayes Design and Advertising
Front cover image: iStock/ tostphoto

Contents

Notes on Contributors   v
Acknowledgments   x

PART I   Introduction, Theory, and the Transnational Sites of Contestations

1   Spatial Imaginaries and Geopolitics in US–China Rivalry   3
Salvador Santino F. Regilme Jr

2   The US, China, and the Implications of Uneven and Combined Development   26
James Parisot and Jake Lin

PART II   Geographies of Rivalry: Spatializing US–China Relations

3   Southeast Asia and the Militarization of the South China Sea   47
Salvador Santino F. Regilme Jr

4   South Asian Contestations and India's Strategic Role: An Advaita Account   73
Deepshikha Shahi

5   Northeast Asia and China's Pursuit of Greatness   97
Jing Sun

6   Africa and US–China Rivalry: Between Webs and Bases   116
Lina Benabdallah

7   Latin America and the Caribbean: How the Belt and Road Initiative Diminished US Influence   138
Juan E. Serrano-Moreno

8   The Middle East and Changing Superpower Relations   160
Chien-Kai Chen and Ceren Ergenc

9   Arctic Interests: How China Is Challenging the US   181
Cameron Carlson and Linda Kiltz

10   Europe's Role in US–China Strategic Competition   206
Richard Maher and Till Schöfer

PART III Conclusions

11   Conclusions: Reframing the Puzzle of US–China Rivalry   233
Salvador Santino F. Regilme Jr

Index   245

Notes on Contributors

Lina Benabdallah is Assistant Professor of Politics and International Affairs at Wake Forest University, USA. She is the author of *Shaping the Future of Power: Knowledge Production and Network-Building in China-Africa Relations* (University of Michigan Press, 2020). Her research has appeared in *International Studies Quarterly, International Studies Reviews, The Journal of International Relations and Development, Third World Quarterly, African Studies Quarterly, Project on Middle East Political Science*, as well as in public facing outlets such as *Foreign Affairs*, the *Washington Post's Monkey Cage*, and *Foreign Policy*. Dr Benabdallah was a Johns Hopkins University China Africa Research Initiative Research Associate, a Senior Associate at the Center for Strategic and International Studies' Africa Program and is a co-editor of *PS: Political Science and Politics*.

Cameron (Cam) Carlson serves as the Dean for the College of Business and Security Management at the University of Alaska Fairbanks, USA. He is the founding director for both the Homeland Security and Emergency Management undergraduate and graduate programs as well as the Director of the Center for Arctic Security and Resilience, where he now serves as the assistant director. He retired as a Lieutenant Colonel from the US Army in 2006 after 25 years on active duty. Dr Carlson has authored and co-authored numerous articles on the Arctic region, specific to defense and human security-related issues as well as homeland security and emergency management education. Additionally, his research has focused on the science of teaching and learning, and online instruction. His ongoing scholarly work includes support for the recently conducted Arctic Security Forces Roundtable, an international senior level defense forum and as the Project Lead/Principal Investigator for the Arctic Defense Security Orientation.

Chien-Kai Chen is Associate Professor of International Studies at Rhodes College, USA. He received his PhD degree in political science from Boston University. Focusing on the region of East Asia, his academic interests bridge international relations and comparative politics. He has been teaching and conducting research on Chinese government and politics, China's foreign policy, comparative political economy of East Asia, China–Taiwan–US relations, and so on. He is the author of *Political Economy of China-Taiwan Relations: Origins and Development* (Lexington Books, 2018), and his articles have appeared in such peer-reviewed journals as *Asian Survey*, *Journal of Contemporary China*, *South Asia Research*, *Journal of Current Chinese Affairs*, *East Asia: An International Quarterly*, *Strategic Review for Southern Africa*, *American Journal of Chinese Studies*, and *International Journal of China Studies*.

Ceren Ergenc is Associate Professor of China Studies at Xi'an Jiaotong-Liverpool University, China. She received her PhD degree in political science from Boston University. Her research interests include local governance, urban politics, and social and industrial policy making with an area focus on, but not limited to, contemporary China and East Asia. Her research includes both qualitative and quantitative methodologies developed based on over a decade of fieldwork. Her research appeared in peer-reviewed journals such as *Territory, Politics and Governance*, *Journal of Chinese Political Science*, and *East Asia*. She is the editor of *ASEAN as Method: Re-centering Processes and Institutions in Contemporary Southeast Asian Regionalism* (Routledge, 2020).

Linda Kiltz is Program Coordinator for the homeland security program in the College of Business and Security Management at the University of Alaska Fairbanks, USA, where she teaches and designs courses in emergency management and homeland security. She has a PhD in Public Administration and Policy from Portland State University. Her research interests are focused on the impacts of climate change on critical infrastructure, particularly food and water systems and human security. She also conducts research on the Scholarship of Teaching and Learning in the fields of emergency management and homeland security. She is an editor of *Critical Issues in Homeland Security: A Casebook* (Routledge, 2014). Her research has appeared in *Homeland Security Affairs Journal*, *Journal of Homeland Security and Emergency Management*, *Journal of Human Security*, and *Journal of Homeland Security Education*. She has over 15 years of experience in higher education designing and teaching courses in public administration, homeland security, emergency management, criminal justice, and nonprofit management. She has over two decades of leadership experience while serving in law enforcement, in the US Army, and in various nonprofit organizations.

Jake Lin is Assistant Professor in the Department of Political Science, University of Texas, USA. He is also an associate fellow in the Faculty of Sociology, Bielefeld University, Germany. He has been the recipient of European Research Council (ERC) Starting Grant fellowship 2019–2021 at Bielefeld University, Japan Society for the Promotion of Science postdoctoral fellowship 2017–2019 at Tokyo University of Foreign Studies, after receiving his PhD in International Relations from Victoria University of Wellington, New Zealand. His current research explores labor migration and social policy reconfiguration in Global China and Vietnam, funded by the ERC Starting Grant 2019–2024. His broader research interests include labor politics and social policy, inequality and capitalism, politics and international relations in China and East Asia. He has published in journals such as *Global Public Policy and Governance*, *Journal of Contemporary Asia*, *International Sociology*, and *Socialism and Democracy*. His most recent book is *Chinese Politics and Labor Movements* (Palgrave, 2019). He is an associate editor of *Journal of Labor & Society*.

Richard Maher is an independent scholar in Daphne, Alabama, USA. Previously he served as Assistant Professor in the School of Politics and International Relations at University College Dublin, Research Fellow in the Robert Schuman Centre for Advanced Studies at the European University Institute, and a Max Weber Postdoctoral Fellow at the European University Institute. His research focuses on European security and defense, the history and theory of European integration, and EU–China relations.

James Parisot is Assistant Professor of Political Science at the University of Texas, USA. He is the co-editor of *American Hegemony and the Rise of Emerging Powers* (Routledge, 2017) and author of the book *How America Became Capitalist: Imperial Expansion and the Conquest of the West* (Pluto, 2019). He has also edited an issue of the *Journal of Historical Sociology* on capitalism and American empire, and is currently working on a book examining the political foundations of US capitalism.

Salvador Santino F. Regilme Jr is a tenured Associate Professor of International Relations based at the International Studies and History section of the Institute of History, Humanities Faculty of Leiden University, the Netherlands. He is the author of *Aid Imperium: United States Foreign Policy and Human Rights in Post-Cold War Southeast Asia* (The University of Michigan Press, 2021), principal co-editor of *Human Rights at Risk: International Institutions, American Power, and the Future of Dignity* (Rutgers University Press, 2022), *American Hegemony and the Rise of Emerging Powers* (Routledge, 2017), and the author of at least 28 peer-reviewed articles in leading social sciences and humanities journals such as *Journal of Global Security Studies*, *Political Geography*, *International Studies Perspectives*, *Third World Quarterly*, *Geoforum*, *International Political Science Review*, and *Human Rights Review*, among many others. He holds a joint PhD in Political Science and North American Studies from the Freie Universität Berlin, and he studied at Yale, Osnabrück, Göttingen, and De La Salle Manila. Before returning to Europe in 2016, he briefly held a tenure track

Assistant Professor in International Relations position at the Department of Political Science at Northern Illinois University. He is the recipient of the 2019 Inaugural Best Conference Paper Award for the Asia-Pacific of the International Studies Association and Honorable Mention for the 2022 Best Scholarly Article Award in Human Rights from the American Sociological Association.

Till Schöfer is a guest lecturer at the Institute for China Studies of the Freie Universität Berlin, Germany. He holds a PhD in Governance from the Hertie School, having previously studied international relations and history at the University of Cambridge, Sciences Po Paris, and the London School of Economics. His research focuses on international trade politics and the foreign policies of emerging economies—primarily Brazil, India, and China. In collaboration with scholars at the University of Maastricht and the Hochschule St. Gallen, he has co-authored a book on the special rights of developing countries in international politics. His work has further been published in *International Affairs* and *Third World Quarterly*.

Juan E. Serrano-Moreno is Assistant Professor at the Institute of International Studies of the University of Chile. He holds a PhD in Political Science from the University Paris I Panthéon-Sorbonne and has taught at various universities in France, Spain, and Chile. He has developed various interdisciplinary research projects on social memory studies, authoritarianism, democratic transitions, and comparative public law. His current research interests comprise China–Latin America relations and Hong Kong´s political system. He is also a founding member of the Association of Spanish Scientists and Researchers in Chile and an attorney member of the Madrid Bar Association.

Deepshikha Shahi is Associate Professor at the O. P. Jindal Global University (JGU), India. She is the Founding Director of the Centre for the Study of Global International Relations at JGU. She likes to perform symptomatological readings of the classical texts to theorise International Relations and to boost transdisciplinary synergies between humanities and social sciences. Her books, *Advaita as a Global International Relations Theory* (Routledge, 2018), *Kautilya and Non-Western IR Theory* (Palgrave Macmillan, 2019), and *Sufism: A Theoretical Intervention in Global International Relations* (Rowman & Littlefield, 2020) employ a series of classical texts to design a "de-centering agenda" in IR that foregrounds the cognitive complementarities between the West and the non-West. Her writings have appeared in the *European Journal of International Relations*, *Cambridge Review of International Affairs*, *Millennium: Journal of International Studies*, *Global Intellectual History*, and *All Azimuth*, among others.

Jing Sun is Professor in the Department of Political Science at the University of Denver, USA. His areas of expertise are Japanese politics, Chinese politics, and East Asian international relations. He is the author of two books: *Red Chamber World Dream: Actors, Audience, and Agendas in Chinese Foreign Policy* (The University of Michigan Press, 2021) and *Japan and China as Charm Rivals: Soft Power in Regional Diplomacy* (The University of Michigan Press, 2012). His articles have appeared in peer-reviewed journals including *Asian Survey*, *Journal of Contemporary China*, *Asia Policy*, *Journal of Japanese Studies*, and *Journal of International Communication*, among others.

Acknowledgments

This edited volume is the outcome of the collaborative efforts of many people. I greatly appreciate colleagues who prepared chapters for this volume. I thank the peer reviewers for their constructive suggestions and insights, which were crucial in improving the manuscript. This project would not be possible without the support of Bristol University Press, especially the acquisitions editor, Stephen Wenham, and his very reliable colleagues. I thank Stephen Wenham for supporting this project and his colleagues, including Zoe Forbes, for their guidance throughout the writing and publication processes. A writing project like this requires research time and institutional support. I thank the Institute for History, Leiden University, for supporting my research leave during the fall/winter semester 2022–2023, while I conducted my research at the Netherlands Institute for Advanced Study (NIAS) in Amsterdam. Many thanks to the Management Team of the Institute for History at Leiden University and the NIAS Amsterdam for supporting my research projects. Andre Gerrits has been a supportive senior colleague and supervisor at Leiden University, and I am thankful for that. Discussions about global transformations at Leiden University, particularly with my students and colleagues in International Relations, provided some good insights about the big questions of contemporary world politics. Many thanks to my students and colleagues at Leiden. Almost 11 years ago, when I was pursuing my PhD in North American Studies and Political Science at the Freie Universität Berlin, I often felt intellectually isolated, which was not entirely unexpected given the nature of my program. As the only person from the Global South in my cohort at the Kennedy Institute's Graduate School of North American Studies and hailing from the Philippines—a former American Commonwealth—I viewed the US from a quite unique perspective, different from that of my German/European/Global North, middle-class peers. With few exceptions, my colleagues seemed certain that American hegemony's problems were domestic or benign, with little interest in anticipating China's rise or interrogating the durability of American hegemony in light of global structural conditions. This was surprising, as history teaches us that great powers come and go, and it is only a matter of time and circumstance before a great power's dominance could be upended. It was unfortunate that the moral and political failures of US power in global governance were not fully interrogated in that intellectual environment in Berlin. The doctoral curriculum did not dedicate substantial attention to the American empire and its powerful reinforcement of racial, gendered, and material inequalities. Instead, the curriculum focused on America's "Manifest Destiny," ignoring the US-led mass violence in the Philippines in the 1900s and the numerous hypocrisies and deaths caused by US foreign policy. It was not until I continued my PhD at Yale, where American empire actively re-emerged in my intellectual thinking, that I began to grapple with these issues, despite the blatant elitism therein. Nonetheless, I am deeply grateful to Lora Viola for her excellent mentorship during my time as a PhD student in Berlin. Her supervision many years ago helped me to think through the big questions of global politics. Immanuel Wallerstein's public lecture at Yale further stimulated my interest in the topic of American decline and global transformation, and the numerous discussions at the MacMillan Center at Yale inspired me to reflect upon the topic of US power. This volume was completed nearly 12 months since the Putin-led regime in Russia launched its war of aggression in Ukraine. It is unclear how the war will evolve, but it is becoming evident that we are entering a world full of many unprecedented challenges, with seemingly catastrophic, if not apocalyptic, consequences. I hope that this book is useful for its many readers, who I assume, are like me struggling to make sense of the recent past in order to understand the present—and, in doing so, prepare for a challenging future.

PART I

Introduction, Theory, and the Transnational Sites of Contestations

1

Spatial Imaginaries and Geopolitics in US–China Rivalry

Salvador Santino F. Regilme Jr

Introduction

Great power rivalry is back once again (Layne 2012; Buzan and Cox 2013; Mearsheimer 2014; Graaff and Van Apeldoorn 2018; Ikenberry 2018a, 2018b; Lake 2018). In the 21st century, post-COVID-19 pandemic world order, China and the US have emerged as the two most powerful state actors, if several quintessential economic, military, and sociocultural indicators are considered. The economic front is indeed an area of great power contestation. According to the World Bank (2022a), while the US in 2021 had the world's largest gross domestic product (GDP; constant 2015 US dollars [USD]) with 20.3 trillion USD, China recorded 15.8 trillion USD. China's enormous economic wealth that it has accumulated over the last few decades, however, has to be shared by the country's 1.4 billion people. China's 2021 GDP per capita (constant USD for 2015) remains remarkably low at 11,188 USD, compared to the US that has 61,280 USD. Notwithstanding, China has overtaken the US as the world's largest manufacturer of products that are then exported to all countries. Consequently, China has the largest percentage share of the world's exports of goods, with 14.7 percent in 2020, while the US only has 8.1 percent (Razo 2021). Nearly 124 countries recorded China as their top trading partner, while the US was recorded as the top exporter in only 56 countries (Arte 2022).

In global financial governance, China challenges US dominance as the former established the Belt and Road Initiative (BRI), the vast rail, land, and sea global network that connects China to a large number of countries in almost all world-regions (Kuo and Kommenda 2018; Nordin and Weissmann 2018; Jones and Zeng 2019). In a bid to stimulate development outcomes elsewhere, China founded the Asian Infrastructure Investment Bank (AIIB), which is a multilateral financial institution that invests in various economic, social, and sustainable development projects in at least 105 member countries (Kubalkova 2015; Babones et al 2020; Lai 2022). China's BRI and AIIB constitute attempts to upstage the Washington DC-based World Bank and the Manila-based Asian Development Bank, both of which predominantly reflect US interests. Because global dominance is largely contingent upon a country's access to key natural resources that are crucial for industrial production and exports, the so-called "rare earths," which refer to 17 soft heavy metals, are necessary in the manufacturing processes of nearly all electrical technologies, lasers, magnetic devices, and many other industrial work-processes (Ferreira and Critelli 2022). On that aspect alone, China possesses nearly 80 percent of the world's rare-earths imports, while the US has 15.5 percent only, thereby making the latter's industrial capacities highly vulnerable to the former's export policies (Subin 2021; Garside 2021).

In the military dimension, the US retains its position as the world's biggest spender on national defense, with a budget pegged at approximately 778 billion USD in 2020 (39 percent of total world military expenditure), while China is positioned in a distant second with 252 billion USD (Zhang 2021). Although the US is widely considered as having the world's most powerful navy with 300 navy ships and 11 aircraft carriers that are highly mobile and strategically positioned in a wide variety of distant territories, China has 360 navy ships and three aircraft carriers. Even in the Asia-Pacific front, where China is expected to claim naval dominance, the US possesses some clear advantages due to Washington DC's control of many military bases strategically located in Japan, South Korea, Taiwan, Brunei, Guam, Singapore, Indonesia, Australia, and several islands in the Pacific (Arte 2022). US military advantage also includes the recently established 2021 AUKUS Agreement, which functions as a trilateral military security treaty between the US, UK, and Australia. The AUKUS agreement allows the US and the UK to provide Australia with nuclear-powered submarines—a collective pact among allies that could be seen by China as Western attempts to undermine Beijing military ambitions in the Asia-Pacific region (Barnes and Makinda 2022; Wilkinson 2022).

In global governance, while the US remains as the key state actor in a large majority of intergovernmental organizations, China has been actively co-operating with Russia in various key voting issues in the UN Security Council (Machaffie 2022). As the world's largest state contributor to UN peacekeeping missions, China commissions 2,500 peacekeepers as of 2019 and contributes a 12 percent share of the total budget of the UN. China, meanwhile, comes second after the US, which is the UN's largest state donor, with contributions valued at 22 percent (CGTN 2020). Meanwhile, in the international development sector, the US is the world's biggest donor of bilateral foreign aid, with nearly 200 recipient countries and territories. China, however, remains in the second position, and the scope and the purposes of Beijing's foreign aid programs are, however, opaque to public scrutiny (Regilme 2021; Regilme and Hodzi 2021).

In those aforementioned arenas of great power contestation, China's increasing assertiveness is not the only challenge to US dominance; rather, domestic political crises constrain the sustainability of American hegemony (Regilme 2019). Over the last two decades, the US has struggled to resolve multiple transnational crises: transnational non-state terrorism, the 2007/2008 global financial crisis, climate change, the COVID-19 pandemic, as well as the deep political polarization that crippled the government's legitimacy and effectiveness in addressing domestic and global problems such as extreme material inequities, economic insecurity, systemic racism, and gender inequality (Bieler and Morton 2018; McCoy and Somer 2019; Regilme 2020, 2021; Theidon 2020; Zaidi 2021; Albert 2022; Liodakis 2022; Mandelbaum 2022). In response to the 9/11 terror attacks, the US, under the Bush administration, launched its so-called global war on terror, which poured in billions of dollars on militaristic policy strategies that eventually generated widespread human rights abuses—rather than primarily investing in socioeconomic programs that could have uplifted the most marginalized communities within and outside the US (Kutz 2014; Sanders 2017; Regilme 2018a, 2018b; Moyn 2021). Amid the 2007 global financial crisis, the US government provided hefty billion-dollar bailouts to corporate behemoths, while the socioeconomic welfare of the many minoritized groups remained at the bottom of the policy agenda (Helleiner 2011; Blyth 2013a, 2013b). In such crises, the legitimacy and effectiveness of the US as a model for governance have been called into question. The unparalleled US military power appeared to be ineffective in delivering its intended outcomes of fostering peace and economic development in many places in the Global South, where America's violent interventions persisted—including Afghanistan and Iraq. Despite being the world's largest economy in terms of GDP, the US, with its model of neoliberal governance, has been unable to respond effectively to the socioeconomic needs of its most marginalized communities (World Bank 2022b).

During the COVID-19 pandemic, the Trump administration systematically discarded the need for intensified multilateral cooperation for the sake of global public health, while thousands of Americans died amid Trump's disregard for scientific expertise and indifference toward the dignity and health of his constituents (Gramer 2021; Regilme 2022a, 2022b; Sandlin 2022). In an effort to clean up the mess of his predecessor, US President Joseph Biden has sought to intensify US contributions to global governance, reinvigorate his country's economic development, and effectively manage the COVID-19 pandemic (Regilme 2022a, 2022b). Yet, the Biden administration's commitment to sell democratic governance—as the legitimating discourse of US global dominance—both to his domestic constituents and the rest of the world has proven to be difficult. While nearly six in ten surveyed American respondents confirmed that US democracy is in deep trouble and at the risk of collapse (Rose and Baker 2022), global public opinion in 2021 confirmed that 56 percent in 17 Global North countries that are constitutional democracies expressed their discontent with how their political systems were unable to deliver economic growth, demonstrate managerial competence, and foster fairness in the distribution of material wealth (Wike and Fetterolf 2021). Overall, those global and domestic problems faced by the US in the last two decades illustrate the difficulties of maintaining the country's hegemonic status in the international system.

Amid the perception of the tarnished moral appeal of the US as a global power, China has re-emerged as one of the most powerful state actors that could credibly challenge the dominance of the US (and its Western allies) in the post-Cold War international system. Among the re-emerging powers such as India, Russia, and Brazil, China is perhaps the only country that demonstrates the ambition and potential to enhance its military capabilities, economic influence, and social legitimacy in ways that could constrain US influence in many places worldwide. China has become the world's largest manufacturing country and biggest exporter of economic goods, while bolstering its global military apparatus and influence in global governance institutions (Murphy 2022). The Chinese state's ability to deliver rapid economic growth in just a short period of time has been remarkable. After opening up its economy to world trade in the late 1970s, China's economic growth averaged at least 10 percent a year and nearly a billion people escaped extreme poverty—an achievement that is often attributed to Beijing's long-term technocratic planning. Even during the COVID-19 pandemic in 2021, China nonetheless registered 8.1 percent growth—a remarkable rate that is more than twice the rate of economic growth of the US and its Western European allies (Tan 2022). With those remarkable economic success, the Chinese state has been determined in converting that economic power into military might. In 2022, the Chinese Ministry of Finance confirmed a remarkable increase of 7.1 percent in military spending, which is estimated at around 230 billion USD (Cheng 2022)—a rate that is much higher than the 6 percent average in recent years but still remarkably low compared to US military spending of at least 778 billion USD in 2022 (SIPRI 2022). Notwithstanding, China is betting on the potential of innovative and revolutionary technologies such as autonomous systems, quantum, cyber, and biological instruments in a way that could undermine US dominance in the Indo-Pacific region (Horowitz and Kahn 2021).

If indeed the post-Second World War global order faces an accelerated pace of profound global transformation, what is, in theoretical terms, meant by global transformation or shift? In its broadest terms, global shift pertains to "the transformative, transitionary, aggregate, and multidimensional processes whereby a state, or a group of states, actively and strategically challenges the dominant power position of a status quo global hegemon or a leading group of states" (Regilme and Hartmann 2019: 1). There are so many notable ways in which the US—the status quo global power—faces significant challenges that could threaten its fundamental interest of maintaining its dominant power position. In Europe, Putin's militaristic aggressions in Ukraine since early 2022 have intensified the threat of a full-scale, enduring, and extremely devastating war that could spill over to other parts of Europe and beyond—a possibility that could challenge US power in this particular geographical front. In the Asia-Pacific, China's relentless construction and militarization of artificial islands in the disputed South China Sea enables Beijing some significant control in this important maritime route, which more than 60 percent of global trade passes through (Mai and Zheng 2017; Zhang 2017; Ramadhani 2019). Beijing's intensified militaristic showmanship and rhetorical threats of invasion of Taiwan undermine the sustainability of US military dominance, which is underpinned by its treaty alliances with Japan, the Philippines, South Korea, and Thailand, strategic partnerships with Malaysia, Vietnam, and Singapore, as well as a panoply of military bases worldwide (Yeo 2011; Regilme 2022a). While the Biden presidency is committed to providing military aid to Ukraine in a bid to defend US interests in Europe, Beijing has been busy in entrapping traditional US allies in Asia within China's sphere of influence—a pattern demonstrated, for example, by the shift of Thailand's military junta toward Beijing and the Philippines' Duterte presidency amidst its unprecedented support for China's leadership in the region (Chachavalpongpun 2011; Jory 2014; Busbarat 2016, 2017; Pongsudhirak 2016).

Theorizing the puzzle of US–China rivalry

Considering the global context as described in the previous section, this book raises the following core questions: How is great power rivalry and cooperation formed, contested, and transformed across various territorial spaces and geographic scales in the international system? How and why do those patterns of contestations and cooperation manifest and vary in different regions of the world? Both questions constitute the puzzle of US–China rivalry in the era of 21st-century global transformation.

That puzzle was formulated with three global-structural conditions that must be considered in analyzing US–China rivalry. First, the post-Second World War international system is entering a global interregnum. While US hegemony appears to be receding, China has emerged as the world's largest manufacturing country, and its military and political influence are expanding beyond its immediate regional security environments (Arrighi 2007; Wallerstein 2009; Go 2011; Lachmann 2014; Mearsheimer 2014; Chase-Dunn and Podobnik 2015; Brooks and Wohlforth 2016; Chase-Dunn and Friedman 2016; Regilme and Parisot 2017; Schwarzer 2017; Ho-Fung 2018; Regilme 2019; Zaidi 2021; Murphy 2022; Thompson 2022). Both the US and China are the two most powerful yet rivalrous state actors in the international system, even amidst the ongoing COVID-19 pandemic and the seemingly imminent inflation crisis that is hitting Global South and North countries alike. Second, the exact features and conditions of such a great power contestation vary across geographic spaces because each physical space of contestation possesses a unique constellation of actors, institutions, sociocultural factors, economic resources, and historically bounded beliefs that shape, enable, and constrain the processes and trajectory of US–China relations (Cheng and Liu 2021; Maya and Urdinez 2022; Murphy 2022; Schindler and DiCarlo 2022). Third, the ideational and normative foundations of the Western-dominated liberal international order are in deep crisis, while unjust distributive politics has fueled discontent and resentment among the most marginalized sectors of the world's populations (Regilme 2014, 2019; Ikenberry 2018a; Elliott 2019; Babic 2020; Barnett 2020; Oxfam 2020). Systemic hypocrisy—or the mismatch between ideational claims for leadership and actual practices—does not match the actual series of actions of powerful state actors. The US has consistently demonstrated its systemic hypocrisy through its persistent invocation of human rights and democracy promotion, but it has always failed to do so in favor of militarism and unfettered capital accumulation (Acharya 2007; Moyn 2021). China, on the other hand, claims to be focusing on the socioeconomic rights and collective interests of its population. Yet, Beijing's policies have persistently generated the curtailment of civil and political rights in favor of perpetually empowering the very top leaders in Beijing and their allies, while the unprecedented economic growth has also generated remarkable material inequalities across the Chinese society (Inboden and Chen 2012; Kinzelbach 2014; Inboden 2015; Peyrouse 2022; Üngör 2022). In both countries, and nearly all parts of the globe, capitalism is credited for improving the lives of millions of people, yet that same political-economic system is also blamed for extreme inequalities, political polarization, and growing resentment against state institutions (Robinson 2014; Fraser 2015; Mickey et al 2017; Cárdenas-García et al 2021; Gunderson 2022; Liodakis 2022).

Unfortunately, many previous scholarly studies on global transformations and great power contestations often deploy mainstream theories of International Relations (IR), without a nuanced empirical analysis that explicitly teases out the relationship between geographic space and great power contestations (Doshi 2021; Bergsten 2022; Economy 2022;

Friedberg 2022; Rudd 2022). As Sjoberg (2008: 484–485) compellingly maintains, "the tenets of political realism (international anarchy as a foundational assumption), political liberalism (cooperation for gains), and political constructivism (the influence of ideas) are necessary but insufficient to understand and explain global politics"; specifically, "they are missing sufficiently complicated understandings of process and of the relationship between the social and the physical." Hence, this volume offers an alternative approach. Specifically, this book upholds that great power rivalry vary across different geographical spaces and scales, and it seriously considers geographical spatial imaginary to be contingent on social relations that are produced within a particular territory, historical period, and political system (Murdoch and Marsden 1995; Sjoberg 2008; Jessop 2012; Watkins 2015).

Focusing on great power rivalries of 21st century, this book considers spatialization as a key conceptual tool for understanding socio-ideational and material processes and their relationship with geographical physical space (Lefebvre 1991: 26–27; Sjoberg 2008). This book situates the scholarly analysis of the US–China rivalry within the intersections of physical geography, social relations, and global politics from several disciplinary, methodological, and analytic perspectives from various world-regions. In this way, the book offers a truly global yet multiscalar examination of global transformation in the 21st century. This analytic objective responds to recent calls for a more fruitful conversation between Global IR theory and area studies, which allows for a more rigorous probing of mainstream approaches as well as the innovation of new theoretical perspectives that were developed in light of empirical evidence from various parts of the world (Acharya 2014; Regilme 2021; Dian 2022). Indeed, spatialization enables us to make more insightful, theoretically innovative, and evidence-based analysis than the often universalizing and Eurocentric discussion of US–China rivalry. How is that even possible? By asking IR theorists who are also experts of specific world-regions, this book upholds a Global IR approach. As Acharya explains (Acharya 2014: 649), Global IR pertains to the analytic desire that:

- is committed to pluralistic universalism, which recognizes the diversity in political communities;
- is based in world histories, and not just Euro-American historical experiences;
- incorporates and engages with current IR theories and approaches;
- utilizes the evidence and theoretical perspectives from area studies, regions, and distinctive areas of the world;
- disregards exceptionalism; and
- upholds the manifold manifestations of political agency in addition to material power, such as resistance, collective actions, and localized visions of global order.

Beyond the general US–China rivalry debate, recent scholarship that upholds features of Global IR has emerged, and offers innovative theoretical insights that meaningfully contribute to broader puzzles of world politics (for example, Lee 2017; Getachew 2019; Benabdallah 2020; Regilme 2021; Zarakol 2022).

As such, the chapters herein demonstrate that global power shifts and systemic transformations should be theorized and empirically investigated by examining how political contestations are constrained, enabled, and bounded within a given temporal period, material space or geographic place, and social relations. In this way, this volume upholds a scalar and place-based approach to the analysis of US–China rivalry, thereby highlighting the links between intersubjective relations and geographical features that constitute and produce a wide range of repeated as well as dynamic political processes (Sjoberg 2008: 489). This anthology provides a multifaceted and spatially oriented analysis of how China's re-emergence as a global power impacts the dominance of the US as well as the domestic state and non-state actors in various world-regions, including the Asia-Pacific, Africa, South America and the Caribbean, the Middle East, Europe, and the Arctic. This volume offers the core argument that the great power rivalry between the US and China must be examined by considering the many geographic scales at which it is generated, imagined, enacted, and transformed. The volume analyzes the 21st-century's great power rivalry's multiple and, at times, divergent scalar and spatial expressions.

This collaborative project distinguishes itself from current scholarly and policy debates on global governance and global transformations in several ways. First, it highlights the patterns of rivalry as well as cooperation between China and the US, as they manifest in distinctive territorial spaces and varying geographical scales of the contemporary international system. Second, the edited volume showcases the careful deployment of relevant theoretical perspectives to understand a given empirical puzzle emanating from a particular geographical space and scale, thereby demonstrating theoretical pluralism and diversity as well as analytic eclecticism in its approach. Third, departing from popular discussions on global shifts that usually focus on state actors and geostrategic as well as economic issues, the scope of chapters herein illustrate topical diversity, in a way that features issues beyond those that directly concern military security and economics, particularly by considering the underappreciated roles of non-state actors and civil society groups.

State of knowledge: US–China rivalry

This rivalry between the world's two most powerful states has often been characterized in mainstream scholarly and public debates in ways that do not seriously consider how great power rivalry has varying causes and consequences across different world-regions and territorial spaces. This edited volume reflects on how and under which conditions does the US–China competition (and cooperation) vary across regions and territorial spaces and what such variations actually mean for the prospects of war and peace, global cooperation, and human welfare. In the anthology *China's Challenges and International Order Transition* (Feng and He, 2020), the editors interrogated China's external security, political, and economic challenges and their dynamic relationship with the deployment of power, rules, and norms. While the volume by Feng and He (2020) provides an insightful reflection on whether China challenges the current global order, the chapter contributions therein did not fully investigate *how* the China's foreign policy initiatives varied across many parts of the world. Meanwhile, the anthology titled *US–China Foreign Relations* (Ross et al 2020) aimed to investigate the consequences of China's rise on the US, Europe, and Asia, but the book did not adopt a multidisciplinary approach, while it failed to cover other regions of the world in its analysis, notably Asia, the Middle East, and the Arctic (see also similar examples: Doshi 2021; Hass 2021; Bergsten 2022; Vinodan and Kurian 2022). In addition, Dawn Murphy's (2022) *China's Rise in the Global South* is a perceptive account of re-emerging powers' impact in many places in the non-Western world, but that monograph did not cover Southeast Asia, in a way that this book does. Other recently published volumes, however, focus on China as just of one of the other rising powers or as a case study for broadly theorizing great power competition (Nadkarni and Noonan 2013; Thies and Nieman 2017; Regilme and Parisot 2017; Xuetong 2019; Schoen 2020). During the COVID-19 pandemic, however, other re-emerging powers, such as Russia, India, and South Africa, have demonstrated their notable structural weaknesses and limited capabilities in ways that made China appear to be more comparatively resilient and the most credible challenger state of US hegemony. Other recent monographs, meanwhile, focused only on one geographic space of contestation: the case of US–China rivalry in several arenas such as Taiwan (Chen 2017), Thailand (Zawacki 2021), the broader Indo-Pacific Region (Chan 2013; Goldstein 2015), Europe (Ross et al 2020), the global order as whole (Allison 2017), or global finance as an imagined space (Fok 2021). Those aforementioned works, while insightful, did not take a global perspective that compares patterns of contestations across geographic regions.

Other recently published edited volumes pertaining to contemporary China in world politics are analytically innovative, but this book remains distinctive from those outputs. For example, the two volumes, *The China Questions* and *The China Questions 2* (Carrai et al 2019), offer a comprehensive overview of the contemporary US–China bilateral relations and their impacts in world politics. Yet, those two volumes heavily focus on the domestic and foreign politics of China on a thematic policy basis rather than explicitly highlighting how such bilateral dynamics differ across various regions of the world, as it is demonstrated through a spatialization analytic frame as deployed in this volume. Another example is *China and the World* (Shambaugh 2020), which is another notable analysis of US–China relations, but that output does not analytically focus on geographic differentiation of such bilateral power dynamics, as this volume does (see also Thurnston 2021).

While various single-author books and several edited volumes cover some of the issues addressed in this book, none of them combine both the empirical scope *and* analytic ambitions of this project. This anthology provides a much-needed eclectic forum for examining US–China rivalry through a variety of disciplinary and theoretical perspectives as well as spatially oriented analyses, thereby making it possible to develop theoretically informed and empirically rich perspectives of the issue that are so crucially needed.

This volume demonstrates topical diversity and one of the few studies on US–China rivalry that explicitly theorizes on *geographic space* and *spatialization* as the core analytic frames for investigating the multifaceted expressions of global power transitions and transformations in the 21st century. The volume emerges out of frustration at the narrow scope of existing work on the topic, whereby so much of the influential scholarship deploys mainstream theories of IR without an explicit theorization and empirical analysis of the role of geographic space and its material as well as ideational-social dimensions. Additionally, this anthology features chapter contributions by a diverse range of established and emerging scholars, coming from a wide variety of institutional affiliations (located in the Global South and the Global North) and disciplinary perspectives (humanities, social sciences, and public policy), thereby enabling opportunities to situate the book in multiple scholarly, disciplinary, and political conversations. Remarkably, the volume features one chapter focusing on the African continent and one chapter about the Arctic region, considering that both geographical spaces are often discarded and misunderstood in mainstream IR literature as well as public debates on global transformations and US–China rivalry.

Summary of chapters

The organizational logic of the book is divided into three main sections. Part I of the book highlights the broader analytic issues and theoretical perspectives pertaining to the rivalry and cooperation between the US and China. In addition to this introductory chapter, Part I features the political economy-oriented chapter written by sociologist James Parisot and political scientist Jake Lin. The two authors take the perspectives of political geography and international relations as a way of investigating how the scholarly debates on uneven and combined development help us reflect on the implications of

US–China rivalry in a world underwritten by global capitalist logics. Parisot and Lin contend that economic development instigated by the rise of China and US hegemony should be understood by highlighting the agential roles of exploitative transnational capitalists and the world's working populations—an analytic strategy that overcomes the analytic limitations of mainstream IR literature's state-centrism. This insightful chapter suggests that the debate about US–China rivalry should not be about choosing which hegemon is "better" for world politics; rather, our discourses should refocus instead on democratizing world politics through the intensified inclusion of working-class interests in the formation of domestic and foreign policies.

Part II, on the other hand, features chapters that focus on US–China bilateral relations in various world-regions. Through the deployment of spatialization, these chapters demonstrate the distinctive geographies of US–China bilateral relations, particularly in ways that differ from the often-simplistic characterizations of great power competition offered by international media outlets and mainstream IR theorists.

Chapter 3 focuses on the Southeast Asian region as a geographic site of rivalry between the US and China. I ask why the claimant states in the South China Sea dispute, especially China, have recently increased militarization activities and public diplomacy efforts, particularly in unprecedented ways that were relatively absent in the previous decades. The chapter focuses on the increased militaristic and public diplomacy assertiveness of Beijing and its impact on Washington's strategic interests in the Southeast Asian region. I underscore three notable findings. First, the confluence of China's economic growth in recent decades vis-à-vis the domestic power struggle within the regime of Xi Jinping likely amplified enduring Chinese insecurity. Thus, it highlights Beijing's increased strategic resolve to militarize the disputed South China Sea region, which is fast becoming a spatial site of great power competition between the US and China. Second, Southeast Asian countries' foreign policies and domestic public perception of US power in the region suggest stronger support for continued US military and political assertiveness under the Biden presidency. Third, the chapter calls for smaller claimant states (for example, Philippines, Brunei, Indonesia, Malaysia, Taiwan, and Vietnam) to cooperate with each other and use multilateral bodies to call for a more peaceful resolution of the dispute.

Focusing on South Asia, IR scholar Deepshikha Shahi acknowledges the complexity of international relations as sets of multiple practices with diverse actors as well as multifarious patterns of competition and cooperation. Understanding US–China relations in South Asia requires the analytic departure from traditional Western realism, which considers the sphere of "the international" as governed by dualisms and oppositions. In Chapter 4, Shahi deploys the non-dualistic Global IR theory inspired by the Indian philosophy of Advaita to evaluate India's strategic response to the ongoing

US-China competition in the South Asian region. In doing so, Shahi offers six fundamental principles of Advaita in order to tease out the complexities of contemporary quadrilateral interactions of non-state and state actors between India, Pakistan, China, and the US in the imagined geographical space of South Asia. Shahi highlights the diverse realities of such interactions, in ways that traditional IR theory failed to appreciate; those realities experienced by actors in South Asia, however, are still bounded to the same core reality—that of *single hidden connectedness*, or the holistic interdependence of global politics.

Focusing on the East Asian region, meanwhile, political scientist Jing Sun underscores in Chapter 5 how physical geography has shaped China's quest for great power status and what such a quest means for other state actors, particularly the US. This sense of geography functions as a useful social construct that is relevant for framing Chinese national identity and security in ways that are instrumental to the state. Jing Sun underscores a spectrum view of *tianxia* (All under Heaven) as a spatial-positioning idea, which includes accommodation and domination on opposite sides of the range. The author introduces *tianxia* as a Chinese philosophical concept that imagines a utopian world with a benevolent and effective leader positioned between Heaven and Earth, ruling one's subjects through the mandate of Heaven. As such, Jing Sun explains that *tianxia* functions both as spatial concept and moral instrument that are used to explain and justify the supposedly harmonious and cooperative spatial and normative positionings of all living beings on land. China's rapid and dramatic economic growth, and its consequential accumulation of political influence, poses a challenge to the traditionally land-based conception or interpretation of *tianxia*. To further reinforce its economic growth, Beijing seeks to secure its control over its nearby maritime regions, thereby facilitating the necessity to reframing the idea of *tianxia* as a way of legitimizing its overreaching maritime claims that have been persistently disputed by other neighboring states. This conceptual reframing emerges as a useful discursive technique that bolsters Chinese leaders' domestic political motivations of resurrecting sensibilities of Chinese greatness, or also known as the "Chinese Dream." Yet, this recent reframing of justificatory narratives of Chinese ascendancy and influence in the maritime region generated fear and insecurity among less militarily powerful states in the Northeast Asian region. Moreover, China's maritime expansion consequently challenges the enduring dominance of US military power in those aforementioned regions. As such, the US recalibrated its security strategy in the region, thereby pushing the White House to rebrand its expanded militarism in the region as part of its "Indo-Pacific" strategy. Jing Sun emphasizes that this geography-inspired contestation between two powerful states is besieged with uncertainties, and that conflict could undermine the relative stability in the Northeast Asian region. Competing Chinese political actors deploy alternative interpretations of *tianxia*, whereby the more China's geographical positioning is emphasized, the more assertive one's discursive construction of China's global aspiration would become. In this regard, the regime of Xi Jinping has been justifying its rapid maritime expansion and militaristic activities through the invoked shift of *tianxia* from land to maritime regions. Consequently, this intensified militarization of disputed maritime regions such as the South China Sea facilitated the emergence of militarization by, and insecurity among, regional neighbors and also the increased securitization by the US.

Analyzing US–China relations in the African region, political scientist Lina Benabdallah commences her investigation by acknowledging the broader context that the US–China rivalry has spilled over beyond the officially recognized borders of both states. In her innovative approach to analyzing Chinese power abroad, Benabdallah contends that our understanding of Beijing's influence in Africa should transcend the simplistic counting of the number of ports, bridges, and other infrastructure projects built by Chinese enterprises and funded by Beijing. Alternatively, the author focuses the investigation on party-to-party diplomacy as a site of China's foreign policy making in Africa, whereby a relational approach is deployed in order to tease out the mechanisms or instruments of social and human capital as well as professional network-building opportunities. Benabdallah highlights the fundamental difference between the US and China in their foreign policy approaches in Africa: whereas US state leaders primarily invest in counterterrorism initiatives with their African counterparts, China focuses on building relations and social capital with elites, government officials, and civil servants. China's approach is indeed remarkable, considering that Benabdallah acknowledges how scholars of relationality and *guanxi* maintain that investments in deepening and expanding personal as well as professional networks between Chinese and African elites are crucial to uncovering the advantages and weaknesses of Chinese influence in Africa. Benabdallah provides empirical evidence on how Chinese influence is generated through the creation of social exchange platforms as well as training opportunities that eventually serve as elite capture mechanisms.

In Chapter 7, legal scholar and IR analyst Juan E. Serrano-Moreno focuses on the ongoing US–China relations in Latin American and Caribbean countries. Specifically, Serrano-Moreno claims that the participation of many states in the BRI illustrates how China has been seeking to fill the apparent void left by the US presence in its traditional sphere of influence. The author contends that the BRI serves as an ambiguous and flexible cooperation platform for initiating investments, infrastructure projects, and trade transactions with China. Serrano-Moreno argues that it is unclear if the BRI has beneficial effects for the people in the region, but it does have concrete diplomatic advantages for Beijing. Through a critical examination of the relevant literatures and official documents pertaining to the BRI, the author highlights two key factors for the initiative's success. First, the BRI offers partner governments to choose or craft their degree of involvement with Chinese actors. Second, the BRI reinforces the rhetoric of regional connectedness, and that initiative addresses the enduring infrastructural deficits in the region. For Serrano-Moreno, the BRI can also be considered as a discursive strategy that frames China as a benevolent and equal partner in the region through its insistence that it is part of the semi-periphery in the modern capitalist world-system.

In Chapter 8, IR scholars Chien-Kai Chen and Ceren Ergenc explore contemporary US and Chinese foreign policies in the Middle East, particularly the structural conditions upon which those policies are produced, implemented, and eventually changed. In promoting their interests, including oil extraction as a way of fulfilling energy needs, Beijing and Washington DC adopt differing policy approaches. Whereas Beijing is less assertive and non-interventionist, the US adopts a more militaristic, blatantly assertive, and interventionist strategy. In their analysis, the authors use the concept of "path dependence" from the historical institutionalist literature, which pertains to the patterns of reproducing and constraining consequences of the decisions and actions made in the past on the outcomes that are currently being produced and those that will be generated in the future. Using a scalar and place-based approach, the authors examine how repeated dialogical interactions between the actors from the US, China, and the Middle East have created and sustained varying "paths" that the US and China have been traversing in the region in terms of foreign policy. In addition, the chapter discusses how the US withdrawal from Afghanistan in 2021 could shape a new political-economic climate in the region and a new "critical juncture" or opportunity for China to shift from its non-interventionist path toward more involvement and assertiveness in regional security issues.

In Chapter 9, security and defense studies scholars Cameron Carlson and Linda Kiltz investigates US–China relations in region that is perhaps the least studied by many scholars—the Arctic region. Carlson and Kiltz begins with a contested geographical frontier as an ideal backdrop where one could analyze inter-state relations. The authors maintain that the Arctic Council and its constituent member states are legitimate Arctic actors, with significant geographical claims and long-standing relationships with the Arctic as a contested region. The Council is composed of eight member states, including Sweden, the US, Denmark, Finland, Norway, Iceland, Canada, and Russia. Each of those member states has claimed sovereignty over the lands within the Arctic region and have had single decision-making authority over policies therein. Yet, China has presented itself as "near-Arctic state," even though the country is remarkably distant and thousands of miles away from the nearest Arctic territorial region. Carlson and Kiltz advance the claim that China views the Arctic as a new strategic frontier with its seabed and space construed as ungoverned or under-governed public areas. The authors underscore evidence that Chinese military pronouncements admit that the "great powers" are in a position to contest other states' territorial claims over global public spaces such as the Arctic. While the Arctic Council does not deal directly with policy issues concerning military security, an opportunity for China to reinforce its interests in the Arctic could emerge, while the rest of the traditional Arctic states might be preoccupied with other foreign policy issues elsewhere.

In the final empirical chapter, governance and IR scholars Richard Maher and Till Schöfer examine contemporary Europe, which, they claim, is neither the core site nor the quintessential prize of US–China competition. Although the important flashpoints of great power rivalry could be in the Asia-Pacific region, both the US and China consider Europe as a foremost strategic partner, and Europe indeed has served as an increasingly contested space for economic competition between the two powerful states. Maher and Schöfer uses the case study of Huawei's presence in Europe's fifth generation (5G) wireless networks in extrapolating important insights about US–China competition in Europe. In doing so, the authors find three key findings. First, Europeans' desire to deepen their economic relationship with China stands in conflict with their enduring dependence on the US for defense and security guarantees. Second, Western European countries are unlikely to stand in blatant opposition against China despite the apparent convergence of views between the US and Europe. Third, despite internal conflicts within Europe, which in turn could prevent it from emerging as a cohesive actor in US–China rivalry, Europe is likely to retain its capacity to influence the dynamics of its immediate region, oppose US and Chinese demands, and perhaps shape US–China competition elsewhere in some ways.

The aforementioned chapters illustrate the multiple and spatially contingent expressions of US–China rivalry in the 21st century. Some chapters focus on disputing claims of ownership on geographic regions (South China Sea and the Arctic), while others focus on economic affairs, social capital, discourses, and the weaponization of international institutions. Taken as a whole, the perspective developed by bringing these analyses together, I hope, is something bigger and more useful than each taken individually. Hence, the chapters illustrate the careful use of theoretical and analytic frameworks to understand the evidence from a particular region, which enables the contributor to illustrate accurately the particular expression of US–China rivalry that is bounded within a particular geographic space, temporal condition, and social context. I do not claim that this anthology successfully completes the task of bringing perspectives from political geography in the key theoretical debates in IR pertaining to US–China rivalry. I do, however, hope that this anthology inspires other scholars to be mindful of the analytic advantages and possibilities of using spatialization as well as other concepts from political geography in our analyses of global transformations and great power rivalry.

References

Acharya, A. 2007. "State Sovereignty after 9/11: Disorganised Hypocrisy." *Political Studies* 55(2): 274–296.

Acharya, A. 2014. "Global International Relations (IR) and Regional Worlds." *International Studies Quarterly* 58(4): 647–659.

Albert, M. 2022. "COVID-19 and the Planetary Crisis Multiplicity: From Marxist Crisis Theory to Planetary Assemblage Theory." *Theory & Event* 25(2): 332–363.

Allison, G. 2017. *Destined for War: Can America and China Escape Thucydides's Trap?* Boston: Houghton Mifflin Harcourt.

Arrighi, G. 2007. *Adam Smith in Beijing: Lineages of the Twenty-First Century*. London: Verso.

Arte. 2022. *USA vs China: Mapping the World*. https://www.youtube.com/watch?v=sdlFiFmQ_SM

Babic, M. 2020. "Let's Talk about the Interregnum: Gramsci and the Crisis of the Liberal World Order." *International Affairs* 96(3): 767–786.

Babones, S., Åberg, J. and Hodzi, O. 2020. "China's Role in Global Development Finance: China Challenge or Business as Usual?" *Global Policy* 11(3): 326–335.

Barnes, J. and Makinda, S. 2022. "Testing the Limits of International Society? Trust, AUKUS and Indo-Pacific Security." *International Affairs* 98(4): 1307–1325.

Barnett, M. 2020. "COVID-19 and the Sacrificial International Order." *International Organization* 74(S1): E128–147.

Benabdallah, L. 2020. *Shaping the Future of Power: Knowledge Production and Network-Building in China–Africa Relations*. Ann Arbor: University of Michigan Press.

Bergsten, C.F. 2022. *The United States vs. China: The Quest for Global Economic Leadership*. Cambridge: Polity Press.

Bieler, A. and Morton, A. 2018. *Global Capitalism, Global War, Global Crisis*. New York: Cambridge University Press.

Blyth, M. 2013a. *Austerity: The History of a Dangerous Idea*. New York: Oxford University Press.

Blyth, M. 2013b. "Paradigms and Paradox: The Politics of Economic Ideas in Two Moments of Crisis." *Governance: An International Journal of Policy, Administration, and Institutions* 26(2): 197–215.

Brooks, S.G. and Wohlforth, W. 2016. "The Rise and Fall of the Great Powers in the Twenty-First Century: China's Rise and the Fate of America's Global Position." *International Security* 40(3): 7–53.

Busbarat, P. 2016. "'Bamboo Swirling in the Wind': Thailand's Foreign Policy Imbalance between China and the United States." *Contemporary Southeast Asia* 38(2): 233–237.

Busbarat, P. 2017. "Thai–US Relations in the Post-Cold War Era: Untying the Special Relationship." *Asian Security* 13(3): 256–274.

Buzan, B. and Cox, M. 2013. "China and the US: Comparable Cases of 'Peaceful Rise'?" *The Chinese Journal of International Politics* 6(2): 109–132.

Cárdenas-García, J.F., Soria De Mesa, B., and Castro, D. 2021. "Capitalism Has No Clothes: The Unexpected Shock of the COVID-19 Pandemic." *Perspectives on Global Development and Technology* 19(5–6): 545–564.

Carrai, M.A., Rudolph, J., and Szonyi, M. (eds). 2019. *The China Questions: Critical Insights into a Rising Power*. Cambridge, MA: Harvard University Press.

CGTN. 2020. "China and UN in Graphics: A Contributor to World Peace." https://news.cgtn.com/news/2020-09-18/China-and-UN-in-graphics-A-contributor-to-world-peace-TPwjeqR1cs/index.html

Chachavalpongpun, P. 2011. "Competing Diplomacies: Thailand amidst Sino-American Rivalry." *Southeast Asian Affairs*: 306–319.

Chan, S. 2013. *Looking for Balance: China, the United States, and Power Balancing in East Asia*. Palo Alto: Stanford University Press.

Chase-Dunn, C. and Podobnik, B. 2015. "The Next World War: World-System Cycles and Trends." *Journal of World-Systems Research* 1(1): 349–380.

Chase-Dunn, C. and Friedman, J. 2016. *Hegemonic Decline*. New York: Routledge.

Chen, D.P. 2017. *US–China Rivalry and Taiwan's Mainland Policy: Security, Nationalism, and the 1992 Consensus*. Heidelberg: Springer.

Cheng, E. 2022. "China Will Raise Defense Spending by 7.1% in 2022, Faster than Last Year." *CNBC*, March 4. https://www.cnbc.com/2022/03/05/china-defense-spending-to-rise-by-7point1percent-in-2022-says-finance-ministry.html

Cheng, H. and Liu, W. 2021. "Disciplinary Geopolitics and the Rise of International Development Studies in China." *Political Geography* 89: 102452.

Dian, M. 2022. "The Rise of China between Global IR and Area Studies: An Agenda for Cooperation." *Italian Political Science Review/Rivista Italiana di Scienza Politica* 52(2): 252–267.

Doshi, R. 2021. *The Long Game: China's Grand Strategy to Displace American Order*. New York: Oxford University Press.

Economy, E. 2022. *The World According to China*. London: Polity Press.

Elliott, L. 2019. "World's 26 Richest People Own as Much as Poorest 50%, Says Oxfam." *The Guardian*.

Feng, H. and He, K. 2020. *China's Challenges and International Order Transition: Beyond "Thucydides's Trap."* Ann Arbor: University of Michigan Press.

Ferreira, G. and Critelli, J. 2022. "China's Global Monopoly on Rare-Earth Elements." *The US Army War College Quarterly: Parameters* 52(1): 57–72.

Fok, J. 2021. *Financial Cold War: A View of Sino-US Relations from the Financial Markets*. Hoboken: John Wiley & Sons.

Fraser, N. 2015. "Legitimation Crisis? On the Political Contradictions of Financialized Capitalism." *Critical Historical Studies* 2(2): 157–189.

Friedberg, Aaron. 2022. *Getting China Wrong*. London: Polity Press.

Garside, M. 2021. "U.S. Rare Earths Global Production Share 2021." *Statista 2022*. https://www.statista.com/statistics/1294394/share-of-global-rare-earths-production-in-the-united-states/

Getachew, A. 2019. *Worldmaking after Empire: The Rise and Fall of Self-Determination*. Princeton: Princeton University Press.

Go, J. 2011. *Patterns of Empire*. New York: Cambridge University Press.

Goldstein, L. 2015. *Meeting China Halfway: How to Defuse the Emerging US–China Rivalry*. Washington, DC: Georgetown University Press.

Graaff, N. and Van Apeldoorn, B. 2018. "US–China Relations and the Liberal World Order: Contending Elites, Colliding Visions?" *International Affairs* 94(1): 113–131.

Gramer, R. 2021. "Trump Mounts Last-Minute Attempt to Starve Funding for Foreign Aid, Global Vaccine Efforts." *Foreign Policy*. https://foreignpolicy.com/2021/01/15/trump-last-minute-cut-funding-foreign-aid-vaccines-diplomacy-rescission-billions-congress-biden-transition/#

Gunderson, J.R. 2022. "When Does Income Inequality Cause Polarization?" *British Journal of Political Science* 52(3): 1315–1332.

Hass, R. 2021. *Stronger: Adapting America's China Strategy in an Age of Competitive Interdependence*. New Haven: Yale University Press.

Helleiner, E. 2011. "Understanding the 2007–2008 Global Financial Crisis: Lessons for Scholars of International Political Economy." *Annual Review of Political Science* 14(1): 67–87.

Ho-Fung, H. 2018. "Global Capitalism in the Age of Trump." *Contexts* 17(3): 40–45.

Horowitz, M. and Kahn, L. 2021. "DoD's 2021 China Military Power Report: How Advances in AI and Emerging Technologies Will Shape China's Military." *Council of Foreign Relations*, November 4. https://www.cfr.org/blog/dods-2021-china-military-power-report-how-advances-ai-and-emerging-technologies-will-shape

Ikenberry, G.J. 2018a. "The End of Liberal International Order?" *International Affairs* 94(1): 7–23.

Ikenberry, G.J. 2018b. "Why the Liberal World Order Will Survive." *Ethics and International Affairs*: 1–13.

Inboden, R.S. 2015. "The EU's Human Rights Dialogue with China: Quiet Diplomacy and Its Limits/China's Human Rights Lawyers: Advocacy and Resistance." *Cambridge Review of International Affairs* 28(3): 514–516.

Inboden, R.S. and Chen, T. 2012. "China's Response to International Normative Pressure: The Case of Human Rights." *The International Spectator* 47(2): 45–57.

Jessop, B. 2012. *Cultural Political Economy, Spatial Imaginaries, Regional Economic Dynamics*. Lancaster University CPERC Working Paper Series. https://www.lancaster.ac.uk/cperc/docs/Jessop%20CPERC%20Working%20Paper%202012-02.pdf

Jones, L. and Zeng, J. 2019. "Understanding China's 'Belt and Road Initiative': Beyond 'Grand Strategy' to a State Transformation Analysis." *Third World Quarterly*: 1–28.

Jory, P. 2014. "China Is a Big Winner from Thailand's Coup." *East Asia Forum*. http://www.eastasiaforum.org/2014/06/18/china-is-a-big-winner-from-thailands-coup/

Kinzelbach, K. 2014. *The EU's Human Rights Dialogue with China*. New York: Routledge.

Kubalkova, P.G. 2015. "Asian Infrastructure Investment Bank." *China Quarterly of International Strategic Studies* 1(4): 667–685.

Kuo, L. and Kommenda, N. 2018. "What Is China's Belt and Road Initiative?" *The Guardian*, July 30. https://www.theguardian.com/cities/ng-interactive/2018/jul/30/what-china-belt-road-initiative-silk-road-explainer

Kutz, C. 2014. "How Norms Die: Torture and Assassination in American Security Policy." *Ethics & International Affairs* 28(4): 425–449.

Lachmann, R. 2014. "The United States in Decline." *Political Power and Social Theory* 26.

Lai, C. 2022. "If It Is Not Socialisation, Then What? China's Institutional Statecraft in the Asian Infrastructure Investment Bank." *China: An International Journal* 20(3): 1–22.

Lake, D.A. 2018. "Economic Openness and Great Power Competition: Lessons for China and the United States." *The Chinese Journal of International Politics* 11(3): 237–270.

Layne, C. 2012. "This Time It's Real: The End of Unipolarity and the Pax Americana." *International Studies Quarterly* 56(1): 203–213.

Lee, C.K. 2017. *The Spectre of Global China: Politics, Labor, and Foreign Investment in Africa*. Chicago: University of Chicago Press.

Lefebvre, H. 1991. *The Production of Space*. Translated by D. Nicholson-Smith. Oxford: Blackwell.

Liodakis, G. 2022. "The Imperative Transformation beyond the Capitalism Pandemic." *Perspectives on Global Development and Technology* 20(5–6): 478–491.

Machaffie, J.P. 2022. "Russian–Chinese Cooperation at the United Nations Security Council: Costly Signalling and Trust Building in the Strategic Partnership." *China Report* 58(4): 431–447.

Mai, J. and Zheng, S. 2017. "Xi Personally behind Tough Stance on South China Sea Dispute." *South China Morning Post*, July 28. http://www.scmp.com/news/china/policies-politics/article/2104547/xi-personally-behind-island-building-south-china-sea

Mandelbaum, M. 2022. *The Four Ages of American Foreign Policy*. New York: Oxford University Press.

Maya, J.C.G. and Urdinez, F. 2022. "Geopolitics and Geoeconomics in the China–Latin American Relations in the Context of the US–China Trade War and the COVID-19 Pandemic." *Journal of Current Chinese Affairs* 51(1): 3–12.

McCoy, J. and Somer, M. 2019. "Toward a Theory of Pernicious Polarization and How It Harms Democracies: Comparative Evidence and Possible Remedies." *The ANNALS of the American Academy of Political and Social Science* 681(1): 234–271.

Mearsheimer, J.J. 2014. "Can China Rise Peacefully?" http://www.eastlaw.net/wp-content/uploads/2016/09/Can-China-Rise-Peacefully_-_-The-National-Interest.pdf

Mickey, R., Levitsky, R., and Way, L.A. 2017. "Is America Still Safe for Democracy? Why the United States Is In Danger of Backsliding." *Foreign Affairs* 96: 20–29.

Moyn, S. 2021. *Humane: How the United States Abandoned Peace and Reinvented War*. New York: Farrar, Straus & Giroux.

Murdoch, J. and Marsden, T. 1995. "The Spatialization of Politics: Local and National Actor-Spaces in Environmental Conflict." *Transactions of the Institute of British Geographers* 20: 368–380.

Murphy, D. 2022. *China's Rise in the Global South: The Middle East, Africa, and Beijing's Alternative World Order*. Palo Alto: Stanford University Press.

Nadkarni, V. and Noonan, N.C. (eds). 2013. *Emerging Powers in a Comparative Perspective: The Political and Economic Rise of the BRIC Countries*. London: Bloomsbury Publishing.

Nordin, A.H.M. and Weissmann, M. 2018. "Will Trump Make China Great Again? The Belt and Road Initiative and International Order." *International Affairs* 94(2): 231–249.

Oxfam. 2020. *Time to Care: Unpaid and Underpaid Care Work and the Global Inequality Crisis*. Oxford: Oxfam International. https://oxfamilibrary.openrepository.com/bitstream/handle/10546/620928/bp-time-to-care-inequality-200120-en.pdf

Peyrouse, S. 2022. "China's Impact on Democracy and Human Rights in Central Asia." *Security and Human Rights*: 1–16.

Pongsudhirak, T. 2016. "An Unaligned Alliance: Thailand–U.S. Relations in the Early 21st Century." *Asian Politics & Policy* 8(1): 63–74.

Ramadhani, E. 2019. "Is Assertiveness Paying the Bill? China's Domestic Audience Costs in the South China Sea Disputes." *Journal of Asian Security and International Affairs* 6(1): 30–54.

Razo, C. 2021. "Evolution of the World's 25 Top Trading Nations." *UNCTAD*. https://unctad.org/topic/trade-analysis/chart-10-may-2021

Regilme, S.S.F. 2014. "Bringing the Global Political Economy Back In: Neoliberalism, Globalization, and Democratic Consolidation." *International Studies Perspectives* 15(3): 277–296.

Regilme, S.S.F. 2018a. "A Human Rights Tragedy: Strategic Localization of US Foreign Policy in Colombia." *International Relations* 32(3): 343–365.

Regilme, S.S.F. 2018b. "Does US Foreign Aid Undermine Human Rights? The 'Thaksinification' of the War on Terror Discourses and the Human Rights Crisis in Thailand, 2001 to 2006." *Human Rights Review* 19(1): 73–95.

Regilme, S.S.F. 2019. "The Decline of American Power and Donald Trump: Reflections on Human Rights, Neoliberalism, and the World Order." *Geoforum* 102: 157–166.

Regilme, S.S.F. 2020. "COVID-19: Human Dignity under Siege amidst Multiple Crises." *E-International Relations*. https://www.e-ir.info/pdf/85067

Regilme, S.S.F. 2021. *Aid Imperium, United States Foreign Policy and Human Rights in Post-Cold War Southeast Asia*. Ann Arbor: University of Michigan Press.

Regilme, S.S.F. 2022a. "Aid Imperium, United States Foreign Policy and Human Rights in Post-Cold War Southeast Asia." *The Diplomat*. https://thediplomat.com/2022/03/americas-aid-imperium-and-human-rights-in-southeast-asia/

Regilme, S.S.F. 2022b. "United States Foreign Aid and Multilateralism Under the Trump Presidency." *New Global Studies*. https://doi.org/10.1515/ngs-2021-0030

Regilme, S.S.F. and Hartmann, H.S. 2019. "Global Shift." In S. Romaniuk, M. Thapa, and P. Marton (eds) *The Palgrave Encyclopedia of Global Security Studies*. Cham: Palgrave, pp 1–5.

Regilme, S.S.F. and Hodzi, O. 2021. "Comparing US and Chinese Foreign Aid in the Era of Rising Powers." *The International Spectator* 56(2): 114–131.

Regilme, S.S.F. and Parisot, J. (eds). 2017. *American Hegemony and the Rise of Emerging Powers: Cooperation or Conflict*. London: Routledge.

Robinson, W.I. 2014. *Global Capitalism and the Crisis of Humanity*. New York: Cambridge University Press.

Rose, J. and Baker, L. (2022) "6 in 10 Americans say U.S. Democracy is in Crisis as the 'Big Lie' Takes Root." *NPR*, January 3. https://www.npr.org/2022/01/03/1069764164/american-democracy-poll-jan-6

Ross, R., Tunsjø, Ø. and Wang, D. (eds). 2020. *US–China Foreign Relations: Power Transition and its Implications for Europe and Asia*. London: Routledge.

Rudd, K. 2022. *The Avoidable War: The Dangers of a Catastrophic Conflict between the US and Xi Jinping's China*. New York: Public Affairs.

Sanders, R. 2017. "Human Rights Abuses at the Limits of the Law: Legal Instabilities and Vulnerabilities in the 'Global War on Terror'." *Review of International Studies* 44(1): 1–22.

Sandlin, E.W. 2022. "The Trump Administration Versus Human Rights: Executive Agency or Policy Inertia?" *Human Rights Review* 23: 1–27.

Schindler, S. and DiCarlo, J. 2022. "Towards a Critical Geopolitics of China–US Rivalry: Pericentricity, Regional Conflicts and Transnational Connections." *Area*.

Schwarzer, D. 2017. "Europe, the End of the West and Global Power Shifts." *Global Policy* 8(S4): 18–26.

Schoen, D. 2020. *The End of Democracy?: Russia and China on the Rise, America in Retreat*. New York: Simon & Schuster.

Shambaugh, D. (ed). 2020. *China and the World*. New York: Oxford University Press.

SIPRI. 2022. "Military Spending by Country 2022." *World Population Review*, April 15. https://worldpopulationreview.com/country-rankings/military-spending-by-country

Sjoberg, L. 2008. "Scaling IR Theory: Geography's Contribution to Where IR Takes Place." *International Studies Review* 10(3): 472–500.

Subin, S. 2021. "The New US Plan to Rival China's Dominance in Rare Earth Metals." *CNBC*, April 17. https://www.cnbc.com/2021/04/17/the-new-us-plan-to-rival-chinas-dominance-in-rare-earth-metals.html

Tan, C.K. 2022. "China GDP Growth Slows to 4.0% in Q4 amid COVID, Property Woes." *Nikkei Asia*, January 17. https://asia.nikkei.com/Economy/China-GDP-growth-slows-to-4.0-in-Q4-amid-COVID-property-woes

Theidon, K. 2020. "A Forecasted Failure: Intersectionality, COVID-19, and the Perfect Storm." *Journal of Human Rights* 19(5): 528–536.

Thies, C.G. and Nieman, M.D. 2017. *Rising Powers and Foreign Policy Revisionism: Understanding BRICS Identity and Behavior through Time*. Ann Arobor: University of Michigan Press.

Thompson, W.R. 2022. *American Global Pre-Eminence*. New York: Oxford University Press.

Thurnston, A. (ed). 2021. *Engaging China: Fifty Years of Sino-American Relations*. New York: Columbia University Press.

Üngör, Ç. 2022. "A 'Human Rights' of Our Own? Chinese and Turkish Encounters with a Western Concept." *Diogenes*. https://doi.org/10.1177/03921921221103717

Vinodan, C. and Kurian, A.L. 2022. *US–China Relations in the 21st Century*. Abingdon: Routledge.

Wallerstein, I. 2009. "The Eagle Has Crash Landed." *Foreign Policy*, November 11. https://foreignpolicy.com/2009/11/11/the-eagle-has-crash-landed/

Watkins, J. 2015. "Spatial Imaginaries Research in Geography: Synergies, Tensions, and New Directions." *Geography Compass* 9(9): 508–522.

Wike, R. and Fetterolf, J. 2021. "Global Public Opinion in an Era of Democratic Anxiety." *Pew Research*, December 7. https://www.pewresearch.org/global/2021/12/07/global-public-opinion-in-an-era-of-democratic-anxiety/

Wilkinson, T. 2022. "Is AUKUS Really an 'Alliance'?" *Melbourne Asia Review* 9. https://melbourneasiareview.edu.au/is-aukus-really-an-alliance/

World Bank. 2022a. *Data for China and the United States*. https://data.worldbank.org/?locations=CN-US

World Bank. 2022b. *GDP for China*. https://data.worldbank.org/indicator/NY.GDP.MKTP.CD?most_recent_value_desc=true

Xuetong, Y. 2019. *Leadership and the Rise of Great Powers*. Princeton: Princeton University Press.

Yeo, A. 2011. *Activists, Alliances, and Anti-U.S. Base Protests*. New York: Cambridge University Press.

Zaidi, S.M.S. 2021. "American Global Supremacy Under Threat? The Chinese Factor." *Politics & Policy* 49(2): 502–528.

Zarakol, A. 2022. *Before the West: The Rise and Fall of Eastern World Orders*. Cambridge: Cambridge University Press.

Zawacki, B. 2021. *Thailand: Shifting Ground Between the US and a Rising China*. London: Bloomsbury.

Zhang, F. 2017. "Assessing China's Response to the South China Sea Arbitration Ruling." *Australian Journal of International Affairs* 71(4): 440–459.

Zhang, Z. 2021. "Explainer: US-China Rivalry: Who Has the Stronger Military?" *South China Morning Post*. https://www.scmp.com/news/china/military/article/3140681/us-china-rivalry-who-has-stronger-military

2

The US, China, and the Implications of Uneven and Combined Development

James Parisot and Jake Lin

This chapter responds to the theme of "geographies of rivalry" and international relations by exploring the implications of recent debates over uneven and combined development (U&CD) for the US and China within global capitalism. On one hand, the two powers remain deeply economically interlinked. On the other, recent discussions of, for instance, a "new Cold War" have brought to light tensions between the two world powers. Thus, this chapter asks two major questions. First, what can a U&CD perspective help us understand about global politics and world power? Second, how can this help us make sense of the complex intertangles between the US and China?

In recent years, a wide variety of studies have begun to explore the implications of the critical idea of U&CD for explaining the dynamics of global power. Justin Rosenberg, in particular, has been developing it as a framework for making sense of international relations from a perspective engaging with Marxism (Rosenberg 1996, 2009, 2013, 2019).[1] At the same time, this perspective has been criticized for, perhaps, trying to do more than it can. In this regard, the first section of this chapter examines this debate, suggesting that while the concept of U&CD can play a key role in framing questions of global power, its uses are limited, as it is a helpful concept, not a comprehensive approach or theory.

Second, this chapter uses this concept to explore questions of the US, China, and their geographics of conflict. Beginning with an overview of the political economy of the US, the chapter suggests that U&CD is useful for developing a narrative of the rise of American world dominance and its possible contemporary decline, and the uneven dynamics of this question. This framework makes it possible to link together the ways capitalist class power and neoliberalism intersect with the dynamics of U&CD globally as class relations are shaped both by forces within states, and by movements on uneven and multilayered international scales. That being said, the argument presented here also notes the limits of a U&CD approach, as it is a useful tool within a broader framework but limited as an overall approach to making sense of global power relations.

Following this, the chapter examines the rise of China and the contemporary dynamics of the Chinese political economy. First, it briefly discusses China's uneven pathways toward capitalist development, which were concomitantly driven by other great powers under global capitalism. After this, through a global lens, it looks at the ways in which the uneven development of US and Chinese power have shaped tension and conflict between the powers. Lastly, we conclude by raising the question of the democratization of US–China relations and the future of global capitalism.

The concept of uneven and combined development

Going back especially to Rosenberg's attempt to begin to expand on Trotsky's idea of U&CD in the 1990s, recent years have seen a revival of engagements with U&CD as a framework to make sense of "the international" in history (Rosenberg 1996). It has formed, in many regards, as a reaction to perspectives on international relations that neglect a way of explaining how "the international" is one of many spatial scales of world politics. In simple terms, scholars using a U&CD approach have employed it as an alternative to perceived problematic limits of other perspectives. Realists, for instance, tend to view states as "black boxes," competing for power and survival on the global stage. Liberals, by contrast, have tended to emphasize the way that a liberal international order has held states together, controlling and regulating the potential for global conflict and war. Meanwhile, constructivists, from another perspective, have highlighted the ideational aspects of world power. While realism is helpful for understanding potential sources of international conflict and violence, liberalism helps explain why states cooperate in global capitalism, and constructivism provides a space to think about the role of ideas in world politics, each risks becoming ahistorical, without social content. U&CD is a starting point for solving this problem, and for building a historical sociology of international relations (or, perhaps, a historical sociology that can bridge the levels of the domestic and the international) (Rosenberg 2006).

The premises of the approach go back to Trotsky, most significantly, although not exclusively, in *The History of the Russian Revolution*, first published in Germany in 1930 (Trotsky 1980). For the author, the "peculiarities" of

Russia were determined not by "internal" or "external" factors alone—within borders or outside them—but by the place of Russia in the broader contours of world history as shaped by both localized and international forces. In what he called the "privilege of historical backwardness," less advanced countries were forced, by the pressure of their lack of advancements, to follow those countries which had reached ahead in capitalist development. And, "although compelled to follow after advanced countries, a backward country does not take things in the same order" (Trotsky 1980: 5). Rather, "under the whip of external necessity their backward culture is compelled to make leaps" (Trotsky 1980: 5). From this angle, from the "law of universal unevenness" comes the "law of combined development" (Trotsky 1980: 5–6).

In other words, all human history, going back so far as to the ways societies shaped themselves as reactions to the ecological and climactic conditions in which people lived, to the specific political and economic advances and social structures that were built in different regions, is uneven. This is a "law" or regular pattern in historical development. And as different societies with varying social structures interact, so the ones that find themselves behind are compelled to catch up, and even potentially advance beyond, others. Trotsky's focus, though, was particularly on the ways that pressures from *capitalism* cased this process to occur: it is not clear if he believed it could be extended beyond this. This leads to combined development, in which a previously "backwards" society will take on aspects of the more advanced in historically distinct ways, while also holding on to the legacy of the past. What forms is "an amalgam of archaic with more contemporary forms" (Trotsky 1980: 6). Trotsky wrote this specifically to make sense of the case of Russia. The unevenness of Russia's history and unevenness of its place in the development of capitalism, and the combined nature of its nascent industrial capitalist development within a Tzarist state, under international pressure to catch up, set the specific conditions for the Russian Revolution. The pieces of capitalism that formed in Russia, and the class composition of the Russian bourgeoisie and working class, along with the form of state, were the result of uneven and combined pressures.

More broadly, these insights have been expanded upon to explain a variety of phenomenon, and have become a paradigm for critical theorizing and explanations of world power, historically and today. Anievas and Nişancıoğlu, for instance, have, perhaps most ambitiously, tried to rethink the question of the rise of the West through a U&CD perspective (Anievas and Nişancıoğlu 2015). Their perspective provides a clear overview of a U&CD approach, along with its limits. Drawing from Trotsky, the authors note that unevenness is an empirical observation; an ontological starting point for thinking about human history. People historically reacted in different ways to their natural environment and built different types of societies—and modes of production—at different rates and in many ways. And given that societies are not isolated creations, but interact with neighbors and other states and modes of life, so societies shape each other. What are often termed "international" relations are really "inter-social" relations. The "internal" workings of a given social group are shaped by "external" pressures which are internalized (Anievas and Nişancıoğlu 2015: 44–47). The uneven and combined contours of history make it possible to break down the artificial conceptual separation between the internal workings of a country and states outside, to show how history has been shaped by interaction between social forces on many spatial scales. For instance, in the example they highlight in their book, Europe was not made in Europe alone, but through Europe's relations with the rest of the world.

The authors acknowledge that U&CD does not provide a "theory" of how modes of production operate, so much as a way of thinking that helps us conceptualize how particular countries, modes of production, and so on are shaped by inter-social processes (Anievas and Nişancıoğlu 2015: 58). This is also where the perspective, in general, is open to criticism. Neil Davidson, for instance, has criticized Anievas and Nişancıoğlu's approach, suggesting that the category of U&CD is useful for explaining ways countries, and uneven locations within countries, such as Russia—the case Trotsky developed his formulations specifically to understand—developed overlapping historical layers. But it does not work as a transhistorical approach to history (Davidson 2018). Rather, the "combined" aspect, in which a non-capitalist mode of production is compelled to catch up with a capitalist one in uneven and combined ways, in which old modalities of life and the organization of production articulate with the new, is a particular phenomenon unique to the development of capitalism in world history.

More general criticisms of U&CD have been taken up by Rioux, among others (Rioux 2015). Expanding from Neil Smith's argument that the concept of U&CD lacks explanatory power, Rioux argues U&DC approaches too often "take for granted what needs to be theorized" (Rioux 2015: 484). To put it differently, it might be suggested that U&CD is a concept that can fit with theoretical approaches, but as a framework itself cannot explain social developments. That history is uneven is not wrong, but it does not tell us how unevenness was socially produced. And to say, at least with the rise of capitalism, countries were compelled to catch up with industrial production, and so on does not tell us specifics about how/why modes of production form and transform. In the case of the capitalist mode of production, for instance, historical materialist theories of social and political change that start by analyzing the labor process, how this relates to the state, class, gender, race, and so on, and how these dimensions have changed over time, have a different starting point than U&CD.

What U&CD *does* present is a useful concept for beginning to think about international/inter-social relations that does not reify an abstract construction of the "internal" and "external" workings of states, but makes possible a starting point for thinking about how countless spatial scales—shaped by different layers and process of history—interact. It also provides an alternative to theories of international relations that neglect to bring together the ways social factors, such as class, are shaped and in turn shape the contours of world power. Coupled with a social theory of change, it can be useful, but its explanatory power should not be overstated. It is a concept that can provide a lens for thinking about a particular aspect of international power in a way that allows for space to connect social relations and modes of production with international power as part of a broader historical materialist perspective. For purposes of this chapter, U&CD is a helpful concept to document the developmental pathways of the US and China in a way that balances spatially oriented factors within and between states in the context of global capitalism. From the rise of the US as the world's top industrial power in the 19th and 20th centuries, to the rise of China in the 20th and 21st, capitalist development in both countries was shaped by the position of each within the world economy, as well as domestic circumstances including the structure of the state, and class relations and the labor market. And while Trotsky's original account of U&CD was used to make sense of the particularities of Russia's transition to capitalism, and the specific class relations that formed as a result, U&CD can also be a helpful concept to make sense of the rise of capitalism in the US, China, and elsewhere.

As well, it can be extended to help us make sense of contemporary capitalist international relations in a way that does not see states as "things" that act as atomistic individuals, or black boxes carried by singular national interests, but complex, relational processes that stretch across borders in a multilayered international system. Both the US and China are, in very different ways, both national and global powers. Both are characterized by high degrees of spatial unevenness domestically, as well as pressures from combined international development. In the case of China, this has meant using the "privilege of historical backwardness" to catch up, and become an innovative technological leader and capitalist country in its own right. In the case of the US, the world's last remaining superpower after the end of the USSR and Soviet bloc, it has meant cooperating and competing on a global level in a way that has both aided China's rise while, at the same time, pushed back against it.

The rise, and possible fall, of American global dominance

From the beginning of its rise to eventual position of global superpower, the shape of American power was formed by the uneven and combined position of its place in world history. Following the American Revolution, the elite shaped the creation of a new national government that would be molded by the domestic unevenness of the country itself, reflecting a class structure which included slavery, merchant capitalism, capitalist speculation in bonds and western land, along with the small farmer family and independent urban shop (Parisot 2019). The post-revolutionary state was set up to both support state-level and national economic development through, for instance, the creation of a more coherent financial system, along with allowing space for states to pursue developmental projects (although the federal state did invest, somewhat, in infrastructure as well). Merchants, meanwhile, maintained the US's position in the world economy, made possible by the early American state's diplomatic efforts, as, for instance, plantation slavery grew as domestic unevenness was encouraged due to the US's combined position in the world economy.

As Smith discussed, the transforming shape of the American empire consisted of changing imperial geographies (Smith 2003). As the US formed as the world's most powerful industrial power by the late 19th and early 20th centuries, its spatial/geographical logic of expansion pushed both the colonization of Hawaii, Puerto Rico, Guam, Cuba, and the Philippines, along with more "informal" types of economic power, particularly as US corporate capitalism would, eventually, spread globally. But even US economic imperialism via multinational corporations, as would be more characteristic of the post-Second World War world order, would have a territorial logic; after all, corporations are physical forces when settling, selling on world markets, and so on.

Finance would also characterize a central part of the American post-Second World War sphere of power. By institutionalizing the dollar as world money, so other countries would grow to be dependent on the value of the US dollar: as many are still today (Block 1978; Desai 2013). The uneven and combined pressures from the Cold War would also characterize the development of the global political economy in the postwar period. Just as the USSR pushed industrialization to catch up, as Trotsky discussed, with the aid of foreign capital, so the US would support the rebuilding of Europe, and the rise of industrial powers including Japan as part of its broad Cold War strategy (Panitch and Gindin 2012: 106–107). The results of this unevenness returned when the short-term strategies characterizing US foreign and domestic policy in the 1950s and 1960s conflicted with long-term pressures in the uneven and combined world economy.

The trajectory of events is well-known. As Brenner has discussed, one reason that American corporations began to see profit rates fall was due to the rise of German and Japanese economic competition: the result of their combined catch-up with US producers in the Cold War context (Brenner 2006). This would go along with what Panitch and Gindin referred to as the "contradictions of success" (Panitch and Gindin 2012: 111–131). Some aspects of this included the contradiction between the US dollar's expansion and the limited supply of gold the US held, which created a tension as investors began to worry that the dollar would no longer be convertible, leading the Nixon administration to, first, suspend convertibility, then float the dollar. American capitalists, symbolized by Reagan's famous breaking of the air traffic controllers' union, would wage war on worker unions, already in decline before the 1970s. Next, to combat "stagflation" Paul Volker would implement the famous "Volker Shock," increasing interests rates dramatically. The US would also use its position of power to reconfigure the value of the dollar with the 1985 Plaza Accord in an attempt to increase the international position of US producers in a competitive global economy. The result was "neoliberalism." But what that means has been a source of great debate.

David Harvey argued that neoliberalism was "a *political* project to re-establish the conditions for capital accumulation and restore the power of economic elites" (Harvey 2005: 19; emphasis in original). As noted, in Trotsky's original formulations of U&CD, class power and state power were inseparable and internationally constituted: class structures in particular countries are shaped by both domestic conditions of struggle and conflict as well as the position of the country in the uneven international system and combined reactions by social classes to national and international pressures.

Conceptualizing neoliberalism in class terms, in this context, it can be argued, was a global process in which the US took a central role, but different countries engaged with the class politics of neoliberalism in specific ways. In the case of American capital, neoliberal globalization was, as Panitch and Gindin have argued, anchored in the power of the US state (Panitch and Gindin 2012). The relative autonomy of the capitalist state meant that state officials through organizations such as the North American Free Trade Agreement and the World Trade Organization (WTO) could act to create the conditions for the further global spread and deepening of American corporations and banks across the world, creating more opportunities for capitalist profit through neoliberal globalization as the geography of American economic power shifted. One central aspect of this has been the shifting form of capital. While, as Panitch and Gindin have suggested, it is likely too simple to argue that financialization is the result of the "real" economy declining, sending capital into the artificial realm of finance—as finance and production are deeply linked—so increasingly finance has been the center of US profit formation, from the early 1980s to mid-2000s increasing from around 10 percent to around 30 percent of US profits (Panitch and Gindin 2012; Weissman 2013).

On one hand, by recent numbers, the US still remains the world's most powerful country. The Department of Defense estimates in 2022 the US will spend US$715 billion on the military, still over three times China's yearly estimated spending (Department of Defense 2021). The US also retains troops in at least 175 countries and has military bases in 80, although the effectiveness of US military power for US dominance as a whole is unclear (Regilme and Parisot 2021). And while it has been relatively declining since the post-Second World War era, the US remains the world's most powerful economy. As well, neoliberalism has entailed a remaking of the elite class–state relationship as through everything from "right to work" laws undercutting unions, to decreased taxes on corporations and the wealthy, the American state has facilitated a concentration of capitalist power at the top.

That being said, one of the challenges in making sense of US decline is the question of unevenness. While the result of the combined and uneven development of global capitalism, including the rise of "emerging powers," most significantly China, has meant some degree of relative American decline, "decline" itself is a highly uneven process. On one hand, for instance, for Wall Street bankers investing in stocks and even crypto currencies, profits are far from declining, and for instance, in 2021, eight of the ten richest people on the planet were Americans. On the other hand, for the American working and middle class, decline has been setting in for decades. As Lachmann has discussed, elite power in itself has a complex relationship with possible decline (Lachmann 2020). While he argues international pressures play a role, the trajectory of American decline is being shaped by the way the domestic elite react to domestic and global pressures. In other words, simply because the US has some of the most powerful capitalists on the planet does not necessarily mean American global power as a whole will persist. In fact, as the elite work to consolidate their power, they may undermine the larger project of American hegemony, protecting their class interests at the expense of broader national and international policies that would strengthen US global power.

In 2020 about 10.8 percent of American workers were in unions (US Bureau of Labor Statistics 2021). As well, wages for American workers have been stagnant for decades (Gould 2020). American capital has replaced rising wages and allowing workers a share in productivity increases with giving workers access to larger amounts of credit. As American capitalists continue to accrue large profits, so neoliberalism has entailed a large shift in class power away from the American working and middle classes toward the capitalist elite. In other words, while the rich have continued to get richer, working-class Americans have been the victims of their success.

In this context, the US has been characterized by increasing geographical/spatial segregation domestically. Since the 1980s, for instance, workers in the American rust belt have seen their share of wages decline, both in relative and real terms (Mendieta-Muñoz et al 2021). In general, wage growth has decoupled with productivity growth nationally. Especially in rust belt zones, workers have found their livelihoods stripped away, and the labor market has shifted from more stable, higher-paying industrial jobs to less secure, more precarious, lower-paying service sector jobs. In other words, while *parts* of the United States—particularly the amount of billionaires—don't seem to be in absolute decline by any means—and as American capital has been generating profits through, for example, finance and international cross-border production networks exploiting the uneven pool of global capitalism's labor market—for many American workers, the American economy has been in steep decline for decades.

In summary, the question of possible American decline is both domestically uneven and shaped by the uneven contours of the global economy. It also is dependent upon the combined dynamics of global capitalism, particularly the ways that rising powers have reshaped the global economy by using the "privilege of historical backwardness" to potentially catch up, and perhaps even eventually surpass, American economic power. This will depend on many factors, including the specific ways that unevenness, combined-ness, and class relations shape each other. It will also shape the dynamics of global conflict, particularly as China pushes its way up the global hierarchy, creating new means of cooperation and conflict in international politics.

Authoritarian capitalism and the rise of China

The rise of China is a continued process of contradiction and unevenness across time and space presided over by the authoritarian state (Hildebrandt 2013). Historically, the Chinese state since 1949 has experienced major swings in ideology from Mao Zedong to Xi Jinping. The Chinese Communist Party (CCP) was initially more aligned with Soviet Russia in Mao's time. Most of the elite had studied or visited Russia before the 1960s, including Mao Zedong and Deng Xiaoping. China's swing toward the capitalist path was driven both internally and externally. After the experimental socialist reform in the 1950s, with land redistribution in rural areas and the nationalization of industrial and commercial sectors in urban areas, China was turned toward one of those "really existed socialist" states by and large based on the Soviet model. It was, however, far from ideal socialism. The transition was brutal and violent. For example, the land reform from the 1930s through to the 1950s resulted in countless attacks on not just landlords, but rich and poor peasants, particularly women (Hinton 1983; DeMare 2019). Through this period of the socialist experiment, new forms of social hierarchy were established. The spatial rural–urban division was sustained by the notorious Household Registration system, which continues to date albeit in a less rigid way. Spatial separation and redistribution by the state had facilitated mass resources extraction and "state capitalist primitive accumulation" from rural areas to support the improved lifestyle of the urban working classes and party elite, which paved the way for a full-blown capitalist boom after Mao (Wen 2004, 2013; Day 2008; Hung 2016).

China's rise to a capitalist power was also driven by other great powers. It was initially associated with the debate about Khrushchev and Stalin, which eventually led to escalated diplomatic dispute in 1960, and provided the condition for the China–US cooperation in the Cold War. While China remained ideologically socialist and hostile to the imperialist US in its domestic propaganda, its shift toward the US was inevitable considering its class relations. Rural–urban division and the new urban working class's disapproval of industrial socialization poorly managed by the CCP (Perry and Lu 1997) had led to the radicalization of politics and resurrection of class struggle, epitomized by the disastrous Cultural Revolution of 1966–1976. Within mainland China, capitalism was never disappeared at the state and societal levels. On one hand, it was disguised in the state capitalism, in which the state dominated the accumulation and allocation of capital and produced state-led consumerism by greater control over people's consumption (Gerth 2020). Inside the CCP elite a small group of pre-1949 industrialists had been well protected as "Red Capitalists" in Mao's time and beyond. For example, industrialist Rong Yiren was appointed as vice-mayor of Shanghai in 1957 and vice-president of the People's Republic of China in 1993. On the other hand, geographically located in East Asia, China has always been economically and culturally close to the region, and strong ties to the Chinese diaspora, such as in Hong Kong, Taiwan, Singapore, Malaysia and Indonesia, provided the Chinese with reliable access to capitalist resources even during the Mao period, and acted particularly as a catalyst for the "Reform and Opening Up" by Deng.

The opening of China to the capitalist world under Deng Xiaoping after 1979 followed a spatial sequence with the Special Economic Zones, such as Shenzhen, liberalized first as the intersection between the capitalist core and the underdeveloped periphery in mainland China. These Special Economic Zones are spatially close to Hong Kong, Macao, Taiwan, and Southeast Asia, and were designed to mobilize the resources of the Chinese diaspora from those regions, who were well connected to the West, including the US, and brought the majority of foreign direct investment, technology, and management knowledge into China (Smart and Hsu 2004). Joining the WTO in 2001 was a critical step to become further integrated into global capitalist supply chains with a development strategy heavily reliant on the millions of low-waged rural migrants working in the global factories around the coastal provinces (Lin 2019b). In 2003, China surpassed the US to become the number one foreign direct investment inflow country in the world. China's exports as a percentage of gross domestic product jumped from 25 percent in 2002 to 39 percent in 2006, making it the "sweatshop of the world." Its annual trade in goods passed the US$4 trillion mark for the first time in 2013 to become the world's largest trading nation, overtaking the US in what Beijing described as "a milestone" for the country. In 2010,

China also overtook the US to become the largest capital market for initial public offerings, replaced Japan to become the second largest economy, and was expected to overtake the US as the largest economy by the late 2020s.

The rise to the second largest economy, however, is inherently uneven, benefiting the powerful and elite much more than the working and lower classes at the expense of social and environmental wellbeing under Chairman Jiang and Hu's administrations. By 2013, China was an upper-middle-income economy, but already a highly unequal society measured by income Gini coefficient, worse than most of the newly industrialized countries, such as South Korea, and developed countries including the US (Lin 2019a). The net worth of the 70 richest delegates in China's National People's Congress rose to 565.8 billion yuan (US$89.8 billion) in 2011, wealthier than the US congressmen combined (Bloomberg 2012). The representative numbers of workers and peasants in the National People's Congress dropped drastically, from 51.1 percent in 1975, to less than 4 percent in 2003 (Kerswell and Lin 2017). Rural poverty and mass land expropriation drove 50–66 million peasants away from their rural homelands between 1990 and 2002 (Hsing 2010: 32). The number of rural to urban migrant workers had increased to about 290 million by 2018 (National Bureau of Statistics 2020). In urban China, privatization of less strategic state-owned enterprises rendered 36 million urban workers unemployed between 1990 and 1999 (Huang 2005: 346) alongside the dismantling of the work-unit based welfare system. Labor unrest became explosive in urban China, with the total number of labor disputes jumped sharply from about 8,000 per year in 1993, to more than 80,000 in 1995 during the beginning of the reform of state-owned enterprises, before exceeding 850,000 a year in 2012 (Lin 2019b).

Xi Jinping's coming to power in 2012 initially gave hope that the issues of uneven development and rampant corruption would be tackled, but became characterized by his more authoritarian rule internally and more confrontational stance with the West. Xi rolled out a range of industrial and social policies under his leftist rhetoric with limited effects. In 2014, the central government introduced comprehensive reform of the divisive Household Registration institution to allow more migrants to become urban residents and to be included into the integrated social insurance system, covering healthcare, unemployment and pensions. However, observers contend that it has enabled more sophisticated and subtle state control and surveillance of labor mobility (Chen and Fan 2016; Dong and Goodburn 2019). Despite the extension of state welfare to the marginalized, it has enabled more marketization into social protection, which becomes the instrument to sustain ruling legitimacy and political control (Pan 2020; Lin and Nguyen 2021). Xi's declaration of nation-wide elimination of absolute poverty in 2021 was immediately contradicted by Premier Li's remarks that about half of the population had their monthly wages below US$160. Xi's much anticipated new social policy of "common prosperity" proved to be more rhetoric as he clarified that the government should not make promises it could not deliver on and avoid the trap of "welfarism and helping the lazy."

In contrast to the meager commitment to social protection, China's spending on security maintenance and defense have been rising rapidly under Xi in response to growing class inequality and unrest inside the country and his ambitious nationalist foreign policy (Economy 2018; Regilme 2018). China's annual spending on domestic security has more than tripled since 2007, reaching US$193 billion in 2017 (Nikkei Asia 2018), even more than its national defense budget in 2021 at US$183.5 billion with a 6.6 percent increase over the previous year (CSIS 2021). Since 2010, the annual increase in China's security and military spending has outpaced its annual gross domestic product growth, reflecting the priority of bolstering police and armed forces for regime stability. The statistics also reflect Xi's heightened suppression of civil society and increasingly unyielding positions in international disputes from territory to trade issues. For example, despite the liberalization of the Household Registration system to narrow the rural–urban divide, uneven development in China has evolved into more extreme forms of "terror capitalism" in Xinjiang to support China's competitive position in global supply chains (Roberts 2020; Byler 2022). Moreover, Xi has committed an enormous amount of resources to his flagship foreign policy, the Belt and Road Initiative (BRI), which encourages surplus capital, especially state capital, to explore new overseas markets for profit, mostly in poor Global South nations with less transparent governance. The 70 BRI "corridor economies" projects that had already been executed, in implementation, or planned, were estimated to amount to US$575 billion by 2018 (World Bank 2018).

US–China relations and the recurring crisis

It is clear by now that the relative rise and fall of China and the US are temporally and spatially uneven yet interconnected and are driven by the compulsive expansion of global capitalism within a nation-state-centered world system that is prone to recurring crisis. However, unevenness itself does not tell us a lot about what drives the two great powers to confront and cooperate with each other at specific historical moments. From a historical materialist perspective, the US–China simultaneous competitive and cooperative relationship is an integral part of the historically continuous "cycles of hegemony" in the nexus of comparative superiority in the world economy (Xing and Bernal-Meza 2022). The competitive aspect of China–US relations is underscored by the rivalry essentially between two different variations of capitalism competing for the core with their own sphere of influence on the periphery. The cooperative aspect is driven by compromises and shared interests among the elites in order to sustain the broader global capitalist accumulation at the expense of the working classes at home and abroad. It is in their mutual interest, as Xing and Bernal-Meza (2022) argue, to protect the exploitative accumulation by free market access and trade while avoiding economic stagnation through forming a system of coordination leading to a relatively peaceful imperialist world order.

The collusion of the US political and business elite with the CCP since the late 1970s plays a primary role in shaping the relatively peaceful and lucrative period of neoliberal globalization made possible by free trade, dismantling collective labor power, and reconfiguring welfare programs across the Global North and South. China's conflict with the Soviet Union in 1960s led to deteriorated relations, and the normalization of US–China relations under Nixon and Mao in 1972. China subsequently had much room for maneuver during the Cold War. China's market reform and integration into world capitalism would not have been possible without a nod from the US, which conversely contributed to the US defeating the Soviet Union in the Cold War. The end of US–Soviet rivalry means that an opening China had to shift its foreign policy, which brought the latent antagonisms in the relationship with the US to the forefront. The US focus on the "war on terrorism" after 2001 quietened the "China threat" voices for a decade or so, providing a peaceful environment for the rise of China, with growing economic influence across the world (Breslin 2021), and a pretext for the CCP to suppress pluralism, such as turning Xinjiang into a policed state in the name of anti-terrorism (Byler 2022).

The peaceful and friendly so-called "Chimerica" (Ferguson 2007) period is underscored by ever closer economic and trade relations. China's milestone entry to the WTO in 2000 is significant given that the US practically endorsed a new China-centered global supply chain system dependent on the cheap labor sweatshops by removing the human rights issue from trade negotiation under Clinton's administration supported by American multinational corporations. While free trade has led to the rise of a wealthy Chinese state, it has produced hyper inequality and the new rural migrant working classes. It has enriched American multinational corporations, while also resulting in increasing struggles for the middle and working classes in the US, with 560,000 job losses in the US manufacturing sectors due to direct competition with imports from China between 1999 and 2011 (Meltzer and Shenai 2019: 8). This period also saw the simultaneous dual development process in which the Chinese economy became increasingly industrialized, while the US economy became more deindustrialized and financialized.

The global financial crisis of 2008 is a turning point after decades of hyper accumulation under neoliberal globalization. As China became the largest US foreign creditor after the crisis, the view that the "US is in decline" gained popularity among the nationalist elite in China while the "China threat" voices regained traction in the US. In November 2011, President Obama's "Pivot Toward Asia" signaled a move to counter China's growing clout in the Asia-Pacific region. Trade tensions emerged initially from February 2012, as the US trade deficit with China rose to an all-time high of US$295.5 billion in 2011. The Trump administration ushered in a new era of open confrontation with China, by announcing sweeping tariffs on Chinese imports, worth at least US$50 billion in March 2018, increasing to U$200 billion worth of Chinese goods in May 2019. Xi's government, of course, retaliated. The US Congress subsequently passed a series of legislation to challenge China's human rights issues, such as a bill supporting the Hong Kong protests in 2019, and a bill designating China's abuse of Uyghurs as genocide in 2021. China retaliated by sanctioning US officials and human rights non-governmental organization activists. The Trump administration's justification of a shifted China foreign policy due to the ideological difference between an authoritarian regime and a liberal democracy, particularly highlighting China's violation of "the level playing field," clearly misses the point as China has always been authoritarian, before and after the market reform (Hung 2020). The authors contend that the current US–China rivalry is essentially between two imperial powers competing for the world market. For example, the US increasingly is concerned that China is moving up in the global supply and value chains, which would result in China's greater share of global market and surplus. The US thus has responded to China's "Made in China 2025" initiative with coercive sanctions against the Chinese tech sector, such as Huawei, and to the BRI with its own "Build Back Better" policy. Even though tensions are building up, as shown in the rhetoric of the "New Cold War" and "de-coupling," the majority of the transnational capitalist class (Harris 2021) still hope to extend their prime time of stability to as long as possible by continued lobby to governments in both states. Despite the historic high levels of inequality, with mounting challenges from poverty and climate change under the converging broken authoritarian neoliberal systems, the elite from both countries increasingly turn to alternative strategies—from the ultra-rich's race to the space in the US (Valentine 2012) to the princelings in China hiding their enormous wealth in developed countries (Shambaugh 2015).

The current more confrontational turn of US–China relations, epitomized in the trade wars, however, has masked the deeper contradiction and prolonged crisis of neoliberal capitalism in the global political economy, which was hijacked by the elite for their own interests and ruling legitimacy from both hegemons at the expense of the suffering working populations. Most of the current economic problems, from the US's trade deficit, to China's slower growth, are the symptoms of the deeper structural crises of world capitalism. One of the root problems, as Klein and Pettis (2020) observe, is that the ever increasing and now skyrocketing profit rate of world capitalism is unsustainable because the working populations as the central forces of consumption are underpaid, which is the very result of exploitative capitalist production and reproduction, leading to the rich getting richer. While this process is geographically bounded by national boundaries, it is directed and dominated by transnational capital with global ramifications. Low wages combined with free trade are systemic transfers of wealth from Chinese workers to the CCP state, which suppress consumption and push up asset prices and debt levels internally, and dump cheap goods into the world market. Concurrently, while the US businesses profit immensely from trading with China, the US economy suffers from hyper financialization and job losses that affect millions of middle- and working-class families. Trade wars are thus essentially class wars (Klein and Pettis 2020) as the conflict between economic classes within the US, even more so in China, orchestrated by the elite in both countries, has distorted the global economy and threatens international peace. The conflict is not between the US and China as two peoples, but between the intra-capitalist cartels and the working populations in both countries. The volatile US–China relations and recurring crisis of global capitalism have reproduced each other, which has global ramifications on regional stability and prosperity.

Conclusion

Drawing from the insight of U&CD theory coupled with a critical political economy approach, this chapter has shed new light on the nature of US–China relations and shows that the rise and fall of the two hegemons are shaped by social and political movements on a wide variety of spatial scales.

The current conflictual US–China relations are integral to the historical cycles of collusion and confrontation, with narratives predominantly constructed under state-centric diplomacy, by and large excluding the voices of the ordinary working populations. These state-dominant narratives serve the elite's interests in both countries when they see fit to sustain maximized access to the world market and capital accumulation in the global economy. The dual approach suggested by this chapter demystifies some of the diagnosis and treatment of conflict by conventional international relations theories, such as realists' notion of Thucydides's trap that sees wars between the two states are inevitable, liberals' conviction that closer economic ties would certainly bring more democracy and peace to the international order, and constructivists' continued faith on the role of liberal norms and institutions in reshaping the world.

It is vital to democratize and socialize inter-state relations by having more working-class and everyday actors' voices included in the discussion of international relations and in the processes of making domestic and foreign policies. This is especially the case since, as a U&CD approach shows, processes of international relations are also processes of shifting class relations, and just as societal class formations and movements shape international politics, so political actors at the top shape the abilities and conditions under which resistance from below can emerge to organize. A more democratic approach to US–China relations would require the rejection of the disastrous choice between either the two hegemons sealing the devil's deal and forming a cartel that prevents vicious competition in global capitalism or their entering full-blown military confrontation to settle the inter-imperialist rivalry. Neither cooperation nor confrontation between elites of the two hegemons can salvage global capitalism from recurring crisis. The ultimate solution would need to involve addressing the root cause of rising inequality and class conflict *within* both countries and changing the current unjust global trade regime dominated by the transnational capitalist class at the expense of the welfare of working populations.

Note

[1] For a full bibliography of these debates see the website of the Sussex U&CD Working Group: https://unevenandcombineddevelopment.wordpress.com/writings/

References

Anievas, A. and Nişancıoğlu, K. 2015. *How the West Came To Rule: The Geopolitical Origins of Capitalism*. London: Pluto Press.

Block, F. 1978. *The Origins of International Economic Disorder: A Study of United States International Monetary Policy from World War II to the Present*. Berkeley: University of California Press.

Bloomberg. 2012. "China's Billionaire-lawmakers Make US Peers Look Like Paupers." *Bloomberg*. https://www.bloomberg.com/news/articles/2012-02-26/china-s-billionaire-lawmakers-make-u-s-peers-look-like-paupers

Brenner, R. 2006. *The Economics of Global Turbulence*. New York: Verso.

Breslin, S. 2021. *China Risen? Studying Chinese Global Power*. Bristol: Bristol University Press.

Byler, D. 2022. *Terror Capitalism: Uyghur Dispossession and Masculinity in a Chinese City*. Durham: Duke University Press.

Chen, C. and Fan, C.C. 2016. "China's Hukou Puzzle: Why Don't Rural Migrants Want Urban Hukou?" *China Review* 16(3): 9–39.

CSIS. 2021. "Understanding China's 2021 Defense Budget." *CSIS*. https://www.csis.org/

Davidson, N. 2018. "The Frontiers of Uneven and Combined Development." *Historical Materialism* 26(3): 52–78.

Day, A. 2008. "The End of the Peasant? New Rural Reconstruction in China." *Boundary 2* 35(2): 49–73.

DeMare, B. 2019. *Land Wars: The Story of China's Agrarian Revolution*. Stanford: Stanford University Press.

Desai, R. 2013. *Geopolitical Economy: After US Hegemony, Globalization and Empire*. London: Pluto Press.

Department of Defense. 2021. "Defense Budget Overview: United States Department of Defense Fiscal Year 2022 Budget Request." https://comptroller.defense.gov/Portals/45/Documents/defbudget/FY2022/FY2022_Budget_Request_Overview_Book.pdf

Dong, Y. and Goodburn, C. 2019. "Residence Permits and Points Systems: New Forms of Educational and Social Stratification in Urban China." *Journal of Contemporary China* 29(125): 647–666.

Economy, E.C. 2018. "China's New Revolution: The Reign of Xi Jinping." *Foreign Affairs* 97(3): 60–74.

Ferguson, N. 2007. "Not Two Countries, But One: Chimerica." *The Telegraph*. https://www.telegraph.co.uk/comment/personal-view/3638174/Not-two-countries-but-one-Chimerica.html

Gerth, K. 2020. *Unending Capitalism: How Consumerism Negated China's Communist Revolution*. Cambridge: Cambridge University Press.

Gould, E. 2020. "State of Working America Wages 2019: A Story of Slow, Uneven, and Unequal Wage Growth Over the Last 40 Years." *Economic Policy Institute*. https://www.epi.org/publication/swa-wages-2019/

Harris, J. 2021. "Behind the US–China Cold War." *Race & Class* 63(3): 43–62.

Harvey, D. 2005. *A Brief History of Neoliberalism*. Oxford: Oxford University Press.

Hildebrandt, T. 2013. *Social Organizations and the Authoritarian State in China*. Cambridge: Cambridge University Press.

Hinton, W. 1983. *Shenfan: The Continuing Revolution in a Chinese Village*. New York: Random House.

Hsing, Y.T. 2010. *The Great Urban Transformation: Politics of Land and Property in China*. Oxford: Oxford University Press.

Huang, Y. 2005. *Selling China: Foreign Direct Investment during Reform Era*. Cambridge: Cambridge University Press.

Hung, H. 2016. *The China Boom: Why China Will Not Rule the World*. New York: Columbia University Press.

Hung, H. 2020. "The US–China Rivalry Is about Capitalist Competition." *Jacobin*. https://www.jacobinmag.com/2020/07/us-china-competition-capitalism-rivalry

Kerswell, T. and Lin, J. 2017. "Capitalism Denied with Chinese Characteristics." *Socialism and Democracy* 31(2): 33–52.

Klein, M.C. and Pettis, M. 2020. *Trade Wars Are Class Wars*. New Haven: Yale University Press.

Lachmann, R. 2020. *First-Class Passengers on a Sinking Ship: Elite Politics and the Decline of Great Powers*. New York: Verso.

Lin, J. 2019a. "Precarity, Cognitive (Non-)Resistance and the Conservative Working Class in China." *Journal of Contemporary Asia* 49(4): 568–585.

Lin, J. 2019b. *Chinese Politics and Labor Movements.* New York: Palgrave Macmillan.

Lin, J. and Nguyen, M.T.N. 2021. "The Cycle of Commodification: Migrant Labour, Welfare, and the Market in Global China and Vietnam." *Global Public Policy and Governance* 1(3): 321–339.

Meltzer, J.P. and Shenai, N. 2019. "The US-China Economic Relationship: A Comprehensive Approach." SSRN 3357900. https://papers.ssrn.com/sol3/papers.cfm?abstract_id=3357900

Mendieta-Muñoz, I., Rada, C., Schiavone, A. and von Arnim, R. 2021. "Dualism and Payroll Shares across US States." *Regional Studies.* https://e-tarjome.com/storage/panel/fileuploads/2022-10-31/1667207076_e-tarjome-e17250.pdf

National Bureau of Statistics. 2020. Rural Migrant Workers Monitoring Report 2019. http://www.stats.gov.cn/tjsj/zxfb/202004/t20200430_1742724.html

Nikkei Asia. 2018. "China Spending Puts Domestic Security Ahead of Defense" *Nikkei Asia.* https://asia.nikkei.com/Spotlight/China-People-s-Congress-2018/China-spending-puts-domestic-security-ahead-of-defense

Pan, J. 2020. *Welfare for Autocrats: How Social Assistance in China Cares for its Rulers.* Oxford: Oxford University Press.

Panitch, L. and Gindin, S. 2012. *The Making of Global Capitalism: The Political Economy of American Empire.* New York: Verso.

Parisot, J. 2019. *How America Became Capitalist: Imperial Expansion and the Conquest of the West.* London: Pluto Press.

Perry, E. and Lu, X. 1997. *Danwei: The Changing Chinese Workplace in Historical Perspective.* Armonk: ME Sharpe.

Regilme, S.S.F. 2018. "Beyond Paradigms: Understanding the South China Sea Dispute Using Analytic Eclecticism." *International Studies* 55(3): 213–237.

Regilme, S.S.F. and Parisot, J. 2021. "Contested American Dominance: Global Order in an Era of Rising Powers." In S.A.H. Hosseini, J. Goodman, S.C. Motta, and B.K. Gills (eds) *The Routledge Handbook of Transformative Global Studies.* New York: Routledge, pp 181–193.

Rioux, S. 2015. "Mind the (Theoretical) Gap: On the Poverty of International Relations Theorising of Uneven and Combined Development." *Global Society* 29(4): 481–509.

Roberts, S.R. 2020. *The War on the Uyghurs.* Princeton: Princeton University Press.

Rosenberg, J. 1996. "Isaac Deutscher and the Lost History of International Relations." *New Left Review* I: 215.

Rosenberg, J. 2009. "Basic Problems in the Theory of Uneven and Combined Development: A Reply to the CRIA Forum." *Cambridge Review of International Affairs* 22(1): 107–110.

Rosenberg, J. 2006. "Why Is There No International Historical Sociology?" *European Journal of International Relations* 12(3): 307–340.

Rosenberg, J. 2013. "The 'Philosophical Premises' of Uneven and Combined Development." *Review of International Studies* 39(3): 569–597.

Rosenberg, J. 2019. "Trotsky's Error: Multiplicity and the Secret Origins of Revolutionary Marxism." *Globalizations* 17(3): 477–497.

Shambaugh, D. 2015. "The Coming Chinese Crackup." *Wall Street Journal*.

Smart, A. and Hsu, J.Y. 2004. "The Chinese Diaspora, Foreign Investment and Economic Development in China." *The Review of International Affairs* 3(4): 544–566.

Smith, N. 2003. *American Empire: Roosevelt's Geographer and the Prelude to Globalization*. Berkeley: University of California Press.

Trotsky, L. 1980. *The History of the Russian Revolution*. New York: Monad Press.

US Bureau of Labor Statistics. 2021. "A Look at Union Membership Rates across Industries in 2020." https://www.bls.gov/opub/ted/2021/a-look-at-union-membership-rates-across-industries-in-2020.htm

Valentine, D. 2012. "Exit Strategy: Profit, Cosmology, and the Future of Humans in Space." *Anthropological Quarterly* 85(4): 1045–1067.

Weissmann, J. 2013. "How Wall Street Devoured Corporate America." *The Atlantic*. https://www.theatlantic.com/business/archive/2013/03/how-wall-street-devoured-corporate-america/273732/

Wen, T. 2004. *Women daodi yao shenme* [What Do We Want?]. Beijing: Huaxia Chubanshe.

Wen, T. 2013. *Baci weiji: Zhongguode zhenshi jingyan 1949–2009* [Eight Crises: The Real Experience of China, 1949–2009]. Beijing: Dongfang chubanshe.

World Bank. 2018. "Belt and Road Initiative." https://www.worldbank.org/en/topic/regional-integration/brief/belt-and-road-initiative

Xing, L. and Bernal-Meza, R. 2022. "China-US Rivalry: A New Cold War or Capitalism's Intra-Core Competition?" *Revista Brasileira de Política Internacional* 64(1).

PART II

Geographies of Rivalry: Spatializing US–China Relations

3

Southeast Asia and the Militarization of the South China Sea

Salvador Santino F. Regilme Jr

Introduction

One of the greatest puzzles in the academic study and contemporary practice of international politics is whether the rise of China, as a re-emerging global power, would be peaceful amidst the perception of declining US dominance (Christensen 2006; Mearsheimer 2006; Starrs 2013; Monteiro 2014: 122–126; Regilme and Parisot 2017a; 2020; Regilme and Hartmann 2018). Considered as the "most important rising power" (Hameiri and Jones 2015: 3), China, with its expanding sphere of influence in world politics, will "undoubtedly be one of the great dramas of the twenty-first century" (Ikenberry 2008: 23). Despite the countervailing discourses from some Chinese political elites who advocate a more pacifist tone, some Western scholars, pundits, and policy makers warned that China's political ascendancy is inevitably dangerous (Mearsheimer 2006; Regilme 2019; Regilme and Parisot 2020). This sense of insecurity is felt more increasingly in the Southeast Asian region, where many of the smaller countries have traditionally depended upon the US leadership and security guarantees. The South China Sea[1] (or the SCS hereafter)—a marginal sea area that is partially surrounded by Northeast (China and Taiwan) and Southeast (Malaysia, the Philippines, Brunei, Indonesia, Singapore, and Vietnam) Asian countries—has become one of the most visible maritime geographic spaces of conflict in the region. In Southeast Asia, four out of ten countries therein are active claimants of a part of the SCS region: Vietnam, the Philippines, Malaysia, and Brunei.

As one of the world's highly militarized site of inter-state territorial conflicts, the SCS is economically significant for the global economy primarily because a large chunk of annual world trade output passes through this maritime area. The US interest in the dispute is discursively sold as about "ensuring freedom of navigation," considering that "half the world's commercial shipping passes through the SCS—$5 trillion a year—and US warships regularly transit the region on their way to and from the Persian Gulf, Southwest Asia and the Indian Ocean" (Spitzer 2012: 8). The UN Conference on Trade and Development emphasizes the economic significance of the SCS, because nearly 60 percent of maritime trade comes through the Asia-Pacific, and at least one-third of the global trade needs to pass through the SCS (Jennings 2021: 6). The SCS is important also for Europe, because the disputed maritime region links Southeast and Northeast Asian markets to the Indian Ocean, which serves as the transit point for goods to Europe (Jennings 2021: 6). Due to its global economic significance amidst conflicting territorial claims, the SCS is described as a regional problem that could potentially result in a large-scale global conflict (Fravel 2014; Mastanduno 2014).

This chapter[2] addresses the following key puzzle: Why did claimant states, especially China, recently increase militarization activities in the SCS region, in unprecedented ways that were relatively absent in the previous decades? I offer three substantive propositions. First, the enduring Chinese military insecurity from American dominance in Southeast Asia has been recently amplified by the confluence of China's economic rise, and more importantly, the domestic political considerations within the Xi Jinping-led regime. I offer a domestic politics-oriented approach in explaining the strategic resolve of Beijing to militarize the disputed SCS region. Second, although many countries in the region uphold a "hedging foreign policy strategy," which refers to their strategic engagement "both" with China and the US, the Southeast Asian countries' recent patterns of foreign policy behavior and perceptions suggest that the US remains the preferred security guarantor amidst the re-emergence of China as a regional power. Third, notwithstanding such a perception of Southeast Asian states toward the US, I demonstrate that Washington's long-term commitment of upholding its security guarantees to its Southeast Asian partners is hindered by the US's need to strategically engage with Beijing. Such a motivation for engagement stems from the need to protect broader American interests in global governance—or interests that are perceived to be much more consequential to its goal of maintaining its long-term position in the international system.

The SCS dispute is widely seen as part of the broader policy and scholarly debates on the US hegemony vis-à-vis rising or re-emerging powers, including China. As Michael Yahuda (2013: 446) argues, "China's new assertiveness in the South China Sea has arisen from the growth of its military power, its 'triumphalism' in the wake of the Western financial crisis and its heightened nationalism." Mainstream International Relations contributions to the SCS dispute and the rise of China debates have always been driven by the deliberate use or defense of a (single) paradigm—including realism (Christensen 2006; Glaser 2011a; Kirshner 2012; Mearsheimer 2014; Regilme and Parisot 2017b: 5–6), liberalism (Hughes 1995; Buzan 2010; Ikenberry 2011) or even historical materialist orientation (Parisot 2013; Starrs 2013), among several dominant approaches or paradigms.

The goal herein is not to discredit those important works; rather, this chapter distinguishes itself from those mono-paradigmatic approaches by underscoring the role of various domestic factors within SCS claimant states as well as the broader transnational dynamics involving the US and its long-standing hegemonic influence in Pacific Asia. Recognizing the explanatory limitations of employing a singular International Relations paradigm, this chapter employs instead analytic eclecticism, which constitutes a "middle-range causal account incorporating complex interactions among multiple mechanisms and logics drawn from more than one paradigm" (Sil and Katzenstein 2010: 19; see also Cornut 2015; Regilme 2021). In that way, I acknowledge the complexity and confluence of various factors that can account for the sudden increase in foreign policy assertiveness and militarization activities of China and other Southeast Asian claimant states in the SCS maritime region.

Considering the Biden presidency's divided policy attention, largely generated by intensified US involvement in Europe due to the Russian war of aggression in Ukraine amid the unstable domestic politics in the US, SCS claimant states' tenacity to rely on the US security umbrella is likely to become weary over time. Thus, I underscore the explanatory power of examining the interactions between "ideas" and "material interests" in the study of international politics. Such interactions can be seen in two ways:

- how the Southeast Asians' self-reinforcing positive "perceptions" of the US push for a balancing and hedging strategy toward China; and
- how the considerable limitations in the "material capabilities" and the "range of foreign policy concerns" (beyond Southeast Asia) of the US undermine the credibility of Washington's commitment to its Southeast Asian partner states.

This chapter is organized as follows. I begin by characterizing the increasing militarization in the SCS maritime region, an outcome brought by strategic interests (material), yet smaller Asian states have renewed their strategic military ties to the US as a response to China's land reclamation activities, a development triggered by those countries' long-standing affinity to the US (ideational). Next, it discusses the causes and consequences of increased military and construction activities in the disputed maritime region and argues that strategic material interests and recent changes in domestic politics in Beijing primarily shape the highly insecure security environment in East Asia, especially Southeast Asia. The third section discusses how and why the SCS dispute becomes a litmus test for the continuing rivalry for regional hegemony in the Asia-Pacific region between the US and China. I explain how domestic politics and economics, particularly in China, as well as public and elite perceptions (pro-US socialization of East Asian elites) play a crucial role in the patterns of inter-state diplomacy in regard to the SCS dispute. Finally, the chapter discusses the broader theoretical and policy implications of an analytically eclectic approach on the SCS dispute.

The recent militarization of the South China Sea

Many foreign policy observers and political elites in the Asia-Pacific region view the SCS to be in a precarious situation, compared to the last few decades. Whereas the territorial dispute during the last three decades or so largely focused only on marginal backlashes in inter-state public diplomacy, China today has aggressively implemented "dredging operations for land reclamation works … at seven disputed reefs and shoals," and the "naval and air force facilities are being established: new piers and wharves, extended airstrips, and military garrisons with radar installations and coastal artillery" (Yoon 2015: 1). In the Spratly Islands, several hundreds of miles from the Chinese mainland's coastline, "Chinese dredgers are spewing up torrents of sand from the sea bed, turning reefs into new islands" (Marcus 2015).

As the US Pacific Fleet Commander Harry Harris stated, "China was using dredges and bulldozers to create a 'great wall of sand' in the South China Sea" (Brunnstrom and Takenaka 2015). In mid-June 2015, the Chinese foreign ministry reported that the land reclamation activities in the seven reefs in the SCS region would end soon and announced that it would begin establishing infrastructures in those reclaimed lands "for defence, but also maritime search and rescue, disaster relief and research" (BBC 2015a). Amidst the COVID-19 global pandemic on March 2022, US Indo-Pacific Commander John Aquilino confirmed that "China has fully militarized at least three of several islands it built … arming them with anti-ship and anti-aircraft missile systems, laser and jamming equipment and fighter jets in an increasingly aggressive move that threatens all nations operating nearby" (Associated Press 2022: 1). In 2021, nearly 300 Chinese maritime militia vessels were found roaming and monitoring the Spratly Islands at any given time as a way of Beijing's intensified territorial claims (Hale 2021: 1). According to the Pew Research Center, based on a cross-national survey of 15,313 respondents from ten Asia-Pacific countries (April 6–May 27, 2015), the majority of the respondents from the Philippines (91 percent), Japan (83 percent), Vietnam (83 percent), South Korea (78 percent), Australia (63 percent), Malaysia (45 percent), and Indonesia (41 percent) confirmed that they are "very/somewhat concerned" about the territorial maritime disputes with China (Pew Research Center 2015). On July 28, 2015, the Chinese navy "conducted live firing drills" in the SCS, which involved "more than 100 naval vessels, dozens of aircrafts, several missiles launch battalions of the Second Artillery Corps, as well as unknown number of information warfare troops" (The Ministry of National Defense, People's Republic of China 2015). In other words, "China's growing naval power" facilitated the emergence of a perception of overwhelming "capability and evident willingness to enforce its claims more assertively" (Ciorciari and Weiss 2012: 63). Since the start of Xi Jinping's leadership, China has demonstrated more confidently its military capabilities in the SCS region and expressed escalatory foreign policy rhetoric in ways that were not observable in previous years (Poh 2017: 158; see also Chang-Liao 2016).

Those unilateral actions by Chinese authorities have triggered serious complaints from other Northeast (particularly Japan and Taiwan) and Southeast Asian (especially Vietnam and the Philippines) states, many of them hinting that the probability of a military confrontation in the region are much higher than in previous decades. Even a non-claimant Southeast Asian state such as Singapore expressed its discontent over Chinese assertiveness in the SCS region; specifically, Singaporean Prime Minister Lee Hsien Loong upheld the SCS ruling in The Hague in 2016 and called for freedom of navigation rather than Chinese control of the maritime area (Yahya 2018). Ann Marie Murphy clearly described the various remarkable ways in which Beijing has been vigorously undermining other Southeast Asian states' activities in the SCS region:

> China's maritime assertiveness not only produces disequilibrium in the system but also directly threatens the national interests of four states under discussion. China has ousted Philippine fisherman from Scarborough Shoal and taken physical control of it. Beijing has denied Vietnam fisherman access to traditional fishing grounds, deployed an oil exploration rig to waters within Vietnam's EEZ, and used force against Vietnamese ships sent to protect those waters. China has physically interfered with Indonesian efforts to arrest Chinese ships caught fishing illegally in Indonesia's EEZ. China has made numerous incursions into Malaysian waterways and planted a Chinese flag in Malaysia's EEZ. (Murphy 2017: 172)

In response to Chinese land reclamation projects, smaller SCS claimant states started to bolster their military defence capabilities and have welcomed an increased presence of US naval and other military forces in their own territories—a development that was markedly absent in the last 20 years since the end of the Cold War. The brewing anxiety among Asian states over the recent Chinese activities in the SCS region is reflective of a much broader trend (Cheng and Paladini 2014: 187): "Since 2010, China has been perceived by the Western world as adopting an increasingly assertive posture in safeguarding its maritime interests." In fact, Zhou Fangyin (2016: 869, 871), a prominent foreign policy strategist from the Chinese Academy of the Social Sciences, acknowledges that "since 2010 the situation in the South China Sea, which had been calm during the post-Cold War era, has become more volatile"—a transformation of Beijing's earlier stance of "keeping a low profile" to a "striving for achievement" mode (2016: 871). Thus, the emergence of Chinese-made artificial islands in the disputed SCS region and the Chinese military build-up therein intensified a sense of insecurity among Southeast Asian states including two notable non-SCS claimant states in the broader Asia-Pacific region, particularly Japan and Australia.

The recent Chinese militarization of the SCS dispute is a quite unprecedented development in the US-dominated East Asian order. Minjiang Li (2015: 362–363) argues that the 2000s, or the pre-Xi Jinping era, witnessed a much more multilaterally engaged Chinese foreign policy even in regard to the SCS issue. In the 1990s, Beijing was generally "prepared to shelve the sovereignty issue, work towards a peaceful resolution of the dispute based on international law, and jointly develop the natural resources with other claimants" (Storey 1999: 99). For example, Beijing provided "consistent political support" to the Association of Southeast Asian Nations (ASEAN), by active participation in its various regional security dialogues (Storey 1999). The Chinese government and the ASEAN member countries committed to the Declaration on the Conduct of Parties in the SCS (DOC), which contributed to the relative peace and stability in the disputed maritime territory (Li 2015: 363). In November 2011, during the ASEAN–China Summit in Bali, Indonesia, Beijing committed to providing RMB3 billion to establish the ASEAN–China Maritime Cooperation Fund for projects supportive of the DOC in addition to its participation in multilateral negotiations with the ASEAN claimant countries on drafting a Code of Conduct on the SCS (Li 2015: 363). Even as early as 2002, ASEAN and China "signed the Declaration on the Conduct of Parties in the SCS with a view to enhancing peace, stability, economic growth, and prosperity in the region," and Beijing even "acceded to the Treaty of Amity and Cooperation one year later" (Thang 2011: 63). Indeed, the pre-Xi Jinping regime witnessed a more diplomacy-oriented approach to the SCS dispute, an observation that is also shared by prominent Chinese legal scholars (Shicun and Huaifeng 2003: 311), who enumerated various diplomatic instruments which China and ASEAN have used prior to 2010. Accordingly, all those instruments were "important contributions to maintenance and promotion of regional peace, security and progress," and they "have set up a landmark in the history of Sino-ASEAN relations" (Shicun and Huaifeng 2003: 311).

There are three key domestic political factors that drove Chinese foreign policy strategy in the SCS region to a more assertive and militaristic stance. The first key factor refers to the broader domestic change whereby the politicians at the top of the Communist Party leadership have been experiencing fundamental challenges to their domestic legitimacy. As Kurlantzick (2011: 6) describes such a development, the death of Deng Xiaoping (China's top leader until the 1990s) witnessed the emergence of "successive leaders—who were younger or lacked military experience—[who] did not enjoy the same wide-ranging authority." Because of the increasing military capabilities of the Chinese military, the People's Liberation Army (PLA) "has begun to view itself as the most important guarantor of China's safety and national interests" (Kurlantzick 2011: 7). In response, as early as 2010, top Communist Party officials began asserting Chinese interests beyond its territory, a strategy that could bolster their nationalist credentials and domestic authority. On July 2010, during an ASEAN summit in Hanoi, Chinese Foreign Minister Yang Jiechi expressed his dissatisfaction with US Secretary of State Hillary Clinton's call for respecting the norm of "freedom of navigation" in the SCS region. Yang reminded ASEAN leaders that "China is a big country and other countries are small countries, and that's just a fact," while he looked down on the foreign affairs minister of Singapore, which is one of America's closest allies in the Asia-Pacific region (Pomfret 2010: 9). This incessant desire for the Chinese Communist Party politicians to bolster its nationalist credentials, together with the increasing economic power and military capabilities of the Chinese state, facilitated the emergence of Chinese assertiveness in the SCS dispute.

The second factor pertains to the change in the top leadership in Beijing in 2012 and the internal political struggles within the Chinese state, both of which reinforced the increased military and political assertiveness of Beijing over the SCS issue. Indeed, Xi Jinping's ascendancy in 2012 to the top leadership of the state marked a transformative episode in Chinese foreign policy, especially in regard to the SCS dispute. The reliance on militarization emerged from Xi's instrumentalization of China's increasingly strong economic and military instruments as a way to influence global politics in a way that is attuned to perceived interests of Beijing (Lam 2014). Such a strategy was quite evident in regard to territorial disputes involving China. Although the SCS dispute has been an on-and-off episode, the SCS issue emerged as a critical juncture for Chinese foreign policy in regard to territorial disputes. In fact, the official Chinese government document called *Study Times* (released by the Central Party School, the top political academy of the Communist Party) specifically lauded President Xi for his policies in the SCS region:

[President Xi] personally steered a series of measures to expand [China's] strategic advantage and safeguard the national interests. ... On the South China Sea issue, [Xi] personally made decisions on building islands and consolidating the reefs, and setting up the city of Sansha. [These decisions] fundamentally changed the strategic situation of the South China Sea. (Mai and Zheng 2017)

The increase in the number of military and civilian activities in the SCS reflected the core ideational foundations of Chinese foreign policy. For example, the Communist Party in 2012 "reclassified the South China Sea as a 'core national interest', placing it alongside such sensitive issues as Taiwan and Tibet"—which "means China is prepared to fight to defend it" (Marcus 2015: 6). Moreover, such a transformation in policy focus coincided with the naval doctrinal changes since Xi Jinping took power. According to the strategy document released by the Chinese navy in 2015, China "will shift its focus to 'open seas protection', rather than 'offshore waters defence'" (BBC 2015b: 2). According to US intelligence sources, Chinese authorities have built around 800 hectares of dry land in the disputed Spratly Island region, which many suspected could be easily used for naval and military purposes. In addition, China's PLA has commissioned "regular security patrols" in the SCS, "reflecting its increasing capability and the heightening concern of the Chinese leadership to strengthen China's territorial claims in the area through a military presence" (Cheng and Paladini 2014: 193).

These political developments suggest that "the new Chinese leadership is widely seen to be more confident in handling major power relations and more inclined to assert China's interests than its predecessors," whereby the current Chinese leadership has assertively bolstered a foreign policy paradigm that emphasizes a "new type of great power relations" (*xinxing daguo guanxi*), where the aim is to put China at the center of global governance (Chan and Li 2015). Such a foreign policy agenda coincided with the 18th Party Congress Report in China that emphasizes the need of making the country a "maritime power" through several strategies:

> (1) formulating an effective control, management and protection of previously neglected maritime domain, particularly the ECS [Eastern China Sea] and SCS; (2) exerting significant influence on regional and international maritime regulations and practices with assertive maritime diplomacy; (3) becoming a powerful maritime economy through effective use of maritime resources within and outside of China's sovereign space. (Chan and Li 2015: 42)

The unprecedented framing of its assertive military strategy is motivated by Xi Jinping's need for consolidating his power, especially by "demonstrating his image as a strongman, who is willing to take tough political and military action to protect China's interests" and by paying "more attention to the military than his two predecessors" (Chan and Li 2015: 43). Because of China's economic slowdown, Xi Jinping's regime has bolstered nationalist rhetoric in its SCS issue-oriented public diplomacy in order to divert the public's attention from the regime's recent failure to effectively sustain a high level of equitable economic growth, which is a crucial source of the Communist Party's legitimacy (Nye and Ramani 2015). Consequently, the increasing militarization of the SCS and the intensification of public diplomacy disputes boosted Xi Jinping's "prestige and authority for his domestic reform agenda, along with an assumption that the United States is extremely unlikely to intervene at this moment in time" (Sun 2014). China did not participate in the special arbitral tribunal constituted under Annex VII to the 1982 United Nations Convention on Law of the Sea (UNCLOS) proceedings in The Hague in the years 2015 and 2016, as initiated by the Philippine government—a policy option showing Beijing's preference for unilateralism and remaking the status quo (Permanent Court of Arbitration 2015). The ruling intensified the political resolve of China to defend its territorial claims, while the specifications of the Permanent Court of Arbitration (PCA) judgment motivated the Duterte-led Philippine government to abandon the ruling and restart a clean slate in its negotiations and deliberations with Beijing (Zhang 2017: 441). When the PCA ruled in favor of the Philippines, Beijing openly defied the court judgment and expanded its militaristic footprint in the SCS through the "fortification of military outposts in the Spratly Islands ... constructed reinforced aircraft hangars on Subi, Mischief and Fiery Cross reefs," thereby increasing "the PLA's power-projection capability in the SCS" (Shah 2017: 6).

The third factor refers to Beijing's disinterest in working with ASEAN, which could facilitate the resolution of disputes among member states and with external actors (Huan and Emmers 2016: 90). There are three factors that undermine ASEAN's potential for facilitating effective dispute resolution mechanisms in the SCS issue. First, the Chinese government has prudently preferred to deal with each claimant state on a bilateral basis, as such a mode of diplomacy weakens the bargaining position of smaller states such as the Philippines and Vietnam. Second, because several ASEAN members are also SCS claimant states with conflicting and converging interests, it is difficult for the regional body to act as a neutral mediator. Finally, because China is not a member of ASEAN, any potential dispute mechanism emanating from ASEAN could be seen as illegitimate to the extent that it is likely designed to promote the interests of ASEAN member states. As such, Beijing exploited the absence of a shared position between ASEAN members in regard to the SCS, considering that generating a common ASEAN approach to the dispute is important in matching "Beijing's 'divide and conquer' approach" (Jaknanihan 2022: 16). Meanwhile, it is very likely that China will continue to defy any form of institutionalized dispute resolution mechanisms, especially in the context of ASEAN and the recently concluded PCA ruling in The Hague.

In recent years, the Chinese government has been committed to bolstering the rhetorical persuasiveness of its territorial claims, particularly the highly disputed "nine-dashed line," which was an arbitrary demarcation line that Beijing refers to in its claims for large parts of the SCS. China's PLA Deputy Chief of Staff General Wang Guanzhong made an exhaustive elaboration of the "nine-dashed line" during the 2015 Shangri-La Dialogue (Sun 2014). In recent years, Chinese military documents and officials' speeches have framed China as a maritime power, although Beijing's top diplomats have undermined the militaristic rhetoric surrounding the SCS issue. Ouyang Yujing, head of the Chinese foreign ministry's department of boundary and ocean affairs, contended that the SCS issue and the recent construction of artificial islands must be seen in light of China's role in "maritime search and rescue, disaster prevention and mitigation, marine scientific research, meteorological observation, ecological environment preservation, safety of navigation and fishery production" (Graham-Harrison 2015). Similarly, Chinese defense ministry spokesperson Yang Yujun argued that: "Looking from the angle of sovereignty, China's development of construction on its islands is no different at all from all the other types of construction going on around the country," and "island building" was "beneficial to the whole of international society" because of reasons pertaining to humanitarian and environmental protection purposes (BBC 2015b; see also BBC 2015a). Even China-based policy scholars supported Beijing's recent foreign policy changes on the SCS issue, including the Chinese Academy of Social Sciences' Xu Liping, who contended that "it's obviously unfair for the West to question China's intentions in its reclamation projects … it shows that the West has willfully misjudged the situation in the South China Sea" (Graham-Harrison 2015). Yet the worrying trend about China's claim in the SCS region is not only the ambitious territorial claims invoked in the nine-dashed line principle but also China's strategic nuclear capabilities that could challenge American power in the region, especially in the control of sea lines of communications and the commercial routes in the SCS (Koda 2016: 93–96). In her systematic study of all public speeches of the 39 Politburo members of the Chinese Communist Party (2013–2018), political scientist Oriana Mastro (2021) shows that these highly influential political elites persistently invoked cooperative themes ("cooperation and political solutions") in addressing their country's claims in the SCS, while the statements of one lone member, Xi Jinping, constitute nearly half of the total number of statements construed with competitive themes ("sovereignty, military, freedom, tension, and non-regional countries/the United States").

Consequently, Beijing's assertive foreign policy likely facilitated a "rally 'round the flag'" effect (Oneal and Bryan 1995), which increased domestic nationalism in mainland China, thereby diverting the Chinese population's focus on the economic and socioeconomic problems at home. One likely factor for strategically increasing Chinese assertiveness in the SCS region is that the "the Communist Party of China (CPC) wants an external conflict to divert attention of the Chinese people from numerous domestic tensions," a goal that is inspired by the fact that "the large majority of [the] Chinese [population] are convinced that the SCS is indisputably part of China" (Meyer 2016: 7). To be exact, there are several principal domestic problems that the Communist Party is extremely concerned about: corruption within the government, economic slowdown, pollution in urban areas, economic inequality, and demographic imbalance, among many others (Laliberte 2016). Those problems undermine the Chinese state's legitimacy. While the Communist Party appears committed to address those problems head-on, diverting the population's attention toward perceived security threats abroad could somehow lessen the dissatisfaction with the problems at home.

The increased militarization of the SCS facilitated the prevailing perception of insecurity among smaller Southeast Asian claimant states' political elites. Indeed, "in recent years, China's ties with many regional countries have experienced a turn for the worse," which "was largely due to the fact that Beijing has demonstrated more readiness to utilize hard power in pursuit of its security interests in the South China Sea" (Li 2015: 360). Consequently, the Philippine government has vigorously welcomed increased US military presence within its territory. As one of the only two Mutual Defense Treaty allies of the US in Southeast Asia (the other is Thailand, a non-claimant state in the SCS dispute), the Philippines has reaffirmed its strategic military partnership with the US in November 2011 through the Manila Declaration, whereby increased "rotational deployment" of US naval surveillance in the archipelago and its nearby maritime areas has been welcomed. Such a demand for "rotational deployment" of US forces was fortified in the 2014 Enhanced Defense Cooperation Agreement between the US and the Philippines, which is a ten-year pact that formally allows American forces to temporarily station military troops and resources within the archipelago (Agence France Presse 2014). In April 2015, US Defense Secretary Ashton Carter announced that Manila and Washington will sponsor annual military exercises near the Spratly Islands in SCS, and he upheld America's "desire to ensure there were no changes in the status quo by force or that territorial rows were militarized" (Brunnstrom and Takenaka 2015).

Because of the emergence of assertive Chinese foreign policy rhetoric and actions in the SCS region, the other smaller countries in the region started to change their approach to the SCS dispute. It was in April 2012 when the Philippine navy dispatched BRP *Gregorio del Pilar*, one of the most modern warships in the region and a decommissioned ship from the US Coast Guard, in order to reprimand several Chinese fishing vessels that were spotted in the Scarborough Shoal—a territory that is claimed by China, Taiwan, and the Philippines (Chan and Li 2015). For the Philippine navy, the goal was to arrest the Chinese fishermen. Yet, two powerful Chinese maritime surveillance ships eventually hindered the Philippine forces—an act that led to the Chinese state's eventual control of the Scarborough Shoal. Since the takeover of the Shoal in 2012 by the Chinese authorities, the SCS region has been the source of various public diplomacy disputes, increasing military presence (China, the US, and other Southeast Asian claimant states), and the build-up by Chinese authorities of artificial islands and infrastructures in various reef regions in the SCS. As Philippine Foreign Affairs Secretary Albert Del Rosario (2011–2016) maintained at that time, China's activities in the disputed maritime region are "threats to regional peace and stability" (Felongco 2013). Despite Philippine President Duterte's (2016–2022) pro-China public pronouncements during the early years of his term, 3,800 Filipino and 5,100 US armed forces personnel initiated in March 2022 "large-scale military drills, in show of strength as China grows increasingly assertive in the disputed South China Sea and Russia's war with Ukraine rages on" (Venzon 2022: 1–2).

Other Pacific Asian states have also fostered new (or renewed) strategic military partnerships in the aim of countering China. Although a non-SCS claimant state, but a Mutual Defense Treaty ally nonetheless of the US, Japan has recently fostered closer military cooperation with the Philippines in the wake of China's assertiveness in the SCS and Senkaku territorial dispute with Japan. On January 2021, the Japanese government submitted a diplomatic note to the UN dismissing Beijing's maritime baseline claims and condemning its attempts to constrain "freedom of navigation and overflight"—that protest emerged amidst other diplomatic condemnations in the UN issued by the UK, France, Germany, Australia, the US, the Philippines, Vietnam, and Indonesia (Haver 2021: 2–3). Earlier than that, under Prime Minister Shinzo Abe, the Japanese government has been busy garnering support from other non-Asian powers in order to undermine China's attempts to change the status quo in the territorial boundary make-up of the region. Largely generated by Shinzo Abe's lobbying during the 2015 G7 meeting in Germany, the G7 leaders issued a joint statement that advocated for "maintaining a rules-based maritime order and achieving maritime security," and that the established powers "are committed to maintaining a rules-based order in the maritime domain based on the principles of international law, in particular as reflected in the UN Convention on the Law of the Sea [UNCLOS]" (Panda 2015). The joint statement came as a remarkable development considering that many of the G7 countries' leaders have, in the past, consistently avoided directly addressing the SCS dispute. The Philippines and Vietnam upgraded in January 2015 their bilateral ties in the form of a "strategic partnership" and advocated that "'concerned parties' should adhere to the ASEAN-China Declaration on Conduct of Parties in the South China Sea, conclude a Code of Conduct, exercise restraint, and resolve disputes peacefully in accord with international law, including the United Nations Convention on the Law of the Sea" (Thayer 2015). Vietnam's increasingly strained relationship with China began in June 2011, when Hanoi accused Beijing of "deliberately cutting the cables of oil exploration vessels in the western Spratly Islands, calling the second incident a 'premeditated and carefully calculated' attack" (Ciorciari 2012: 61). The Philippines has also intensified its negotiations for strategic partnership agreements with South Korea, Japan and Vietnam, particularly in terms of military, political, and economic cooperation. Indeed, the "growing Chinese assertiveness in the South China Sea in recent years has led to a growing convergence of strategic interests between Manila and Hanoi" (Thayer 2015)—a development that emerged amidst the deterioration of China–Vietnam bilateral ties (Amer 2014). Malaysia's Prime Minister Mahathir bin Mohamad planned for the government authorities to continue occupying a handful of islands in the SCS. He also recommended that "foreign warships" should be avoided in the SCS and should be replaced instead by smaller boats that are supposed to guard it from pirates (Jaipragas 2018; *The Straits Times* 2018). Amidst the increasing unilateral assertiveness of Chinese claims in the SCS, "the United States has moved to strengthen defense ties with ASEAN states that share concerns about China," a strategy that even led the Obama administration to resume military ties with Kopassus, or the Indonesian special forces unit (Buszynski 2012: 148).

The South China Sea and the challenges to US–China bilateral relations

What makes the current SCS dispute fundamentally different in the way previous claimant and other stakeholder states approached such an issue in the past? I contend that the SCS dispute could be a possibly dangerous source of inter-state conflict among claimant states and great powers—a development that only emerged in recent years. Political elites within and far beyond the region perceive the current conflict "not" merely as an intra-Asian affair but as a critical issue on great power rivalry. That is the case because, as Buszynski (2012: 139–140) maintains, the SCS dispute "has started to become linked with wider strategic issues relating to China's naval strategy and America's forward presence in the area." Similarly, arguing that the US and China are "caught in a security dilemma," Adam Liff and G. John Ikenberry (2014: 89) maintain that "self-understood defensively oriented policies are generating insecurity and military responses on the other side that make both countries less secure and trigger new rounds of competition." Hence, the SCS dispute demonstrates the strategic military competition and rivalry between the

US and China; yet the increasing economic links and deeply embedded identifications and affinity of secondary states in the Asia-Pacific region influence the patterns of their foreign policies.

There are several reasons for why many political elites in the region view the SCS dispute in the context of US–China rivalry. First, many smaller states in the region began viewing the increased Chinese activities in the SCS as part of Beijing's unprecedented assertion of its influence in the region. For that reason, US Defense Secretary Ashton Carter lamented the ongoing land reclamation in the SCS: "It is unclear how much farther China will go. That is why this stretch of water has become the source of tension in the region and front-page news around the world" (Graham-Harrison 2015). Carter further called on "China to limit its activities and exercise restraint to improve regional trust" (Brunnstrom and Takenaka 2015: 2). In May 2015, Chinese President Xi Jinping introduced his "Asia for Asians" security framework (Ford 2015). Such a framework has been operationalized in two ways:

- China has made the SCS land reclamation project as a way to challenge US military primacy in the region; and
- China established the Asian Infrastructure Investment Bank with US$50 billion initial capital as a way of undermining US leadership in regional economic governance in the Asia-Pacific.

Those patterns of foreign policy behaviour of Beijing demonstrate that its land reclamation activities in the region are just part and parcel of a broader global strategy that seeks to undermine US dominance, and quite possibly, to demonstrate to its Asian neighbors that its reliance upon the US for regional security is no longer tenable.

Second, the foreseeable future of US leadership is likely to encounter unprecedented challenges due to the increased dominance of China. Particularly because of China's artificial islands, Washington DC would find it difficult to defend unconditionally US hegemony unless it opts to be susceptible to military confrontation and conflict with Beijing (Burgess 2016: 113). Whereas other influential scholars (Ikenberry 2001, 2011; Nye 2013) remain optimistic as to the continuity of America's influence in Asia, rapid economic and political developments that are quite favorable to China are quite compelling, so much so that Beijing's eventual hegemonic role in the Asia-Pacific region is possible. Economically, notwithstanding their political reliance on Washington, many Asia-Pacific countries' largest trading partner in the last few years has been China. In fact, China was the biggest trading partner of ASEAN countries in 2013, with 14 percent of total trade within the region, while the US ranked only fourth with a meagre 8 percent (ASEAN 2014). Having China as its largest trading partner since 2012, the Philippines had to momentarily tone down its criticism of

Beijing in its land reclamation activities in 2012, amidst the deep setbacks in banana imports and local tourism (Higgins 2012). China's rapidly increasing economic power is likely to motivate Beijing to strongly pull Asian states away from Washington's sphere of influence. Consequently, the SCS dispute became a "material symbol of Southeast Asian uncertainties and insecurities vis-à-vis China" (Ba 2011: 279). Worried about US commitment in the region, Japan is forging much higher and unprecedented levels of security cooperation with two SCS claimant countries: the Philippines and Vietnam (Grønning 2017). Apparently departing from the hub-and-spoke system of US-led security alliances in the Asia-Pacific region, the Japanese government calls this renewed cooperation with the Philippines and Vietnam a strategic partnership. That partnership includes the establishment of intensive diplomatic exchanges, regularization of strategic security dialogues, intensifying the frequency of interactions and meetings of high-level executive government officials, diplomatic assistance in regard to territorial disputes with Beijing, support for maritime security, and intensive military training collaboration (Grønning 2017: 2).

Although Southeast Asian states are still likely to invoke primarily US security guarantees, that form of reliance is quite tenuous. Many Southeast Asian states still continue to "hedge" in this broader US–China rivalry. Evelyn Goh (2005: xiii) describes the key elements of hedging in the region as:

- indirect or soft balancing whereby the aim is to form a coalition that can undermine Chinese influence;
- complex engagement with China at various dimensions; and
- general strategy of engaging several great powers for them to engage in the Asian regional order.

Although Vietnam continues to be firm in asserting its territorial claims, the Philippine government under President Duterte (2016–2022) appears to be cautiously hedging by discarding the PCA ruling in The Hague and de-escalating blatant public criticisms of Beijing's foreign policy. The reinvigorated security cooperation of the Philippine government with the US and Japanese governments shows how Manila is carefully reaffirming its strategic interests in the SCS region without publicly undermining Beijing.

Why is it then that smaller Asian states continue to hedge in issues such as economic cooperation and trade but not fully rely on China for military security? First, it is likely that the entrenched pro-US norm socialization of political and military elites in the region might be driving hedging tendencies among states in the region. While states' intentions are quite hard to discern (Glaser 2011b: 3; Rosato 2015), identity politics is more likely to play a substantial influence in reinforcing the deep-seated biases of Southeast Asian political elites "who appear to see the United States in a relatively positive light" (Hamilton-Hart 2012: 4). This apparently dominant pro-US sentiment among Asia-Pacific, especially Southeast Asian, foreign policy and political elites is prevalent despite the uncertainty of the general public on whether the demise of US dominance in the region is imminent.

The second reason is that the general domestic public within those hedging Asian states uphold a more favorable view of the US. Notably, the Pew Research Center notes that domestic publics in the broader Asia-Pacific region view increased Chinese economic investments as a prospective liability, granting Beijing too much power over their political economies (Silver et al 2019: 2). As the two largest economies in Southeast Asia, the Philippines and Indonesia both registered 49 percent and 48 percent of their surveyed domestic public, respectively, who viewed China as an overall threat despite increased economic opportunities (Silver et al 2019). In the same Pew survey, the large majority of respondents in the Philippines (84 percent) and Indonesia (67 percent) expressed their preference for the US over China as the core economic partner. In the *State of Southeast Asia 2022 Survey Report* with a total of 1,677 respondents from ten ASEAN member countries, 57 percent of the total number of respondents in the entire region preferred the US over China when asked this question (43 percent for China): "If ASEAN was forced to align itself with one of the two strategic rivals, which should it choose?" (Seah et al 2022: 32). In the same 2022 survey, respondents from three out of four Southeast Asia-based claimant states in the SCS dispute remarkably preferred US over China in terms of strategic alignment: 57 percent in Malaysia, 83.5 percent in the Philippines, and 73.6 percent in Vietnam (Seah et al 2022: 32). Only the tiny claimant state Brunei had 64.2 percent of the total surveyed respondents therein who preferred China over the US. Meanwhile, the Manila-based Social Weather Station confirmed that 70 percent of the total number of Filipino respondents asked in December 2016 confirmed that they had "much trust" in the US (ABS-CBN News 2017). That finding denotes those pro-American sentiments in the Philippines are likely to be more entrenched than fleeting, especially when one considers that the survey was conducted at the height of Philippine President Rodrigo Duterte's anti-US rhetoric and political uncertainties triggered by the 2017 election victory of Donald Trump in the US.

Third, the US has enduring and formal institutional and legal ties with many smaller Asian states involved in territorial disputes with China. To be sure, it is politically costly for high-ranking US government officials to publicly abandon supportive diplomacy toward its Asian allies, even though the US seems most likely unwilling to engage in a full-blown war against China very soon just because of the SCS dispute. As the US Secretary of State Hillary Clinton declared in July 2010 during the ASEAN Regional Forum, "the United States has a national interest in freedom of navigation, open access to Asia's maritime commons, and respect for international law in the South China Sea" (Landler 2010). US strategic relations with China's neighboring countries are even positively reinforced because, as Michigan-based scholar John Ciorciari (2015: 245–246) notes, "Beijing is encased by the spokes of the US-led alliance system and regional institutions designed partly to constrain rising powers." Those spokes are likely to persist, at least in the short term, especially under the Biden presidency that is publicly committed to constrain China's re-emergence as the dominant state actor in the Asia-Pacific.

The region is currently quite divided when it comes to fully depending on the US for security guarantees (Graham 2013). The US has remained to be the only great power that has formal military alliances with key Asia-Pacific nations (Thailand, the Philippines, South Korea, Japan, Australia, and New Zealand), positively unique bilateral relations with Taiwan, a beneficial security agreement with Singapore, and a productive relationship with Malaysia, Indonesia, and Vietnam—in conjunction with a relatively long history of joint and regular military training exercises with military forces in the region (The Heritage Foundation 2015). Although Beijing lacks enduring formal and informal military and diplomatic agreements with Southeast Asian states in ways that Washington DC has, China has been consistently and vigorously intensifying its trade and economic cooperation with Southeast Asian countries (Ratner and Kumar 2017). Southeast Asian states may see Beijing's commitment in economic cooperation as favorable in the long run compared to the unpredictable foreign policy decisions of the regularly changing leadership in the White House.

The need for Washington to constructively engage with Beijing, especially in bigger issues of global governance, undermines a full and unconditional commitment of the US to its Asian allies. The future of the international financial system and global trade relations remains a core concern, which compels Beijing and Washington to engage with each other. As the IMF revealed in 2014, "for the first time in more than 140 years, the US has lost the title of the world's largest economy—it has been stolen by China" (Carter 2014). As the US became a debtor nation, China's "enormous currency reserves potentially convert China into a major global governance actor in the field of international financial markets" (Gu et al 2008: 277). It is possible that Washington DC could give up its hegemony in the Asia-Pacific, by strategic necessity, should Beijing strongly demand it as a condition for further engagement in issues of bilateral concerns as well as those that are global in scope. Beyond issues of global economic importance, one may take into account other compelling issues, including the Russian war of aggression in Ukraine, economic crisis instigated by record-breaking inflation rate, domestic polarization within the US, and the COVID-19 pandemic—all of which are likely to divert Washington's supposedly full and undivided attention in territorial disputes and quest for hegemony in the Asia-Pacific. Indeed, the sheer population and economic size of China, together with its ambitions for a more influential role at the global policy-making table, means that "many global problems will be insoluble without Chinese global engagement" (Gu et al 2008: 288). China may be a "partial power" in a broad range of global issues (Shambaugh 2013), and that makes it less likely that US security guarantees to its Asian allies are unconditional should the SCS dispute escalate to a military confrontation. In contrast to political elites in Washington, the American public, however, is quite likely to support the Philippines instead of China, primarily because of the former's political identity as a democratic state; after all, "identity does play an important role in how security policy is constructed" in the US (Hayes 2009: 977). Of course, the conditions under which democratic identity plays a role vis-à-vis the long-term interest in engaging with China are open to further empirical scrutiny.

Although it is unlikely that China will soon overtake the US in global military dominance, Washington's hegemonic leadership in the Asia-Pacific region is quite likely to be increasingly contested. The second largest in the world, China's military defense budget has increased significantly in 2020, for the 26th consecutive year (SIPRI 2021). If such trends continue, then China is likely to push out the US from dominating the region, not only because of Washington's divided foreign policy attention elsewhere beyond Asia but because of the projected military capacities of China that would continue to dominate the Pacific Rim. To be sure, the goal for China's People's Liberation Army Navy is "to dominate in contested territorial waters and to be able to push any hostile forces well beyond the 'first island chain'—that is, beyond the Philippines, Taiwan and the Japanese archipelago" (*The Economist* 2014: 6).

Conclusion

What are the policy and political implications of the increasing militarization of the SCS dispute? The answer to that question depends on one's positionality in this dispute, especially when one considers that "theory is always for someone and for some purpose" (Cox 1981: 129). Nonetheless, I provide herein some tentative recommendations on moving forward amidst rising tensions in the SCS region. It is very unlikely that China would give up its territorial claims, especially that the continued legitimacy and political survival of the Communist Party of China primarily depends on continued economic growth—and the SCS appears to be crucial to such growth due to its significance in world trade and the plausible natural resources that it could offer. In the short term, smaller SCS claimant states are likely to be better off by realizing that depending upon US security guarantees alone would be a fatal option. The political uncertainty in American domestic politics vis-à-vis the growing demand for US military support for Europe amidst the Russian war of aggression in Ukraine suggest that the reliability of US foreign policy on the SCS is at best unclear. Instead of blatantly and persistently antagonizing Beijing through media tirades and military exercises in the SCS region, smaller SCS claimant states instead, at least in the next few years, may adopt a foreign policy hedging strategy in respect to the US–China rivalry. Smaller claimant states may find ASEAN and other regional multilateral forums as ways to find shared interests in ensuring freedom of navigation and demilitarization of the region, and in doing so, negotiating and bargaining with Beijing in a much better position than through a bilateral mode. Through these collective bodies, smaller claimant states could credibly advocate for a peaceful resolution of a long-running but now intensely militarized territorial dispute. That approach acknowledges two underemphasized yet important observations:

- all claimants seem to have legitimate material stakes in the SCS region; and
- that the SCS conflict is an asymmetric one, where it is unlikely that a small claimant state could make a credible stance against the growing military and economic influence of Beijing.

Most importantly, any potential conflict resolution framework should assess and prioritize the welfare of claimant states' marginalized populations, whose livelihood and wellbeing depend on free, responsible, and equitable access to the supposedly rich natural resources of the SCS region. After all, China's rapid economic growth strengthened its appetite for military control over the SCS region, which is a crucial gateway for the world economy as well as a hub for valuable maritime resources, while long-time US military dominance in the region has always aimed to ensure the interests of American capitalist hegemony.

Notes

[1] I use the term "South China Sea" only because this is the most widely known name for the region. It does not necessarily mean that I prefer China as the supposed rightful claimant.
[2] This chapter is an updated version of an earlier peer-reviewed, open-access article: Regilme, S.S.F. 2018. "Beyond Paradigms: Understanding the South China Sea Dispute Using Analytic Eclecticism." *International Studies* 55(3): 213–237. The earlier article was published in CC-BY license.

References

ABS-CBN News. 2017. "'Very Good' Trust in US Dips; China, Russia Ratings Now Positive: SWS." *ABS-CBN News*, March 2. http://news.abs-cbn.com/ news/03/02/17/very-good-trust-in-us-dips-china-russia-ratings-now-positive-sws

Agence France Presse. 2014. "US and Philippines Sign Ten-Year Defence Pact." *Al Jazeera.* http://www.aljazeera.com/news/asia-pacific/2014/04/us-philippines- sign-ten-year-defence-pact-20144284332171232.html

Amer, R. 2014. "China, Vietnam, and the South China Sea: Disputes and Dispute Management." *Ocean Development & International Law* 45(1): 17–40.

ASEAN. 2014. "ASEAN Trade by Selected Partner Country/Region 2013." *ASEAN.* http://www.asean.org/images/2015/January/external_trade_statistic/table19_asof04 Dec14.pdf

Associated Press. 2022. "China Has Fully Militarized Three Islands in South China Sea, US Admiral Says." *The Guardian,* March 21. https://www.theguardian.com/world/2022/mar/21/china-has-fully-militarized-three-islands-in-south-china-sea-us-admiral-says

Ba, A.D. 2011. "Staking Claims and Making Waves in the South China Sea: How Troubled are the Waters?" *Contemporary Southeast Asia: A Journal of International and Strategic Affairs* 33(3): 269–291.

BBC. 2015a. "China to 'Complete' South China Sea Land Reclamation." *BBC.* http://www.bbc.com/news/world-asia-china-33144751

BBC. 2015b. "Chinese Navy to Focus on 'Open Seas', Paper Says." *BBC.* http://www.bbc.com/news/world-asia-china-32880477

Brunnstrom, D. and Takenaka, K. 2015. "U.S. Defense Chief Warns against Militarization of Territorial Rows in Asia." *Reuters.* http://www.reuters.com/chapter/2015/04/08/us-usa-japan-carter-idUSKBN0MZ02V20150408

Burgess, S.F. 2016. "Rising Bipolarity in the South China Sea: The American Rebalance to Asia and China's Expansion." *Contemporary Security Policy* 37(1): 111–143.

Buszynski, L. 2012. "The South China Sea: Oil, Maritime Claims, and U.S.–China Strategic Rivalry." *The Washington Quarterly* 35(2): 139–156.

Buzan, B. 2010. "China in International Society: Is 'Peaceful Rise' Possible?" *Chinese Journal of International Politics* 3(1): 5–36.

Carter, B. 2014. "Is China's Economy Really the Largest in the World?" *BBC.* http://www.bbc.com/news/magazine-30483762

Chan, I. and Li, M. 2015. "New Chinese Leadership, New Policy in the South China Sea Dispute?" *Journal of Chinese Political Science* 20(1): 35–50.

Chang-Liao, N.-C. 2016. "China's New Foreign Policy under Xi Jinping." *Asian Security* 12(2): 82–91.

Cheng, J.Y.S. and Paladini, S. 2014. "China's Ocean Development Strategy and its Handling of the Territorial Conflicts in the South China Sea." *Philippine Political Science Journal* 35(2): 185–202.

Christensen, T.J. 2006. "Fostering Stability or Creating a Monster? The Rise of China and US Policy toward East Asia." *International Security* 31(1): 81–126.

Ciorciari, J.D. 2012. "Institutionalizing Human Rights in Southeast Asia." *Human Rights Quarterly* 34(3): 695–725.

Ciorciari, J.D. 2015. "A Chinese Model for Patron–Client Relations? The Sino-Cambodian Partnership." *International Relations of the Asia-Pacific* 15(2): 245–278.

Ciorciari, J.D. and Weiss, J.C. 2012. "The Sino-Vietnamese Standoff in the South China Sea." *Georgetown Journal of International Affairs* 13(1): 61–69.

Cornut, J. 2015. "Analytic Eclecticism in Practice: A Method for Combining International Relations Theories." *International Studies Perspectives* 16(1): 50–66.

Cox, R. 1981. "Social Forces, States and World Orders: Beyond International Relations Theory." *Millennium* 10(2): 126–155.

The Economist. 2014. "At the Double." *The Economist*. http://www.economist.com/news/china/21599046-chinas-fast-growing-defence-budget-worries- its-neighbours-not-every-trend-its-favour

Fangyin, Z. 2016. "Between Assertiveness and Self-Restraint: Understanding China's South China Sea Policy." *International Affairs* 92(4): 869–890.

Felongco, G. 2013. "Philippines Alarmed over Militarisation in South China Sea." *Gulf News*. http://gulfnews.com/news/asia/philippines/philippines-alarmed- over-militarisation-in-south-china-sea-1.1203797

Ford, P. 2015. "A Newly Modest China? Official's Reassurances Raise Eyebrows in US." *The Christian Science Monitor*. http://www.csmonitor.com/World/Asia- Pacific/2015/0107/A-newly-modest-China-Official-s-reassurances-raise-eyebrows- in-US

Fravel, M.T. 2014. "Territorial and Maritime Boundary Disputes in Asia." In S. Pekkanen, J. Ravenhill, and R. Foot (eds) *The Oxford Handbook of the International Relations of Asia*. Oxford: Oxford University Press, pp 524–546.

Glaser, C. 2011a. *Rational Theory of International Politics: The Logic of Competition and Cooperation*. Princeton: Princeton University Press.

Glaser, C. 2011b. "Will China's Rise Lead to War? Why Realism Does Not Mean Pessimism." *Foreign Affairs* March/April: 80–91.

Goh, E. 2005. *Meeting the China Challenge: The U.S. in Southeast Asian Regional Security Strategies*. Washington, DC: East-West Center.

Graham, E. 2013. "Southeast Asia in the US Rebalance: Perceptions from a Divided Region." *Contemporary Southeast Asia: A Journal of International and Strategic Affairs* 35(3): 305–332.

Graham-Harrison, E. 2015. "South China Sea Islands are Chinese Plan to Militarise Zone, Claims US." *The Guardian*, May 30. http://www.theguardian.com/world/2015/ may/30/us-claims-south-china-sea-islands-are-beijing-plot

Grønning, B.E.M. 2017. "Japan's Security Cooperation with the Philippines and Vietnam." *The Pacific Review* 31(4): 1–20.

Gu, J., Humphrey, J., and Messner, D. 2008. "Global Governance and Developing Countries: The Implications of the Rise of China." *World Development* 36(2): 274–292.

Hale, E. 2021. "China uses Maritime Militia to Assert Claim on South China Sea." *Al Jazeera*. https://www.aljazeera.com/news/2021/11/19/china-supports-maritime-militia-to-assert-south-china-sea-claim

Hameiri, S. and Jones, L. 2015. "Rising Powers and State Transformation: The Case of China." *European Journal of International Relations* 22(1): 72–98.

Hamilton-Hart, N. 2012. *Hard Interests, Soft Illusions: Southeast Asia and American Power*. Ithaca: Cornell University Press.

Haver, Z. 2021. "Japan Latest Nation to Contest Beijing's South China Sea Claims." *Voice of America*, January 23. https://www.voanews.com/a/east-asia-pacific_japan-latest-nation-contest-beijings-south-china-sea-claims/6201116.html

Hayes, J. 2009. "Identity and Securitization in the Democratic Peace: The United States and the Divergence of Response to India and Iran's Nuclear Programs." *International Studies Quarterly* 53(4): 977–999.

The Heritage Foundation. 2015. *Asia 2016 Index of US Military Strength*. http://index.heritage.org/military/2015/chapter/op-environment/asia/

Higgins, A. 2012. "In Philippines, Banana Growers Feel Effect of South China Sea Dispute." *The Washington Post*. http://www.washingtonpost.com/world/asia_pacific/in-philippines-banana-growers-feel-effect-of-south-china-sea-dispute/2012/06/10/gJQA47WVTV_story.html

Huan, A. and Emmers, R. 2016. "What Explains the Success of Preventive Diplomacy in Southeast Asia?" *Global Change, Peace & Security* 29(1): 77–93.

Hughes, C. 1995. "China and Liberalism Globalised." *Millennium* 24(3): 425–445.

Ikenberry, G.J. 2001. "American Power and the Empire of Capitalist Democracy." *Review of International Studies* 27(5): 191–212.

Ikenberry, G.J. 2008. "The Rise of China and the Future of the West." *Foreign Affairs* January/February: 57–72.

Ikenberry, G.J. 2011. *Liberal Leviathan: The Origins, Crisis, and Transformation of the American World Order*. Princeton: Princeton University Press.

Jaipragas, B. 2018. "Forget the Warships: Malaysian PM Mahathir's Peace Formula for South China Sea." *South China Morning Post*, June 19. https://www.scmp.com/week-asia/geopolitics/chapter/2151403/forget-warships-malaysian-pm-mahathirs-peace-formula-south

Jaknanihan, A. 2022. "Stiffening the ASEAN Spine in the South China Sea." *The Interpreter*, March 25. https://www.lowyinstitute.org/the-interpreter/stiffening-asean-spine-south-china-sea

Jennings, R. 2021. "Why the EU Sides with Southeast Asia in the South China Sea Dispute." *VOA News*, August 21. https://www.voanews.com/a/east-asia-pacific_why-eu-sides-southeast-asia-south-china-sea-dispute/6209828.html

Kirshner, J. 2012. "The Tragedy of Offensive Realism: Classical Realism and the Rise of China." *European Journal of International Relations* 18(1): 53–75.

Koda, Y. 2016. "Maritime Security in the Region: SCS and ECS as Key Arenas for Converging Political Interests." *Asia-Pacific Review* 23(2): 86–108.

Kurlantzick, J. 2011. "The Belligerents." *The New Republic.* https://newrepublic.com/chapter/82211/china-foreign-policy

Laliberte, A. 2016. "China's Domestic Problems." *Diplomat and International Canada.* http://diplomatonline.com/mag/2016/10/chinas-domestic-problems/

Lam, W. 2014. "China's Soft-Power Deficit Widens as Xi Tightens Screws Over Ideology." *China Brief*, December 5. http://www.jamestown.org/programs/ chinabrief/single/?tx_ttnews%5Btt_news%5D=43160&tx_ttnews%5BbackPid%5D= 25&cHash=d5d24d2f82c5981963c0180d300e62cd#.VXa4WmCOXjR

Landler, M. 2010. "Offering to Aid Talks, U.S. Challenges China on Disputed Islands." *The New York Times.* http://www.nytimes.com/2010/07/24/world/ asia/24diplo.html

Li, M. 2015. "The People's Liberation Army and China's Smart Power Quandary in Southeast Asia." *Journal of Strategic Studies* 38(3): 359–382.

Liff, A.P. and Ikenberry, G.J. 2014. "Racing toward Tragedy? China's Rise, Military Competition in the Asia Pacific, and the Security Dilemma." *International Security* 39(2): 52–91. http://www.mitpressjournals.org/doi/pdfplus/10.1162/ ISEC_a_00176

Mai, J. and Zheng, S. 2017. "Xi Personally Behind Tough Stance on South China Sea Dispute." *South China Morning Post.* http://www.scmp.com/news/china/policies- politics/chapter/2104547/xi-personally-behind-island-building-south-china-sea

Marcus, J. 2015. "US–China Tensions Rise Over Beijing's 'Great Wall of Sand'." *BBC.* http://www.bbc.com/news/world-asia-32913899?OCID=fbasia

Mastanduno, M. 2014. "Realism and Asia." In S. Pekkanen, J. Ravenhill, and R. Foot (eds) *The Oxford Handbook of the International Relations of Asia.* Oxford: Oxford University Press, pp 25–44.

Mastro, O. 2021. "What are China's Leaders Saying about the South China Sea?" *The Interpreter.* https://www.lowyinstitute.org/the-interpreter/what-are-china-s-leaders-saying-about-south-china-sea

Mearsheimer, J.J. 2006. "China's Unpeaceful Rise." *Current History* 105(690): 160–162.

Mearsheimer, J.J. 2014. "Can China Rise Peacefully?" *The National Interest*, October 25. http://www.eastlaw.net/wp-content/uploads/2016/09/Can-China-Rise-Peacefully_-_-The- National-Interest.pdf

Meyer, P.K. 2016. "China's Discourse Involving the South China Sea Disputes: A Non-Chinese Approach to International Affairs." *East West Institute.* https:// www.eastwest.ngo/idea/china%E2%80%99s-discourse-involving-south-china-sea- disputes-non-chinese-approach-international-affairs

The Ministry of National Defense, People's Republic of China. 2015. *Chinese Navy Conducts Live Firing Drill in South China Sea.* http://eng.mod.gov.cn/ TopNews/2015–07/28/content_4611603.htm

Monteiro, N.P. 2014. *Theory of Unipolar Politics.* New York: Cambridge University Press.

Murphy, A.M. 2017. "Great Power Rivalries, Domestic Politics and Southeast Asian Foreign Policy: Exploring the Linkages." *Asian Security* 13(3): 165–182.

Nye, J. 2013. "Limits of American Power." *Political Science Quarterly* 117(4): 545– 559.

Nye, J. and Ramani, S. 2015. "Interview: Joseph Nye." *The Diplomat.* http://thediplomat.com/2015/06/interview-joseph-nye/

Oneal, J.R. and Bryan, A.L. 1995. "The Rally Round the Flag Effect in U.S. Foreign Policy Crises, 1950–1985." *Political Behavior* 17(4): 379–401.

Panda, A. 2015. "G7 Leaders Call for 'Rules-Based' Maritime Order, Condemn North Korea." *The Diplomat.* http://thediplomat.com/2015/06/g7-leaders-call-for- rules-based-maritime-order-condemn-north-korea/

Parisot, J. 2013. "American Power, East Asian Regionalism and Emerging Powers: In or against Empire?" *Third World Quarterly* 34(7): 1159–1174.

Permanent Court of Arbitration. 2015. "Press Release: Arbitration between the Republic of the Philippines and the People's Republic of China." http://www.pca-cpa.org/shownews.asp?nws_id=518&pag_id=1261&ac=view

Pew Research Center. 2015. "How Asia-Pacific Publics See Each Other and Their National Leaders." *Pew Research Center,* September 2. http://www.pewglobal.org/2015/09/02/how-asia-pacific-publics-see-each-other-and-their-national-leaders/

Poh, A. 2017. "The Myth of Chinese Sanctions over South China Sea Disputes." *The Washington Quarterly* 40(1): 143–165.

Pomfret, J. 2010. "U.S. Takes a Tougher Tone with China." *The Washington Post.* http://www.washingtonpost.com/wp-dyn/content/chapter/2010/07/29/ AR2010072906416.html

Ratner, E. and Kumar, S. 2017. "The United States is Losing Asia to China." *Foreign Policy.* https://foreignpolicy.com/2017/05/12/the-united-states-is-losing-asia- to-china/

Regilme, S.S.F. 2019. "The Decline of American Power and Donald Trump: Reflections on Human Rights, Neoliberalism, and the World Order." *Geoforum* 102: 157–166.

Regilme, S.S.F. 2021. *Aid Imperium: United States Foreign Policy and Human Rights in Post-Cold War Southeast Asia.* Ann Arbor: University of Michigan Press.

Regilme, S.S.F. and Hartmann, H. 2018. "Mutual Delegitimization: American and Chinese Development Assistance in Africa." *The SAIS Review of International Affairs.* http://www.saisreview.org/2018/03/30/china-america-development-assistance/

Regilme, S.S.F. and Parisot, J. (eds). 2017a. *American Hegemony and the Rise of Emerging Powers: Cooperation or Conflict.* London: Routledge.

Regilme, S.S.F. and Parisot, J. 2017b. "Introduction: Debating American hegemony—Global Cooperation and Conflict." In J. Parisot and S.S.F. Regilme (eds) *American Hegemony and the Rise of Emerging Powers, Cooperation or Conflict.* Abingdon: Routledge, pp 3–18.

Regilme, S.S.F. and Parisot, J. 2020. "Contested American Dominance: Global Order in an Era of Rising Powers." In S.A. Hamed Hosseini, J. Goodman, S.C. Motta, and B.K. Gills (eds) *The Routledge Handbook of Transformative Global Studies.* Abingdon: Routledge, pp 181–193.

Rosato, S. 2015. "The Inscrutable Intentions of Great Powers." *International Security* 39(3): 48–88.

Seah, S., Lin, J., Suvannphakdy, S., Martinus, M., Puong Thao, P.T., Seth, F.N. and Thi Ha, H. 2022. *The State of Southeast Asia: 2022 Survey Report.* Singapore: ISEAS-Yusof Ishak Institute. https://www.iseas.edu.sg/wp-content/uploads/2022/02/The-State-of-SEA-2022_FA_Digital_FINAL.pdf

Shah, D.P. 2017. "China's Maritime Security Strategy: An Assessment of the White Paper on Asia-Pacific Security Cooperation." *Maritime Affairs: Journal of the National Maritime Foundation of India* 13(1): 1–13.

Shambaugh, D. 2013. *China Goes Global: The Partial Power.* New York: Oxford University Press.

Shicun, W. and Huaifeng, R. 2003. "More than a Declaration: A Commentary on the Background and the Significance of the Declaration on the Conduct of the Parties in the South China Sea." *The Chinese Journal of International Law* 2(1): 311–319.

Sil, R. and Katzenstein, P. 2010. *Analytic Eclecticism in the Study of World Politics.* Basingstoke: Palgrave Macmillan.

Silver, L., Devlin, K., and Huang, C. 2019. "China's Economic Growth Mostly Welcomed in Emerging Markets, but Neighbors Wary of Its Influence." *Pew Research Center.* https://www.pewresearch.org/global/2019/12/05/chinas-economic-growth-mostly-welcomed-in-emerging-markets-but-neighbors-wary-of-its-influence/

SIPRI. 2021. "World Military Spending Rises to Almost $2 trillion in 2020." *SIPRI*, April 26. https://www.sipri.org/media/press-release/2021/world-military-spending-rises-almost-2-trillion-2020

Spitzer, K. 2012. "The South China Sea: From Bad to Worse." *Time.* http://nation.time.com/2012/07/15/the-south-china-sea-from-bad-to-worse/

Starrs, S. 2013. "American Economic Power Hasn't Declined—It Globalized! Summoning the Data and Taking Globalization Seriously." *International Studies Quarterly* 57(4): 817–830.

Storey, I.J. 1999. "Creeping Assertiveness: China, the Philippines and the South China Sea Dispute." *Contemporary Southeast Asia* 21(1): 95–118.

The Straits Times. 2018. "Let Malaysia Continue Occupying Islands in South China Sea: PM Mahathir." *The Straits Times,* June 20. https://www.straitstimes.com/asia/se-asia/ pm-mahathir-let-malaysia-continue-occupying-islands-in-south-china-sea

Sun, Y. 2014. "China's New Calculations in the South China Sea." *East European Politics and Societies* 1–2. http://scholarspace.manoa.hawaii.edu/bitstream/ handle/10125/33116/APB%20no.%20267.pdf?sequence=1

Thang, N.D. 2011. "Fisheries Co-operation in the South China Sea and the (Ir)relevance of the Sovereignty Question." *Asian Journal of International Law* 2(1): 59–88.

Thayer, C. 2015. "The Philippines and Vietnam Forge a Strategic Partnership." *The Diplomat.* http://thediplomat.com/2015/03/the-philippines-and-vietnam-forge-a- strategic-partnership/

Venzon, C. 2022. "U.S., Philippines Begin War Games as South China Sea Spat Lingers." *Nikkei Asia*, March 28. https://asia.nikkei.com/Politics/International-relations/U.S.-Philippines-begin-war-games-as-South-China-Sea-spat-lingers

Yahuda, M. 2013. "China's New Assertiveness in the South China Sea." *Journal of Contemporary China* 22(81): 446–459.

Yahya, Y. 2018. "Singapore, Australia Share Common Interests in South China Sea Issue, Says PM Lee." *Straits Times.* https://www.straitstimes.com/politics/singapore- australia-share-common-interests-in-south-china-sea-issue-says-pm-lee

Yoon, S. 2015. "Why is China Militarising the South China Sea?" *NTU Rajaratnam School of International Studies.* https://www.rsis.edu.sg/rsis-publication/rsis/ co15113-why-is-china-militarising-the-south-china-sea/#.VWhVmWCOXjQ

Zhang, F. 2017. "Assessing China's Response to the South China Sea Arbitration Ruling." *Australian Journal of International Affairs* 71(4): 440–459.

4

South Asian Contestations and India's Strategic Role: An Advaita Account

Deepshikha Shahi

Although US President Bill Clinton had nonchalantly floated the imagery of South Asia as "the most dangerous place in the world" in the wake of the nuclear tests by India and Pakistan in 1998, his views were outrightly rejected by India (Babington and Constable 2000). Besides, China emerged as a stabilizing force in the region as it instigated its shuttle diplomacy between India and Pakistan not only after the nuclear tests in 1998 but also after the Mumbai attack in 2008. Even as the disputed Kashmir remains a nuclear flashpoint (notwithstanding the US offer to "help" resolve this lingering issue), several topical incidences—for example, the Doklam standoff, Pulwama attack, Ladakh clash, Taliban takeover, arms race, trade war, pandemic blame-game, and Russia–Ukraine crisis—have triggered fresh patterns of quadrilateral interactions between four key (non-)state actors in South Asia, namely, India, Pakistan, China, and the US. While the competitive and cooperative trends underpinning these quadrilateral interactions are difficult to fathom in terms of traditional Western realism (which considers the sphere of "the international" as fraught with dualistic self-other enmity), this chapter evokes a non-dualistic Global International Relations (IR) theory inspired by the Indian philosophy of Advaita to appraise India's strategic response to the ongoing US–China rivalry in South Asia: unlike the dualistic Western IR theories based on a fundamental self–other distinction, the non-dualistic Advaita Global IR theory ties the self and the other together with a globe marked with single hidden connectedness. Since India is increasingly recognized as a rising power in world politics, a systematic study of its strategic response to the ongoing US–China rivalry in

South Asia is decisive for making sense of the overall global transformations. The chapter is divided into three sections. The first section illustrates the historical trajectory of geopolitical rivalries in South Asia. The second section identifies the topical issues that have cropped up as departure points in this conventional historical trajectory. Finally, the third section employs the Advaita Global IR theory (which refutes the Western style of IR hooked on the fixed logic of self–other enmity, friendship, or neutrality) to facilitate an improved investigation of these topical issues, thereby providing an alternative intellectual framework to interpret the contemporary postures of US–China contestations in world politics.

Demarcating the historical trajectory

South Asia is home to one of the world's oldest civilizations, the Indus valley civilization, that flourished around 2500 BCE and extended along modern-day India, Pakistan, and Afghanistan. Over the millennia, the South Asian political communities carved their own geopolitical cultures. At present, these geopolitical cultures—proliferating in segregated territories of India, Pakistan, Afghanistan, Bangladesh, Bhutan, Nepal, Sri Lanka, and the Maldives—function as distinct "geographical imaginations about self and other in the world," thereby permitting a specific self (or political actor) to momentarily recognize "its enemies and the strategies it deems necessary to preserve its existence, identity, and capacity for maneuver" (Toal 2017: 39). In order to obtain a holistic overview of these geopolitical cultures, it is mandatory to analyze them at three levels—"global" (world politics), "local" (regional politics), and "national" (domestic politics).

At the global level, the distinct conceptual construct of "South Asia" emerged only after the decolonization of British India in 1947 (Wagner 2021). Historically, British colonizers ruled India, Pakistan, Bangladesh, and Sri Lanka (former "Ceylon") and formed protectorates in Bhutan and the Maldives. They did not directly rule but heavily influenced the foreign policies of Afghanistan and Nepal. In 1947, they divided British India into two self-governing territories: India and Pakistan. In 1965, they granted freedom to the Maldives and left this region. However, they retained a crucial zone called the British Indian Ocean Territory (Diego Garcia), where they continue to allow the US military presence. Since 1965, some shifts in the international borders have occurred. Pakistan received 10 percent of the Rann of Kutch from India in 1968, but lost its eastern extension which turned into Bangladesh in 1971. Also, India and Bangladesh switched 51 Bangladeshi enclaves in India and 111 Indian enclaves in Bangladesh. It is anticipated that the partition of the Indian subcontinent into India, Pakistan, and Bangladesh "may not be history's last word in political geography there"; perhaps, it is unwise to assume that this "British paradigm will last forever" (Kaplan 2014). But it is safe to say that, "fairly extensively," the "international borders between the eight nations of South Asia are British creations" (Snedden 2016: 8).

When the Second World War led to the collapse of colonialism, South Asia, a site of several erstwhile colonized countries, was seen as the leader in the development of the so-called Third World (Hilali 2006). In the ensuing Cold War between the First World (US-led capitalist bloc) and Second World (Soviet Union-led communist bloc), South Asia stayed a "peripheral" site (McMahon 2006): the US–Soviet Union superpower rivalry molded the strategic choices of the region, but the region itself was not the primary showground in this rivalry; it was only with the 1979 Soviet intrusion in Afghanistan that the region captured the Cold War spotlight. To discuss the pressures unleashed by the Cold War bloc politics, the South Asian leaders met at the Asian Relations Conference held in New Delhi on March 23, 1947 and decided to follow the doctrine of *nonalignment*. Suggesting to keep away from the bloc politics of groups aligned against each other, which had led to world wars and which might again lead to disasters on a vaster scale, Jawaharlal Nehru, then serving as minister for external affairs in the interim Indian government, exclaimed:

> The countries of Asia can no longer be used as pawns by others; they are bound to have their own policies in world affairs. Europe and America have contributed very greatly to human progress, and for that we must yield them praise and honour. ... But the West has also driven us into wars ... and even now ... there is talk of further wars. ... In this atomic age, Asia will have to function effectively in the maintenance of peace. Indeed, there can be no peace unless Asia plays her part ... all of us in Asia are full of our own troubles. Nevertheless, the whole spirit and outlook of Asia are peaceful. ... We have arrived at a stage in human affairs when the ideal of One World ... seem[s] to be essential. ... We, therefore, support the United Nations structure. ... But in order to have One World, we must also ... think of the countries in Asia co-operating together for that larger ideal. (Copeland et al 2012: 618)

Patently, the US misperceived nonalignment as "neutrality," "Nehru's naivete about the Soviets," and "Nehru's negative attitudes toward the United States": the US claimed that Nehru failed to realize that the Cold War was about values and morality, not just about power and influence; nonetheless, Nehru made it clear that he "liked Americans personally [but] resented at times their lack of imagination and their difficulty in understanding why other countries could not imitate the American way of life" (McMahon 1996: 40–42). In a bid to craft an *Asian way* of life that could accomplish the larger ideal of One World at the regional level, Nehru renewed his plea for establishing a South Asian federation:

> The emergence of the independent nations in Asia naturally leads to what might be called an Asian way of looking at the world. I do not say that there is one Asian way, because Asia is a big continent, offering different viewpoints. However, it is a new angle, and is a change from the Europe-centred or any other view of the world. (Nehru 1961: 280–281)

What, then, was the new angle, the Asian way that differed from the Europe-centred or any other way of looking at the world? Simply put, the Asian way of looking at the world entailed constructing a *concentric-geopolitical-structure* equipped with *panchsheel-functional-principles*. Borrowing from Mahatma Gandhi's premeditations on "oceanic-circles," Nehru (1946: 323–327) planned a concentric-geopolitical-structure resting on the larger ideal of One World overlaying "two or three Asian federations" with India at "the centre of a very big federation." To establish coordination between the global (One World), local (Asian), and national (Indian) wings of this concentric-geopolitical-structure, Nehru recommended an active implementation of the panchsheel-functional-principles which included the norms of nonalignment, non-interference, sovereign equality, territorial integrity, and peaceful coexistence/cooperation for mutual benefit. Noticeably, the same panchsheel principles had founded the 1954 agreement between India and the Tibet region of China. Though these principles were violated in the 1962 Sino-India war fought over a disputed border in the Himalayan mountains of Aksai Chin, India remained committed to these principles while promoting regional cooperation in South Asia.

The seeds of the concentric-geopolitical-structure were sown at the Asian Relations Conference held in New Delhi in 1947 (Haas 1989). But the institutionalization of South Asian regionalism was deferred due to the nationalist undercurrents. In the 1950s, India and Pakistan sought to protect their projected national interests by chasing differing policies in reaction to the Cold War. Pakistan joined the US-sponsored defense deals, South-East Asia Treaty Organization and Central Treaty Organization, whereas India remained tilted toward the Soviet Union. However, the events beyond South Asia acted as a catalyst in reassuring regional cooperation. The creation of another Asian federation in 1967, the Association of South East Asian Nations, presented the prospect of a parallel South Asian regional organization. In the stressful state of affairs caused by the 1971 Indo-Pak war and the 1979 Soviet intrusion in Afghanistan, the hope for peace arose from the ideas of a South Asian regional organization. These ideas were pushed by the Bangladesh president, Ziaur Rahman, who approached India,

Pakistan, Nepal, and Sri Lanka in 1977–1980 to explore the possibilities for regional cooperation.

Responding to Ziaur Rahman's propositions, India's prime minister, Indira Gandhi, asserted: "We adhere to the panchsheel principles and regional cooperation has to fit into that scheme" (Michael 2013: 1944). In line with the panchsheel principles, Bangladesh drafted the proposal for the South Asian Association for Regional Organization (SAARC). Despite persistent pitches to formalize SAARC at the regional level, the political hurdles kept escalating at the national level. While the draft proposal for forming SAARC, as put forth by Bangladesh, was instantly accepted by Bhutan, Nepal, Sri Lanka, and the Maldives, both India and Pakistan exhibited reluctance (Iqbal 2006). Given the protracted history of bilateral disputes in the region, Pakistan had doubts about India's maneuvers to exploit SAARC to fuel its own regional hegemony, whereas India had qualms about its neighbours' trickeries to misappropriate SAARC to gang up against it (Mitra 2003). So, India stressed the restriction of regional cooperation to specific issue-areas and pronounced two preconditions: exclusion of bilateral issues from deliberative discussions; and unanimity as the basis of all decisions (Muni and Muni 1984: 109).

After a series of conscientious consultations, on December 8, 1985, the SAARC Charter was finally approved by India, Pakistan, Bangladesh, Bhutan, Nepal, Sri Lanka, and the Maldives. Owing to the disruptive domestic politics under the People's Democratic Party of Afghanistan, Mujahideen, and Taliban regimes, Afghanistan acquired a formal entry into SAARC only in 2007. The rationale behind forming SAARC was to develop a geopolitical culture where the South Asian political communities (related to various governments and international non-governmental organizations) could work in partnership to cultivate sustainable peace and accelerate economic growth. Still, after 36 years of its existence, neither "political mistrust" has watered down, nor "economic integration" has driven into full swing in South Asia (Kumar and Goyal 2016). Sandy Gordon notes:

> The degree of poverty and instability in South Asia has multiple global effects. First, it consumes substantial global resources for refugee assistance, food programs, peace keeping and making ... [for example] in Afghanistan now, previously in Bangladesh, and more recently in Sri Lanka – and development assistance provided by the World Bank. Second, South Asia is one of the least stable sub-regions of the globe. ... This is in part due to the unstable borders created by the British colonial enterprise ... and in part due to the failure of governance in many regional countries ... the competition between India and Pakistan over Kashmir has contributed to ... the failure of the ... SAARC. ... This regional dissonance has ... attracted

outside ... interference, and acted to leverage sub-regional tensions into global ones ... [for example] China's ability ... to "interfere" in India's troubled "backyard". (Gordon 2012: 53)

The Chinese interference has incited "tempered rivalries" between India and China, India and Pakistan, and the US and China, thereby changing the entire South Asian geopolitical landscape (Percival 2013). At the outset, the US–China rivalries in South Asia may look like a "decade-long sprint," not a "superpower marathon" (Beckley and Brands 2021). Yet, the evolving era of US–China rivalries does not match the patterns of the past (Medeiros 2021). In what follows, the new patterns of quadrilateral interactions between India, Pakistan, China, and the US have been scrutinized so as to detect the departure points in the customary South Asian geopolitical cultures.

Detecting the departure points

Despite Nehru's clever sponsoring of the panchsheel-functional-principles as spiritual strategies to insulate South Asia from the Cold War rivalries, Pakistan dexterously exploited the US fear of communist expansion in Asia and forged a military alliance with it so as to offset "India threat"; likewise, India entered into a quasi-alliance with the Soviet Union so as to counterbalance the "China threat" (Ganguly 2010). Furthermore, Pakistan and China signed a border delimitation agreement in 1963, that is, a year after the 1962 Sino-India war. As per this agreement, Pakistan relocated the Trans-Karakoram tract, a territory in Kashmir that India demanded, to China, thereby converting the bilateral Kashmir dispute into a trilateral one (Tourangbam 2020). While Pakistan intensified its connections with China irrespective of the strong US support (during the 1971 Indo-Pak war) or weak US support (during the 1965 Indo-Pak war), it also played a frontline role for the US in post-1979 Afghanistan. In the light of these fluctuating dynamics, India cautiously calibrated its international relations with an aim to attain a "major power status" (Nayar and Paul 2003). India welcomed the post-Cold War multipolarity and initiated multiple off-and-on cooperative ventures with various countries, including the US, China, and Pakistan. Yet, amidst the fears arising from the unresolved border disputes and China's growing links with Pakistan, India considered the acquisition of nuclear capabilities as key to attaining a major power status. When India devised its "nuclear triad" (with capacities to launch nuclear missiles via air, land, and sea), it provoked not only Pakistan but also China (which owned a huge stockpile of nuclear arsenals) to follow suit, thereby putting South Asia on a "short fuse" (Bidwai and Vanaik 2002). With the rise of China and India as global powers, the South Asian geopolitical landscape has undergone a sweeping transformation. Tanvi Madan elaborates:

> The landscape today is different. The region is ... the primary site of one major power competition – that between China and India. [T]he crucial global competition expected to define the coming era – US–China rivalry – involves a country abutting South Asia. And Beijing has been increasing its presence ... in almost every South Asian country and in the Indian Ocean region. ... Other major powers, which have existing strategic or economic equities in the region or, in some cases, their own concerns about China's rising influence and behavior, will also play a role. These include Japan, Russia, and the European Union (as well as particular European countries, such as France and the United Kingdom). Unlike in the Cold War, South Asia and the Indian Ocean region will be a significant arena of major power competition. ... Smaller states in the region will hope to exercise agency and take advantage of major power rivalries while insulating themselves from any fallout. Together, these two dynamics will shape the geopolitical landscape of the region. (Madan 2021: 1)

To review the geopolitical landscape of the region, it is critical to examine how the topical issues—for example, the Doklam standoff, Pulwama attack, Ladakh clash, Taliban takeover, arms race, trade war, pandemic blame-game, and Russia–Ukraine crisis—have ruptured the familiar "strategic chain" between India, Pakistan, China, and the US: here, the ideational formulation of strategic chain indicates "the degree to which actions taken with regard to one country might have unintended second- or third-order effects on other countries in the chain" (Einhorn and Sidhu 2017: 14). In this context, it is pivotal to bear in mind that these manifold "unintended second- or third-order effects" authenticate the perennial thread of *single hidden connectedness* running through the visibly distinct yet invisibly shared destinies of myriad (non-)state actors in South Asian politics in particular and in world politics in general.

To begin with, one can observe a deviation from the elemental "Cold War mentality," whereby Washington and Moscow tended to rigidly align with Pakistan and India respectively. Today, Moscow's "India-centric Soviet-era policy outlook" is getting swiftly replaced with a more diversified approach which includes Pakistan–Russia as well as Sino-Russia pacts (Pant 2017). Besides, "Washington and Beijing are more deeply invested in India and Pakistan respectively, just as they are viewed with greater distrust in Pakistan and India respectively" (Sun 2020: 4). From the US perspective, the habitual practice of calculating the relative strategic importance of India/Pakistan/China is becoming obsolete: instead of proclaiming that "it is China, not India, that will be the power of the future in Asia, and that the United States should adjust its policies accordingly" (Gordon 1995: 879), the new mantra is to acknowledge that "Washington's policymakers need a better understanding of both the opportunities for and the limitations on American power in the area" (Cohen 2000), and "like China, the United States needs to marry its capabilities and proposals with the development priorities and domestic needs of ... [various] South Asian states" (Pal 2021). While the US and China compete-cooperate to acclimatize their capabilities/proposals with the priorities/needs of the South Asian states, India and Pakistan compete-cooperate to derive optimum advantage from the US/Chinese capabilities/proposals and, therefore, take on a more upfront attitude in articulating their priorities/needs.

Of late, India and Pakistan displayed a highly upfront attitude in response to the warlike events in Doklam, Pulwama, Ladakh, Kabul, and Kyiv. In 2017, when China marched ahead to break the 1988–1998 border accords and build a network of roads to boost its armed presence in Doklam—a tranquil Himalayan grazing area adjoining the trijunction between India, China, and Bhutan—the Indian army, at Bhutan's request, intervened to stop the Chinese People's Liberation Army, thereby prompting a standoff between the two Asian giants having disputed borders in the regions spread across 37,000 sq km of unpeopled Aksai Chin and over 84,000 sq km of Arunachal Pradesh with about 1.4 million people. As China's civil society probed the determination of its leaders to protect its territories, India's "conservative civil society" backed the boycott of Chinese goods in the aftermath of the crisis (Mj 2018). Finally, the "diplomatic tango" between India and China led to the withdrawal of troops; India officially declared: "There was an understanding that where we have differences, it is important that differences should not become disputes" (Chengappa and Krishnan 2017: 5). Even if some analysts hailed the end of the crisis as "India's diplomatic victory" (Sajjanhar 2017), others maintained that the lowering of tensions became possible due to "international diplomacy", including US diplomacy (Cherian 2021).

Later, in 2019, India and Pakistan were on the brink of war when Pakistan-based militant group, Jaish-e-Mohammad, claimed responsibility for a suicide attack in Kashmir's Pulwama which killed 40 Indian security forces. While India summoned Pakistan's top envoy and targeted the alleged terrorist camps at Balakot, Pakistan warned of retaliation if India took military action against it. Eventually, the governments of India and Pakistan decided to "give peace a chance" (Mohan 2019), and civil society activists on both sides of the border engaged in dialogues to resolve the differences (Narayan 2019). After closely monitoring the post-Pulwama situation along the border, India's Ministry of External Affairs (2022) issued a press release: "[B]oth the armies have exercised restraint in the interest of maintaining peace." But then again, in 2020, India found itself trapped into a strategic quagmire of "crisis after the crisis" when China hurled near-simultaneous incursions in Ladakh, a territory hitherto regulated by India; both sides deployed tens of thousands of troops and came close to war; however, after suffering casualties, the talks between the armies led to a mutually agreed disengagement process (Tarapore 2021). While the Ladakh clash reinforced the trust deficit between India and China (Philip 2021), the dramatic fall of Kabul to the Taliban bolstered the Pakistan-based anti-India terrorist groups, thereby burdening the 2021 ceasefire agreement between India and Pakistan (Singh 2021).

As the murky clouds of trust-deficit loom large over India–China and India–Pakistan relations, the US has exposed the political will to selectively cooperate as well as compete with China in matters of crisis-management. Just as China has noticed the limits of its crisis-management capabilities/proposals in the face of its lack of neutrality in India's viewpoint (Sun 2020), the US has taken cognizance of India's priorities/needs (for example, India's strong security posture after the Pulwama attack) and realized that its role as a neutral third party is fading away (Noor 2020). Obviously, the US and China share a common neutral gesture in not contending to mediate the bilateral conflicts between India and Pakistan. Still, when it comes to the supplying of arms for crisis-management, the US and China fiercely compete with each other: "the US wants to boost India's firepower against China" (Tiwari 2021), whereas "China moves to counter India with arms sales to Pakistan" (Hille et al 2022).

In principle, India speculates that neither US–China trade war (Chadha et al 2021) nor India–China trade war (Crabtree 2020) might be profitable for it. Hence, India cooperates with China within the Brazil, Russia, India, China, South Africa (BRICS) format to weaken the Washington Consensus (Ban and Blyth 2013), and cooperates with the US within the Quadrilateral Security Dialogue (QUAD) format to preempt the Beijing's supremacy in the Indo-pacific region (Parthasarathy 2021). Nonetheless, this does not indicate India's relentless enmity/friendship/neutrality with the US, China, or Pakistan. India cooperates with the US in the QUAD format but defies the US warning against purchase of Russian S-400 missiles. India cooperates with China within the BRICS format but opposes China's Belt and Road Initiative and the China–Pakistan Economic Corridor. Likewise, India cooperates with Pakistan to allow shipments across the border to help relieve desperate food shortages in Afghanistan, but withstands the suspended trade relations with Pakistan after the 2019 stripping of the statehood and special constitutional status of the Indian-controlled section of Kashmir (Hashim 2022).

The strategic entanglements in these quadrilateral interactions reached new heights with the outbreak of the global pandemic: the US and India blamed China for COVID-19 (Sharma 2020), and China blamed the US, India, and Pakistan for COVID-19 (Chaudhary 2020; Horsley 2020). On top of that, the Russia–Ukraine crisis—which has regenerated the old ideological debates on "US-backed democracy versus China-backed autocracy" (Rainsy 2022)—went a step further in deepening the divides between these countries: while India, Pakistan, and China, considering the 2022 battle of Kyiv as "also an Asian crisis" (Ching 2022), abstained on a UN Security Council resolution on Russia's actions in Ukraine, the US deplored Russia's "aggression" in the strongest terms and appealed to vote against Russia (Roy 2022). Since the messy patterns of competition-cooperation in these quadrilateral interactions cannot be neatly defined by means of Western realism which presupposes fixated international enmities (or friendships or rivalries), the next section awakens the Advaita Global IR theory to assess the altered geopolitical landscape of South Asia.

Delineating the Advaita account

A methodical comprehension of the altered geopolitical landscape of South Asia (and of India's strategic situation therein) requires a priori knowledge of the prevalent Asian worldviews. Some of these Asian worldviews have contributed to the literature on Global IR that seeks to expand the theoretical boundaries of Western IR (including Western realism). In fact, Global IR seeks to incorporate the so far neglected non-/post-Western IR thinking by pursuing multiple pathways, such as: redefining existing IR theories and methods and building new ones from societies hitherto ignored as sources of IR knowledge; showing a commitment to pluralistic universalism, integrating the study of regions and regionalisms into the central concerns of IR; grounding in world history; avoiding ethnocentrism and exceptionalism irrespective of source and form; and admitting a broader concept of agency with material-ideational elements that include resistance, normative action, and local constructions of global order (Acharya 2014). According to the dualistic Western IR theories, different peoples (with their distinct geopolitical imaginings about the mutually separated self and other) either live in one world of globalizing capitalism centered on a single hegemonic power (US/China?) (Hurrell 2007), or live in many worlds with many voices (pluriverse), including the unheard anti-hegemonic indigenous voices (Querejazu 2016). In contrast to these either-or imaginings, the non-dualistic Global IR theories propose that the visibly different peoples are invisibly intertwined in a world which is at once "one-and-many": that is to say, the "visible time–space divisibility of many worlds" constantly coincides with the "invisible time–space indivisibility of one world"; thus, there are no rigid oppositional relations between "individual vs. individual," "state vs. state," or "individual vs. state."

Deriving from an ancient Indian philosophy, the non-dualistic Advaita Global IR theory asserts that the realm of "the international" is an amalgamation of "phenomena" (that is, world-in-appearance with visible self–other distinction) and "noumena" (that is, world-in-itself with invisible oneness). Here, the phenomenal many-ness and noumenal oneness are not two separated existential zones, but two continuous cognitive zones of the same time–space indivisibility that governs the *single hidden connectedness* of the globe. In this state of global connectedness, the self/other located at a fleeting time–space moment does not bear permanent selfhood/otherhood; instead, the self and other remain varyingly yet continually subsumed in each other via a third dimension, that is, invisible oneness; so, the self–other pluralities are to be perceived as non-mutually-binary interlinked categories (Shahi 2018). Since the Advaita Global IR theory does not accept time–space divisibility, it does not define the self–other in terms of their relations to bounded time–space categories of nation, civilization, culture, and so on. Above and beyond the nation-, civilization-, or culture-based enmity, friendship, or neutrality, the Advaita Global IR theory enables the "momentary self" to remain unaffected by the vagaries of time–space settings and act as a disinterested observer in the changing world.

In the practical domain, the Advaita Global IR theory calls for a fundamental reconceptualization of world politics along a set of six principles. In what follows, an attempt has been made to activate these principles to grasp the complexities of current quadrilateral interactions between India, Pakistan, China, and the US in South Asia:

1. The world as a political entity is perpetually connected.

The Advaita Global IR theory puts emphasis on the time–space indivisibility, thereby conveying a picture of a perpetually connected world. In this perpetually connected world, different parts, or, say, different time-space bounded categories (for example, the US, China, India, and Pakistan) have different understandings of specific political scenarios (for example, Doklam, Pulwama, and Ladakh). But these understandings are built on limited time–space exposures and, therefore, manufacture partial and fragmented narratives of the political scenarios. Considering the imperfections of the limited time–space exposures and partial-fragmented narratives, the Advaita Global IR theory solicits a strictly *responsible political action*: in a scenario of war, a responsible political action is not about making a rationalist/realist case for war on the basis of chances to "maximize power" or "balance power"; it is also not about making a reflectivist case for war on the basis of chances to reshuffle "knowledge-power-equations"; it is, rather, about "foregrounding the hidden stakes" inherent in waging a war that shatters global connectedness. To be sure, Gandhi (1967: 390) subscribed to the Advaita vision of global connectedness when he avowed: "I believe in Advaita [that is, 'non-duality'], I believe in the essential unity of man and, for that matter, all that lives. Therefore, I believe that if one man gains spiritually, the whole world gains with him and, if one man falls, the whole world falls to that extent." Though Nehru tried to push this Advaita vision by backing a model of "One World" overlaying "Asian federations" with India at "the centre of a very big federation," his unwillingness to let go of Kashmir gave a setback to Gandhi's legacy. Carol Becker comments:

> By the time of his death, Gandhi's fasts, political negotiations, and actions of militant nonviolence [as Advaita tactics to restore peace] had helped to transform British rule and determine the conditions for India's independence. ... [However, around] this time Gandhi was horrified by the rage ... accompanying the antagonisms between India and Pakistan, which arose for many reasons, among them ... Prime Minister Jawaharlal Nehru's unwillingness to let go of Kashmir. ... As long as Gandhi was still alive, some felt India would never become the "modern", aggressive, forward-looking, powerful state ... [according to them,] a new India ... [could emerge], not with "militant nonviolence", but with military strength. (Becker 2006: 79)

In recent years, the rise of new India has largely hinged on the amplification of military strength. But as long as Kashmir remains volatile and life on any side of the borders remains vulnerable (as exemplified in Doklam, Pulwama, and Ladakh), India's competences to preserve the ideal of a perpetually connected world (One World) will remain challenged, regardless of its morally high-sounding "extended neighbourhood" or "neighbourhood first" diplomatic outreach policies.

2. The constituents of the world (individuals, nation states, classes, communities, cultures, peoples, ecology, and so on) are diverse sub-realities essentially pertaining to the same core reality, that is, single hidden connectedness.

When the Advaita Global IR theory paints a picture of a perpetually connected world, it also affirms that the constituents of the world (that is, diverse individual and institutional political actors) remain willingly or unwillingly interconnected through a *strategic chain of action*: that is to say, the harms and healings of all the individual/institutional political actors are reciprocally tangled. Unlike Western realism, wherein a self (or a political actor who is separated from the other) can gain power by treating the other as an object to be harmed and suffer from that harm =, Advaita demonstrates how the strategic chain of action ensures that the self's act of harming the other can in effect be an act of harming the self. Explaining how this phenomenon manifested itself in the post-Doklam Sino-India trade war, Maira Qaddos remarks:

> [The] boycott of Chinese goods [by India's "conservative civil society"] could help India less but harm more in the course of resolution of Doklam issue. It was a mistaken belief that by boycotting Chinese products, India would be able to pressurize China. Boycott may harm China but its magnitude was overrated by those who were demanding it. It would not be of that much help to India because India is in dire need of those products especially pharma items, smart phones and information technology apparatus. India cannot afford to get these products from other countries with its weaker economy because in that case it will have to make a compromise on low quality products at higher rates. So, India would think twice before putting a ban on Chinese products and vice versa. (Qaddos 2018: 67)

While the strategic chain of action ensures that the self's act of harming the other can in effect be an act of harming the self, it also suggests that the self's act of healing the other can in effect be an act of healing the self. This insight became detectable during the Indo-Pak Pulwama tussles: it was not only Pakistan's prime minister Imran Khan who decided to release the imprisoned Indian pilot in a peaceful gesture intended to ease hostilities (Prakash 2019), but also the Indian experts who agreed that—even if the "security first" and "offensive defense" doctrines of India's prime minister Narendra Modi could apply calibrated diplomatic-economic pressures on Pakistan—a full-scale Indo-Pak/Sino-India war could create a "loss-loss scenario" for all (Chaulia 2022). On the contrary, if India, Pakistan, and China could operate together to "build economic stability," it could potentially allow the China–Pakistan Economic Corridor and India's connectivity with eastern neighbors all the way from Turkey to Singapore, thereby promising economic growth for all (Banik and Raman 2019).

3. The relations between the constituents of the world cannot be understood by following a rigid unit-of-analysis or level-of-enquiry: individuals and institutions at any political level (local, international, or global) bear the same symptom of connectedness.

The Advaita Global IR theory views the constituents of the world (that is, state and non-state actors) as miscellaneous time–space categories pertaining to the same global connectedness. Therefore, both state and non-state actors, as they work at various political levels, remain equally influential in their capabilities to impair or repair global connectedness. In the wake of a crisis situation (which threatens to impair global connectedness), different state and non-state actors publicize varied observations/perceptions/(re)actions. These observations/perceptions/(re)actions can move in "bottom-up direction" (from local to global) or "top-down direction" (from global to local), thereby contributing to aggravate or ameliorate the crisis situation. In view of this predictability, the Advaita Global IR theory maintains that the state actors can resolve a crisis situation only if their crisis-management measures echo with the hopes of local–global non-state actors. To solve a crisis situation, Advaita advises a proactive synchronizing of state and non-state actions: contrary to the realist line of reasoning whereby the state remains the primary political actor, the Advaita Global IR theory emphasizes that the derailment of crisis-management measures can be preempted if the state and non-state actors work in consistent cooperation with each other. Analyzing how a proactive synchronizing of state and non-state actions mobilizes China's tricky involvement in some of the South Asian states, Deep Pal reports:

> China has been emboldened to assert its interests in South Asia more directly because of profound changes in its relationships with states in the region. Over the past decade, it has developed a greater variety of interests and … more channels of influence. … China floods a country not just with investment but also with strategic messages designed to influence public opinion, there is often little space left for counter-narratives, especially in countries that lack independent media or have weak civil societies. (Pal 2021: 2, 11)

While China has developed a "new model of state–civil society relations" that combines the pluralistic aspect of democratic governance with the state control mechanisms prevalent in authoritarian regimes (Teets 2014), India considers the reviving of Pakistan's weak civil society as a "sensible course" that can empower Pakistan to dodge the perilous strategic choice between radical Islamists and US-sponsored military generals who still call the shots on its foreign policy (Chellaney 2010). Nevertheless, India itself appears to be wavering between a pro-government "conservative civil society" (Mj 2018) and an anti-government "moderate civil society" (Feyyaz 2019) when it comes to policy designing on diverse issues related to trade war or inter-state war. In general, a proactive synchronizing of state and non-state actions is desirable in South Asia where the "pluralistic civil society" (as non-state actor) includes both civil and uncivil elements which may positively or negatively contribute to the crisis-management measures (Sahoo 2021).

4. The diversity among the constituents of the world is a partial reality depending on analytical priorities and heuristic attitudes, calling for advancement in the intellectual capabilities to reveal the hidden connectedness across diversities.

The Advaita Global IR theory comprehends the varied observations, perceptions, and (re)actions (or partial-fragmented narratives) of different state and non-state actors as fleeting snapshots of a crisis situation, that is, a sort of "halfway house" that can be amended in the overall journey of resolving crisis and realizing global connectedness. From this standpoint, a meticulous process of resolving crisis requires a gradual subration of all falsifiable distinctions: here, "subration" implies continual cancellation of all falsifiable distinctions in the outwardly clashing positions of different state and non-state stakeholders so as to extract their inwardly common connections (Shahi 2018). During the Russia–Ukraine crisis, India largely depended on the process of subration to clarify its strategic posturing vis-à-vis the crisis. When India abstained on the US-sponsored UN Security Council resolution on Russia's actions in Ukraine, the US interpreted India's position as "unsatisfactory" (as India did not take the US side) and "unsurprising" (as India seemed to take Russia's side) (Brunnstrom and Martina 2022): here, the US tried to contain India in its classic realist dualistic "us versus them" conundrum. Nevertheless, India cancelled these falsifiable distinctions by announcing that its abstention was a strategy to keep open the opportunity to reach out to both Russia and Ukraine and persuade them "to continue to engage despite the situation" (Gupta 2022). Soon thereafter, when India began to increase its import of Russian oil, despite the imposition of economic sanctions on Russia in the aftermath of the crisis, the US construed India's position as "somewhat shaky" (Chaudhury 2022). But then again, India cancelled these falsifiable distinctions by expounding how India, like other European countries, decided to purchase increased Russian oil because Russia was offering oil at a discounted rate; also, India compared its outwardly disinterested role in the Russia–Ukraine crisis with Europe's outwardly disinterested role after the Taliban takeover (Wintour 2022). The more India cancelled these outwardly falsifiable distinctions, the more it extracted their inwardly common connections: despite distinctions in logical justification of abstention from the UN Security Council vote, the nonaligned stance of India and China formed their inwardly common connections. It was steadily shown how the Russia–Ukraine crisis brought India, China, and Pakistan onto the same page (Mahapatra 2022). However, even if the Russia–Ukraine crisis brought India, China, and Pakistan onto the same page, this fleeting convergence may prove futile if India fails to utilize it "to resolve the border disputes with China, [Pakistan, and other non-state stakeholders] through give-and-take, or seek to promote peace in South Asia" (Chattopadhyay and Vanaik 2022).

5. The intellectual realization of "connectedness" can make a powerful case for reinterpreting diversities in political identities, thereby creating new ethical space for condemning divisive domestic, international, and global politics.

The Advaita Global IR theory treats not only the "varied observations/perceptions/(re)actions" but also the "varied national/civilizational/cultural identities" of state and non-state actors as fragmented halfway-houses that can be surpassed in the overall journey of resolving crisis and realizing global connectedness. Unlike Western realism that grapples with the identitarian issues of "self–other difference" (Tsygankov and Tsygankov 2022), the Advaita Global IR theory revisits the identity question by underlining the possibility to dissolve "self–other differences," especially during the crisis situations. The crisis situation caused by the global COVID-19 pandemic offered the possibility to dissolve self–other differences and to uncover the interconnectedness of diverse national-, civilizational-, and cultural-identities whose shared destinies lay in a human spirit capable of showing resilience, effectiveness, and leadership. To some extent, this human spirit stimulated the South Asian leaders as they realized that the pandemic had exposed the region to an "interconnectedness [where] … if the vulnerable remains at risk, everyone remains at risk" (Bishop and Roberts 2020: 22). Given the interconnectedness, the US, China, India, and Pakistan made efforts to provide relief to the South Asian victims of COVID-19. Despite the blame-game—whereby the US and India blamed China, and China blamed the US, India, and Pakistan for COVID-19—each of these countries cooperated in distributing millions of vaccines in the region. However, these cooperative infrastructures soon became marred with the geopolitical rivalries between India and China, India and Pakistan, and the US and China. Bhagya Senaratne records:

> The scale of Chinese assistance since the onset of the pandemic has reinforced the insecurities that India and the United States have regarding the increased engagement by China in countries such as Maldives, Pakistan, and Sri Lanka. Thus, the emerging trend whereby the United States and India are partnering with one another to counter China's activities has continued. … From the perspective of the small states in the region, the increased presence of China to provide [COVID-19] assistance … and counterbalance Indian dominance in the extended Indian Ocean region is identified as being a positive outcome of the power rivalry between China, India, and the United States. (Senaratne 2020: 9)

Against the backdrop of the global pandemic, the South Asian geopolitical rivalries have stirred "vaccine nationalism." Gauging India's experiments with vaccine nationalism as a strategic tool, Niladri Chatterjee, Zaad Mahmood, and Eleonor Marcussen argue:

> India's vaccine nationalism has taken a different turn. The scientific ability to innovate vaccines has been used as a marker of pre-eminence

and for the construction of national identity. Indian pharmaceutical companies are major manufacturers of vaccines distributed worldwide, particularly those for low-income countries, supplying more than 60 per cent of vaccines to the developing world. ... The Indian Prime Minister has stated that India's vaccine production will be used for the benefit of all humanity to fight the Covid-19 pandemic ... [but] India has announced assistance of vaccines to neighbouring countries and supplied Bhutan, Maldives, Nepal and Bangladesh as "gifts" or grants in line with New Delhi's "Neighbourhood First" policy. ... It is undeniable that India's vaccine gifts will serve to polish its global image and earn her goodwill, especially in South Asia where it is often criticized for its "big brother" behaviour. (Chatterjee et al 2021: 360–361)

As long as the promise of India (or other countries) to provide COVID-19 care and serve humanity will keep fanning the fire of nationalism or regionalism, it will go on adding to the surge of divisive racism and xenophobic sentiments which have affected the minority groups within countries across the world (Elias et al 2021). Perhaps, what the world needs is an enforceable "COVID-19 agreement" that could regulate vaccine manufacturing and global trade by creating layers of interdependence, thereby reducing the fears of those vaccine-producing countries which worry that sharing their output might deprive their "own populations" (Bollyky and Bown 2020.

6. The connected nature of the world is not an unfulfilled political goal to be realized, but an unrealized intellectual quest to be explored.

According to the Advaita Global IR theory, the more the non-centric invisible oneness beneath the geocentric visible many-ness of lives is taken seriously, the more responsible humankind will be in nurturing a sustainable post-pandemic world. Contrary to Western realism that exploits the idea of "outer power" (hard/soft/smart power) to secure survival and/or hegemony in world, Advaita introduces the notion of "inner power" to uncover hidden oneness across the apparent many-ness of the world. However, this agenda to uncover hidden oneness across apparent many-ness is not a hegemonic (or an authoritarian) enterprise. Though Advaita assumes the many-ness of observations/perceptions/(re)actions/identities as amendable halfway-houses, it embraces them as apparent forms of realities. In practice, Advaita makes an intellectual appeal to process these many-ness of observations/perceptions/(re)actions/identities as dynamic interconnectivities, not static binaries. In so doing, it condemns any politicized authoritarian attempts to tame many-ness in the name of oneness. When the Chinese foreign minister Wang Yi visited India in March 2022 and officially denounced the image of a "unipolar Asia," his statement sounded very much in line with the pro-Advaita intellectual insight that "there is no singular idea of Asia" and that Asia is a "contested notion" (Acharya 2010: 1001). But Wang Yi's message was widely processed in India as an "art of deception" that characterized China's past geostrategic culture (Banerjee 2022). As India stresses the need to "mov[e] away from the prison of its past image, and transform ... itself into a country that decides and shapes international discourse, and takes firm decisions" (Jaishankar 2020), it must keep an open mind and also allow other state or non-state stakeholders in South Asia (including China, Pakistan, and the US) to move away from the prisons of their past images (as India's foes/friends), while dialogically engaging with them and processing their observations/perceptions/(re)actions/identities as dynamic interconnectivities, not static binaries. Until India tactically commits itself to such bilateral/multilateral dialogues for resolving different crisis situations, the Advaita visualizations of "one-and-many Asia" and "one-and-many world" will remain an unrealized intellectual quest.

In contrast to the state-centric approach of Western realism that seems to be better at explaining risks/dangers than offering solutions (Johnston 2020), the aforementioned six principles of Advaita Global IR theory enable us to take into account both state and non-state transactions happening in national domestic politics, local regional politics, and global world politics for not only providing a more nuanced analysis of the complexities of quadrilateral interactions between India, Pakistan, China, and the US in South Asia, but also to put forward some suggestions for a more responsible political action based on an understanding of the single hidden connectedness which ensures that the degree to which the strategic actions of harms/healings are taken with regard to one country is bound to have unintended effects on other countries that are collectively involved in determining South Asia's role in shaping global transformations.

Conclusion

The dualistic portrayal of self–other relations in terms of rigid animosity, friendship, or rivalry in orthodox Western IR theories (for example, realism, liberalism, and constructivism) seem inadequate in their ability to capture the new patterns of quadrilateral interactions between the key (non-)state actors in South Asia, namely, India, Pakistan, China, and the US. Against this backdrop, the present chapter employs the non-dualistic Advaita Global IR theory—which presumes the presence of a single hidden connectedness beneath all self–other distinctions in world politics—to challenge the conventional understandings of geopolitical cultures in South Asia. The chapter shows that the non-dualistic geographical spatial imaginary of Advaita—wherein the realm of "the international" is seen as an amalgamation of "phenomena" (that is, world-in-appearance with visible self–other distinction) and "noumena" (that is, world-in-itself with invisible oneness)—offers an alternative explanation of how the key (non-)state actors in South Asia have engaged themselves with several concurrent competitive and cooperative tendencies, thereby forming, deforming, and transforming the entire South Asian geopolitical landscape.

References

Acharya, A. 2010. "Asia is Not One." *The Journal of Asian Studies* 69(4): 1001–1013.

Acharya, A. 2014. "Global International Relations (IR) and Regional Worlds: A New Agenda for International Studies." *International Studies Quarterly* 58(4): 647–659.

Babington, C. and Constable, P. 2000. "India Rebuffs Clinton on Nuclear Controls." *The Washington Post*. https://www.washingtonpost.com/wp-srv/WPcap/2000-03/22/093r-032200-idx.html

Ban, C. and Blyth, M. 2013. "The BRICs and the Washington Consensus: An Introduction." *Review of International Political Economy* 20(2): 241–255.

Banerjee, A. 2022. "Wang Yi Visit and the Chinese Art of Deception." *India Today*. https://www.indiatoday.in/news-analysis/story/wang-yi-visit-and-the-chinese-art-of-deception-1931553-2022-03-30

Banik, N. and Raman, G.V. 2019. "Reading Between the Lines, from Pulwama to the Balakot Airstrike." *The Wire*. https://thewire.in/security/pulwama-balakot-airstrike-india-pakistan

Becker, C. 2006. "Gandhi's Body and Further Representations of War and Peace." *Art Journal* 65(4): 78–95.

Beckley, M. and Brands, H. 2021. "Into the Danger Zone: The Coming Crisis in US–China Relations." *American Enterprise Institute*. https://www.aei.org/wp-content/uploads/2020/12/Into-the-Danger-Zone.pdf?x91208

Bidwai, P. and Vanaik, A. 2002. *South Asia on a Short Fuse: Nuclear Politics and the Future of Global Disarmament*. New Delhi: Oxford University Press.

Bishop, J. and Roberts, A. 2020. "Geopolitics: Resilient and Sustainable Globalization." In *Challenges and Opportunities in the Post-COVID-19 World*. Geneva: World Economic Forum, pp 20–23. https://www3.weforum.org/docs/WEF_Challenges_and_Opportunities_Post_COVID_19.pdf

Bollyky, T.J. and Bown, C.P. 2020. "The Tragedy of Vaccine Nationalism: Only Cooperation Can End the Pandemic." *Foreign Affairs* 99(5): 96–108.

Brunnstrom, D. and Martina, M. 2022. "U.S. Calls India's Position Over Ukraine 'Unsatisfactory' but Unsurprising." *U.S. News & World Report*. https://www.usnews.com/news/world/articles/2022-03-25/u-s-calls-indias-position-over-ukraine-unsatisfactory-but-unsurprising

Chadha, R., Pohit, S., and Pratap, D. 2021. "The US–China Trade War: Impact on India and Other Asian Regions." *Journal of Asian Economic Integration* 3(2): 144–168.

Chatterjee, N., Mahmood, Z., and Marcussen, E. 2021. "Politics of Vaccine Nationalism in India: Global and Domestic Implications." *Forum for Development Studies* 48(2): 357–369.

Chattopadhyay, K. and Vanaik, A. 2022. "No to Russian Imperialist Aggression, No to US/NATO Interference." *Spectre*. https://spectrejournal.com/no-to-russian-imperialist-aggression-no-to-us-nato-interference/

Chaudhary, S. 2020. "China Blames India & Pakistan for COVID-19 Pandemic; Gives Clean-Chit to Original Epicenter – Wuhan." *Eurasian Times*. https://eurasiantimes.com/covid-19-originated-in-central-india-pakistan-not-in-the-city-of-wuhan-chinese-researchers/

Chaudhury, D.R. 2022. "India 'Shaky' in Dealing with Russia: Joe Biden." *The Economic Times*. https://economictimes.indiatimes.com/news/international/world-news/india-shaky-in-dealing-with-russia-joe-biden/articleshow/90383420.cms?from=mdr

Chaulia, S. 2022. *Crunch Time: Narendra Modi's National Security Crises*. New Delhi: Rupa Publications.

Chellaney, B. 2010. "The China-India-Pakistan Triangle: Scenarios for the 21st Century." *CERI Strategy Papers*, Centre D'études et de Recherches Internationales. https://www.sciencespo.fr/ceri/sites/sciencespo.fr.ceri/files/n8_17092010.pdf

Chengappa, R. and Krishnan, A. 2017. "India-China Standoff: All You Need to Know about Doklam Dispute." *India Today*. https://www.indiatoday.in/magazine/cover-story/story/20170717-india-china-bhutan-border-dispute-doklam-beijing-siliguri-corridor-1022690-2017-07-07

Cherian, J. 2021. "Revisiting Pulwama: Frosty Relations with Pakistan after the Pulwama Terror Attack." *Frontline*. https://frontline.thehindu.com/cover-story/relationship-with-pakistan-after-pulwama-terror-attack-diplomacy-foreign-affairs-india/article33904802.ece

Ching, C. 2022. "In Ukraine Response, Asia Struggles to Balance Relations with U.S., Russia, China." *NBC*. https://www.nbcnews.com/news/world/ukraine-response-asia-us-russia-china-rcna17976

Cohen, S.P. 2000. "A New Beginning in South Asia." *Brookings*. https://www.brookings.edu/research/a-new-beginning-in-south-asia/

Copeland, L., Lamm, W., and McKenna, S.J. 2012. *The World's Great Speeches: Fourth Enlarged (1999) Edition*. New York: Dover Publications.

Crabtree, J. 2020. "Why a Trade War with China is a Bad Idea for India." *Financial Policy*. https://foreignpolicy.com/2020/06/29/trade-war-china-bad-idea-india-border-skirmish-boycott/

Einhorn, R. and Sidhu, W.P.S. 2017. "The Strategic Chain Linking Pakistan, India, China, and the United States." *Brookings*. https://www.brookings.edu/research/the-strategic-chain-linking-pakistan-india-china-and-the-united-states/

Elias, A., Ben, J., Mansouri, F., and Paradies, Y. 2021. "Racism and Nationalism During and Beyond the COVID-19 Pandemic." *Ethnic and Racial Studies* 44(5): 783–793.

Feyyaz, M. 2019. "Contextualizing the Pulwama Attack in Kashmir: A Perspective from Pakistan." *Perspectives on Terrorism* 13(2): 69–74.

Gandhi, Mohandas Karamchand. 1967. *The Collected Works of Mahatma Gandhi*. New Delhi: Publications Division.

Ganguly, S. 2010. "South Asia after the Cold War." *The Washington Quarterly* 15(4): 173–184.

Gordon, S. 1995. "South Asia after the Cold War: Winners and Losers." *Asian Survey* 35(10): 879–895.

Gordon, S. 2012. "Why South Asia Matters in World Affairs." *Policy* 28(1): 53–56.

Gupta, S. 2022. "How India's Abstention from UNSC Vote is Different from China." *Hindustan Times*. https://www.hindustantimes.com/india-news/how-india-s-abstention-from-unsc-vote-is-different-from-china-101645844281926.html

Haas, M. 1989. *The Asian Way to Peace: A Story of Regional Cooperation*. New York: Praeger.

Hashim, A. 2022. "Pakistan Allows First Shipment of Indian Wheat to Afghanistan." *Aljazeera*. https://www.aljazeera.com/news/2022/2/22/pakistan-allows-first-shipment-of-indian-wheat-to-afghanistan

Hilali, A.Z. 2006. "Cold War Politics of Superpowers in. South Asia." *The Dialogue* 1(2): 68–108.

Hille, K., Bokhari, F., and Parkin, B. 2022. "China Moves to Counter India with Arms Sales to Pakistan." *Financial Times*. https://www.ft.com/content/b505d504-6447-4ffb-bb7d-3a33db837c9a

Horsley, J.P. 2020. "Let's End the COVID-19 Blame Game: Reconsidering China's Role in the Pandemic." *Brookings*. https://www.brookings.edu/blog/order-from-chaos/2020/08/19/lets-end-the-covid-19-blame-game-reconsidering-chinas-role-in-the-pandemic/

Hurrell, A. 2007. "One World? Many Worlds? The Place of Regions in the Study of International Society." *International Affairs* 83(1): 127–146.

Iqbal, M.J. 2006. "SAARC: Origin, Growth. Potential and Achievements." *Pakistan Journal of History and Culture* 37(2): 127–140.

Jaishankar, S. 2020. "External Affairs Minister in Conversation at Raisina Dialogue 2020: The India Way." *Ministry of External Affairs, Government of India*. https://mea.gov.in/interviews.htm?dtl/32305/External_Affairs_Minister_in_Conversation_at_Raisina_Dialogue_2020__The_India_Way

Johnston, S.A. 2020. "The Pandemic and the Limits of Realism." *Foreign Policy*. https://foreignpolicy.com/2020/06/24/coronavirus-pandemic-realism-limited-international-relations-theory/

Kaplan, R.D. 2014. "Rearranging the Subcontinent." *Forbes*. https://www.forbes.com/sites/stratfor/2014/12/24/rearranging-the-subcontinent/?sh=2ef92ccd790d

Kumar, R. and Goyal, O. 2016. *Thirty Years of SAARC Society, Culture and Development*. New Delhi: SAGE.

Madan, T. 2021. "Major Power Rivalry in South Asia." *Council on Foreign Relations*. https://cdn.cfr.org/sites/default/files/report_pdf/DPmadanOct21_final%20for%20CMS.pdf

Mahapatra, C. 2022. "Why is India's Approach to the Ukraine Crisis under Spotlight?" *Firstpost*. https://www.firstpost.com/world/why-is-indias-approach-to-the-ukraine-crisis-under-spotlight-10427291.html

McMahon, R.J. 1996. *The Cold War on the Periphery: The United States, India, and Pakistan*. New York: Columbia University Press.

McMahon, R.J. 2006. "U.S. Policy toward South Asia and Tibet during the Early Cold War." *Journal of Cold War Studies* 8(3): 131–144.

Medeiros, E.S. 2021. "The Changing Context of Great Power Competition." *Council on Foreign Relations*. https://www.jstor.org/stable/resrep31130.4

Michael, A. 2013. *India's Foreign Policy and Regional Multilateralism*. New York: Palgrave Macmillan.

Ministry of External Affairs, Government of India. 2022. "Border Dispute Between India and Pakistan." March 21. https://pib.gov.in/PressReleaseIframePage.aspx?PRID=1807600

Mitra, S. 2003. "The Reluctant Hegemon: India's Self-Perception and the South Asian Strategic Environment." *Contemporary South Asia* 12(3): 399–418.

Mj, V. 2018. "The Ascent of Conservative Civil Society in India." *Carnegie*. https://carnegieeurope.eu/2018/10/04/ascent-of-conservative-civil-society-in-india-pub-77372

Mohan, R. 2019. "Give Peace a Chance." *Deccan Chronicle*, March 10. https://www.deccanchronicle.com/nation/current-affairs/110319/give-peace-a-chance-1.html

Muni, S.D. and Muni, A. 1984. *Regional Cooperation in South Asia*. New Delhi: National Publishing House.

Narayan, R. 2019. "India-Pak Ties: Young Citizens Discuss Way Forward." *The Quint*. https://www.thequint.com/news/hot-news/india-pak-ties-young-citizens-discuss-way-forward

Nayar, B.R. and Paul, T.V. 2003. *India in the World Order: Searching for Major-Power Status*. Cambridge: Cambridge University Press.

Nehru, J. 1946. "Inter-Asian Relations." *India Quarterly* 2(4): 323–327.

Nehru, J. 1961. *India's Foreign Policy: Selected Speeches, September 1946–April 1961*. Publications Division, Ministry of Information and Broadcasting, Government of India.

Noor, S. 2020. "Pulwama/Balakot and The Evolving Role of Third Parties in India-Pakistan Crises." *Stimson*. https://www.stimson.org/2020/pulwama-balakot-and-the-evolving-role-of-third-parties-in-india-pakistan-crises/

Pal, D. 2021. "China's Influence in South Asia: Vulnerabilities and Resilience in Four Countries." *Carnegie Endowment for International Peace*. https://carnegieendowment.org/2021/10/13/china-s-influence-in-south-asia-vulnerabilities-and-resilience-in-four-countries-pub-85552

Pant, H. 2017. "The Changing Contours of Russia's South Asia Policy". *ORF*. https://www.orfonline.org/wp-content/uploads/2017/07/ORF_IssueBrief_193_India-Russia.pdf

Parthasarathy, G. 2021. "Quad's China Strategy." *The Tribune*. https://www.tribuneindia.com/news/comment/quads-china-strategy-258837

Percival, B. 2013. "China, India and the United States: Tempered Rivalries in Asia." *S. Rajaratnam School of International Studies*. https://www.jstor.org/stable/resrep05795?seq=1

Philip, S.A. 2021. "As Trust Deficit Lingers, India & China Prepare for Another Harsh Winter Deployment in Ladakh." *The Print*.

Prakash, T. 2019. "Pulwama and Its Aftermath: What Is Different This Time?" *Australian Outlook*. https://www.internationalaffairs.org.au/australianoutlook/pulwama-aftermath-different-this-time/

Qaddos, M. 2018. "Sino-Indian Border Conflict and Implications for Bilateral Relations." *Policy Perspectives* 15(2): 57–69.

Querejazu, A. 2016. "Encountering the Pluriverse: Looking for Alternatives in Other Worlds." *RevistaBrasileira de Política Internacional* 59(2): 1–16.

Rainsy, S. 2022. "The Battle Between Democracy and Autocracy, From Russia to Cambodia." *The Diplomat*. https://thediplomat.com/2022/03/the-battle-between-democracy-and-autocracy-from-russia-to-cambodia/

Roy, S. 2022. "Explained: What India's Abstention on UNSC Vote over Russia's Invasion of Ukraine Means." *The Indian Express*. https://indianexpress.com/article/explained/explained-india-abstains-unsc-vote-russia-invasion-ukraine-7791712/

Sahoo, S. 2021. "Civil Society in South Asia." In *Oxford Bibliographies Online in Political Science*. https://www.oxfordbibliographies.com/view/document/obo-9780199756223/obo-9780199756223-0212.xml

Sajjanhar, A. 2017. "The Doklam Crisis Ends: A Diplomatic Victory for India." *ORF*. https://www.orfonline.org/expert-speak/the-doklam-crisis-ends-a-diplomatic-victory-for-india/

Senaratne, B. 2020. "The COVID-19 Pandemic and the Power Rivalry in South Asia." *The National Bureau of Asian Research*. https://www.nbr.org/publication/the-covid-19-pandemic-and-the-power-rivalry-in-south-asia/

Shahi, D. 2018. *Advaita as a Global International Relations Theory.* London: Routledge.

Sharma, U. 2020. "67% Indians Blame China for COVID-19, 50% say Calling it 'Chinese virus' not Racist: Survey." *The Print.* https://theprint.in/india/67-pc-indians-blame-china-for-covid-19-50-pc-say-calling-it-chinese-virus-not-racist-survey/396496/

Singh, R. 2021. "Risk Assessment and Escalation Management in India-Pakistan Conflicts." *ORF.* https://www.orfonline.org/wp-content/uploads/2021/12/ORF_IssueBrief_511_Escalation-India-Pakistan-1.pdf

Snedden, C. 2016. "Shifting Geo-Politics in the Greater South Asia Region." *Daniel K. Inouye Asia-Pacific Center for Security Studies.* http://www.jstor.org/stable/resrep14025.

Sun, Y. 2020. "China and South Asia Crisis Management in the Era of Great Power Competition." *Norwegian Institute of International Affairs.* https://www.jstor.org/stable/resrep25750

Tarapore, A. 2021. "The Crisis After the Crisis: How Ladakh will Shape India's Competition with China." *Lowy Institute.* https://www.lowyinstitute.org/publications/crisis-after-crisis-how-ladakh-will-shape-india-s-competition-china

Teets, J.C. 2014. "Civil Society under Authoritarianism: The China Model." *Cambridge Core.* https://www.cambridge.org/core/books/civil-society-under-authoritarianism/civil-society-in-china/FE8003E3FE2E05D16EAB264E9D1BF40D

Tiwari, S. 2021. "US Wants to Boost India's Firepower Against China; Here Are 5 Weapons That Could Give Delhi a Decisive Edge Over Beijing." *Eurasian Times.* https://eurasiantimes.com/us-wants-to-boost-indias-firepower-against-china-five-weapons/

Toal, G. 2017. *Near Abroad: Putin, the West and the Contest over Ukraine and the Caucasus.* New York: Oxford University Press.

Tourangbam, M. 2020. "The China-India-Pakistan Triangle: Origins, Contemporary Perceptions, and Future." *Stimson.* https://www.stimson.org/2020/the-china-india-pakistan-triangle-origins-contemporary-perceptions-and-future/

Tsygankov, A.P. and Tsygankov, P.A. 2022. "The Global and the Nationally Distinctive in IR Theory." *Vestnik RUDN. International Relations* 22(1): 7–16.

Wagner, C. 2021. "The Remaking of South Asia. Geopolitical Implications of the COVID-19 Pandemic." *Friedrich Ebert Stiftung.* http://library.fes.de/pdf-files/iez/18515.pdf

Wintour, P. 2022. "India Defends Buying Discounted Russian Oil Despite Appeal by Truss." *The Guardian*, March 31. https://www.theguardian.com/world/2022/mar/31/india-defends-buying-discounted-russian-oil-despite-appeal-by-truss

5

Northeast Asia and China's Pursuit of Greatness

Jing Sun

Introduction

This chapter examines how geography has shaped China's pursuit of great power status and what it means to other countries, especially the US. It argues that geography serves as a social construct for Chinese national identity as well as a security concept for its interest. China's geographical positioning is undergoing a transformation from imagining the country as a land-based yellow middle kingdom to a maritime blue superpower.

This chapter stresses a spectrum view of *tianxia* (All under Heaven), a foundational Chinese worldview as well as a spatial-positioning concept. Various political actors offer competing interpretations of *tianxia* ranging from accommodation to domination. Political geography has shaped this debate—the more China's physical positioning is highlighted, the more assertive one's interpretation of China's global aspiration would become. The Chinese government has been leaning toward an increasingly aggressive execution, interpreting the country's rapid maritime expansion as a modern shift of *tianxia* from land to sea. This has caused anxiety among neighbors and confrontation with the US.

This chapter's analysis proceeds as follows: it starts by introducing *tianxia* (All under Heaven)—a Chinese philosophical view that imagines an ideal world where a benevolent and powerful leader sitting between Heaven and Earth, ruling his subjects by heeding the mandate of Heaven. *Tianxia* is both spatial and moral, as it portrays harmonious positionings of all living creatures on the land—people, fauna, and flora.

The chapter then examines how China's rapid ascendancy has challenged this historical concept. Echoing Salvador Regilme's chapter on the militarization of the South China Sea (SCS), this chapter points out that China has been aggressively pursuing the goal of becoming a deep blue power. As Beijing seeks to project its influence to the sea, it needs to expand *tianxia*, a traditionally land-based concept, to justify its vast maritime claim as well. Regilme argues that Xi Jinping's domestic agenda of boosting nationalism is partly responsible for Beijing's militant activities in the vast waters of the SCS. Following this proposition but looking through a more long-term and normative lens, this chapter suggests that the conceptual expansion of *tianxia* serves the Chinese leader's domestic agenda of rejuvenating Chinese greatness, also known as the "Chinese Dream." But Xi's dream has stirred up fear and anxiety among China's neighbors. It also brings the country on a collision course with America, the region's hegemon by default. To counter China's geographical reimaging, the US has emphasized its own "Indo-Pacific" expansion to blunt a blue Chinese *tianxia*. This geographical contesting process between two superpowers is riddled with uncertainties. Short of finding a conceptual reconciliation, it may greatly endanger peace and stability in Northeast Asia.

From "Middle Kingdom" to "All under Heaven"

Chinese history has an enduring preoccupation with geography, physical and imaginative. *Zhongguo*, the Chinese word for the country, started as a geographical description: it means the "Middle Kingdom." The term first appeared in Chinese scripture in the 11th century BC during the early Western Zhou Dynasty. At its genesis, the term referred to the flat region centering Luoyi, the capital city of the Zhou kingdom (Yang 2017). As the Zhou Dynasty expanded, rulers of neighboring kingdoms accepted the nominal legitimacy of the Zhou kings over their jurisdictions. The word *Zhongguo* began to acquire value-based semiotic significance. It no longer just meant a geographical center but a moral one as well. The term *Zhongguo* began to allude to borders, physical and moral. It pictured a superior kingdom separated from hostile and inferior others.

One may perceive this governing structure as consisting of multiple concentric circles: the inner-most circle represents *Tianzi* (son of heaven)—the king or the emperor who claimed to possess the mandate of heaven to rule. The next ring was the internal court governing the land controlled by the supreme ruler. The circles would then expand to include auxiliary courts and tributary kingdoms. Both maintained independence from the son of heaven. The auxiliary courts would traditionally send their heirs apparent to the capital cities of the Chinese kingdoms or empires as hostages. As a result, they were not as autonomous as tributary kingdoms, as the latter's responsibilities to the Chinese supreme rulers were primarily financial and thus more symbolic. Beyond these concentric circles would be the land run by hostile and barbaric tribes collectively known as Di to the North, Rong to the West, Man to the South, and Yi to the East.

Such territorial and normative elements jointly constituted Sino-centrism during the Western Zhou era. The Zhou kings were at the core. Ring by ring, political actors were further and further away from the center—both in distance and in legitimacy. Outside the king's authority scope were the four groups of "barbarians" in four directions. Though these groups were diverse in ethnic and cultural compositions, the *Book of Documents*, an ancient Chinese literature, used four directional exonyms, Yi, Di, Rong, and Man, to present a general designation of culturally inferior groups residing at the peripheral four corners of the Middle Kingdom.

When Western Zhou declined, multiple kings would rename their own kingdom capital cities *Zhongguo* to legitimize their moral authority. This perception would strengthen during the Han Dynasty. Sima Qian, the founding father of Chinese historiography, had chapters for *yiyu* (foreign countries) and recorded exchanges, official and unofficial, between the Han Dynasty with these *yiyu waiwang* (foreign ones with aliens) (Sima 90BC). These records would constitute the country's earliest accounts rudimentarily resembling international relations today.

The power of the moral hierarchy embedded in *Zhongguo* is enduring. Even ethnic groups living in China's border regions claimed to be the concept's rightful proprietors. For example, both Liao and Jin groups proclaimed to be rulers of *Zhongguo*, so did the Chinese rulers of the Song Dynasty during the same era. During the Yuan Dynasty, Emperor Kublai Khan also referred to his Mongol Empire as *Zhongguo* (Li et al 1370). All these examples indicate that the term's utility in justifying legitimacy. This is a time when "China," physical and moral, existed in a plural form. That land that would constitute what is China today consisted of multiple "Chinas" competing for moral supremacy. In 1689, the Qing Empire signed the Treaty of Nerchinsk with the Tsardom of Russia. In the treaty, *Zhongguo* was first used in an international treaty as a formal reference to the state of China. From Western Zhou to Qing—after more than 2,600 years, the "Middle Kingdom" officially entered diplomatic vocabulary.

The Sino-centric visualization of territorial and governing hierarchy of Sino-centrism bordering four barbarians has a Chinese name to it: *tianxia*. This word is well known to the Chinese and those ruling China for thousands of years. But its exposure to the West is quite recent. It attracted Western popular attention a little over two decades ago, thanks to the international release of a Chinese blockbuster movie, *Hero*. The movie, inspired by a true historical event that happened more than two thousand years ago, depicts an assassin who gives up his mission of killing the Emperor of Qin. Instead, the assassin offers the emperor a piece of advice and then self-sacrifices himself by accepting being executed. What is his advice?

The assassin urges China's first unifier to rule with compassion for *tianxia*. Upon hearing the assassin's last words, the emperor cannot hold back his tears. He laments that the only person who truly understands him is the one that attempts to kill him.

The English subtitle describes *tianxia* as "our land" belonging to the Chinese people. This translation is misleading. It imposes nationalism and ensuing Western hierarchical world order, products of the Treaty of Westphalia in 1688, to a Chinese philosophy more than two thousand years ago. The translators probably forced themselves into a cage because the assassin repeatedly claims that he has "two Chinese characters" for the emperor as advice. Apparently, the translators were hunting for two English words as well to make this numerical description consistent, resulting in a misinterpretation of the essence of *tianxia*—a key message of the movie.

Tianxia, which literally means "All under Heaven," is not about the mutually exclusive "we–they" feeling as connotated by the translated English phrase "our land." *Tianxia* means nothing about nationalist pride or a country's position in a hierarchical world. It is entirely different in substance and implications that nationalism entails. "Our land" suggests a more nativist, nationalist call about sole ownership of territories. This is not what *tianxia* implies. Instead, *tianxia* is the traditional Chinese worldview, of which China is a part. A responsible leader's position is central to this Chinese imaginary. He is someone that rules with vision and compassion, a calming authority that guides people in a time of great uncertainties.

An emphasis on "All under Heaven" stresses the spirit of self-sacrifice, which is palpable in the movie *Hero*. The assassin abandons his mission at the last moment for the sake of the masses—that is, he chooses to forgo his personal desire so that people's sufferings may come to an end. In doing so, he becomes a selfless hero to all. The emperor, whose life is spared, also becomes a hero. He laments that people call him a tyrant. But all he wants is working to achieve a harmonious world where violence cedes to exist.

These messages remain politically attractive today. The Chinese government eagerly promoted *Hero*, a Kungfu movie, to audience nationwide. It even offered subsidies to allow government employees and students to watch it. This was unusual because the movie contained ample violence and sexually suggestive scenes. To the Chinese government, the movie's political messages were too enticing not to be propagated. Meanwhile, *Hero* received raving reviews in the West, becoming the first movie to earn the top position at the American box office and earning US$177 million worldwide. It also collected nominations for Golden Globe and the Academy Awards and won accolades at other film awards. Thanks to a mistranslation, the message catering to the Chinese authorities is largely absent in the Western market, allowing viewers there to enjoy the plot and beautiful cinematography without being disturbed by its political implication.

The movie was a precursor to what would unfold in coming years: voices of Chinese authority, leadership, and self-sacrifice are getting louder in the official media. As a recent exam, in June 2021 China's national news agency Xinhua published an account of Chinese President Xi Jinping's foreign policy. The lengthy article begins with the title "For a Better World—Xi Jinping's '*Tianxia*' Compassion" (Zheng and Han 2021). It stresses how China's paramount leader has been "shouldering the mission of maintaining world peace as his personal responsibility." There is no mentioning of China vis-à-vis anyone else. Rather, it is about morally positioning the country and its supreme leader as a central force for the global public good. Such a framing of *tianxia* is in line with the concept's traditional interpretation. It is not about "China versus the world." Rather, it is about a selfless, benevolent Chinese leader taking care of a suffering world. It is about legitimacy based on personal moral superiority—the communist boss is China's new emperor.

Debating "All under Heaven": accommodation to domination

President Xi's version of "All under Heaven" has a contemporary name to it—the "Chinese Dream." It is about reimaging a world led by the moral authority of a rejuvenated China. Ever since Jiang Zemin, each Chinese Communist Party chief has created his own pet slogan. For Jiang, it was "Three Represents"—meaning that the Chinese Communist Party should represent advanced social productive forces, advanced culture, and the fundamental interest of the Chinese people. Jiang's successor, Hu Jintao, was associated with the "Harmonious Society" and "Scientific Development" slogans. When Xi Jinping took charge, he began to promote the "Chinese Dream."

All the three slogans allegedly were the brainchildren of Wang Hujing, a senior policy advisor who thrived under three generations of leadership and earned the online moniker of "Mentor of the Nation" (*guoshi*). The slogans he designed for Jiang and Hu focused on internal politics. They also highlighted problems that the country needed to tackle: how to reconcile a market economy with one-party rule, and how to address rising inequality amid rapid development. The new slogan he tailor-made for Xi is different: it is future-oriented. It offers a moral compass for a confident country aspiring for global eminence. The adjective "Chinese" does not imply territoriality. Rather, it implies the origin of values that will benefit everyone. Indeed, Xi proclaims to the world that the Chinese Dream is also the World Dream (Liaowang 2015). It is China's "*tianxia* 2.0".

The Chinese leader's dream motto is vague in substance. He promotes it as a pursuit of "the great rejuvenation of the Chinese nation" (Xi 2012). But other than this grandiose vision, there is no authoritative clarification of what would constitute this great rejuvenation, how China will get there, and what the Chinese pursuit for greatness means to the rest of the world. In the absence of Xi's definitive explanation, to decipher his Chinese dream has become a booming industry. Political actors have offered competing interpretations in a self-serving manner (Lam 2015).

Political geography comes into play in the competing interpretations of Xi's "*tianxia* 2.0." The more China's physical positioning is stressed, the more assertive one's interpretation of the Chinese Dream would become. On this assertive end, the rhetoric is unapologetically Sino-centric, chauvinistic, and racially nativist. One representing voice is that of Liu Mingfu, an armchair strategist from the National Defense University. In his book titled *The China Dream: Great Power Thinking and Strategic Posture in the Post-American Era*, Colonel Liu proclaims that the time has come for China to replace America as the world's top military power. By using Japan as an example, he warns Asian countries that the only way to get along with China is to know their place—they are living next to a gigantic neighbor, the strongest country in the world that keeps getting stronger. Hence, they need to get used to seeing their influence dwindle (Liu 2010). Liu's voice is extreme; even Luo Yuan, another Chinese military hawk, comments that Liu's view that China is already leading the world is not a fact but reflects "the gap between a promising ideal and reality" (Zhang 2010). Of course, to China's suspicious neighbors, Liu's view represents what a nightmare could look like—Chinese military readying itself for a geopolitical showdown with America, the default hegemon.

In contrast to this territorial interpretation of *tianxia*, another view emphasizes a morality-based world order. According to this view, Xi's dream of a new *tianxia* sounds more traditionalist: it emphasizes moral authority and leadership compassion. Xu Jilin, a history professor from East China Normal University, is a leading voice in this camp. Professor Xu contends that the Chinese Dream should embody a decentered, nonhierarchical new universalism. He envisions the Chinese Dream as open and tolerant. By rejecting both Sino- and European centrism, this benevolent "All under Heaven" opposes the creation of any civilizational hegemony. Instead, the future should look like "huddled masses" from all countries under an open sky, with China being one in a crowd but taking pride in being the creator of this new, accommodating *tianxia* (Xu 2015).

Where on this spectrum would one place China's official navigation for its rightful place in the world? Over the years Xi and the country's propaganda machines have been adding components to this dream, ranging from the goals the People's Republic seeks to achieve by its one hundredth anniversary in 2049 to current policies like the One Belt One Road Initiative, sustainable development, and anti-corruption campaigns, among others. Various efforts are made to bend and weld the two ends of the interpretive spectrum: Sino-centrism and territorial expansion in substance but packaged in open, benevolent rhetoric.

The ever-growing and conflictual components of Xi's dream—nationalism, strengthening of party control, leading the world in a liberal economic order, has attracted scholarly attention (Saich 2017). One buzzword, though, stands out in the country's propaganda effort—*dandang*, which can be translated as the courage to take charge. This new foreign policy posture would be a major departure from Deng Xiaoping's low-profile diplomacy.

One prominent example highlighting such a departure happened in January 2017, when America's new president refused to attend the World Economic Forum in Davos, Switzerland. Xi decided to go and offered a major speech, in which he defended free trade. Without naming the Trump administration, he likened those pursuing protectionism to "locking oneself in a dark room." The speech earned him the moniker the "New Davos Man"—a rich, powerful, and pro-trade global ultra-elite, who also happens to be a communist.

Xi's act could be framed as *dandang* in practice. Under Trump, America was showing signs of retrenching and retreating. It was abandoning its legitimation of issues like human rights and good governance abroad (Regilme 2019). Chinese authorities sensed an opening for their country to assume leadership on the world stage. Pro-government intellectuals are cheerleading this new Sino-centrism. Without the slightest sense of irony, a professor for Chinese Renmin University penned an op-ed for the official media, praising China for being a selfless righteous power leading the world in combating the COVID-19 pandemic. In this opinion piece, the author made repeated references to the word "*dandang*" as China's "great power moral character" in contrast to "a specific country" that is "busy 'delinking' and 'building walls'" (Diao 2020). It would not take a genius to figure out which "specific country" this scholar was bashing.

People beyond China may remember the country's relations to the COVID-19 pandemic differently. According to the Pew Research Center, China's popularity in the West has dropped precipitously since 2020, amid its cover-up at the pandemic's onset, human rights abuses in Xinjiang and Hong Kong, threats to Taiwan, and meddling in other countries' democratic processes. To China's neighbors and countries in the West, Xi's "Chinese Dream" is nightmarish, not dreamy. One major change is Beijing's growing assertiveness on territorial claims, especially those projected to the oceans. China has sent more than 40 piracy control missions to the Gulf of Aden, established a permanent military base in Djibouti at the Horn of Africa, signed a new security agreement with the Solomon Islands, and launched three aircraft carriers in nine years. Among all these military buildups, most alarming to China's neighbors has been the country's turbo-charged speed of reclaiming land in the Spratly Islands area. Though China was a relative latecomer to the land reclamation game in the SCS, it rapidly outpaced other claimants. According to the data released by the United

States Department of Defense, by 2015 China has reclaimed 2,900 acres of land at seven of its eight Spratly outposts. By comparison, Vietnam as the runner-up of this race reclaimed only 80 acres, followed by Malaysia at 70 acres, the Phillipines at 14 acres, and Taiwan at eight acres (United States Department of Defense, 2015).

Dreaming blue: China's new great power frontier

China's roaring maritime expansion is quite new. European powers like Portugal, Spain, and England established their empires through sea-bound conquests. America fulfilled its Manifest Destiny by territorial acquisitions from sea to shining sea. China is different. Throughout its history, dynastic rulers' focus was on securing the land rather than the ocean. Western Zhou, the "middle" kingdom, was in China's heartland. The landlocked kingdom was distant from any shoreline. Later dynasties expanded their borders to the sea. But ruling elites' preoccupation remained locked to the country's land area. It was Mount Tai and the Yellow River that served as sacred worshipping sites for emperors. In 219 BC, Emperor Qin Shihuang, the first ruler that unified China, led the entire imperial court to summit Mount Tai and proclaimed the unity of his empire, setting up a tradition for future emperors to follow. The ocean, by contrast, had a peripheral and somewhat mystic position in Emperor Qin Shihuang's imagination. The only significant mentioning was about the emperor allegedly sending Xu Fu, a court sorcerer, to the East Sea twice in search of the elixir for life. Xu and his entire fleet of young boys and girls never returned from the second mission. Historical accounts of this transient sea-bound exploration were filled with inconsistencies. Many historians dismissed the episode as mythology (Chinese State Council Information Office 2009). Other notable emperors like the Wudi of Han Dynasty and Taizhong of Tang Dynasty were famous for defending China from incursions from the north or conquering the vast land lying to the country's west. Seafarers remained marginal players as one dynasty replaced another.

There was one major exception: a remarkable maritime exploration happened in the 15th century. Led by Admiral Zheng He, the Chinese treasure fleet made seven voyages reaching Southeast Asia, the Indian subcontinent, the Persian Gulf, and Eastern Africa. These voyages are collectively known as "Zheng He Xia Xiyang." "Xiyang," or "Western Oceans," implies that these maritime explorations differed from the more familar east-bound routes leading to Korea and Japan, China's immediate neighbors.

These voyages were not examples of Chinese colonialism. Unlike Western voyages that sought to establish permanent settlements, Zheng He's voyages were about showcasing China's superiority and recruiting members to pay homage to the Ming suzerainty. This purpose was an established component of the Chinese empire's tributary system. Zheng's fleet were heavily militarized. They occasionally engaged in armed conflicts. But the Ming vessels brought along many treasures and exchanged them with goods and even exotic animals that the locals would offer. While demonstrating Chinese grandeur, these voyages did little to permanently establish Chinese imperial power.

Assured that China had no viable threat in that vast region, the Ming rulers shifted their attention back to the northern inland area, where skirmishes with the Manchus were getting more and more intense. Today, the Chinese educational authorities use Zheng He's voyages to boost patriotism and national pride. History textbooks compare Zheng's voyages chronologically with those by Western explorers like Ferdinand Magellan, Christopher Columbus, and Vasco da Gama to prove that the Chinese fleet was bigger, better, and stronger. The government claims that the absence of Chinese colonies was a testament of China's "peaceful" nature—Zheng's fleet proves that China has always been a messenger of peace and prosperity. Some scholars would go so far as to claim the voyages represent Chinese soft power (Shen 2016; Zou 2018).

Despite effusive official praises, there are scholarly voices lamenting that China missed boarding the ship of becoming a maritime world power (Zhang 2014). Zheng He's voyages would be imperial China's first but also last effort of sailing beyond the country's immediate waters. After the seventh voyage, such seafaring trips ended abruptly. Pirates from coastal China, Japan, and Korea would make the Eastern Sea a continued annoyance for the Middle Kingdom. But the rulers' attention once again turned inland. The Ming court would restore its "Sea Ban" (*haijin*) on all private maritime trade. Zheng He's voyages cracked open China's door to exploring the deep blue. But the door quickly swung back.

The ocean would remain dormant for China's rulers until the mid-19th century. Then, just as abruptly, it became a major front exposing the Chinese empire's precipitous decline. It was defeated by two maritime powers—Britain from the West and Japan from the East, losing Hong Kong to the former and Taiwan to the latter. These humiliating defeats forced Chinese revolutionaries and intellectuals to think blue again—the country's rejuvenation must lie in becoming a maritime power. Sun Yat-sen, modern China's founding father, was a major proponent for this view. In his eyes, it was the ocean, not land, that would decide the rise and fall of powers. Sun criticized the ruling elites' entrenched mentality of prioritizing land-based security over the maritime one. He warned fellow revolutionaries that China's decline led to its loss of "maritime privileges" (*haiquan*). Sun further stressed that future leaders must raise national awareness of a systemic ocean concept, and that a strong navy and capability of cultivating maritime resources would be key to China's self-strengthening process (Huang 2020).

Modern China's founding father may have had ambitious maritime plans. But foreign invasions and civil wars would force main political forces in China to continue focusing on land-based conquests. The country's venturing to the ocean remained a remote aspiration. After the founding of the People's Republic in 1949, Mao's naval strategy locked in on a singular target—Taiwan, a remnant issue of a grand land-based struggle between the communists and nationalists. The Chinese navy was small in scale. It lacked the ability to project power beyond the country's immediate waters. Deng Xiaoping, Mao's successor, led the country onto a drastically different path of reform and open-door policy. However, Deng was less ambitious on maritime exploration. Instead, he urged the military to "make way" for economic reform, resulting in the dismissal of more than a million personnel and the cutting of the budget. Deng argued conservatively that the Chinese navy should focus on "defending (the country's) immediate waters" (Jiang 2014). The country's only noted maritime achievement during this period was its two Antarctic explorations in 1985 and 1989.

Ocean's allure: from democracy to supremacy

As China opened its door to the world, anti-establishment, pro-reform forces began to revitalize popular maritime awareness. In 1988, China Central Television broadcast a six-part documentary, *River Elegy* (*heshang*), a fierce attack on the country's inward-looking mentality.

The documentary attributed China's decline to its land-based conservatism. It offered harsh criticisms of traditional Chinese semiotic symbols like the Yellow River, dragon, and the Great Wall, denouncing them as representing an outdated "Yellow Civilization." Its concluding episode, titled "The Azure," called for the Chinese nation to head for a "Blue Civilization" of liberation and freedom. The documentary captivated millions of viewers. A national debate ensued on the urgency of China becoming a maritime civilization. The documentary received blessings from Zhao Ziyang, the reformist party chief at the time. Zhao openly claimed that he was a fan of the show. He presented the documentaries to visiting foreign guests and urged everyone to watch it.

River Elegy made a loud but transient splash. One year later, the government would violently suppress a massive pro-democracy movement and sack Zhao. The reformer party chief would spend the remaining years of his life under house arrest. The victorious conservatives denounced *River Elegy* as propagating "bourgeois liberalization," "nihilism," and "a blueprint for anti-revolutionary activities" (Wang 2018). Producers of the documentary were forced into exile. China's democratic voyage toward a democratic, liberal "Blue Civilization" was not to happen. What emerged as its replacement is an adrenaline-filled military march to the sea.

Two events in the 1990s prompted the Chinese leadership to speed up military modernization with a focus on upgrading naval capabilities: the first Gulf War and the 1996 Taiwan Strait Crisis. The first Gulf War, a conflict fought more than five thousand kilometers from China, unexpectedly accelerated Beijing's pace of military modernization. America's swift victory over the Iraqi forces stunned the Chinese military. Scenes like laser-guided missiles firing from military vessels and fighter jets taking off from aircraft carriers stunned the Chinese leaders, many of whom were still believers in Mao's "People's War" strategy—that is, prevailing over enemies by mobilizing a huge amount of manpower. The Gulf War showed that technologically sophisticated weaponries could quickly incapacitate a large Iraqi army equipped with outdated weapons—many from China. As one Chinese general commented, the overwhelming American military superiority driven by technology "completely beat our military to an awakening moment" (*Sohu News* 2022). Documentaries examining the importance of technology in modern warfare became required teaching materials at Chinese military academies. A proud military was shellshocked and humbled.

The 1996 Taiwan Strait Crisis further exposed the capability gap between the American and Chinese naval forces. This time, the Chinese military no longer needed to learn their lessons by watching from afar. The Americans arrived at their doorstep. During the height of the crisis, American President Bill Clinton dispatched two US aircraft carriers, USS *Nimitz* and *Independence*, to the Taiwan Strait to deter the Chinese forces. Under the American pressure, the Chinese navy backed off. It scaled down its military maneuver and issued the "Three Nos" pledge: no missile to fly over Taiwan, no crossing of the median line of the Taiwan Strait, and no invasion of any island controlled by Taiwan (*VOA News* 2014). In the wake of such a humiliating encounter, the country's naval modernization has become multi-pronged, encompassing aircraft carriers, anti-ship missiles, submarines, amphibious ships, and enhanced training programs of combatants for operations away from home waters, and so on. The speed has been impressive: modern attack submarines rose from three in 1999 to 36 in 2019. During the same period, modern surface warships grew from nil to 48. Fourth generation fighter jets increased from 52 to 837. Developments as such led multiple military experts from America and Australia to warn that the US navy has lost its military primacy in the region (Townshend et al 2019).

America's repositioning effort: pivoting to Asia and merging two oceans

China's pursuit of a maritime "All under Heaven" has agitated the region. The most remarkable tension is the one with the US, the default Pacific hegemon. China's naval capability upgrade and land reclamation certainly caught American attention. After all, it was Harry Harries, commander of the US Pacific fleet, that coined the phrase "Great Wall of Sand" to describe the Chinese government's large-scale land reclamation in the SCS (Harries 2015). As China repaints its sphere of influence in blue, the US government has intensified its own repositioning effort. It started with President Barack Obama's "Pivot to Asia" initiative, rebalancing military, diplomatic, and economic resources away from Europe and the Middle East, America's traditional focal points, to East and Southeast Asia. The "Pivot" campaign had multiple components to boost America's presence in the region—diplomatic, economic, social, as well as military. It also sought to continue engaging with China—for example, the "100,000 Strong" initiative to increase dramatically the number and diversify the composition of American students studying in China (United States Department of State 2009). However, the Chinese government saw the "Pivot" agenda as part of a grand geopolitical confrontation. Beijing used the American campaign as justification to accelerate its own military buildup. Dai Bingguo, Chinese President Hu Jintao's chief diplomatic advisor, allegedly told Secretary of State Hillary Clinton that America should "pivot out of here" (Clinton 2014). At this point, China's "All under Heaven" has become explicitly territorial. Beijing is aiming for a transfer of hegemonic ownership. It sees itself as the new sea lord of the region.

The Trump administration continued America's global repositioning. On one hand, it abandoned a key component of Obama's "Pivot to Asia" agenda on Trump's first day in office—the Trans-Pacific Partnership. As a candidate, Trump bashed this proposed trade agreement of 14 countries in the Pacific Rim not involving China as a "rip off" of America. However, Trump maintained and expanded another geopolitical concept that became popular during the Obama presidency—the increased usage of "Indo-Pacific" as a way to replace "Asia-Pacific." To be sure, "Indo-Pacific" was not a newly invented geographical description. But its usage by American diplomats has increased tremendously in recent years whereas the framing of "Asia-Pacific" is dwindling. The Chinese government is viewing this enlarged geographical concept with open hostility. Its foreign ministry spokesman, Zhao Lijian, explicitly identified America's increased usage of this concept as evidence of the US "trying to contain China" (*China News* 2021).

America replacing Asia-Pacific by Indo-Pacific has enlarged the regional map. It serves at least two strategic purposes: first, it made an apparent connection with India, the world's largest democracy, and emphasized shared democratic values. Second, the new concept encompasses two oceans. This geographical-ideational map covers the Indian Ocean as well as the Pacific Rim, recruiting countries from multiple continents. The "Indo-Pacific" concept represents a new American initiative—building a democratic alliance to cage a rising China.

America was not the first one to conjure up a geographical visual juxtaposed with values. In 2007, the Japanese Foreign Minister Taro Aso proposed the establishment of an "Arc of Freedom and Prosperity." The proposed arc goes from South Korea to Japan, and then to Taiwan, Southeast Asia, India, and curves upward to Europe, forming a circle with China and Russia ostensibly excluded. This geographic imagery had holes: some countries in Southeast Asia and the Middle East were not democracies. They were included in this "art of freedom" nonetheless. Aso's arc map had a short shelf-life. The first Shinzo Abe administration lasted for only one year. The new administrations led by the Democratic Party of Japan ditched it. The Democratic Party of Japan government instead attempted to construct its own ill-conceived "East Asian Community"—a proposed regional bloc bonding countries as varied as Japan and North Korea. This proposal never took off. One decade later, America picked up from where Aso left, replacing Asia-Pacific with Indo-Pacific to adapt to new security situations.

Titan showdown: Chinese dream versus American dream

The Indo-Pacific region has looked increasingly like a battlefield of two grand visions harbored by two world powers. At its genesis, China was avoiding the imagery of a titan showdown. The "Chinese Dream" even sought to build an ideational connection with its more famous cousin—the American Dream. In 2013, Xi told Obama that the Chinese Dream "is connected to the American Dream and the beautiful dreams people in other countries may have" (Xi 2013). Obama stayed silent on any dreamlike connection with China. America did not even acknowledge the Chinese concept, let alone endorse it.

Fast-forwarding to today, any superficial bonding of the two dreams is gone. The lone comparable factor is a desire to amass power, as one Chinese scholar stated that only great powers like China and American "dare to have national dreams" (Shi 2013). This argument is ironic—for a China that loves to propagate the message of equality, it now saw having a national aspiration as a privilege for great powers. Smaller and weaker countries cannot afford such a grand fancy.

China's propaganda machines no longer refrain from attacking America. In the summer of 2019, Chinese viewers noticed that in the country's definitively dull prime-time news program *Xinwen Lianbo* (News Simulcast), hosts began to use slangs to mockingly berate America, calling the country's policies "absurd enough to make people spit meal," claiming that America was "a stick swirling shit," "a liar so despicable that he does not even blush when lying," and that the famed American Dream is the "American Nightmare." Beijing's propaganda attacks have become increasingly vitriolic, even vulgar and personal on occasions. For example, China and America have been busy shaming each other's handling of the COVID-19 crisis. China's state broadcaster CCTV denounced the then US Secretary of State Mike Pompeo as an "enemy of mankind" for his accusations of the Chinese cover-up of the outbreak. In the same denouncement, Pompeo also collected titles like "stumbling block," "accomplice," and someone "whose name shall be condemned for thousands of years" (CCTV Editorial 2020). To shame America's chief diplomat in such a public fury was unprecedented. Beijing's gloves were off. *Xinwen Lianbo*'s America-bashing has become so regular that netizens have begun to refer to it as "CCTV's Daily Curse" (*Yangshi Meiriyima*). They are certainly entertained when the CCTV's hosts describe American politicians as "lotus spitting" and "tornado gulping"—all slang to describe someone who talks impressively but acts little (*China News* 2020).

Going rhetorically ballistic or, in the Chinese language, the so-called "Wolf Warrior" diplomacy, continued under the Biden administration. Two months into Biden's presidency, Xi sent Chief Diplomatic Advisor Yang Jiechi and Foreign Minister Wang Yi to Alaska to meet their American counterparts, Secretary of State Antony Blinken and National Security Advisor Jake Sullivan. It quickly escalated into a face-to-face spar. In his opening remarks, Blinken presented a list of American concerns on issues ranging from Xinjiang to Hong Kong to Taiwan and to China's intimidation of its neighbors. Blinken also vowed that America will speak to China "from a position of strength." In response, Yang broke the protocol of having a three-minute introductory speech. Instead, he lectured the American side for 20 minutes. Among many angry words Yang vented out, one line quickly went viral—he told his American hosts:

> Let me say here that, in front of the Chinese side, the United States does not have the qualification to say that it wants to speak to China from a position of strength. The U.S. side was not even qualified to say such things even 20 years or 30 years back, because this is not the way to deal with the Chinese people. (Nikkei 2021)

The Chinese translator expressed Yang's original phrase, "Zhongguoren buchi zheyitiao," as "This is not the way to deal with the Chinese people." This was a markedly polite version of what Yang said. Back in China, an online competition commenced to see who could better translate it to reflect its blunt and assertive nature—ranging from "Chinese people do not eat this, and you know what I am saying" to multiple versions that include profanity. The sentence also appeared on all kinds of commodities overnight—from t-shirts to mugs and cellphone cases, and so on. It would be hard to image that "this is not the way to deal with the Chinese people" could become so wildly popular. That translation sounded neither catchy nor macho. To

China's nationalist netizens, it was those ruder translations that better captured the contemptuous nature of Yang's words. According to the Chinese media, people were applauding their national TV hosts and diplomats' irate outbursts to America, calling such acts "*nudui*" and "*dalian*"—internet memes for "furiously refuting" and "slapping in face," respectively. The real picture of the public responses to this propaganda trend is hard to gauge, though, as the official media framing is most certainly selective.

One century after Sun Yat-sen, China's America-educated founding father, urged the country to head for the deep blue, it has indeed set sail. Instead of becoming a force of peace, though, China's maritime expansion has an explicitly military undertone. It has instigated fear and anxiety among neighbors. A grand geopolitical showdown, wrapped up as a competition between two superpowers' dreams, is keeping the region on edge.

Conclusion

This chapter historicizes China's spatial-imaging effort by first examining the geographical root for the country's name—*Zhongguo*, or the Middle Kingdom. It shows how the term's implication shifted from claiming territoriality to justifying supreme governing legitimacy. A combination of territorial and ideational imaginaries led to the creation of the *tianxia*, or "All under Heaven", concept. This concept remains a potent semiotic framing in contemporary China. In fact, the "Chinese Dream" slogan may be perceived as Chinese ruler Xi Jinping's effort of imagining a world led by the moral authority of a rejuvenated China. Xi's campaign, however, is filled with inconsistencies, internal and external. Inside China, contesting interpretations emerge on what exactly a modern "All under Heaven" international order should look like—ranging from unapologetically Sino-centric chauvinism to one that imagines a "huddled masses" under an open sky. The Chinese government's diplomatic practices are leaning toward a more assertive execution of the *tianxia* concept, causing anxiety among countries near and far.

The chapter then examines China's belated awakening to maritime exploration and its political and social impacts. Early revolutionaries looked to the ocean and founded a new opportunity of redefining Chinese national identity: that is, to replace its land-based worldview with one that emphasized maritime expansion. This sea-bound endeavor brought new promises for a nation hungry for a modern national purpose. However, the country's march to the ocean was intermittent, disrupted by foreign invasions and domestic conflicts. The founding of the People's Republic did not lead to an immediate prioritization of maritime expansion. The first two generations of Chinese leaders continued the tradition of looking inward and focusing on securing its land borders. After the country opened its door, a call for transforming China into a "blue civilization" quickly crashed as a political dissenting movement.

Starting from the 1990s, awed by America's military technologies and humiliated in the 1996 Taiwan Strait Crisis, China renewed its effort of maritime expansion. This time, the expanding process became more consistent, driven by a rising state aiming for enlarging its security perimeter. The COVID-19 pandemic has not slowed down China's efforts to assert its dominance in the region. A sluggish economy, a rapidly ageing population, the eruption of popular dissent on the government's draconian lockdown policy, coupled with international condemnation on human rights abuses in Hong Kong, Xinjiang, and its threat to Taiwan, all heightened Xi's anxiety of seeing China under siege on numerous fronts. As Regilme et al point out in other chapters, all these domestic and international problems that China faces add more incentives for Beijing to double-down on its aggressive foreign policy, also known as the "wolf warrior" diplomacy.

Driven by a mixture of pride and fear, China is making the oceans the new front of its own manifest destiny. China's heavily armed maritime expansion has incited anxiety among its neighbors. Packaged as a key component of the "Chinese Dream" concept, China's militant march to the sea has put it on a collision course with America. To counter China's assertiveness, America has been busy rekindling the Indo-Pacific concept, a strategic framing that is both a geographical encirclement and a political alliance that highlights democracy—jointly to cage China. A grand contest of two superpower dreams has increasingly looked like a stress test for countries in the region and beyond.

References

CC Editorial "Guoji Ruiping" [Insights on World] by China Central Television . 2020. "Renlei gongdi; Qiangu maming" [Enemy of the State; Someone Whose Name Shall be Condemned for Thousands of Years]. https://finance.sina.com.cn/wm/2020-04-27/doc-iirczymi8703138.shtml

China News. 2020. "Yangshi meiri yima: meiguo zhengke 'koutulianhua' 'tunge xuanfeng'" [CCTV's Daily Curse: American Politicians Pretend They Could Spit Lotus or Gulp Down a Tornado]. https://news.creaders.net/china/2020/05/17/2225767.html

China News. 2021. "Mei tiqian 30nian jiemi yintaizhanlve wenjian, Zhao Lijian zhichu qizhong sandacuowo" [Zhao Lijian Points Out Three Mistakes in American Indo-Pacific Strategy Declassified 30 Years Earlier Than Original Deadline]. https://www.chinanews.com.cn/gn/2021/01-13/9386065.shtml

Chinese State Council Information Office. "Xu Fu dongdu chuanshuo" [Folklores of Xu Fu's maritime journey to the East], http://www.scio.gov.cn/ztk/xwfb/09/8/Document/656389/656389.htm

Clinton, H. 2014. *Hard Choices*. New York: Simon & Schuster.

Diao, D.M. 2020. "Zhongguo kangyi zhangxian daguo dandang" [China's Effort of Combating Pandemic Demonstrates Great Power Responsibility] in *Sheke Dongtai* [New Developments in Social Sciences], http://www.nopss.gov.cn/BIG5/n1/2020/1103/c219544-31916315.html

Harries, H. 2015. Speech delivered to the Australian Strategic Policy Institute. https://www.cpf.navy.mil/leaders/harry-harris/speeches/2015/03/ASPI-Australia.pdf

Huang, S.L. 2020. "Sun Zhongshan Haiyang qiangguo sixiang tanlun" [Research on Sun Yat-sen's Maritime Power Theory] in *Tuanjiewang* [Solidarity Net]. http://www.tuanjiewang.cn/2020-11/12/content_8895097.htm

Jiang, T.Y. 2014. "Deng Xiaoping dui Mao Zedong junshisixiang de jicheng he fazhan" [Deng Xiaoping's Continued Practice and Development of Mao Zedong Military Thought] in *Renminwang* [People's Daily Net]. http://cpc.people.com.cn/n/2014/0813/c69113-25459367-3.html

Lam, W.W.L. 2015. *Chinese Politics in the Era of Xi Jinping: Renaissance, Reform, or Retrogression?* London: Routledge.

Li, Shanchang and Song Lian. 1370. *Yuanshi juan* [History of Yuan]. http://www.guoxue.com/shibu/24shi/yuanshi/yuasml.htm

Liaowang. 2015. "Zhongguomeng gongming shijiemeng" [Chinese Dream Echoes World Dream] in *Xinhuawang* [Xinhua Net]. http://www.xinhuanet.com//politics/2015-01/06/c_127363511.htm

Liu, M.F. 2010. *Zhongguomeng: zhongguo de mubiao, daolu ji zixinxin* [Chinese Dream: China's Goals, Path, and Self-Confidence]. Beijing: Zhongguo Youyi Publishing.

Nikkei Asia, March 19, 2021. "How it happened: transcript of the US-China opening remarks in Alaska." https://asia.nikkei.com/Politics/International-relations/US-China-tensions/How-it-happened-Transcript-of-the-US-China-opening-remarks-in-Alaska

Regilme, S.S.F. 2019. "The Decline of American Power and Donald Trump: Reflections on Human Rights, Neoliberalism, and the World Order." *Geoforum* 102: 157–166.

Saich, T. 2017. "What Does General Xi Jinping Dream About?" in *Ash Center Occasional Papers*. https://ash.harvard.edu/files/ash/files/what_does_xi_jinping_dream_about.pdf

Shen, R. 2016. "Haiwai jidi: zhenghe xiaxiyang lishijingyan yu xianzai qishi" [Overseas Bases: Historical Experience and Contemporary Implications of Zhenghe's Western Ocean Voyages]. *Journal of Shanghai University* 33(2): 67–77.

Shi, M.Z. 2013. "Zhongguomeng qubieyu meiguomeng de qida tezheng" [Seven Differences between the Chinese Dream and the American Dream] in *Huanqiu* [The Globe], https://opinion.huanqiu.com/article/9CaKrnJAFzV

Sima, Q. 90BC. "Dayuan liezhuan" [Treatise on Dayuan] in *Shi Ji* [Records of the Grand Historian], vol. 123, no. 63., Guoxuewang [Chinese Studies Net]. http://www.guoxue.com/book/shiji/0123.htm

Sohu News. 2022. "Haiwanzhanzheng daxing zhongguo" [The Gulf War Woke Up China]. https://www.sohu.com/a/526692363_819718

Townshend, A., Thomas-Noone, B. and Steward, M. 2019. "Averting Crisis: American Strategy, Military Spending and Collective Defense in the Indo-Pacific" United States Studies Centre at the University of Sydney. https://www.ussc.edu.au/analysis/averting-crisis-american-strategy-military-spending-and-collective-defence-in-the-indo-pacific

United States Department of Defense. 2015. "Asia-Pacific Maritime Security Strategy." https://dod.defense.gov/Portals/1/Documents/pubs/NDAA%20A-P_Maritime_SecuritY_Strategy-08142015-1300-FINALFORMAT.PDF

United States Department of State. 2009. "100,000 Strong Educational Exchange Initiative." https://2009-2017.state.gov/100k/index.htm

VOA News. 2014. "Jiemishike: Liu Liankun shaojiang taihai diyijiandiean" [Confidential Information Revealed: Lieutenant Liu Liankun and Top Espionage Case in Cross-Taiwan Strait Relations]. https://www.voachinese.com/a/taiwan-spy-in-china-20140413/1892276.html

Wang, A.Y. 2018. "Gaige kaifang yilai zhongguogongchandan lingdaofandui lishixuwuzhiyi de Shijian he jingyan" [Practice and Experience of the Chinese Communist Party Combating Historical Nihilism in the Reform and Open-Door Era]. *Journal of Marxism Studies* 5: 130–140.

Xi, J.P. 2012. "Speech at the 'Road to Rejuvenation' Exhibition." In *Qiushi* [Seeking Truth], http://www.qstheory.cn/zhuanqu/2021-03/03/c_1127162387.htm

Xi, J.P. 2013. Remarks by President Obama and President Xi Jinping of the People's Republic of China after bilateral meeting, June 8.

Xu, J.L. 2015. "Xintianxia: chongjian zhongguo de neiwaizhixu" [New "All under Heaven": Reconstruction of China's Internal and External Orders] in *Aisixiang* [Passion for Philosophical Thoughts]. http://m.aisixiang.com/data/91702.html

Yang, S.M. 2017. "Hezun-zuizao jilu 'zhongguo' yici de qingtongqi" [Hezun – the Earliest Bronze Device with the Word "China" Inscribed]. *Chinese Artifacts Information*. http://www.kaogu.cn/cn/kaoguyuandi/kaogusuibi/2017/0727/59046.html

Zhang, J.G. 2014. "Zhenghe xiaxiyang weishenme bei jiaoting" [Why was Zhenghe's Western Ocean Voyages Halted]. *Sina History*. http://history.sina.com.cn/bk/mqs/2014-08-03/232796855.shtml

Zhang, J.J. 2010. "Ying taoguangyanghui liangshaojiang fandui zhuiqiu shijie diyi junshiqiangguo" [Low Profile is Needed; Two Lieutenant Generals Oppose Pursuit of the World's Top Military Power Status] in *Huanqiu* [The Globe]. https://mil.huanqiu.com/article/9CaKrnJn4wf

Zheng, H.G. and Han, L. 2021. "Weile geng meihao de shijie" [Toward a Better World – Xi Jinping's 'Tianxia' Compassion] in *Xinhuawang* [Xinhua Net]. http://www.xinhuanet.com/politics/leaders/2021-06/30/c_1127612909.htm

Zou, Z.H. 2018. "Zhenghe xiaxiyang yu mingchao de 'qilin' waijiao" [Zheng He's Western Ocean Voyages and Ming Dynasty's 'Giraffe Diplomacy']. *Journal of East China Normal University* 2(50): 1–11.

6

Africa and US–China Rivalry: Between Webs and Bases

Lina Benabdallah

Introduction

In December 2022, the *China Daily* newspaper ran an opinion piece titled "Will Americans Imitate China's Approach to Africa?"[1] The article was making reference to the US–Africa Summit organized by the US in Washington DC hosting several African state leaders. Summit diplomacy has become a staple in China–Africa relations as Beijing hosted the first Forum on China-Africa Cooperation (FOCAC) in the year 2000 and there have been eight editions of the summit since then.[2] It is in this context that the author of this *China Daily* article and many others have wondered if the US was mimicking China's foreign policy approach in Africa. To be able to understand if Beijing has been socializing the US in transforming its approach to Africa by imitating its own, we have to first understand what summit diplomacy tells us about the values and norms underpinning Beijing's approach in Africa.

In June 2021, Uganda's President Museveni appointed the new Party Secretary for the country's ruling party, the National Resistance Movement (NRM), Richard Todwong. A few moments after the announcement, the party's website shared that China congratulated the new Party Secretary for his appointment (National Resistance Movement 2021b). As it turns out, in 2019, Todwong had participated in a three-month training at Peking University sponsored by the Chinese government for elites to learn about governance from Communist Party of China (CPC) experts. In an interview with Xinhua about the training, he highlighted how "African leaders could learn governance philosophy of the CPC, as the party is committed to a people-centered philosophy of development" (Xinhua 2021a). Similarly, at the 100th anniversary of the CPC (in July 2021), Todwong filmed a video message congratulating China, thanking the CPC for its mentorship, resources, and friendship with African political parties, and stating that the NRM will continue to "walk in the footsteps of the Communist Party" to achieve development and wellbeing for the Ugandan people (National Resistance Movement 2021b).

By contrast, the news of Todwong's accession as the head of the NRM did not make it to US news outlets despite having also trained in the US before going to China. Such variance suggests a difference in China's relational approach that puts a premium not only on training African elites but also on setting up mechanisms to follow (celebrate, for example) the political achievements of African elites trained in China. This one example shows the importance that Chinese foreign policy makers put on investing in human/social capital and network-building with not only high-level but also middle- and low-level officers and civil servants from across Africa. In this way, the chapter starts from the position that China's influence in Africa comes not only from Chinese investments in physical infrastructure buildings (as seen in the construction of ports, parliaments, and presidential palaces) but it is also produced and manufactured through the creation of platforms for exchanging expertise which also serve as elite capture mechanisms. China's network approach goes beyond hosting delegations, trainings, and elite capture programs, and also activates those personal and professional bonds in order to build a more expansive network of close ties.

This sits in a stark contrast with the approach of the US in Africa where military interests have been prioritized post-9/11 (see Miles 2012; Moore and Walker 2016). Even a simple account of the number of high-level visits (presidents, for instance) to Africa in the last ten years shows an acutely imbalanced high-level diplomacy in favor of China. Indeed, the Chinese foreign minister has made it a routine to target the African continent for his first trip abroad every year (Scarfe 2022). Moreover, during the Trump administration, Africa was deprioritized in significant ways (Abrahamsen 2018). For instance, US–Africa trade fell to approximately US$41 billion in 2018, down from a high of US$100 billion in 2008. Similarly, US foreign direct investment in Africa decreased from US$50.4 billion in 2017 to US$43.2 billion in 2019. This "14% decline came at a time when other countries like China were increasing their investments in the region" (Owusu and Carmody 2020). Trump's Africa policy was also tainted by the Muslim ban which inflicted travel restrictions on students, diplomats, businesspeople, and tourists from several African countries to the US. It is also during this time that the "debt trap" narrative became a heuristic description of Chinese investments in Africa for many US politicians, further harming the relations with African partners.[3]

Even more to the point, on July 1, 2021, the CPC celebrated its 100th anniversary, marking the occasion with a series of celebrations, congratulatory messages from party leaders from across the globe, and hopeful declarations about the next hundred years, as well as several consultation meetings. The 100th anniversary served as an opportunity to accomplish at least three important goals for the CPC: first, taking advantage of the opportunity to display the CPC's leadership in fighting poverty and success in achieving high levels of development in a short period of time; second, to showcase that the CPC has many friends and admirers from all around the globe with political party leaders stating their willingness to learn from China's experience; and, third, to expand the CPC's outreach by inviting more party leaders to engage with, learn from, and dialogue with the CPC on various fronts. Related to this third goal, on July 8, 2021, the CPC hosted the "World Political Parties Summit" with the participation of leaders of over 500 political parties from around the globe. During the summit's keynote speech, President Xi Jinping was explicit about an outward focus going forward, stating that the CPC will be "pressing ahead with the Chinese-style modernization to make new contributions to humanity's search for ways to modernize."

In that same speech, Xi Jinping put a premium on the role of the party (the CPC) in leading the path in charting these "new contributions" that China will make to global development and prosperity. In that way, he pledged that "CPC will work with political parties of all countries to promote state-to-state coordination and cooperation through party-to-party consultation and cooperation and bring into better play the due role of political parties in global governance" (Xi Jinping Keynote Address at the CPC and World Political Parties Summit 2021). Not only in this speech but across the gamut of foreign policy, party-to-party diplomacy has become an increasingly important tool for Xi Jinping's government to increase global awareness of China's development path, its governance model, and its aspiration for building a "community with a shared future for mankind."

Africa has, since Mao's era, been an important player for China's party-to-party diplomacy. Today, Africa is even more important for the aspirations laid out by President Xi Jinping than it has been in the past. Geographically speaking, the continent represents an ideal partner for Beijing to push China's core interests with the maritime silk road. Diplomatically speaking, Africa remains the continent where China is most positively viewed compared to anywhere else in the world, which constitutes an opportunity for Chinese diplomatic efforts. African party leaders, elites, as well as citizens of different walks of life often express their aspirations to model their policies after China's development success and to learn from China's experiences eradicating extreme poverty, achieving economic growth, social stability, and political prestige (see Carrozza and Benabdallah 2022). Africa is viewed by Chinese leadership as a prospect for China's development and governance models to introduce and implement a viable alternative to the Western-centric models. Therefore, making sure that the CPC maintains close consultation mechanisms with as many political parties in Africa as possible occupies a key position in Chinese diplomatic strategy (Benabdallah 2020). By contrast, the US has for a long time banked on its soft power to create a somewhat organic (not state-engineered) environment for US democracy, values, and culture to be attractive across the Global South, Africa included. Yet, as we have seen in recent studies there is a significant growing trend of backsliding democracy in the continent which has pushed US policy makers to think about a more hands-on approach to spreading US influence in the Global South (and Africa). An example of this can be seen in the recently organized summit for democracy which was hosted by the Biden administration with an eye on curbing China's influence by playing up the role of civil society organizations, youth leadership, and grassroots movements in upholding democratic ideals. A total of 17 African countries were invited to participate in the summit, which ended up alienating a large number of African partners who thought the summit organizer alienated them by stigmatizing them as not worthy of an invitation (see Levinson 2021). The summit was calculated by the Biden administration as a move to curb China's influence in the world by highlighting American foreign policy priorities in terms of democratic values, norms of transparency, human rights respect, abidance by the rule of law, and concern for the environment. The summit was a strategic opportunity to contrast what a so-called Western rules-based order could offer different from what China offers. Unfortunately, when it comes to US–China competition in Africa, US foreign policy is still struggling with making its existing initiatives more visible and struggling even more with finding a brand for its approach to the continent that can be distinguished from China's summit diplomacy and other people-to-people exchange programs.

In order to better understand the dynamics, patterns, and characteristics of these exchanges and their implications both for China–Africa relations and for US–China rivalry, this chapter explores China's competitive advantage over the US by looking into China–Africa party-to-party ties and examines the strengths and weaknesses of China's party-to-party diplomacy in Africa. It begins with an overview of China–Africa party-to-party relations, including party diplomacy during Africa's anti-colonial struggles and Xi Jinping's thought and the Chinese governance model. It continues by explicating the drivers, characteristics, and contents of China–Africa party exchanges, before discussing some of the challenges that China's party diplomacy has faced in light of the COVID-19 pandemic. It then uses case studies and examples to illustrate China's party diplomacy in Africa and continues to discuss the implications and potential future dynamics of party-to-party diplomacy for China–Africa diplomatic relationships. All in all, Beijing's network approach in its diplomacy with African states has been a successful strategy to counterbalance its weakness in terms of engaging civil society organizations and grassroots movements. By contrast, the US has mostly focused on two fronts in its approach to Africa: militarily cooperating on counterterrorism programs and diplomatically by engaging members of African civil society organizations. The approaches by China and the US in Africa are vastly different but one has influence on the other. In the conclusion, the chapter summarizes these overlapping areas and discusses what US–China rivalry means for Africa and Africans.

Overview of China–Africa party-to-party relations

There are two channels within the Chinese governance structure that are typically associated with developing and maintaining China's influence abroad. The smaller of the two is the United Front Work Department (UFWD), which comprises "a network of civic and business associations, student groups, Chinese-language media, academic institutions, and politicians, which is used to intimidate, surveil, and co-opt the overseas Chinese community" (Newlin and Kostelancik 2020). The UFWD has recently also acquired its own publication outlet, the *Journal of United Front Science*, which was founded in 2017 two years after Xi Jinping declared that the "United Front Work is a branch of science." The current UFWD mission statement, which addresses overseas work, is explained in a recent document, stating that the UFWD should devote itself and its resources "to maintaining and promoting China's reunification, realizing the great rejuvenation of the Chinese nation, enhancing the friendly cooperation and exchanges between the Chinese people and the people of the world, and promoting the building of a community of human destiny" (Ranade 2021: 2). Here, we see that the UFWD has a broad enough scope that it can include engaging with elites from all different ranks, but it does not officially conduct China's party-to-party diplomacy. As such, most of the party-to-party work that UFWD does is informal. On top of this, the UFWD has very little relevance to examining China's influence in Africa, given that it is mostly active in Europe, the US, and Australia.

The main government channel that is typically associated with the exercise of China's party diplomacy is the International Department of the Communist Party of China (中共中央對外聯絡部, Zhonggong zhongyang duiwai lianluobu, ID-CPC hereafter) which was formed in 1951 and evolved from the third section of the UFWD.[4] The ID-CPC's original goal was strictly to work with foreign communist parties as well as national liberation movements from Africa (Bing 2017: 55). Its mission, then, was limited by both politics and geography. However, over the years, the ID-CPC's engagements have expanded, and it has built a network "to maintain contact with 400 parties in over 160 countries." The International Department is headed by Minister Song Tao (since 2015), working alongside four vice-ministers and two assistant ministers.⁵ In working with this network, the ID-CPC "holds regular meetings with its foreign counterparts, provides training for foreign cadres, and sponsors party schools abroad" (Hackenesch and Bader 2020: 1). Speaking about the importance of the work done by the ID-CPC to legitimate and expand China's central government's influence, ID-CPC minister Song Tao (2019) explained that "the fundamental task of the Party's external work is to solidify the Party's position as the ruling party and safeguard the security of socialism with Chinese characteristics". The external work of the ID-CPC, then, is closely related to its internal work and the CPC's overarching goals. One of the key advantages of ID-CPC over other government channels is that it "not only provides access to high-level decision-makers in formal government functions, but it also allows for engagement with influential political actors outside the realm of regular foreign affairs diplomacy, such as power-brokers operating behind the scenes or future political leaders" (Song Tao 2019). The ID-CPC therefore plays a vital role not only in providing necessary connections to external party officials for the CPC, but it has also become an unsurpassable vehicle for the CPC to share success stories, practical experience, and expert knowledge from its own governance model with elites across the globe.

Party diplomacy during Africa's anti-colonial struggles

China–Africa party-to-party exchanges date back to Mao's era, perhaps most notably at the time the 1955 Bandung Conference. Attended by 29 African and Asian countries, the conference at Bandung can be understood as a "watershed in CPC political relations in Africa" as Premier Zhou Enlai, who led the Chinese delegation, was able to interact with delegations from Egypt, Ethiopia, Liberia, Libya, and soon-to-be-independent Sudan and Ghana (Eisenman 2018: 4). What started mostly as the CPC providing rhetorical support for fellow Bandung attendees, over the intervening decades became more tangible, including equipment support, medical team visits, and military trainings. These early party-to-party diplomatic relations were not as regular or substantial as they are today but were still both materially and symbolically meaningful.

Early CPC interactions with African political elites and revolutionary leaders served several ideological purposes, including, most importantly, obtaining official recognition of the People's Republic of China as the legitimate government of China and limiting the Soviet Union's influence in the Cold War "Third World." Initial efforts at elite capture were successful for Beijing. In the late 1950s and early 1960s,

> the CPC's political outreach in Africa achieved impressive results. Beijing sent 144 missions to African countries and received 405 African

delegations. ... By 1964, political outreach and host diplomacy had paid dividends with 15 of 35 independent African countries choosing to recognize Beijing, rather than Taipei—up from only seven in 1960. (Eisenman 2018: 9)

The expansion of Beijing's party-to-party diplomacy was more than just reaching more countries—it also reached more parties. The ID-CPC went beyond its initial engagement with only leftist or left-leaning parties to engage with parties across the political spectrum. In a move which stands uneasily next to Beijing's typical position of engaging only in state-to-state diplomatic relations, the ID-CPC's mandate is to work with *all* political parties, including opposition parties to governments that the CPC recognizes. Along these lines, a 1982 policy coming from the CPC's 12th National Congress identified four guiding principles for the ID-CPC's party diplomacy with the intent of building a new sort of inter-party relations with as many partners across the world as possible (Zeng 2015). Those four principles are mutual respect, independence, non-interference in each other's internal affairs, and complete equality.

Chinese diplomacy has seen a significant payoff coming from this strategy. As a result of the ID-CPC's expanded mandate, "by 1988, over 40 political parties from Sub-Saharan Africa had established relations with the CPC" (Zhong 2013). The expansion was successful all over the continent, where in recent years, the "CPC has established relations with 81 African parties both in and out of power" (Zhong 2013). Still, the early 1990s saw a retraction of the number and frequency of party-to-party interactions between China and Africa, owing to democratization movements across Africa and a related ambivalence about China (Zhong 2013). This retraction was short-lived, however, reversing in the early 2000s with renewed energy around China–Africa party-to-party exchanges by both Chinese and African officials.

The "new" party-to-party exchanges that are common this millennium have moved away from the sort of legitimacy-seeking which featured heavily in early Chinese engagements in Africa. If earlier engagements were mostly concerned with the legitimacy and stability of the CPC and its image abroad, the face of Chinese party-to-party interactions is very different now (Eisenman 2018: 12). The CPC which is leading China–Africa party-to-party exchanges now exhibits a more confident, stronger voice more interested in leadership, mentoring, and sharing the China governance model than looking for approval. This has practical implications as well: the "old" CPC looked to support the parties which were in power at the time to obtain and maintain their support for Mao, and the "new" CPC is involved with as many parties as possible, looking to establish positive relationships with any party that happens to come to power.

This forward-looking strategy not only motivates the ID-CPC to engage with more parties, but also to have a stronger view of how to interact with the leaders of the future. As such, the Chinese government has been developing programming to interact with, and build good working relationships with, the next generation of political elites across the continent. This programming combines educational scholarships for hundreds of young African elites and professionalization trainings located in the CPC's Beijing-based party school. These exchanges build and strengthen ties between African party officials and their Chinese counterparts. While there are too many examples to discuss in the scope of this chapter, the remainder of this paragraph includes a few highlights. In the time since Beijing's 2011 recognition of the independence of South Sudan, China has extended more than 4,000 short-term trainings and educational scholarships to party members in the new country (Kuo 2017). Many of the South Sudanese party members attended the CPC's party school for lessons on cadre management, tax collection, media relations, organizational structure for parties, and relations between national and local level civil services. Similarly, China's ambassador to Uganda related that around 500 people from Uganda attend trainings in China each year (Xinhua 2019). These efforts in South Sudan and Uganda mirror many across the continent. For example, since 2007, the Ningbo Polytechnic's campus (in Zhejiang Province, China) has hosted over a thousand trainees from 48 countries in the African continent. After African party members attend these trainings in China, they often exhibit "a willingness to work with China and view China's internal policies favorably in the future" (Nakkazi 2018).

Drivers, characteristics, and contents of China–Africa party exchanges

Drivers

As mentioned in Xi Jinping's speech, engaging political party leaders from Africa and the Global South more generally can be seen as an opportunity for the CPC to market its governance model as an alternative that African governments can source their inspiration from, rather than Western models which may have failed them in the past. Party-to-party diplomacy, especially through exchanges organized by the ID-CPC, is a particularly strong tool to reach these global outreach goals for the CPC. In fact, one can group the motivations behind enhancing party-to-party relations into three main drivers: ideological, commercial, and *guanxi*/network-building.

Ideological drivers

Convening training workshops, seminars, and delegation visits with African political party representatives and senior cadres can provide appropriate spaces for Chinese government officials to share CPC norms and values regarding governance, party leadership structure, the party's relations to the army, to the public, to surveillance technology, or to social media and so on. Party diplomacy in this way can be more efficient than public diplomacy (typically carried out via state-owned media messaging or through events hosted by Confucius Institutes).[6] Getting access to senior cadres of ruling (as well as non-ruling) political parties opens up chances for one-on-one focused consultations and discussions of China's success story. Among these success stories that the ID-CPC has been boasting about during its exchanges with foreign party representatives are China's development, poverty eradication, and economic growth over the last few decades.

Building off and expanding on this approach, party-to-party diplomacy events have recently been framing China's development success as an alternative to the development frameworks that have long been pushed by international institutions including the International Monetary Fund and the World Bank. In fact, the "right to development" has now pretty much became a signature aspect of China's discourse around global human rights where instead of staying silent about human rights, as China had for a long time, now there is a reclaiming of defining human rights along the lines of economic development rather than the mainstream liberal way of understanding human rights. Party-to-party diplomacy is therefore an appropriate and even optimal tool to communicate China's interpretations (or characteristics) of concepts such as the right to development as a human right and the equality of all countries. As the right to development stands in direct contrast to a Western/liberal notion of rights based on individual freedoms, its promotion underscores an ideological driver to engage in exchanges that allow the CPC to introduce its values and norms as an alternative to liberal values, which are often viewed as dominant.

Commercial drivers

In addition to the ideological drivers for enhancing party-to-party diplomacy as a tool of China's foreign policy conduct toward African states, there is also a practical and commercial component to the delegation visits and exchanges. When delegations of senior political parties are invited to China for exchanges or trainings, there is typically a show-and-tell component to the visits with tours of various facilities, offices, and production plants. Typically, political party trainings which touch on topics such as the use of technology in safe city and smart city projects also present opportunities for Chinese tech companies to market their products to African elites during their visits. Of course, there is no denying here that the ideological and commercial drivers bleed into each other as the distinctions between the two are rather arbitrary and used only to enhance our understanding of what is at stake.

We can see across media reports that a number of African party members who travel to China return to their home countries impressed with the ways that China utilizes surveillance equipment to improve the government's ability to control the internet and to track and reduce crime. For example, Anthony Kpandu of South Sudan, who reports reading parts of the "Concise History of the Chinese Communist Party" daily, led a group of members of the Sudan People's Liberation Movement to China. He returned from the trip and reported being impressed with how drones were used in China to address crime. He was interested in acquiring the technology that he saw in China and mimicking its use. When he got home, he immediately ordered the surveillance drones he had seen used in China for use in South Sudan (Kuo 2017). Like Kpandu, other governments or party members have either ordered or are in the process of ordering facial recognition technology from China to enhance their policing and security operations (Hawkins 2018; Prasso 2019). While it is hard to hold Beijing responsible for any misuse of Chinese technology after it is purchased, it is also difficult to ignore the wide variety of political parties which find China's governance techniques attractive. That said, the example of African politicians acquiring surveillance technology from China after seeing it during party-to-party exchanges highlights both a high level of power and influence on China's part and a willingness to follow and advocate for the Chinese model on the part of African elites. In this way, we can see that party-to-party exchanges can be an effective method for marketing equipment from China to potential buyers in Africa.

Guanxi *and network-building*

The expansive nature of the CPC's menu of party-to-party training workshops for African political leaders provides a variety of chances for networking not only between elite members of political parties on both sides, but also between youth and junior party cadres. Party delegations which visit China for trainings usually stay in China for one to two weeks, though some trainings have more extended timelines. When they are in China, party members from Africa are offered seminars on a wide variety of topics. These seminars provide information about the history of China, the CPC party structure, China's development model, internet governance, and other topics that the CPC can share their knowledge and experience to address. These trainings serve the purpose of building strong diplomatic ties with both current and future leaders of diverse political parties, which in turn serves as a near-guarantee that the CPC's foreign policy makers will find warm reception with future African leaders regardless of their political party or ideological leanings.

The effectiveness of this strategy can be seen in the fact that several current or former heads of African states led party-to-party delegations to visit China before they became presidents of their home states. These leaders include former presidents of three African countries, Mozambique's Guebuza, Namibia's Pohamba, and South Africa's Zuma.[7] Not only did these leaders attend Chinese trainings, if they are anything like the median attendee, they likely had a good experience. African attendees of Chinese trainings typically report a highly positive experience of the training specifically and of their experience getting to know China generally. Training participants frequently speak of their gratitude to the CPC for the opportunity and note that they learned a significant amount about how to manage parties from the CPC officials who led the training. For example, Cyril Ramaphosa, the current president of South Africa, in 2009 in his role as African National Congress General Secretary led a delegation to visit Beijing. During that visit, Ramaphosa conveyed a willingness to learn the things that the CPC would be training party members about. He noted that:

> It is not long since the ANC was founded and became a ruling party, but the CPC has been a ruling party for six decades and has accumulated rich experiences. We would like to learn from each other. Every participant studied hard and had deep discussions and they admitted they gained a lot. (Zhong Weiyun 2013)

Positive reactions like this from African counterparts signal the success of these training workshops both in their own right and in terms of furthering Chinese influence. These results have caused politburo officers and CPC officials to work to increase the number and length of exchanges with party members from Africa.

During the early months of the COVID-19 pandemic outbreak, we saw various expressions of solidarity by African political elites toward China at a time when the Chinese government was both dealing with the impacts of the outbreak domestically and with accusations from European governments and the US Trump administration concerning China's role in the origination of the virus. Those gestures of solidarity expressed included letters of solidarity, equipment donations, decisions not to interrupt flights (such as those conducted by Ethiopian Airlines to China), or even visits such as the one made by Egypt's health minister to China. These are a few of many examples of the ways that building and nurturing *guanxi* through party-to-party exchanges enhances trust-building and strengthen bonds between Chinese and Africa political elites.

Relational networks serve to enhance trust-building and to promote mutual understanding between China and developing states across the Global South. Networks introduce state elites and government officials to new and common sets of values and norms when professionalization trainings are organized. Understanding the centrality of relationality and the processes of expert knowledge production through people-to-people exchanges and social network-building programs are key to unpacking China's rising power status in Africa (and elsewhere in the Global South). These relations are manifested in the case of Chinese foreign policy in steadily increasing quotas for scholarships to international students, people-to-people exchange programs under the Belt and Road Initiative, joint workshops and professionalization training programs offered for elites, civil servants, military officers, and citizens of various developing countries (Benabdellah 2019). Chinese government-sponsored professionalization trainings serve different specialty areas, but they all result in producing expert knowledge whether through seminars, workshops, or joint-navy drills. Across these purposes, they set up relational networks of goodwill and shared values.

Characteristics

As already mentioned, the CPC invites parties across the political and ideological spectrum to participate in party-to-party exchanges. Even if the CPC establishes stronger relationships with parties that fall closer to it ideologically, its strategy has been to engage even with parties that have significant differences with its core ideologies, including democratic-leaning parties, left, right, and center-leaning politicians. This flexibility is a manifestation of the CPC's interest in making sure that it has a good political relationship with any party that is either elected or rises to power across the continent, regardless of political affinity.[8] This also motivates the ID-CPC's practice of engaging with opposition parties in party-to-party exchanges, making a functional exception to China's norm of only pursuing state-to-state diplomacy. Strategically, this helps to protect the stability of China's political and economic interests as well as the strength of its diplomatic ties, promoting China's strategic interests in the case of both anticipated and unanticipated political transitions. Highlighting this makes it possible to understand the key role that party-to-party exchanges play in Chinese diplomacy as well as the wide reach of party-to-party exchange invitations.

Course/training contents

While many party-to-party seminars, workshops, and trainings have different components and speak to different audiences, some key themes are common across these exchanges. Those key themes include the poverty alleviation, party structure and organizational leadership, bureaucracy management, Marxist thought, and civil–military relations. Other topics that appear in party-to-party trainings include relationships between government and media, opposition monitoring on social media, internet censorship, and China's history with Hong Kong and Taiwan.

Across these trainings and seminars, the CPC's use of surveillance technology (especially facial recognition) to monitor political opponents and provide political stability has appealed to authoritarian-leaning governments on the African continent. Historically, the Chinese government has been both thorough and efficient in blocking a number of different forms of opposition—from online platforms such as Twitter, Facebook, or WeChat to in-person protests. This efficiency requires a combination of tactical know-how and technical knowledge, which the Chinese government can share through trainings with other party cadres. Particularly, the CPC shares its techniques for limiting social media-based critiques or challenges to its government. There have been a number of reports that Chinese strategies have been applied in places as diverse as Zimbabwe, Ethiopia, and Sudan, resulting in internet shutdowns and social media blackouts (see Feldstein 2020).

Whether utilized for building party infrastructure or controlling opposition or anything in between, party-to-party exchanges, particularly courses and training, provide unique outlets for norm diffusion, socialization of elites into existing norms, and knowledge production.[9] Some results of such socialization can be found in expressions of solidarity and support by several African political party elites of the CPC. For example, in response to the July 2020 national security law adopted by Chinese government and aimed at Hong Kong, 27 states endorsed a statement read at the United Nations Commission on Human Rights criticizing the law. At the same meeting, 57 countries endorsed a statement read in support of China's decision to pass that law. Almost half of those countries were from the African continent (for a full list see Lawler 2020). Rather than trying to think about how party-to-party exchanges *cause* support for Chinese policy in international organizations, it is helpful to think about the ways that influence and power have a synergistic and circular relationship in producing and maintaining networks between CPC officials and their counterparts in Africa. This being said, there have been a few sporadic critiques of China's tech influence in the continent, especially from Western reporters, although occasionally also from African civil society groups (see Prasso 2019).

Challenges: China's party diplomacy during the COVID-19 pandemic

Given how China's party-to-party exchanges often involve significant travel to meet in person and are intimately built on a relational/network approach that fosters personal bonding among party elites, one might be tempted to assume that the disruptions caused by the COVID-19 pandemic would present the ID-CPC with unique challenges and lead to an inevitable decline in activity as its traditional activities were infeasible. To some extent, this happened at the beginning of the pandemic, as the form of party-to-party exchanges it had sponsored would not work during the pandemic. As explained by Yao Wen, during the early stages of the outbreak, "normal activities of the ID-CPC were completely halted; explaining the situation and sustaining international support were its paramount task" (Yao 2021: 61). While it is a fact that the pandemic has disrupted the CPC's ability to continue to interact directly and physically with senior cadres and elites from various African political parties, rather than stop its activities altogether, the ID-CPC adapted its programming. In fact, the ID-CPC was quick to readjust its role to match what China was going through domestically with the different phases of the health pandemic. In the early months of the pandemic, the ID-CPC slowed down its direct party-to-party engagements in favor of consolidating the party's domestic legitimacy and soliciting support from abroad. During the later phases of the outbreak, the ID-CPC reached out to parties to serve as a diffusion mechanism for a new norm of Chinese governance, sharing the CPC's pandemic management with party officials abroad. By the close of the pandemic emergency in China, the ID-CPC emerged busier than during pre-pandemic times. The numbers of virtual workshops, consultation meetings, and training classes organized by the ID-CPC for engagement with political parties around the world have multiplied.

In the months that followed and as China got a better grip on the pandemic crisis management, the ID-CPC turned its main operations toward diffusing messaging about how the CPC was a source of inspiration and a force of global good in its commitment to provide an alternative way of governance and crisis management during the pandemic. The multitude of meetings hosted by the ID-CPC ensured that there was a continuous interaction on behalf of the CPC and global outreach often resulting in political party cadres from African countries expressing thanks. The ID-CPC continued its global outreach on behalf of the government and, by mid-April 2020, the institution sent letters to "over 310 parties in 128 countries, reaffirming the CPC's commitment to joint efforts against COVID-19 and to the building of a 'community with a shared future for mankind'" (Yao 2021: 63). In addition to the ID-CPC's intensive liaising between the CPC and external parties, during the pandemic, the International Department also provided programming for the Chinese domestic audience, looking to convey to them messaging about the CPC's reputation abroad (Yao 2021: 57).

All in all, despite the challenge that travel restrictions put on the important soft power aspect of China's party diplomacy, especially in light of the success of curated tours for political elites in China, the pandemic actually opened up opportunities for institutions like the ID-CPC to grow, particularly in their party-to-party efforts. The ID-CPC remained highly active and visible in its global outreach during the pandemic and took on an even broader mandate, both expanding its trainings and expanding the audience toward whom they were targeted.

The Forum of China-Africa Cooperation and elite network-building in China–Africa relations

Another important platform for elite network-building in China-Africa relations is FOCAC. FOCAC was launched in 2000 and takes place every three years (see Taylor 2011). It is a forum for Chinese and African officials to discuss the agenda of investments, exchanges, and priorities placed in the next three years. The most recent edition of the Forum, the eighth, took place in Dakar, Senegal in November 2021. It is expected to cement the strong ties between Chinese and African elites as they are still struggling with post-pandemic recovery.

Forum diplomacy is an ideal platform for boosting relations between high-level elites from China and their African counterparts outside of or in addition to the work organized by the ID-CPC. At FOCAC forums, African officials have opportunities to experience China as a serious partner that also takes them seriously, building both interdependence and trust. One of the advantages of this Forum is precisely this direct contact and the art of social relations (informal gatherings such as socials augment trust building). In its early years, FOCAC's focus was almost exclusively commercial and market related. China's strategic goals were to boost economic relations with African states, and, with that, to secure access to previously unavailable or underutilized markets and natural resources. The Forum has since expanded its scope to various areas of diplomacy including media, culture, agriculture, and security, among others.

FOCAC has also since its launch been expanded into a number of other sub-forum diplomacy avenues. For instance, in July 2018, Beijing hosted defense ministers and high-ranking military officials from 50 African states under the auspices of the China Africa Defense and Security Forum (Benabdallah 2020). The Forum lasted two weeks during which African delegations attended seminars, visited Chinese facilities, were introduced to Chinese-made military equipment, and toured several cities in China. But perhaps most importantly, in the two weeks, Chinese military officials had a unique networking opportunity with their African counterparts during which exchanges about common visions for peace and stability, challenges, and aspirations for the future took place (Carrozza and Marsh 2022).

Moreover, in 2019, Beijing hosted another iteration of the security Forum dubbed the China-Africa Peace and Security Forum and invited African defense ministers and high-ranking officials to China for a week. Similar to the previous Forum, this was an opportunity to showcase China's military equipment and technological know-how, as well as to exchange views and visions for regional and global peace and security. For example, during the Forum, African military officials were invited to visit the Special Police College in Beijing that trains anti-terrorism personnel for China's elite armed police force. During the visit, the two sides (African and Chinese) discussed military cooperation and combat-oriented training opportunities for African delegations at the Special Police College (CGTN 2019). From such examples, it is evident that there is a strong element of networking and building strong ties between Chinese and African counterparts which builds from, and builds on, forum diplomacy.

Due in large part to the social dynamics and networking opportunities provided by hosting such high-profile gatherings, both FOCAC and its complements have so far been extremely successful (Benabdallah 2020). During the seventh edition of FOCAC (September 2018), 51 heads of state arrived in Beijing for the summit (Soulé 2020). This was a record high for the number of African heads of states compared to previous FOCAC summits (Kuo 2017). Additionally, as there has lately been an upward trend in the proliferation of sub-forums, held under the umbrella of FOCAC, now we see regular FOCAC-sponsored mini forum meetings on media, security, agriculture, and think tank relations between China and African countries. These sub-forums are an opportunity to bring African civil servants and government officials of various ranks (from high-ranking to middle- or low-level officials) to China for short visits of several days. The visits can serve multiple purposes including showing African officials around, taking them to various Chinese facilities, enterprises, as well as to big cities around the country. Chinese foreign policy makers rely on interagency communication (embassies communicate with relevant actors in various ministries as well as media agencies about trainings for instance) in order to activate their *guanxi* connections and keep a growing network of party-to-party elites. In this way, a *guanxi* approach to power building is a relatively low-cost and potentially high-reward approach, especially in cases where previously trained officers climb leadership ladders.

What this means for Africa's Western partners

While the CPC remains one of the world top ruling parties to dedicate massive amounts of attention to party diplomacy, most African political elites have adopted a pragmatic approach to the rivalries between China and the US or China and other Western powers more broadly. The advantages that the CPC has over European counterparts with African political parties include three very important and unique contexts. On the one hand, the CPC has a history of supporting African revolutionary parties against colonial powers and that support keeps being used today to invoke that China had always been on the right side of history when it comes to Western powers' involvement in the continent. Second, there exist affinities between the CPC's authoritarian governance style and several African political parties that are more willing to learn from the CPC ways of managing, monitoring, and shaping public opinion than to learn how to democratize their political system. Third, the CPC's governance trainings that include components on the use of technology in monitoring government–public relations often also come with marketing typically affordable technology packages that can put in practice what the trainings show at a relatively low cost. By contrast, acquiring technology from Europe or the US is often prohibitive which opens up opportunities for the CPC to take the extra step of linking technology sales to governance and leadership trainings. In addition to this, issues of migration and counterterrorism have pre-occupied European and US agendas for Africa at the detriment of building strong connections with African party elites.

Investing in young leaders such as through the Obama-backed Young African Leaders Initiative (YALI) is one idea for US and European governments to expand their outreach and influence.[10] YALI, which was launched in 2010, is a very successful program that targets young African leaders (between ages 18 and 35) to support them "as they spur growth and prosperity, strengthen democratic governance, and enhance peace and security across sub-Saharan Africa."[11] YALI is a very popular program among African youth as it is viewed as a program that takes African perspectives and agency seriously and engages African youth as equal partners instead of tutees or learners that are talked down at. Programs like YALI could expand to engage all African countries (including in North Africa), and also be more involved in providing education opportunities for young leaders. Over 60 percent of Africa's population is under age 25 and the continent is the world's youngest. This makes opportunities to invest in African youth a very valuable way of investing in the future of African governance, development, and peace.

Another important point to highlight is that party-to-party ties and investment in young leaders are groundwork initiatives that take a long time to achieve. They are not the kind of investments that necessarily yield fast turnaround dividends. It may take a generation or more for the results to show. This is indeed yet another element that the CPC has an advantage in. The International Department has been consistent in its outreach programs. A program like YALI, however popular it is in the eyes of the African youth, is subject to partisan administration politics in the US, mostly due to the fact that interest in African governance is usually viewed through the prism of counterterrorism and other military programs instead of civic leadership programs. In other words, streamlining long-term views and agendas (with budgets) that have a much wider horizon of engagement with African leaders (young and otherwise) will provide a sense of stability and serious commitment to African partners and will send a strong signal of rich and long-term exchanges to Africa's various non-Western partners. A chief example of how domestic politics in the US and partisan divides influence engagement with Africa can be found in the many blows that US diplomacy in Africa suffered after Obama's administration. As explained by Regilme (2022: 2), "the credibility of US commitment to foreign assistance and multilateralism appeared to be at risk, especially during the term of former US president Donald Trump." Indeed the credibility of US commitments to African partners also sustained a step back when Trump decided to withdraw US troops from Somalia in 2020. However soon after Biden took office, the Pentagon signaled the US would resume its operations in Somalia with a few hundred troops to be stationed in the Horn. These policy shifts (from disengagement back to engagement) are often motivated by how the US views itself on the global stage vis-à-vis rising/challenging powers. For Trump, the US would be better off focusing its efforts containing China away from Africa and in areas closer to China geographically. For Biden, and especially in light of Russia's invasion of Ukraine in the early months of 2022, maintaining a presence in the Horn would give the US important logistical leverage in case the conflict with Putin escalated beyond Ukraine's borders (Hansen 2022).

Conclusion

US foreign policy making in the Global South has not built a reputation for prioritizing Africa in a holistic way. Instead, the ebbs and flows of interest in Africa were typically driven by strategic interests of the US in issues where Africa was deemed to be too important to neglect. For instance, in the 1990s, securing shipping lanes for flows of energy imports to the US made Africa rise in importance. Likewise, in a post-9/11 security environment, a myopic view of "good" versus "bad" states skewed US presence in the continent to a few key states and a few key areas of engagement. Unlike the US, China had for decades aimed at building strong ties with different career-level diplomats in order to ensure that it is viewed as a serious partner of African states and a partner that's interested in knowing about the contexts of each of the continent's states that Beijing has official relations with.

The CPC has so far established relations with over 600 political parties and organizations from all corners of the globe and is working to increase the breadth and depth of those networks regularly. Every year, the ID-CPC as well as other relevant agencies engage in hundreds of activities and events that aim at nurturing, strengthening, and expanding these party-to-party connections. From symbolic calls to secretary generals/presidents of the parties, to invitations for senior cadres, training classes for other cadres, as well as various consultation seminars and summits, the CPC's global outreach to political parties around the world is a unique and unmatched diplomacy tool. Indeed, it is hard to think of another government with as big a capacity to interact with as many political parties.

Chinese government-sponsored professionalization trainings and people-to-people exchanges are meant to build connections among high-ranking officers, create an affective bonding, a sense of gratitude toward the Chinese government for covering all expenses, providing mentorship, and for the opportunity to work side-by-side with Chinese elites. Additionally, and perhaps even more interestingly, some of these professionalization trainings (especially those for party officials, government elites, and military personnel) provide opportunities to align ways of thinking and reacting to real security, governance, or development issues as they serve as platforms to challenge African attendees to think from the perspective of their hosts' model of governance, security, development, and so on.

Finally, to circle back to the theme of global transformations in the US–China Rivalry, what we learn from China–Africa party-to-party relations is that there is a significant difference between the way Beijing and Washington DC approach their relations with Africans. On whether the US is being socialized by China to transform its foreign policy making in Africa to be based more on social/human capital investments and less on counterterrorism measures, it is still too early to draw conclusions. It is clear, however, that from the Chinese side the emphasis on network-building and knowledge production will remain prioritized in China–Africa relations for years to come.

Notes

[1] See https://global.chinadaily.com.cn/a/202212/23/WS63a55db4a31057c47eba5e81.html
[2] For more on FOCAC, see Taylor (2011).
[3] See Bräutigam (2020) on a deconstruction of the "debt trap" narrative.
[4] The ID-CPC keeps an open record of multiple diplomatic updates and activities organized with foreign counterparts. The department's website news can be reached through this link: https://www.idcpc.org.cn/english/news/index.html
[5] ID-CPC staff organization: https://www.idcpc.org.cn/english/Profile/leader/index.html
[6] Confucius Institutes are Chinese government-sponsored cultural institutes that offer Mandarin language instructions, host cultural events, and organize competitions for scholarships to China, among other activities.
[7] Inter-party relations promote Sino-African strategic partnership.
[8] The ID-CPC does not only invite ruling political parties but diversifies its exchanges with various parties with different ideological leanings. For instance, the CPC holds exchanges with the Rally of Houphouëtists for Democracy and Peace of Côte d'Ivoire (see ID-CPC 2019b) and Senegal's Alliance for the Republic.
[9] For studies on norm diffusion and socialization processes in military exchanges in and beyond the case of China, see Alden and Large (2015), Atkinson (2006) and Carrozza and Marsh (2022).
[10] Young African Leaders Initiative Info sheet: https://www.usaid.gov/sites/default/files/documents/2.21_FINAL_RLC_One-Pager.pdf
[11] https://yali.state.gov

Acknowledgments

An adapted version of this chapter has been published by the Konrad-Adenauer-Stiftung Foundation.

References

Abrahamsen, R. 2018. "The Geopolitics of America's New Africa Strategy." *Center for International Policy Studies CIPS Blog*. https://www.cips-cepi.ca/2018/12/19/the-geopolitics-of-americas-new-africa-strategy/

Alden, C. and Large, D. 2015. "On Becoming a Norm Maker: Chinese Foreign Policy, Norms Evolution and the Challenges of Security in Africa." *The China Quarterly* 221: 123–142.

Atkinson, C. 2006. "Constructivist Implications of Material Power: Military Engagement and the Socialization of States, 1972–2000." *International Studies Quarterly* 50: 509–537.

Benabdallah, L. 2019. "Contesting the International Order by Integrating It: The Case of China's Belt and Road Initiative." *Third World Quarterly* 40(1): 92–108.

Benabdallah, L. 2020. *Shaping the Future of Power: Knowledge Production and Network-Building in China–Africa Relations*. Ann Arbor: University of Michigan Press.

Benabdallah, L. 2021. "Spanning Thousands of Miles and Years: Political Nostalgia and China's Revival of the Silk Road." *International Studies Quarterly* 65(2): 294–305.

Bing, N.C. 2017. "Barisan Nasional and the Chinese Communist Party: A Case Study in China's Party-Based Diplomacy." *The China Review* 17(1): 53–82.

Bräutigam, D. 2020. "A Critical Look at Chinese 'Debt-Trap Diplomacy': The Rise of a Meme." *Area Development and Policy* 5(1): 1–14.

Carrozza, I. and Benabdallah, L. 2022. "South–South Knowledge Production and Hegemony: Searching for Africa in Chinese Theories of IR." *International Studies Review* 24(1): viab063.

Carrozza, I. and Marsh, N. 2022. "Great Power Competition and China's Security Assistance to Africa: Arms, Training, and Influence." *Journal of Global Security Studies*.

CGTN (China's Global Television Network). 2019. "China-Africa Security Cooperation: African Military Officials Visit Special Police College in Beijing." https://news.cgtn.com/news/794d444e784d4464776c6d636a4e6e62684a4856/index.html

Eisenman, J. 2018. "Comrades-in-Arms: The Chinese Communist Party's Relations with African Political Organizations in the Mao Era, 1949–76." *Cold War History*. https://doi.org/10.1080/14682745.2018.1440549

Feldstein, S. 2020. "Testimony before the U.S.–China Economic and Security Review Commission Hearing on China's Strategic Aims in Africa." *Testimony*. https://www.uscc.gov/sites/default/files/Feldstein_Testimony.pdf

Hackenesch, C. and Bader, J. 2020. "The Struggle for Minds and Influence: The Chinese Communist Party's Global Outreach." *International Studies Quarterly* 64(3): 723–733.

Hansen, S.J. 2022. "What US Re-entry into Somalia Means for the Horn of Africa and for Bigger Powers." *The Conversation*. https://theconversation.com/what-us-re-entry-into-somalia-means-for-the-horn-of-africa-and-for-bigger-powers-183962

Hawkins, A. 2018. "Beijing's Big Brother Tech Needs African Faces." *Foreign Policy*. https://foreignpolicy.com/2018/07/24/beijings-big-brother-tech-needs-african-faces/

International Department of the Communist Party of China website. https://www.idcpc.org.cn/english/Profile/leader/index.html

Kuo, L. 2017. "Beijing is Cultivating the Next Generation of African Elites by Training them in China." *Quartz Africa*. https://qz.com/africa/1119447/china-is-training-africas-next-generation-of-leaders/

Lawler, D. 2020. "The 53 Countries Supporting China's Crackdown on Hong Kong." *Axios*. https://www.axios.com/countries-supporting-china-hong-kong-law-0ec9bc6c-3aeb-4af0-8031-aa0f01a46a7c.html

Levinson, R. 2021. "Biden's 'Democracy Summit' Meets the African Paradox." *The Hill*. https://thehill.com/opinion/international/584702-bidens-democracy-summit-meets-the-african-paradox/

Miles, W. 2012. "Deploying Development to Counter Terrorism: Post-9/11 Transformation of U.S. Foreign Aid to Africa." *African Studies Review* 55(3): 27–60.

Moore, A. and Walker, J. 2016. "Tracing the US Military's Presence in Africa." *Geopolitics* 21(3): 686–716.

Nakkazi, E. 2018. "China Ramps Up Support for African Higher Education." *University World News*, September 7.

National Resistance Movement. 2021a. "Get to Know Your NRM Secretary General." https://www.nrm.ug/news/get-know-your-nrm-secretary-general?fbclid=IwAR3zUGvhQj-BLKp3Gp_MrtL7tRm1WaPyLzI7UOTBhPbfh6OaKbayVClIctQ

National Resistance Movement. 2021b. "NRM SG Richard Todwong Congratulates CPC upon Making 100 Years." https://www.youtube.com/watch?v=F6RE6nWLuVE

Newlin, C. and Kostelancik, T. 2020. "Countering Russian and Chinese Influence Activities." *Center for Strategic and International Studies*. https://www.csis.org/features/countering-russian-chinese-influence-activities

Owusu, F. and Carmody, P. 2020. "Trump's Legacy in Africa and What to Expect from Biden." *The Conversation*. https://theconversation.com/trumps-legacy-in-africa-and-what-to-expect-from-biden-150293

Prasso, S. 2019. "China's Digital Silk Road is Looking More Like an Iron Curtain." *Bloomberg*. https://www.bloomberg.com/news/features/2019-01-10/china-s-digital-silk-road-is-looking-more-like-an-iron-curtain

Ranade, J. 2021. "Xi Jinping Further Strengthens Chinese Community Party's 'Magic Weapon': The United Front Work Department." Center for China Analysis and Strategy. https://ccasindia.org/CCAS-CCP-UFWD.pdf

Regilme, S.S.F. 2022. "United States Foreign Aid and Multilateralism Under the Trump Presidency." *New Global Studies*: 1–25.

Scarfe, J. 2022. "East Africa: Was China's Foreign Minister's Visit a Success or Failure?" *The Africa Report*. https://www.theafricareport.com/167943/east-africa-was-chinas-foreign-ministers-visit-a-success-or-failure/

Song Tao. 2019. "Buduan tuijin dang de duiwai gongzuo lilun he shijian chuangxin" (Continuously Advance Innovations in the Ideas and Practice of the Party's External Work), *Renmin Ribao* (People's Daily), September 28: 15.

Soulé, F. 2020. "'Africa+1' Summit Diplomacy and the 'New Scramble' Narrative: Recentering African Agency." *African Affairs* 119(477): 633–646.

Taylor, I. 2011. *The Forum on China-Africa Cooperation (FOCAC)*. London: Routledge.

Xi Jinping Keynote Address at the CPC and World Political Parties Summit. 2021. "Strengthening Cooperation Among Political Parties to Jointly Pursue the People's Wellbeing." http://en.qstheory.cn/2021-07/08/c_640967.htm#

Xinhua. 2021a. "Interview: Chinese Model of Engagement with African Countries Genuine – Ugandan Party Official." http://www.xinhuanet.com/english/northamerica/2021-04/11/c_139872705.htm

Xinhua. 2021b. "Xi Focus: Xi Urges World Political Parties to Shoulder Responsibility for Pursuit of People's Wellbeing, Progress of Mankind." http://www.xinhuanet.com/english/2021-07/07/c_1310046460.htm

Yao, W. 2021. "Branding and Legitimation: China's Party Diplomacy amid the COVID-19 Pandemic." *The China Review* 21(1): 55–89.

Zeng, A. 2015. "China-Africa Governance Exchanges and Experiences." *Chinese Institute of International Studies*. http://www.ciis.org.cn/english/2015-12/03/content_8424552.htm

Zhong, W. 2013. "Inter-Party Relations Promote Sino-African Strategic Partnership." *Ministry of Foreign Affairs*. https://www.mfa.gov.cn/zflt/eng/zfgx/rwjl/t1102167.htm

7

Latin America and the Caribbean: How the Belt and Road Initiative Diminished US Influence

Juan E. Serrano-Moreno

Introduction

This chapter analyzes how the Belt and Road Initiative (BRI) allowed China to fill the void left by the US in Latin America and the Caribbean (LAC), its traditional sphere of influence, by increasing the region's dependence on the Chinese economy and expanding its diplomatic exchanges. The participation of LAC governments in the BRI has brought about fewer economic benefits to the region than promised and has exposed them to pressure from the US on some vital security and technology issues. However, China has had noticeable gains from the BRI, as this chapter will explain. To understand the geographies of the rivalry in the Americas, one must study the implications of the Chinese initiative in which the promises of infrastructures allowed LAC governments to surmount geographical, cultural, and political distances.

The BRI is an international cooperation platform announced by the Chinese government in 2013 initially oriented to promote connectivity to its neighboring countries by celebrating official forums and the conclusion of non-binding bilateral agreements. The initiative seeks to boost Chinese foreign investment, infrastructures, and trade between China and its partners, especially developing countries that are eager for infrastructures. In 2022, according to the official statements, 144 countries joined the BRI (Xinhuanet 2021), despite no clarity concerning its accession and participation mechanisms. The BRI has progressively expanded its geographical scope, activities, and projects, becoming a fuzzy initiative that is challenging to conceptualize. Since its launch, it has evolved from "an effort to revitalise the connectivity of the Silk Road into a key point for Chinese foreign policy" (Myers 2018: 239) and then to "so omnipresent in Chinese foreign discourse and practice that it is now almost impossible to distinguish it from Beijing's foreign policy" (Rolland 2019: 1).

Although the BRI at its origins did not contemplate the inclusion of LAC, after the celebration in 2018 of the China and Community of LAC States Forum (China-CELAC Forum), LAC countries started to participate (González Jauregui 2020; Oliveira and Myers 2021). The first few participating countries were less exposed to US influence—Cuba, Bolivia, Venezuela, and Ecuador—and China's strategic economic partners in the region—Chile, Uruguay, and Peru (Bórquez and Bravo 2020). In 2023, 24 out of 33 members of the CELAC have joined the BRI. Except for Mexico, the biggest economies of LAC, namely Brazil, Argentina, and Colombia, have participated in the initiative to different degrees. The remaining countries that do not are Paraguay and nine small developing economies in Central America.

After the initially ambivalent attitude of the Trump administration toward the BRI, the US considered that the BRI did not meet international financial standards and transparency and recommended its allies not to join it (Thuy 2020: 216). However, most LAC governments considered that the BRI could bring diplomatic and economic benefits, which shows the increasing influence of Beijing to the detriment of Washington's. The existence of an alternative power in the region, therefore, has an effect of, on the one hand, increasing the political autonomy of LAC governments on the international scene and, on the other hand, reducing their exposure to US influence (Ellis 2017: 38; Jenkins 2017: 194). Based on these observations, this chapter attempts to analyze how China convinced most LAC countries to join the BRI and what LAC countries' motivations and strategies are in an international context characterized by the US–China rivalry.

Despite some academic and media hype that surrounded the participation of LAC countries in the BRI (Oropeza 2018; Zottele and Zottele 2020), recent studies have made clear that there has not been any substantial change in the evolution of trade and investments between China and LAC since 2018 (Ferchen 2021; Jenkins 2021). Therefore, this study does not fully analyze the BRI as a global policy with measurable economic effects. Instead, this study finds that the initiative represents a practical and flexible diplomatic tool that primarily updates and provides coherence to the previous discursive framework of China's regional policies. In other words, the BRI has helped Beijing to rebrand and push forward its agenda for LAC, mainly to guarantee access to crucial commodities imports for the Chinese economy—oil, iron, copper, and soybeans—and to increase the international isolation of Taiwan since LAC is a strategic region for the One-China policy (Long and Urdinez

2021). As Salvador Regilme (2018a, 2018b, 2021) studied the US foreign aid as a way of shaping converging interests between states, the BRI should also be analyzed not only in its material dimension but also in its discursive dimension (Serrano-Moreno et al 2021a, Serrano-Moreno 2021). The connectivity rhetoric of the BRI provides a ground that is ambiguous enough to allow LAC governments to join it, accommodating their needs which in return helps them to counter US pressure. The analysis of the diplomatic weighting of different LAC countries will be discussed later in this chapter.

This study follows the works that question whether the BRI, Brazil, Russia, India, China, and South Africa (BRICS), the Asian Infrastructure Investment Bank (AIIB), and the rest of the Chinese development banks constitute a new international architecture that challenges the international liberal order (Kahler 2013; Knoerich and Urdinez 2019; Lake et al 2021; Telias 2021; Weiss and Wallace 2021). Even if some analysis of the BRI suggests a non-legalistic conception of intergovernmental cooperation, its vagueness and lack of measurable effects question its capacity to build an alternative model of globalization. Instead, this study supports the idea that we are moving toward a multipolar world where the US's ability to shape global politics is diminishing (Regilme and Parisot 2017: 9–10). In other words, the BRI is one of the "trojan horses" used by Beijing to fill the void left by the US after the country ended the Monroe Doctrine and concentrated its efforts in the Asia-Pacific region since the 2010s (Urdinez et al 2016; Ellis 2017). In this regard, the examples of the Chinese loans to Ecuador, Venezuela, and Argentina illustrate how China assisted these countries when they lost their access to international funding. Furthermore, China did not impose conditions related to domestic policies and deregulations as the international financial organizations did in the past, which contributed to the deterioration of the image of the US in the region, which was already considerably damaged by Washington's support for authoritarian regimes in the 1970s and 1980s.

This study analyzes the participation of LAC in the BRI by reviewing the most recent literature in international relations and political economy and using discourse analysis on official diplomatic documents and news. The chapter begins by presenting the significant milestones of the origin and institutionalization of the BRI, followed by a literature review, and then addresses the previous dynamics of the China–Latin America relations. Finally, the chapter analyzes the different degrees and motivations of the participation of the region's countries in the BRI.

Background: the institutionalization of the connectivity rhetoric

The origin of the BRI goes back to the speeches of Xi Jinping in Astana on September 7, 2013 and October 3, 2013 in Indonesia during the Asia-Pacific

Economic Cooperation summit. The initiative was announced a year after the transition of the Chinese Communist Party to new leadership under Xi. The BRI, therefore, represents the emblematic foreign policy of the new president and a central axis of the "Chinese dream of national rejuvenation" (Callahan 2015; Ferdinand 2016). The initiative was officially sanctioned by the State Council of the People's Republic of China with the publication of the document "Vision and Actions on Jointly Building the Silk Road Economic Belt and the 21st Century Maritime Silk Road" (NDRC 2015) on March 28, 2015. The document includes some of the essential principles of Chinese foreign policy, such as mutually beneficial cooperation, the integration of China "in the global economic system," and the promotion of a "multipolar world, economic globalisation, cultural diversity and a greater application of information technologies" within the "global free trade regime and open global economics in the spirit of open regional competition." In addition, five key areas of cooperation are set out: policy dialogue aimed at creating an intergovernmental mechanism for dialogue; connectivity designed to develop an infrastructure network to link the sub-regions of Asia, Europe, and Africa (note that Latin America was not mentioned); unhindered trade to eliminate trade and investment barriers and create free-trade areas between countries; support through financial cooperation and the promotion of stability of the monetary, investment, and credit systems in Asia; and, finally, the exchange between people as a means of friendly cooperation (Huang 2016).

The institutionalization of the BRI continued with its inclusion in the 13th Five-Year Plan 2016–2020 as the chapter "Push Forward Construction of the Belt and Road Initiative." Also, the initiative was included in the Chinese Communist Party Constitution during its 19th National Congress in October 2017. Another significant milestone was the Belt and Road Forum for International Cooperation held in Beijing on May 14 and 15, 2017. Authorities from 57 countries attended the forum, including Argentinean president Mauricio Macri and Chilean president Michelle Bachelet at the time. The presence of state and government heads at the forum shows that the foreign governments considered the BRI an instrument to expand Chinese influence and an opportunity to participate.

Later, between April 25 and 27, 2019, amid the US–China "trade war," the Second Belt and Road Forum for International Cooperation took place in Beijing with 37 governments and heads of state attending, including Chilean president Sebastián Piñera, who at the time was the only head of state from the Americas. In the forum's official document, the Chinese government stated that "it supports the construction of infrastructure in developing countries in Asia, Africa and Latin America" (Office of the Leading Group for Promoting the Belt and Road Initiative 2019: 6–7). Since then, signatories to the Memoranda of Understanding on the BRI have multiplied.

However, since the second forum, the initiative started to decelerate, at least publicly, due to two factors. First, the Chinese government wanted to reduce the tension with the US by "lowering the profile" of the assertive Chinese global policies. The unlimited geographical extension of the BRI can be understood as a symptom of China's "strategic overstretch" (Pu and Wang 2018). Second, the emergency of the COVID-19 pandemic has pushed the Chinese government to concentrate its efforts on "mask diplomacy" and later cooperation in vaccine distribution and production (Telias and Urdinez 2021).

The Western Hemisphere was noticeably absent in the initial BRI documents. Likewise, the second Policy Paper for LAC, published by the Chinese government in 2016, did not mention the BRI (The State Council of PRC 2016). However, the joint communique of the Belt and Road Forum in 2017 specified that the initiative was open to other regions, including South America (Belt and Road Portal 2017). In the Second Belt and Road Forum in April 2019 in Beijing, the official document referred explicitly to the region, stating that the Chinese government "supports the construction of infrastructure in developing countries in Asia, Africa and Latin America." Before that, the invitation for LAC countries to participate in the BRI was formalized by the Chinese Minister of Foreign Affairs, Wang Yi, at the China-CELAC Forum in Santiago on January 22, 2018. A forum which excludes the US and Canada and is considered by China the central multilateral forum for building the relationship with the region raised concerns among the US administration and lawmakers (Ellis 2017: 50–51; González Jauregui 2020). According to Margaret Myers (2018; Oliveira and Myers 2021), the region's inclusion resulted more from lobbying by the LAC governments than the Chinese government's original plan.

The ministers of foreign affairs partaking in the China-CELAC Forum published a special declaration that directly addressed the participation of CELAC members in the BRI. This declaration included the invitation from the Chinese Minister of Foreign Affairs to the members of CELAC to join the initiative and his perception of these countries as "the natural extension of the Maritime Silk Road and ... indispensable participants in the international cooperation of the Belt and Road" (CELAC 2018: 1). As anticipated, the statement also included the general principle that guides the BRI, that is, the "spirit of cooperation, openness, inclusion, mutual learning and shared benefits, (that) seeks to promote coordination, the interconnectivity of infrastructures, the facilitation of trade, cooperation in financial matters and understanding" (CELAC 2018: 1).

Panama was the first LAC country to sign a memorandum of understanding of the BRI in 2017, and Argentina was the last in 2022. Until 2022, 20 LAC countries in total have signed the memoranda. However, the memoranda do not have measurable effects per se. All the memoranda examined have a standard format, include a clause that specifies their non-binding nature, and do not stipulate any institutional mechanisms to meet the stated objectives. The first section of the document establishes the general common goals, such as deepening political and economic ties and respect for national legislation and pre-existing international commitments. The second section identifies five areas of cooperation that reproduce what was indicated previously in other official Chinese government documents, that is, coordination of public policies, facilitation of connectivity, unhindered trade, financial integration, and the exchange between people.

When examining the BRI official documents, the terms "connectivity" and "interconnectivity" are omnipresent and broadly associated with undetermined projects such as airports, ports, railways, telecommunications, and dams, among others. Thus, the connectivity rhetoric outstands as the main discourse frame of the BRI. Indeed, the promotion of connectivity through the construction of infrastructures for the circulation of goods, services, communications, and, to a decreasing extent, people have been a constant in Western countries' speeches and public policies for decades (Castells 2010). The Chinese government has not done anything other than borrowing this framework to reinforce the legitimacy of its foreign policy abroad. As expected, this framework has been particularly effective in regions with infrastructure deficits, such as LAC.

Literature review: smoke and mirrors

Since its inception, promoters of the BRI have stated that the initiative frames hundreds of projects and involves a large-scale investment program, which initially attracted the attention of government officials, academia, and the business community (Yu 2017). In addition, it has been indicated that behind the BRI are concrete objectives such as promoting the renminbi's internationalization, strengthening diplomatic relations, increasing the popularity of China in developing countries, and counteracting the US strategy of containing Beijing (Cheng 2016). Other objectives are related to geopolitical issues, particularly the possibility of reinforcing the China–Russia strategic partnership and counteracting the influence of India by bolstering the alliance between China and Pakistan. For this reason, the most remarkable effects of the initiative have been noted in Eurasia, thanks to the set of infrastructures called the "Eurasian Land Bridge," which links China and Central Europe, as well as the "China-Mongolia-Russia Economic Corridor" (Garlick 2020; Shakhanova and Garlick 2020).

These targets and outcomes have been interpreted widely as a component of China's global strategy to elevate its status of power in the international order, from being a "rule taker to a rule maker" (Zhou and Esteban 2018; Rolland 2019). Therefore, the BRI could be interpreted as one of

China's global policies to shape a model of globalization with "Chinese characteristics" that could challenge US hegemony in providing global public goods. From a legal point of view, Heng Wang (2019) states that the BRI is neither focused on institutions nor is it based on treaties; therefore, it is a substantial change in the Chinese strategy for its adherence to the World Trade Organization. The initiative involves an instrumental view of international law, the top priority of which is to act with the maximum possible flexibility. The Chinese government adopts a proactive and adaptive strategy that seeks to escape the typical regulation of trade treaties and the global financial governance associated with the more developed Western countries. The BRI would represent a Chinese counter-model of multilateralism currently being defined, the specific translation of which is the predominance of bilateral intergovernmental cooperation and soft law.

Other studies have focused on the tangible impact of the BRI, considering economic indicators on trade and direct investment from China to the countries taking part in the initiative. A study by the World Bank shows that BRI strategic economic corridors helped to reduce delivery times and commercial costs in Asia, Europe, and East Africa (De Soyres et al 2018). Nevertheless, there is no conclusive evidence of a positive correlation between a country's participation in the BRI and a significant increase in trade with China and the output of direct foreign investment from China (Baniya et al 2019; Joy-Perez 2019).

The BRI has also been explained as a direct consequence of the overcapacity of the Chinese domestic economy. Therefore, the BRI contributes to the effort to provide new markets for Chinese producers of steel, cement, aluminum, and construction companies (Narins 2016: 284; Jenkins 2018: 606). Ho-fung Hung (2018) linked the BRI to the stimulus package adopted by the Chinese government to tackle the 2009 global financial crisis. Once the effects of this counter-cyclical policy disappeared, Chinese companies needed to transfer their capital outside "in search of profitable investments, just as the overaccumulation of capital has led many capitalist powers to export capital throughout the history of capitalism" (Hung 2018: 2). Thus, the BRI is not more than the continuity of the Chinese government's "Go Out Policy" under another name, adopted at the end of the 20th century, and the consequent support offered to its "national champions" in their conversion to multinational leaders in their respective sectors (Gallagher and Irwin 2014; Gallagher 2016: 51). Following this logic, the BRI can be interpreted as a relabeling of previous capital export strategies (Hung 2015).

Some studies have adopted a constructivist perspective that is worth noting given the flagrant disparity between the lack of specificity of the BRI and its impact on public debates and diplomatic strategies of the formal participating countries and the non-participating ones. Tim Summers questioned the declared novelty of the BRI and pointed to the continuity between the stated objectives and Chinese sub-national public policies previously targeting the bordering countries, which in some cases, like that of the province of Xinjiang, goes back to the 1980s (Summers 2016, 2018). Adopting the logic of global network capitalism, the BRI represents an elevation to a national level of pre-existing connectivity policies that are reinforced by being identified as a high priority by the Chinese government in the eyes of civil servants, officials, and diplomats after the adoption of the "Vision and Actions on Jointly Building the Silk Road Economic Belt and the 21st Century Maritime Silk Road" in 2015.

Similarly, Astrid Nordin and Mikael Weissmann's (2018) study on the narratives of the Chinese elites about the BRI calls for greater attention to its discursive logic. The authors state that there is no consensus among the Chinese elites on what the BRI represents. However, they agree that it is a critical project in the "Chinese dream of national rejuvenation" under the leadership of Xi Jinping and characterize it as "a non-legalistic" project oriented toward the free market and foreign investment and led by national governments (Nordin and Weissmann 2018: 240). The BRI conveys a Sinocentric worldview, where China will play a "stabilizing" role as a defender, promoter, and leader of the capitalist world-system in an ongoing transition toward a more beneficial model for the developing countries allied with China and where the influence of the US is progressively reduced.

Consequently, it is difficult to determine what projects and actions are covered by the BRI and how many countries it includes. Recent developments have emerged, such as the Arctic Silk Road, the Digital Silk Road, and even the Space Silk Road, which make it even more challenging to understand what specific projects are aligned with this cooperation platform. During the first months of 2020, the new "Health Silk Road" was also discussed, even before the COVID-19 pandemic. Further still, China's decision to keep the door open to all the governments who wish to join the BRI, regardless of their geographic location or economic potential, shows the lack of intention to specify fixed terms and criteria to define the initiative's scope.

China–Latin America and Caribbean previous dynamics

In the last two decades, the economic relations and cooperation between China and LAC have intensified considerably, comparable to the relations between China and Africa (Jenkins 2017, 2018). The bilateral trade between LAC and China contributed to consolidating the export-oriented Chinese economic model, helping China to address its structural deficit of natural resources (Gallagher 2016; Myers and Wise 2017; Wise 2020). China's import of raw materials exploded after it entered the World Trade Organization in 2001, allowing LAC countries to win the so-called "commodities lottery," with the price of petroleum, copper, iron, and soybean doubling, or even tripling, from 2003 to 2013 (Gruss 2014; Barton and Rehner 2018). The bilateral trade connected the LAC economies to the Chinese economy (Wise and Chonn Ching 2018), which helped the region to recover quickly from the global financial crisis in 2009 (Gallagher 2016: 41–61) and increased the popularity and prospects for the re-election of supposedly leftist anti-US candidates during the Pink Tide (Campello and Zucco 2016).

The literature has reported on the problems that this increasing economic dependency has caused in LAC countries, especially in terms of a recommodification of exports (Jenkins 2017: 3–4; López and Muñoz 2020) and the resulting deindustrialization described in the already classic work by Gallagher and Porzecanski (2010), *The Dragon in the Room*. Effects came to the fore regarding unemployment in the Central American countries and political polarization in Brazil and Argentina (Jenkins 2015; Urdinez et al, 2018). In other words, China's economic involvement has reproduced the center–periphery relations that traditionally characterized trade with Western economies.

To understand the expectations created by LAC's participation in the BRI, we must recall the well-known infrastructure deficit affecting the region's economies. As the United Nations Economic Commission for Latin America and the Caribbean (UNECLAC) has indicated numerous times, the gap between infrastructure supply and demand discourages economic and social development, and, to overcome it, investments needed to double over the 2012–2020 period (UNECLAC 2014, 2019). At the "Silk and Road Forum" in Paris on December 7 and 8, 2018, Alicia Bárcena, the Executive Secretary of ECLAC at the time, stated that LAC "looks at the BRI with great interest because it offers an opportunity to diversify and improve the quality of their economic relations with China, and specifically it can help attract much-needed investment in infrastructures, industry and services" (CEPAL 2018: ∮3).

Although there is little doubt about the sustained growth of trade between China and LAC in the last two decades, Chinese direct investments in the region and the infrastructure projects awarded by LAC governments to Chinese companies are mainly unknown to the public. The difficulty in calculating the evolution of direct investment from China to LAC is well known among the authors interested in the matter (Jenkins 2017: 184; Jenkins 2018: 154). Moreover, it is known that Chinese capital usually passes through tax havens like Hong Kong, the Virgin Islands, and the Cayman Islands before reaching its destination, so the trail is lost (Hung 2018). However, the data published by the Boston-based think tank the American Enterprise Institute and the Mexico-based Latin America and the Caribbean Network on China indicated that Chinese direct investment in LAC increased steeply after the 2009 global financial crisis and recovered slow but steady growth from 2015. However, this tendency has not changed substantially since the BRI arrived in the region in 2018 (Dussel Peters 2020; Scissors 2020; Jenkins 2021).

In addition, the total investment numbers include the mergers and acquisitions of local businesses by Chinese companies, which are market-driven and do not affect infrastructure development per se. The same is true of the projects that cannot be identified because they are service contracts, concessions, tenders, and other forms of public procurement with different regulations, nomenclature, and advertising in each country. These public contracts also do not necessarily guarantee more and better public infrastructures; their impact depends on the local authorities' regulations and control mechanisms. In most cases, Chinese companies have just begun competing with Western companies, which are more experienced in tender-bidding in the region. In addition, there was no shortage of projects under the BRI label when they were announced and later abandoned according to the evolution of each country's politics. A striking example of this was the erratic railway projects in which Chinese companies participated in Venezuela, Brazil, Peru, Mexico, and Argentina (Leiva 2020).

There is neither evidence of a correlation between the BRI and a change in previous dynamics nor a reduction of the infrastructure deficit. Therefore, a systematic study of the tangible economic impact brought by BRI to LAC could be a difficult task. Consequently, it is more analytically useful to distinguish the levels of participation of the region's governments in the BRI and their motivations.

Motivations and degrees of participation in the Belt and Road Initiative

Two objective indicators of a LAC country's participation in the BRI are the signing of a bilateral memorandum of understanding and the participation of high-level government representatives in the BRI forums. This study found several factors that explain the decision to participate or not in the BRI and the intensity of the participation. The most significant positive factor in joining the initiative is the presence of a previous formal partnership with China: Free Trade Agreement, strategic economic partner official status, and AIIB membership. The main negative factors are the exposure to US influence and domestic political anti-China attitudes. Based on that, LAC countries can be classified into four groups depending on their attitude toward the BRI: enthusiastic, pragmatic, reluctant, and absent (see Table 7.1).

The first group is the most numerous, comprising the countries that joined the BRI without hesitation in the second half of 2018. They can be subdivided into two batches. One batch is the countries traditionally

Table 7.1: Countries' different degrees of participation in the Belt and Road Initiative

Country	Explanatory factors	High-level participation in official forums	Memorandum of understanding: signing date
Countries with an enthusiastic attitude toward the BRI			
Cuba	Anti-US government, ALBA member, and AIIB member	Vice-President, Council of State (2019)	November 11, 2018
Bolivia	Anti-US government, ALBA member, and AIIB member.	Minister of Foreign Affairs (2019)	September 3, 2018
Ecuador	Anti-US government, ex-ALBA member, and AIIB member	n/a	December 12, 2018
Venezuela	Anti-US government and ALBA member	Minister of Economy (2019)	September 14, 2018
Costa Rica	Free Trade Agreement with China since 2011	Minister of Finance and Minister of Agriculture (2019)	September 3, 2018
Chile	Special economic partner status since 2012, Free Trade Agreement with China since 2005, and AIIB member	President (2017 and 2019) and Representative of the executive (2021)	November 6, 2018
Peru	Special economic partner status since 2008, Free Trade Agreement with China since 2009, and AIIB member	Minister of Foreign Trade (2019)	April 28, 2019
Uruguay	Special economic partner status since 2016 and AIIB member	Minister of Foreign Affairs (2019)	August 20, 2018
Countries with a pragmatic attitude toward the BRI			
Brazil	Domestic politics	Secretary of Strategic Affairs (2017)	n/a
Argentina		President (2017) and Minister of Foreign Affairs (2019)	February 4, 2022
Countries with a reluctant attitude toward the BRI			
Colombia	US pressure	Representative of the executive (2021)	n/a
Mexico		President of Morena political party (2019)	n/a

Source: Prepared by the author from the Belt and Road Portal (https://eng.yidaiyilu.gov.cn/), completed with information available from government and national media websites.

opposed to US influence: Cuba, Bolivia, Ecuador, and Venezuela. They are members of the Bolivarian Alliance for the Peoples of Our America (ALBA), except Ecuador, which withdrew in 2018. The other batch is the countries with previous special economic ties with China—Free Trade Agreement, special economic partner status, and/or AIIB membership—that joined the BRI without internal or external resistance: Chile, Costa Rica, Peru, and Uruguay.

The second group is composed of Mexico and Colombia, who adopted a reluctant attitude toward the BRI mainly because of their exposure to pressure from the US State Department. The third group is Argentina and Brazil, which adopted a pragmatic strategy due to the internal political resistance provoked by the advocacy for protectionist policies. The last group comprises countries with small developing economies, that do not participate to any extent in the BRI simply because they maintain diplomatic relations with Taiwan. This group is composed of Paraguay and nine Central American countries: Belize, Bahamas, Guatemala, Haiti, Honduras, Nicaragua, Saint Lucia, Saint Kitts and Nevis, and Saint Vincent and the Grenadines.

It is worth noting that nine CELAC member states currently maintain diplomatic relations with the Republic of China, making LAC a strategic region for the One-China policy (Long and Urdinez 2020). The BRI has substantially contributed to this policy since three Central American countries severed their diplomatic ties with Taiwan and recognized the People's Republic of China before signing the BRI memoranda. Panama did so in June 2017, the Dominican Republic in May 2018, and El Salvador in August 2018 (*South China Morning Post* 2017; *New York Times* 2018a, 2018b). Their expectations of increasing trade and investments thanks to the BRI could explain this diplomatic shift. In other words, the connectivity rhetoric helped push the Chinese agenda.

Within the countries with an enthusiastic attitude toward the BRI, Chile represents a distinctive case. The Andean country, a traditionally open economy, joined the BRI willingly, but at the same time, it has managed to cope with the pressure from the US (Serrano-Moreno et al 2020b). Chile actively lobbied to obtain the invitation to join the BRI in the China-CELCAC forum in Santiago in 2018, and its two former presidents, Bachelet and Piñera, participated in the BRI forums. Since then, Chinese investment has risen with significant operations as the acquisitions of the shares of the CGE, the leading electric distributor, by State Grid from the European company Naturgy; and the obtention of public contracts to build new infrastructures like the extension of Santiago's metro or the extension of the country's principal trade port in San Antonio. However, this trend did not stop the Chilean government in July 2020 from choosing the Australia–Japan route instead of the Chinese one for the transpacific Humboldt internet cable project, a critical infrastructure project for the whole region (Nikkei Asia 2020). The decision was taken a few months after the visit of US Secretary of State Mike Pompeo, who explicitly warned Chile against Huawei for security reasons. Later in 2021, another case put Chile in the crossfire between China and the US: the public tendering for the fabrication of passports and identity cards. The Chinese company Aisino won the tender, but surprisingly the Chilean administration changed its decision after the US warned that this contract might represent a security breach and affect the special migration status of Chilean nationals granted by the US through the Visa Waiver Programme. These examples show how Chile has adopted a pragmatic strategy toward the US–China rivalry by deepening the cooperation with China to facilitate the growing trade, direct investments, and public contracts with Chinese companies while keeping the US content in crucial technological and security decisions.

Besides that, the political proximity of Mexico and Colombia to the US explains why the former did not join the BRI, and the latter did so discreetly in June 2021. Mexico, China's second-largest trading partner in LAC after Brazil, did not join the BRI mainly because doing so would have altered its already complicated diplomatic relations with the US. In addition, the failure of several Chinese projects in the country—the construction of the Chicoasén II dam—exacerbated the friction between Mexico and China. Mexico's possible membership in the BRI and incorporation into the AIIB are vital topics on their bilateral agenda. Although Mexico did not sign the memorandum to join the BRI, under the presidency of leftist Andrés Manuel López Obrador—in office from 2018 to 2024—it is highly likely that the government will strengthen ties with China. Proof of this is the attendance of Yeidckol Polevnsky, president of Morena, López Obrador's political party, at the second BRI forum in 2019 and his public statements on the foreign policy objective to join the BRI as a means to reduce dependency on the US (Xinhuanet 2019).

Colombia's delay in joining the BRI may be due to President Iván Duque Márquez—whose presidential term ran from August 2018 to August 2022—who excluded China from his foreign policy priorities (Bermúdez Liévano 2019). This decision can be explained by Colombia's intense security cooperation with the US, as Colombia is the country that has received the most military aid from the US on the entire continent. During Iván Duque's visit to China in 2019, the government stated the intention to receive Chinese investment in the infrastructure sector; however, this came with no inclination to join the BRI (*Diálogo Chino* 2019). Later, at the height of the pandemic, the Colombian government decided to review its strategy, given the need to strengthen cooperation with China on the public health emergency. On June 23, 2021, the Asia and Pacific High-level Conference on Belt and Road Cooperation was held, with the participation of 28 countries, including governmental representatives from Colombia and

Chile. As expected, the conference's primary subject was cooperation for COVID-19 vaccines (*The Diplomat* 2021). Since then, the election of the leftist president Gustavo Petro on 29 May 2022 has been well received by Beijing and may represent "a new starting point" in the relations between both countries (*China Daily* 2022; EFE 2022).

Finally, Brazil and Argentina adopted a pragmatic strategy to participate in the BRI. Argentina was the last to sign the memorandum of understanding, on February 4, 2022. However, it has always had a strong presence in BRI forums—in the first, Argentinian president Mauricio Macri attended while his chancellor Jorge Faurie attended the forum in 2019—and it is also a prospective member of the AIIB. This reluctance reflects the political tensions surrounding the Chinese trade and investments caused by the recommodification and deindustrialization effects noted earlier (Urdinez et al 2018).

Brazil has not signed the memorandum but has participated partially in the BRI through its Secretary of Strategic Affairs' presence at the 2017 forum. Although presidents Temer and Rousseff at the time were interested in deepening their relations with China, corruption scandals weakened their domestic and foreign policies. Even if the Brazilian President Bolsonaro adopted anti-communist and nationalistic rhetoric during the election campaign in 2018 (*China Daily* 2018), the Brazilian government has no coherent strategy toward China (Gabriel et al 2018). However, the significance of the country's reluctance to participate in the BRI is relative. Brazil is the first Chinese trade partner in the region, and it has other, probably better, channels to manage its economic and diplomatic relations with Beijing. Since 1993, China has considered Brazil a strategic economic partner (Bórquez and Bravo 2020), an active member of the BRICS summits and the only potential founding member of the AIIB in LAC.

The different motivations of each country to participate in the BRI points to the absence of a single explanatory variable. Therefore, pragmatism and opportunism are the only factors in a government's decision to join the BRI since the initiative has no binding effects, accession process, or regulated exit. In some instances, greater cooperation with China has been achieved without formal participation in the BRI, as the case of Brazil shows. This flexibility would avoid political tensions domestically as industrial unions are among the main anti-Chinese interest groups in Argentina and Brazil and internationally, mainly from the US Department of State in Colombia and Mexico.

The BRI memoranda and forums represent more of a diplomatic staging than an effective accession to a new international cooperation platform. Arguably, signing the memoranda could represent a sort of "trophy" for Chinese diplomacy and a concession on the part of LAC governments that can continue cooperating with China by other formal or informal routes. It is observed that, on the one hand, there is a tendency for China to increase the number of participating countries in its official statements and, on the other hand, the lack of publicity by some LAC governments concerning the memoranda signing. In short, the BRI offered enough flexibility to the LAC countries to choose their preferred degree of participation without jeopardizing their relations with the US or increasing domestic political tensions.

Conclusion

The BRI arrived at LAC after China became the region's most significant economic partner at the end of the 2010s. Thus, the initiative represents a diplomatic reflection of the new "new normal" characterized by the growing dependence of LAC economies on China (Jenkins 2018: 655–656). Accordingly, the BRI confirms that China has filled the void left by the US in its traditional sphere of influence and it has deepened its influence among developing countries in the Global South. Although Washington has lobbied against China's growing diplomatic influence in the region, these efforts have obtained little results. This study also concludes that for the mere discursive prospect that China pushes forward via BRI, the relations between LAC and China would not see a radical change in the short term. Indeed, there is no evidence of a correlation between BRI's participation and a substantial increase in Chinese direct investments or an improvement of the infrastructures in the region. This study aligns with previous works suggesting that the growing dependence of LAC economies on China consolidates the region's position in the capitalist world-economy's semi-periphery (Wallerstein 2004; Grell-Brisk 2017; Bernal-Meza and Li 2020; Li 2021; Li and Bernal-Meza 2022).

Consequently, the BRI should not be understood as a new policy, not even as a platform of cooperation, but rather as a transformation in the image of China's strategy in the region. The initiative rather represents a broad discursive framework with the potential to create a coherent narrative based on the connectivity rhetoric for a wide range of projects and policies. The BRI is too ambiguous and volatile to contribute to creating an alternative globalization model theoretically more beneficial for developing countries. On the contrary, the BRI contributes to deepening the current model by accommodating the needs of China as the next first superpower and diminishing US influence.

The participation in the BRI of many countries in the region and its biggest economies, except Mexico, represents a success for Chinese diplomacy because it allowed the development of its ties with the region's governments without a considerable cost. Examining the literature, news, and official BRI documents points to two factors in the BRI's success in

LAC. First, the discursive efficiency of the connectivity rhetoric, and second, the flexibility offered by the ambiguity of the initiative to each government to choose their degree of involvement. This flexibility allowed Colombia to overcome its initial hesitations provoked by US pressures and Argentina and Brazil to counter the domestic industrial interest groups concerned with dependence on the Chinese economy. Also, the BRI can be considered a diplomatic success for China because it contributed to the One China Policy by establishing diplomatic relations with Panama, the Dominican Republic, and El Salvador.

However, the different motivations and degrees of participation in the BRI confirm the absence of a regional strategy to accommodate the US–China rivalry scenario. Each country is navigating on its own, despite the Chinese efforts to deal with the region as a whole through the CELAC multilateral forums. Further research in China–LAC relations should provide case studies on infrastructure projects and investments, considering the concrete political and legal controversies involved. The development of critical mass in LAC academia should contribute to understanding the challenges and opportunities related to the region's increasing dependence on China if it manages to overcome the official diplomatic rhetoric that can lead to unrealistic expectations and harmful misunderstandings.

References

Baniya, S., Rocha, N., and Ruta, M. 2019. *Trade Effects of the New Silk Road: A Gravity Analysis*. Washington, DC: World Bank Group.

Barton, J.R. and Rehner, J. 2018. "Neostructuralism through Strategic Transaction: The Geopolinomics of China's Dragon Doctrine for Latin America." *Political Geography* 65: 77–87.

Belt and Road Portal. 2017. "Joint Communique of the Leaders Roundtable of the Belt and Road Forum for International Cooperation." May 16. https://eng.yidaiyilu.gov.cn/zchj/qwfb/13694.htm. Accessed 16 August 2022.

Bermúdez Liévano, A. 2019. "China's Belt and Road Advances in Latin America's Andean Region." *Diálogo Chino*. https://dialogochino.net/28021-chinas-belt-and-road-advances-in-latin-americas-andean-region/

Bernal-Meza, R. and Li, X. 2020. *China–Latin America Relations in the 21st Century*. Boston: Palgrave Macmillan.

Bórquez, A. and Bravo, C. 2020. "Who are China's Strategic Economic Partners in South America?" *Asian Education and Development Studies* 10(3): 445–456. https://doi.org/10.1108/AEDS-09-2019-0153

Callahan, W.A. 2015. *China Dreams: 20 Visions of the Future*. New York: Oxford University Press.

Campello, D. and Zucco Jr, C. 2016. "Presidential Success and the World Economy." *The Journal of Politics* 78(2): 589–602.

Castells, M. 2010. *The Rise of the Network Society*. New York: Wiley-Blackwell.

CELAC. 2018. "Special Declaration of Santiago of the II Ministerial Meeting of the CELAC-China Forum on the Belt and Road Initiative." January 22. https://celac.rree.gob.sv/documento-oficial/special-declaration-of-santiago-of-the-ii-ministerial-meeting-of-the-celac-china-forum-on-the-belt-and-road-initiative/

CEPAL. 2018. "Chinese Belt and Road Initiative is an Opportunity for Inclusive and Sustainable Investments: ECLAC." December 7. https://www.cepal.org/en/news/chinese-belt-and-road-initiative-opportunity-inclusive-and-sustainable-investments-eclac

Cheng, L.K. 2016. "Three Questions on China's 'Belt and Road Initiative'." *China Economic Review* 40: 309–313.

China Daily. 2018. "No Reason for 'Tropical Trump' to Disrupt Relations with China: Editorial." October 29. https://www.chinadaily.com.cn/a/201810/29/WS5bd702e9a310eff303285424.html

China Daily. 2022. "Colombia's New Leader Seeks Unity." August 9. // global.chinadaily.com.cn/a/202208/09/WS62f1bca3a310fd2b29e71186.html

De Soyres, F., Mulabdic, A., Murray S., Nadia Patrizia Rocha Gaffurri, N.P., Ruta, M. 2018. *How Much Will the Belt and Road Initiative Reduce Trade Costs?* Policy Research Working Paper No. WPS8614. World Bank.

Diálogo Chino. 2019. "El presidente colombiano va a China buscando vender más que petróleo." (The Colombian president goes to China looking to sell more than oil). August 12. https://dialogochino.net/29604-colombias-president-looks-beyond-oil-on-china-visit/?lang=es

The Diplomat. 2021. "China Holds Slimmed-Down Belt and Road Conference." June 25. https://thediplomat.com/2021/06/china-holds-slimmed-down-belt-and-road-conference/

Dussel Peters, E. 2020. *Monitor de la infraestructura china en América Latina y el Caribe 2020 (Chinese infrastructure monitor in Latin America and the Caribbean 2020)*. Mexico, DF: Red América Latina y el Caribe sobre China. Available at: https://www.redalc-china.org/monitor/infraestructura/images/pdfs/menuprincipal/DusselPeters_MonitorInfraestructura_2020_Esp.pdf

EFE. 2022. "Presidente de China felicita a Petro y habla de 'nuevo punto de inicio' en relación bilateral." (President of China congratulates Petro and speaks of 'new starting point' in bilateral relationship). *Noticias Caracol*, June 27. https://noticias.caracoltv.com/politica/elecciones-colombia/presidente-de-china-felicita-a-petro-y-habla-de-nuevo-punto-de-inicio-en-relacion-bilateral-so35

Ellis, R.E. 2017. "Cooperation and Mistrust between China and the United States in Latin America." In M. Myers and C. Wise (eds) *The Political Economy of China-Latin America Relations in the New Millennium: Brave New World*. New York: Routledge, pp 50–74.

Ferchen, M. 2021. "The BRI in Latin America. New Wine in Old Bottle?" In F. Schneider (ed) *Global Perspectives on China's Belt and Road Initiative: Asserting Agency through Regional Connectivity*. Amsterdam: Amsterdam University Press, pp 97–112.

Ferdinand, P. 2016. "Westward ho – the China Dream and 'One Belt, One Road': Chinese Foreign Policy under Xi Jinping." *International Affairs* 92(4): 941–957.

Gabriel, J.P.N., Pires, D.A., and Carvalho, C.E. 2018. "Brazilian Engagement to Asia and the Belt and Road Initiative in 2017: Less Politics, More Trade and Investments." *Estudos Internacionais: Revista de Relações Internacionais Da PUC Minas* 6(1): 26–43.

Gallagher, K.P. 2016. *The China Triangle*. New York: Oxford University Press.

Gallagher, K.P. and Irwin, A. 2014. "Exporting National Champions: China's Outward Foreign Direct Investment Finance in Comparative Perspective." *China & World Economy* 22(6): 1–21.

Gallagher, K.P. and Porzecanski, R. 2010. *The Dragon in the Room: China and the Future of Latin American Industrialization*. Stanford, CA: Stanford University Press.

Garlick, J. 2020. "The Regional Impacts of China's Belt and Road Initiative." *Journal of Current Chinese Affairs* 49(1): 3–13.

González Jauregui, J. 2020. "Latin American Countries in the BRI: Challenges and Potential Implications for Economic Development." *Asian Education and Development Studies* 10(3): 348–358.

Grell-Brisk, M. 2017. "China and Global Economic Stratification in an Interdependent World." *Palgrave Commun.* 3(17087). https://doi.org/10.1057/palcomms.2017.87

Gruss, B. 2014. *After the Boom: Commodity Prices and Economic Growth in Latin America and the Caribbean*. International Monetary Fund Working Paper WP/14/154. https://www.imf.org/external/pubs/ft/wp/2014/wp14154.pdf

Huang, Y. 2016. "Understanding China's Belt and Road Initiative: Motivation, Framework and Assessment." *China Economic Review* 40: 314–321.

Hung, H. 2015. *The China Boom: Why China Will Not Rule the World*. New York: Columbia University Press.

Hung, H. 2018. "The Tapestry of Chinese Capital in the Global South." *Palgrave Communications* 4(65). https://doi.org/10.1057/s41599-018-0123-7

Jenkins, R. 2015. "Is Chinese Competition Causing Desindustrialisation in Brazil?" *Latin American Perspectives* 42(6): 42–63.

Jenkins, R. 2017. "China and Latin America." In S.S.F. Regilme and J. Parisot (eds) *American Hegemony and the Rise of Emerging Powers*. New York: Routledge, pp 182–197.

Jenkins, R. 2018. *How China is Reshaping the Global Economy: Development Impacts in Africa and Latin America.* Oxford: Oxford University Press.

Jenkins, R. 2021. "China's Belt and Road Initiative in Latin America: What has Changed?" *Journal of Current Chinese Affairs* 1(27). https://doi.org/ DOI: 10.1177/18681026211047871

Joy-Perez, C. 2019. "The Belt and Road Initiative Adds More Partners, But Beijing Has Fewer Dollars to Spend." *China Brief*, 19(17). https://jamestown.org/program/the-belt-and-road-initiative-adds-more-partners-but-beijing-has-fewer-dollars-to-spend/

Kahler, M. 2013. "Rising Powers and Global Governance: Negotiating Change in a Resilient Status Quo." *International Affairs* 89(3): 711–729.

Knoerich, J. and Urdinez, F. 2019. "Contesting Contested Multilateralism: Why the West Joined the Rest in Founding the Asian Infrastructure Investment Bank." *The Chinese Journal of International Politics* 12(3): 333–370.

Lake, D.A., Martin, L.L. and Risse, T. 2021. "Challenges to the Liberal Order: Reflections on International Organization." *International Organization* 75(2): 225–257.

Leiva, D. 2020. "BRI and Railways in Latin America: How Important are Domestic Politics?" *Asian Education and Development Studies* 10(3): 386–398.

Li, X. 2021. "The Rise of China and its Impact on World Economic Stratification and Re-stratification." *Cambridge Review of International Affairs* 34(4): 530–550.

Li, X. and Bernal-Meza, R. 2022. "China–US Rivalry: A New Cold War or Capitalism's Intra-Core Competition?" *Revista Brasileira de Política Internacional* 64. https://doi.org/10.1590/0034-7329202100110

Long, T. and Urdinez, F. 2021. "Status at the Margins: Why Paraguay Recognises Taiwan and Shuns China." *Foreign Policy Analysis* 17(1). https://doi.org/10.1093/fpa/oraa002

López, D. and Muñoz, F. 2020. "China's Trade Policy towards Latin America: An Analysis of Free Trade Agreements Policy." *Asian Education and Development Studies* 10(3): 399–409.

Myers, M. 2018. "China's Belt and Road Initiative: What Role for Latin America?" *Journal of Latin American Geography* 17(2): 239–243.

Myers, M. and Wise, C. (eds). 2017. *The Political Economy of China-Latin America Relations in the New Millennium: Brave New World.* New York: Routledge.

Narins, T.P. 2016. "Evaluating Chinese Economic Engagement in Africa versus Latin America." *Geography Compass* 10(7): 283–292.

NDRC (National Development and Reform Commission). 2015. "Vision and Actions on Jointly Building Silk Road Economic Belt and 21st-Century Maritime Silk." March. http://2017.beltandroadforum.org/english/n100/2017/0410/c22-45.html.

New York Times. 2018a. "Taiwan's Diplomatic Isolation Increases as Dominican Republic Recognises China." May 1. https://www.nytimes.com/2018/05/01/world/asia/taiwan-dominican-republic-recognize.html

New York Times. 2018b. "El Salvador Recognises China in Blow to Taiwan." August 21. https://www.nytimes.com/2018/08/21/world/asia/taiwan-el-salvador-diplomatic-ties.html

Nikkei Asia. 2020. "Chile Picks Japan's Trans-Pacific Cable Route in Snub to China." July 29. https://asia.nikkei.com/Business/Telecommunication/Chile-picks-Japan-s-trans-Pacific-cable-route-in-snub-to-China.

Nordin, A. and Weissmann, M. 2018. "Will Trump Make China Great Again? The Belt and Road Initiative and International Order." *International Affairs* 94(2): 231–249.

Office of the Leading Group for Promoting the Belt and Road Initiative. 2019. *The Belt and Road Initiative. Progress, Contributions and Prospects.* https://www.yidaiyilu.gov.cn/wcm.files/upload/CMSydylgw/201904/201904220254037.pdf

Oliveira, G.D.L.T. and Myers, M. 2021. "The Tenuous Co-Production of China's Belt and Road Initiative in Brazil and Latin America." *Journal of Contemporary China* 30(129): 481–499.

Oropeza, A. (ed). 2018. *China: BRI o El Nuevo Camino de La Seda.* México: Universidad Nacional Autónoma de México, Instituto de Investigaciones Jurídicas.

Pu, X. and Wang, C. 2018. "Rethinking China's Rise: Chinese Scholars Debate Strategic Overstretch." *International Affairs* 94(5): 1019–1035.

Regilme, S.S.F. 2018a. "A Human Rights Tragedy: Strategic Localisation of United States Foreign Policy in Colombia." *International Relations* 32(3): 343–365.

Regilme, S.S.F. 2018b. "Does United States Foreign Aid Undermine Human Rights? The 'Thaksinification' of the War on Terror Discourses and the Human Rights Crisis in Thailand, 2001 to 2006." *Human Rights Review* 19(1): 73–95.

Regilme, S.S.F. 2021. *Aid Imperium: United States Foreign Policy and Human Rights in Post-Cold War Southeast Asia.* Ann Arbor, MI: University of Michigan Press.

Regilme, S.S.F. and Parisot, J. (eds) 2017. *American Hegemony and the Rise of Emerging Powers.* London: Routledge.

Rolland, N. 2019. "Beijing's Response to the Belt and Road Initiative's 'Pushback': A Story of Assessment and Adaptation." *Asian Affairs* 50(2): 216–235.

Scissors, D. 2020. "China's Global Investment in 2019: Going Out Goes Small." *American Enterprise Institute – AEI*, January 14. https://www.aei.org/research-products/report/chinas-global-investment-in-2019-going-out-goes-small/

Serrano-Moreno, J.E. 2021. "La retórica de la conectividad de la Iniciativa de la Franja y la Ruta en América Latina." In J. Sahd (ed) *China y América Latina: Claves para el futuro*. Santiago: Centro de Estudios Internacionales Universidad Católica (CEIUC) & Konrad Adenauer Stiftung, pp 151–173.

Serrano-Moreno, J.E., Telias, D., and Urdinez, F. 2021a. "Deconstructing the Belt and Road Initiative in Latin America." *Asian Education and Development Studies* 10(3): 337–347.

Serrano-Moreno, J.E., Pérez Ceballos, A., and De Abreu Negrón, M.G. 2021b. "Beyond Copper: China and Chile Relations." *Asian Education and Development Studies* 10(3): 359–373.

Shakhanova, G. and Garlick, J. 2020. "The Belt and Road Initiative and the Eurasian Economic Union: Exploring the 'Greater Eurasian Partnership'." *Journal of Current Chinese Affairs* 49(1): 33–57.

South China Morning Post. 2017. "Panama Establishes Diplomatic Ties with Beijing in Blow to Taiwan." June 13. https://www.scmp.com/news/china/diplomacy-defence/article/2098038/panama-establishes-diplomatic-ties-china-blow-taiwan

The State Council of PRC. 2016. "China's Policy Paper on Latin America and the Caribbean." November 24. http://english.www.gov.cn/archive/white_paper/2016/11/24/content_281475499069158.htm

Summers, T. 2016. "China's 'New Silk Roads': Sub-national Regions and Networks of Global Political Economy." *Third World Quarterly* 37(9): 1628–1643.

Summers, T. 2018. "Rocking the Boat? China's 'Belt and Road' and Global Order." In A. Ehteshami and N. Horesh (eds) *China's Presence in the Middle East*. New York: Routledge, pp 24–37.

Telias, D. 2021. "El orden liberal, China y América Latina." (The liberal order, China and Latin America). In J. Sahd (ed) *China y América Latina. Claves para el futuro* (China and Latin America. Keys to the future). Santiago: CEIUC & Konrad Adenauer Stiftung, pp 21–44.

Telias, D. and Urdinez, F. 2021. "China's Foreign Aid Political Drivers: Lessons from a Novel Dataset of Mask Diplomacy in Latin America During the COVID-19 Pandemic." *Journal of Current Chinese Affairs*. https://doi.org/10.1177/18681026211020763

Thuy, N.T.T. 2020. "United States Attitudes and Reactions towards China's 'Belt and Road' Initiative." In A. Chong and Q.M. Pham (eds) *Critical Reflections on China's Belt & Road Initiative*. Singapore: Springer, pp 203–221.

UNECLAC. 2014. "The Economic Infrastructure Gap and Investment in Latin America." Santiago: CEPAL. https://www.cepal.org/en/publications/37381-economic-infrastructure-gap-and-investment-latin-america

UNECLAC. 2019. "Panorama Social de América Latina 2018." Santiago: CEPAL. https://www.cepal.org/es/publicaciones/44395-panorama-social-america-latina-2018

Urdinez, F., Mouron, F., Schenoni, L.L., and de Oliveira, A.J. 2016. "Chinese Economic Statecraft and United States Hegemony in Latin America: An Empirical Analysis, 2003–2014." *Latin American Politics and Society* 58(4): 3–30.

Urdinez, F., Knoerich, J., and Ribeiro, P.F. 2018. "Don't Cry for Me 'Argenchina': Unraveling Political Views of China through Legislative Debates in Argentina." *Journal of Chinese Political Science* 23(2): 235–256.

Wallerstein, I. 2004. *World-Systems Analysis: An Introduction.* Duke: Duke University Press.

Wang, H. 2019. "China's Approach to the Belt and Road Initiative: Scope, Character and Sustainability." *Journal of International Economic Law* 22(1): 29–55.

Weiss, J.C. and Wallace, J.L. 2021. "Domestic Politics, China's Rise, and the Future of the Liberal International Order." *International Organization* 75(2): 635–664.

Wise, C. 2020. *Dragonomics: How Latin America Is Maximising (or Missing Out on) China's International Development Strategy.* London: Yale University Press.

Wise, C. and Chonn Ching, V. 2018. "Conceptualising China-Latin America Relations in the Twenty-First Century: The Boom, the Bust, and the Aftermath." *Pacific Review* 31(5): 553–572.

Xinhuanet. 2019. "Interview: Outdated United States Policies Unfit for Today's World Says Mexican Politician." June 15. http://www.xinhuanet.com/english/2019-06/15/c_138145885.htm

Xinhuanet. 2021. "Chinese President Calls for Building Closer Belt and Road Partnership." June 23. http://www.xinhuanet.com/english/2021-06/23/c_1310024161.htm

Yu, H. 2017. "Motivation behind China's 'One Belt, One Road' Initiatives and Establishment of the Asian Infrastructure Investment Bank." *Journal of Contemporary China* 26(105): 353–368.

Zhou, W. and Esteban, M. 2018. "Beyond Balancing: China's Approach towards the Belt and Road Initiative." *Journal of Contemporary China* 27(112): 487–501.

Zottele, E. and Zottele A.C. 2020. *Aproximaciones a la Franja y la Ruta.* Vracruz: Universidad Veracruzana.

8

The Middle East and Changing Superpower Relations

Chien-Kai Chen and Ceren Ergenc

Introduction

The 21st century has witnessed economic, political, and normative transformations as a result of protracted economic crises, technological developments used to overcome these crises, shifts in global value chains, and the consequent shifts in power distribution among great powers and leading regions. The relations between the US and China are among the most contentious dynamics in the contemporary world. With the so-called "rise of China" as a result of China's successful economic reform since the late 1970s, which has turned China into the second largest economy of the world following the US only, scholars and diplomats alike are wondering how the relations between the two powers in our world today will evolve. Many recent developments, such as the revival of the Quadrilateral Security Dialogue between the US, Japan, Australia, and India since 2017, the Sino–US "trade war" since 2018, and the US-led "diplomatic boycott" of China's Winter Olympics in 2022, seem to reveal the emergence of the Sino–US rivalry and the increase of the tension between the two in our international system. In this context of growing Sino–US conflicts, it is both academically and practically important to study their relations in one of the most strategically important regions in our world, the Middle East, which is producing one third of the oil for the whole world.

The Middle East is composed of multiple subregions with distinct political and socioeconomic backgrounds. However, the positions of these subregions in relation to regional and global powers are interconnected, forming the regional relations of the Middle East. Intriguingly, despite the huge strategic importance of the region, the tension between the US and China over the

Middle Eastern issues has not been very high. While the US has been actively taking actions to intervene in regional affairs to protect and promote its interests in the region, China has been adopting a hands-off approach toward the region (that is, a less assertive and non-interventionist policy toward the Middle Eastern countries). Many studies that examine China's responses to such issues as the US invasion of Iraq, the Israeli–Palestinian relations, and the US policy toward Iran even reveal that China has intentionally avoided being too assertive in the Middle East in order to prevent conflict with the US (Lai 2007; Wehrey et al 2010; Chen 2012; Ehteshami et al 2018; Conduit and Akbarzadeh 2019).

However, will the tension between the US and China in the Middle East remain low in the future? Or, more specifically, with the constant growth of the Chinese presence in the region, will the US–China rivalry in the Middle East become significant like that in many other regions and, as a result, will the tension increase? In other words, will China move away from that hands-off approach, becoming more assertive and interventionist on the Middle Eastern affairs and, in the meantime, less hesitant to confront the US in the Middle East whenever there are conflicts of interests between them over the region? To address this question, we will first compare and explain their contrasting policies toward the Middle East in an analytical framework that combines the concept of path dependence with a scalar and place-based analysis.[1] Then, we will explore whether and how the US withdrawal from Afghanistan in 2021, which ended its 20-year war over there, would bring about a new political and economic landscape in the Middle East and as a result create a "critical juncture" that encourages China to become more assertive and interventionist in the Middle East, which in turn would increase the Sino-US tension.

Afghanistan is a cusp state at the intersection of South Asia and the Middle East, with historical and geopolitical ties to both regions. It shares cultural connections with other Middle Eastern subregions and a history of great power rivalry in modern times. Afghanistan has a diverse population that includes many ethnic groups, such as Pashtuns, Tajiks, Hazaras, and Uzbeks. These groups share many cultural and linguistic ties with people in neighboring countries, such as Iran and Pakistan. Afghanistan is a predominantly Muslim country, with Sunni and Shia Islam being the two major sects. These two sects are also represented in many Middle Eastern countries, such as Iran, Iraq, Saudi Arabia, and Syria. Afghanistan's complex history is intertwined with neighboring countries in the Middle East. In ancient times, Afghanistan was part of the Persian empire, and it has been invaded by various regional and colonial powers over the centuries. Its strategic location has made it a battleground for various regional and global powers, including Russia, the US, and China, as will be discussed later in this chapter.

As our study will demonstrate, although China might become a little bit more interventionist as it tries to deal with the aftershocks of the power vacuum left by the US withdrawal from Afghanistan, it will still refrain from being overly assertive in order to preserve its non-interventionist reputation among the countries in the region. Therefore, while there seems to be a critical juncture emerging and, as a result, the tension between the US and China in the Middle East might increase, whether there will be a significant hegemonic competition between the two in the region remains to be seen.

The US policy toward the Middle East

There are four major US interests in the Middle East: protecting the "energy resources and their unrestricted commercial flow to consumers"; preserving the "security and welfare of Israel"; assisting "friendly regimes in the region in order to enhance overall regional stability"; and maintaining the "US political influence and commercial access in the region" (Fuller 1990: 419). Among them, the first one is arguably the most significant that connects all of the other interests together. Simply speaking, the US interests in the Middle East involve a combination of oil, corporate wealth, and national security (Gendzier 2002: 596 and 618), centered on the "pursuit of geo-strategic advantages in control of the region's energy resources—oil and natural gas, the pipelines and sea lanes that connect them to global markets" (Rosenthal 2010: 11). To be more specific, there are three key goals surrounding that combination of interests that the US has been trying to achieve: controlling the "oil and gas resources of the region"; influencing "certain regimes in the region as much as possible, especially Israel, Saudi Arabia, Iraq, Iran, Egypt, and Pakistan"; and preventing the "rise of any popular movements – whether communist, socialist, nationalist, or religious – that might threaten US control of the region's energy resources and the stability of its client regimes" (Rosenthal 2010: 11).

To protect the aforementioned interests, the US has been intervening in Middle Eastern affairs not only politically but also, from time to time, militarily as revealed by its continuous military operations in Afghanistan and Iraq over the past two decades. Although the US has completely withdrawn its forces from the former, its military is still playing an "advisory" role in the latter. How to explain its extremely assertive, interventionist approach toward the Middle East? This question is especially interesting if we compare the US policy to China's, which has been less assertive and relatively non-interventionist. As Gendzier (2002: 600) argues well, "for those seeking to make sense of recent developments in the Middle East, earlier periods compelled attention." Therefore, it is important to examine the US foreign relations in the Middle East before and see how they have affected its policy, as well as the relations, today. Here, the conceptual lens of "path dependence" combined with a scalar and place-based approach toward global politics is one of the best analytical tools to address this question.

Path dependence and the US presence in the Middle East

From a theoretical perspective of "path dependence," the US since the end of the Second World War has been following a path of power politics and interventionism in its relations with the Middle Eastern countries. "Path dependence," associated with "historical institutionalism" that emphasizes "history matters" (Greener 2005: 62), is a theoretical framework resting on the assumption that "choices made in the past influence the menu of options available in the present and future" (Leithner and Libby 2017: 1–2) and that "initial moves in one direction elicit further moves in that same direction" (Marx 2010: 182). In other words, a certain decision you made in the first place would pave a specific path, as compared to other alternative paths, that you are inclined to follow moving forward: it has reproducing and constraining effects on the decision that you are making now, which in turn will have similar effects on the decision that you can make in the future. When it comes to the study of international relations, the concept of "path dependence" is a helpful theoretical tool for scholars to explain the foreign policy that a certain country is currently implementing and predict the policy that it will adopt in the future. As Leithner and Libby (2017: 12–13) point out, although the term "path dependence" is seldom used in foreign policy analyses, the idea that "history is an important explanatory factor in contemporary foreign policy decisions" is popularly accepted in the field.

Here, on top of the concept of "path dependence," we also have to take a scalar and place-based approach toward global politics, which emphasizes the importance of interaction, process, and context in studying international relations (Sjoberg 2008), to examine how the iterative dialogical interactions between the US and other actors in the Middle East and beyond have helped create and maintain that "path." As the rest of this section will demonstrate, the path of power politics and interventionism that the US has been following when it comes to its policy toward the Middle East was forged in the first place by its pursuit of hegemony to protect its national interests in the region and beyond as one of the two superpowers during the Cold War. Most importantly, the US has continued to go down the same path since (and in spite of) the dissolution of the USSR in order to defend its post-Cold War hegemonic position in the region.

A path of power politics and interventionism

The US didn't have significant presence in the Middle East until the Second World War when the US began to station its forces in Egypt and Iran (Foreign

Policy Association 1988: 55). Then, its involvement in the Middle East drastically increased as the end of the Second World War brought about the Cold War between the US and the USSR. Throughout the Cold War, from 1945 to 1991, the two and only superpowers competed with each other over hegemony at each corner of the world, including, but of course not limited to, the strategically important region of the Middle East (Gutfeld and Zumbrunnen 2013: 624).

Against this backdrop, the major concern of the US in the Middle East throughout the Cold War was the Soviet effort to increase its influence over the region in general and the Middle Eastern countries close to its border in particular (Kuniholm 1987: 9). As a result, the most important elements of the US policy toward the Middle East back then consisted of the "balance of power" among the Middle Eastern countries and "containment" against the Soviet expansion in the region (Kuniholm 1987: 18; Fuller 1990: 418). To achieve these goals, the US gradually developed two strategies against the USSR in the region. One involved the development of "strategic airlift forces capable of transporting large numbers of American combat units (and equipment) directly to the Middle East (or to any point on the globe), in record time, without dependence on the good-will of allied or friendly nations for refueling stops in their territories en route" (Gutfeld and Zumbrunnen 2013: 623). The other focused on the development of an "interdependent relationship with Saudi Arabia that would intertwine Saudi fortunes with the well-being of the United States, thus protecting vital American interests in Saudi Arabia and in the Persian Gulf" (Gutfeld and Zumbrunnen 2013: 623).

The strong US support for Israel can be understood in this context as well. Following the 1967 Six-Day War, as well as the 1973 Yom Kippur War, an alliance between the US and Israel emerged, and the issue about the Arab–Israeli conflicts became a key one in the US policy toward the Middle East (Kuniholm 1987: 19). While the "Israel lobby" in the US did play a very important role in the US support for the country, the US effort to pursue a hegemonic position against the USSR in the region is a critical factor that cannot be ignored (Rosenthal 2010: 13–14). Overall, preventing the Soviet expansionism (and pursuing the US hegemony) in the Middle East is a key rationale behind the support for Israel in the 1967 and 1973 wars, as well as other US interventions like the overthrow of the Mossadegh government in Iran, the backing for King Hussein of Jordan and Camille Chamoun of Lebanon, the arming of US "proxies" in the Gulf, and so on (Hubbell 1998: 8).

Staying on the path to defend the US hegemonic position

The US eventually "won" the Cold War and became the hegemon in the Middle East and beyond as a result of the dissolution of the USSR in December 1991. Actually, it is fair to say that, even before the dissolution of the USSR, the 1990–1991 US-led Gulf War against Iraq had already revealed the US hegemonic position in the Middle East. Either way, beginning in the early 1990s, for the first time since the end of the Second World War, the US was the only superpower, or the so-called "hyperpower" (Mohamedi and Sadowski 2001: 11), in the Middle East and beyond. However, despite the dissolution of the USSR, the US's assertive and interventionist approach toward the Middle East, which was forged during the Cold War to prevent the Soviet expansion, still continued (Hubbell 1998: 9). Simply speaking, the US has been largely staying on the same path of power politics and interventionism in the post-Cold War era despite the dissolution of the USSR. According to the studies of "path dependence," a key reason for an actor to stay on a certain path has a lot to do with the "cost" of switching from one path to another, and as those studies have demonstrated, the longer an actor stays on a certain path, the higher the cost of changing the path (Greener 2005: 62; Marx 2010: 184; Leithner and Libby 2017: 3). As Hubbell (1998: 9) observes, since the end of the Cold War, the US has continued to "construct and defend an authoritarian order to resist challenges to its domination" in the Middle East. Actually, the US status as the only superpower in the wake of the dissolution of the USSR might provide even more incentives for the US to stay on that path of power politics and interventionism in order to protect its interests in the Middle East and beyond. By the end of the 1990s, the US had maintained a higher military presence in the Middle East than in the 1980s (Clarke 2017: 148).

While it might still be debatable as to whether that path of power politics and interventionism caused the 9/11 terrorist attacks against the US in 2001, those attacks did keep the US on the path. The 9/11 terrorist attacks were followed by not only the US invasion of Afghanistan but also that of Iraq. According to Clarke (2017: 147 and 149), by 2001, the US "had been the single superpower for slightly over a decade," and its major national security leaders "wanted to keep it that way" and "thought that the swift and decisive victory over al-Qaeda and the Taliban had not been enough to undo the damage done by 9/11 to the superpower reputation of the United States." The constant US military operations in the Middle East since the 9/11 terrorist attacks were frequently criticized inside and outside the US as "dumb wars" (Clarke 2017: 148–151). However, as mentioned, it is hard for the US to change the path of power politics and interventionism toward the region that it has been following for so long. The US had to continue to halt the withdrawal from Afghanistan because of the need to deal with the resurgent Taliban (Clarke 2017: 152). Also, although the US did officially withdraw from Iraq in 2011, it had to send the US troops back in order to fight against the forces of the Islamic State in Iraq and Syria (ISIS) (Clarke 2017: 152). It was not until 2021 that the US completely withdrew from Afghanistan and changed its military mission in Iraq against ISIS from a combat one to an advisory one. To sum up, going down the path of power politics and interventionism, the US has become a hegemonic power in the Middle East that can hardly desert that path without losing its hegemonic status and damaging its huge interests over there that have been protected with that status. As Totten (2013: 14) argues well, the US "can take a bit of a breather, but retirement is decades away."

China's policy toward the Middle East

Being a rising power as a result of its successful economic reform initiated in the late 1970s, China's interests, especially the economic ones, in the Middle East have significantly expanded, which involve not only oil import but also other trade and investment activities like labor export, construction services, engineering projects, business partnerships, bilateral investment plans, and so on (Shichor 2013: 35; Shichor 2017: 109–110). However, as compared to the US approach toward the Middle East that we have discussed in the previous section, China's acts of intervention in the region are still limited. In general, as many scholars have found, China is still taking a less political, business-first, economic approach toward the Middle East while doing some "quasi-mediation diplomacy" (that is, indirect involvement that emphasizes following rather than leading, revising the agenda rather than setting it, and conflict de-escalation rather than conflict resolution) at times in the region (Sun and Zoubir 2018: 224).

This of course does not mean that China plays no role in the Middle Eastern affairs and has no interference at all with the regional issues over there. To China, although intervening in the Middle Eastern affairs is "fundamentally unacceptable," it is "occasionally unavoidable" (Shichor 2013: 32). That being said, it is very obvious that China in the Middle East has tried to be as least assertive as possible and conducted only that "quasi-meditation diplomacy" at most if necessary. More specifically, when it comes to Middle Eastern affairs, encouraging peaceful settlements by the Middle Eastern countries themselves is still China's first and foremost option, with intervention without military force through regional or international organizations as a second but reluctant choice and unilateral intervention, as well as any interference by military force including those multilateral ones, as the option that China has tried to avoid the most (Shichor 2013, 2017).

It is also worth noting that the Middle East is not a homogeneous region but a heterogeneous one where countries have diverse conflicts of political, economic and cultural interests among themselves as revealed by the Israeli–Palestinian conflicts, the Iraq–Iran War, Iraq's invasion of Kuwait, the Yemen crisis, the Syrian crisis, ISIS, Iran's nuclear programs, and so on. Occasionally, countries in the Middle East actually had no problem with or even expected China's intervention given that China is much politically closer to them as compared to the US and other Western powers (Shichor 2013: 38; Shichor 2017: 115). However, even under this circumstance, China still declined to be more assertive and tried to avoid taking sides in order to maintain good relations with all sides (Shichor 2013: 31–32). When it comes to a conflict of interests between two or more countries in the Middle East, China does not want to please one country at the risk of alienating another.

Path dependence and China's presence in the Middle East

So, how to explain China's less assertive, non-interventionist approach? Once again, the conceptual lens of "path dependence" combined with a scalar and place-based approach toward global politics is one of the best analytical tools to address this question. As the rest of this section will demonstrate, China since the early 1950s has been following a path of anti-imperialism and non-intervention when it comes to its policy toward the Middle East, which was forged by the "Five Principles of Peaceful Coexistence" that were initiated by China itself in the first place (that is, mutual respect for sovereignty and territorial integrity, mutual non-aggression, mutual non-interference in each other's internal affairs, equality and mutual benefit, and peaceful coexistence).

The prominent status of the "principle of non-intervention" and the idea of "anti-imperialism" in China's relations with the Middle Eastern countries is manifested by China's first-ever official policy paper toward the region published in January 2016 (Ministry of Foreign Affairs, China 2016). Mentioning the "Arab national liberation movement," China said that it "firmly supports Arab countries' struggle to uphold sovereignty and territorial integrity, pursue and safeguard national interests, and combat external interference and aggression" (Ministry of Foreign Affairs, China 2016: para 2). Also, seeing itself as a country that suffered from imperialism and colonialism as well, China emphasized that it and the Middle Eastern countries all have a "broad consensus" on "safeguarding state sovereignty and territorial integrity" and "defending national dignity" (Ministry of Foreign Affairs, China 2016: para 5). Furthermore, regarding itself as a member of the Global South, China depicted its relations with the Middle East as a "model of South-South cooperation," saying that "both sides have always respected and treated each other as equals and remained brothers, friends and partners no matter what happens on the world arena" (Ministry of Foreign Affairs, China 2016: para 6). When it comes to terrorism, China made it clear that "counter-terrorism operations should comply with the purposes and principles of the Charter of the United Nations and international norms, and respect sovereignty, independence and territorial integrity of all countries" (Ministry of Foreign Affairs, China 2016: para 52). Overall, according to China, it "upholds the Five Principles of Peaceful Coexistence" in its policy toward the Middle East and "respects choices made by the Arab people, and supports Arab states in exploring their own development paths suited to their national conditions" (Ministry of Foreign Affairs, China 2016: para 14).

A path of anti-imperialism and non-intervention

The "Five Principles of Peaceful Coexistence" were first raised by China in its negotiation with India between 1953 and 1954 over the issue about Tibet (Ministry of Foreign Affairs, China 2000a). The principles were officially included in the Agreement on Trade and Intercourse between Tibet Region of China and India that was signed by China and India in April 1954 (Ministry of External Affairs, India 1954; Ministry of Foreign Affairs, China 2000a). One year later, in April 1955, China promoted those same principles in the Asian-African Conference held in Bandung, Indonesia (that is, the "Bandung Conference"), where China and the other 28 countries from Asia, Africa, and the Middle East, many of which just became independent from the colonial rule, got together to show their solidarity against colonialism and promote economic and cultural cooperation among one another, and the principles were eventually incorporated into the resolution of the conference (Ministry of Foreign Affairs, China 2000a; Office of the Historian, Department of State, US nd). Since then, as many official statements issued by China reveal, the "Five Principles of Peaceful Coexistence" has been publicized by China as the guiding doctrine for its foreign relations (Ministry of Foreign Affairs, China 2000a, 2000b). At the core of the "Five Principles" is the norm of "non-intervention," especially in terms of struggle against imperialism/colonialism where powerful countries interfere with the affairs of other weaker countries to their own advantages. According to China, the "Five Principles of Peaceful Coexistence" get rid of the "unfairness" in international relations, are in opposition to "hegemony" and "power politics," and reflect the "common desire of developing countries" (Ministry of Foreign Affairs, China 2000a, 2000b).

The promotion of the "Five Principles of Peaceful Coexistence" by China in the 1950s was against the backdrop of China's status as a less-developed country which had limited economic, military, and political capabilities while facing several internal and external challenges. Territorial integrity was one of the key challenges. As mentioned, the "Five Principles" were first raised by China in its negotiation with India between 1953 and 1954 over the issue of Tibet that China claimed as a Chinese territory. Also, the issue of Taiwan that China regarded as a "renegade province" was an important one, too. At the Bandung Conference held in 1955 where China enthusiastically promoted the "Five Principles," China secured support from many Middle Eastern countries for its claim on Taiwan and its bid for becoming a member of the United Nations (UN; where the Chinese seat was held by Taiwan back then) with its promise to support their position on the issue of Palestine (Khalili 1970: 310). Threats from the "imperialist" forces (that is, the US and, at a later point, the USSR) constituted another key challenge, and the "Five Principles" were used to rally support from the "third-world countries" against the two superpowers back then. Take the Bandung Conference for example again. At the conference, while China made clear its opposition to the "Western 'imperialistic' designs" in the Middle East, many countries in the region agreed to China's position against the US and its idea of anti-imperialism/colonialism in general (Khalili 1970: 310).

In contrast to the US path of power politics and interventionism, China's path of anti-imperialism and non-intervention is a result of China having very few hard and soft capabilities to use in the first place. In other words, without enough capabilities to effectively impose its will on others, China had little choice but to resort to "norm" (that is, the principle of non-intervention) and "morality" (that is, anti-imperialism), both of which were embodied in the "Five Principles of Peaceful Coexistence," to protect its interests in the Middle East and beyond.

Staying on the path to preserve China's non-interventionist reputation

China is still emphasizing the importance of the "Five Principles" in its relations with the Middle East despite the fact that it has changed from that less-developed country to the second largest economy of the world that has huge economic, military, and political power. Here, the reproducing and constraining effects of "path dependence" again play an important role. Following the "path" set by China's enthusiastic promotion of the "Five Principles" in the 1950s, China has not only continued to emphasize the principle of non-intervention and its position against imperialism but also made even more concrete promises along the way. For example, Deng Xiaoping as the chairman of the Chinese delegation to the 6th special session of the UN General Assembly in 1974 claimed in his speech to the UN that China "firmly sees its joint struggle with the third world against imperialism, hegemony, and colonialism as a sacred international duty," "firmly stands by the third world countries," and most importantly, "will never pursue hegemony" (Wu nd). He went so far as to say:

> If one day China should change her color and turn into a superpower, if she too should play the tyrant in the world, and everywhere subject others to her bullying, aggression and exploitation, the people of the world should identify her as social-imperialism, expose it, oppose it and work together with the Chinese people to overthrow it. (Mohan and Power 2008: 23)

Chinese leaders after Deng, including Jiang Zemin, Hu Jintao, and the current leader Xi Jinping, continued to follow the "path," pointing out on various occasions as well that China will never seek hegemony and domination *even if* it becomes strong and has the capabilities to do so (Asian Society 1997; Beijing Review 2009; BBC News 2018). Their words are all repeated in an official white paper entitled "China and the World in the New Era" that was made public by China in September 2019 (State Council, China 2019). In the paper, China emphasized that, with the "Five Principles of Peaceful Coexistence," it has "safeguarded the interests of developing countries, playing an important role in building a fair and equitable international political and economic order." Furthermore, it pointed out that "China will never pursue hegemony or expansion, nor will it seek to create spheres of influence, no matter how international situation changes, how China develops itself."

To understand why China has been largely staying on the same path, we have to examine more closely the "cost" of changing that path of anti-imperialism and non-intervention forged by the "Five Principles of Peaceful Coexistence." To China, the cost involves a huge damage to its reputation as a reliable non-interventionist partner among the Middle Eastern countries that have viewed China's "noninterventionism" more favorably than the "more-muscular US approach" to regional affairs (Wehrey et al 2010: 61). More specifically, given China's constant emphasis on the "Five Principles" over the past seven decades, becoming more assertive and interventionist (or even an attempt to do so) in the Middle East would arguably lead countries in the region (or even the whole Global South) to regard China as not trustworthy and reliable due to its breaking its own long-time promises against interventionism and imperialism, which in turn would make it difficult for China to build more partnerships and strengthen the existing ones in the Middle East to protect and promote whatever interest it might pursue in the region and beyond.

By contrast, maintaining a reputation as a reliable partner that keeps promises would encourage cooperation from others. In terms of Sino-Middle Eastern relations, one key benefit that China has obtained by promoting and then sticking to the "Five Principles of Peaceful Coexistence" is that countries in the Middle East have in general refrained from interfering with those international controversies that China claims as its domestic affairs, such as those about Taiwan, Tibet, and Xinjiang. Here, the issue about Xinjiang is especially relevant to Sino-Middle Eastern relations. The oppression of Uyghur Muslims in Xinjiang by the Chinese government in the name of war on extremism since the 9/11 has caught the attention of many people in the world including those in the Middle East (Roberts 2020). For example, in the wake of China's repression of Uyghurs' protests in 2009, the reformists in Iran criticized their conservative counterparts for "supporting Muslims in Gaza while supposedly snubbing Uyghurs in China" (Ehteshami et al 2018: 8–9). Also, beginning in 2018, the "re-education camps" in Xinjiang that the Chinese government uses to "carry out anti-extremist ideological education" have been a target of criticism from human rights activists all over the world (Westcott and Xiong 2018). However, like the case of 2009, while there are people in the Middle East expressing support for the repressed Uyghurs in Xinjiang, their governments have largely shied away from openly criticizing China for those re-education camps (Ibrahim 2019). It is reasonable to argue that China's refraining from being too assertive on the Middle Eastern issues has been, to a certain degree, encouraging the Middle Eastern countries not to interfere with China's affairs in exchange.

To sum up, going down the path of anti-imperialism and non-intervention set by the "Five Principles of Peaceful Coexistence," an image as a reliable non-interventionist partner has been created and constantly reinforced by China itself among the countries in the Middle East through China's effort to differentiate itself from the US and other Western powers that, according to China, have been engaging in zero-sum power politics in the region for nothing but their own interests. It in turn has created a situation where moving away from that path against interventionism and imperialism will cause huge damage to China's reputation as a reliable non-interventionist partner to the Middle Eastern countries and the Global South in general. As a result, China has continued to refrain from becoming too assertive and interventionist in the Middle East in order to maintain its image as a reliable and trustworthy partner to the Middle Eastern countries as compared to those interventionist "Western powers."

US withdrawal from Afghanistan: a critical juncture?

It is worth pointing out here that, while an analysis based on "path dependence" largely focuses on "how increasing returns or positive feedback loops generated continuity as opposed to change" (Leithner and Libby 2017: 17), it does not completely rule out the possibility of change. According to the studies of "path dependence," a dramatic change might still occur when there is a "critical juncture" in which "something erodes or swamps the mechanisms of reproduction that generate continuity" (Greener 2005: 25; Leithner and Libby 2017: 18). So, has the US withdrawal from Afghanistan in 2021, which ended its 20-year war there, created a "critical juncture" for change? International security issues related to Afghanistan have played a significant role in shaping and reshaping both the US and China's regional and global foreign policies. The developments in Afghanistan since the Cold War were instrumental in spatial shifts in the foreign policies of both the US and China. Both countries have realigned their geographic priorities in response to developments in Afghanistan—the US from the Middle East to East Asia, and China from East Asia to the Middle East. The spatiality of US–China relations evident in their respective Afghanistan policies also demonstrates that contemporary regionalisms are still geographically grounded. Afghanistan is included in South Asia, the Middle East, Asia Pacific, and Indo-Pacific regions at different times depending on the political security needs of the time and policyholder.

US and China in Afghanistan

While both China and the US found themselves involved in Afghanistan's internal and regional affairs in the Cold War years, China has a longer history with Afghanistan for being a regional power. Historically, Afghanistan has always been a security issue for China. During the imperial period, the kingdom of Afghanistan did not welcome China's expansion of its borders toward Central Asia, but there was no conflict of interests for a long time once the borders were finalized after the revolution thanks to China's main diplomatic strategy, Third-Worldism. Even the Sino-Soviet split did not particularly harm the relations between China and Afghanistan that was close to the Soviet Union.

As for the US, after securing the European and Asian boundaries of the West Camp in the early Cold War years, it shifted its focus to the Middle East due to military and energy security issues. Afghanistan was still considered a South Asian country at that point. The spilling over of the internal clashes within Afghanistan to the Middle East would happen only after the dissolution of the Cold War security boundaries across regions. That being said, the Soviet–Afghanistan War that erupted in 1979 was still regarded by the US as a potential threat to its interests in the Persian Gulf region and therefore worthy of intervention. In the meantime, after the initial proxy wars and quasi-conflicts of the 1950s and 1960s, the Cold War came to a stalemate with the protracted Vietnam War in the 1970s. The US decided to tip the power balance by re-establishing diplomatic relations with China. China was open to the idea after long economic isolation following the Sino-Soviet split. This eventually led to a relatively long-term collaboration over Soviet-occupied Afghanistan.

Continuity in the post-Cold War era

While the sudden end of the Cold War constituted a major rupture in global politics, the Sino-US relationship demonstrated continuity from the late Cold War years as the rise of China was yet to constitute a threat to the US global hegemony. The events of 9/11 further converged their national interests against international terrorism. The US invasion of Afghanistan took place after 9/11, and China, like other countries in the region, established relations with the new Afghanistan government supported by the US to take measures against international terrorism. The Shanghai Cooperation Organization, previously called the Shanghai Five, was also established at that time. In the 2000s, China tried to support the stabilization of the country by providing economic assistance to the Afghanistan government. This shows that China's promise of economic support to the Taliban today is a continuation of its main foreign policy principle of prioritizing business relations.

China continued to be involved in Afghanistan economically through the US occupation. In the second half of the 2010s, however, it increased its military-political presence in the country by sending peacekeepers. The reason for this policy change was that the Taliban had increased their attacks against Chinese nationals in retaliation for the Chinese government's tacit approval of the US-backed government in Afghanistan. The safety of Chinese nationals and investments in destination countries has always been a priority for China, but the increasing attacks in Afghanistan (as well as Pakistan) was particularly troubling because these attacks took place at a time when China launched the Belt and Road Initiative (BRI) and made significant investments in the China–Pakistan Economic Corridor. In other instances, China is known to pause its investments and withdraw its nationals from unsafe environments but, in Afghanistan and Pakistan, China collaborates with international peacekeeping operations because the predicament in the region was directly related to the border security of Xinjiang.

The emergence of change

Sino-US relations took a sour turn when the Obama administration identified the "rise of China" as the primary threat to the US global hegemony and launched the Asia Pivot policy in 2011 to reinstate the US as the hegemonic leader of the Asia-Pacific region (Birgbauer 2022). While the US attempted to reinvigorate its relations with the Asia-Pacific allies with initiatives such as Trans-Pacific Partnership and Indo-Pacific regionalism, China responded with both regional and transregional initiatives. The regional initiatives such as the Regional Comprehensive Economic Partnership were to rebuke the US containment strategies in China's own region. The policies with transregional scope such as the BRI aimed to fill in the void created by the US shifting its gaze away from such regions as the Middle East and Africa. The BRI symbolizes both a continuity and change in China's traditional foreign policy principles. It is a continuity for being a primarily economic foreign policy. Yet, it is a proactive, assertive policy program that carries China significantly farther away from its traditional regional sphere of influence.

The US decision to withdraw from Afghanistan, announced first in 2010 and once delayed to 2016, was also a part of the Asia Pivot to reallocate resources in preparation for a perceived upcoming conflict with China in the Asia-Pacific. As a result, China's response was to develop a more assertive Middle East policy. The New Neighborhood Policy announced concurrently with the BRI was the security leg of the economically oriented BRI (Zhang 2022). China began to have even more extensive economic engagement with the Gulf countries, Egypt, Israel, and Iran. Besides, it was more actively involved in regional political and military conflicts such as the Syrian civil war and the Arab–Israeli conflict (Lo and Zhao 2022). One reason why China has become more involved in the Middle East is to fill the vacuum left by the US. The other reason is that the international terrorism threats have spilled over from Afghanistan to the Middle East over the last decades. The evidence that there were Uyghur volunteers participating in the Syrian civil war urges China to reconceptualize the region by merging Afghanistan and the Middle East in its regional policies (Duchatel 2019).

In August 2021, the US finally announced the withdrawal of its troops from Afghanistan after a decade-long delay. Contra the delay in the decision to withdrawal, the actual process was fast, and therefore it left a power vacuum behind. The Taliban immediately claimed power over the rival political factions and took over the government in Kabul. While the Western powers protested the Taliban takeover of the Kabul government, China immediately established contact with the new de facto rulers of Afghanistan to secure a promise from Taliban that they would not intervene in China's domestic affairs in Xinjiang (Johnson 2021). Therefore, the actual withdrawal seems to constitute a critical juncture for not only the US as it intends to shift the focus to its Indo-Pacific strategy but also China as it sways away from its traditional foreign policy principles by meeting a yet-to-be officially recognized government (that is, the Taliban).

More specifically, while the US is planning to re-establish dominance in the Pacific region with its withdrawal from Afghanistan, China is trying to take pre-emptive measure against the aftershocks of the power vacuum created by the US withdrawal. US President Biden expressed that one of the key reasons for the rapid withdrawal from Afghanistan was to focus solely on China as a hegemonic challenger (Green and Scheinmann 2021). In this sense, the US policy toward China since Obama is consistent even when its relations with China seem to have particularly deteriorated during the Trump era. In fact, China's expectation that President Biden would end Trump's trade war with China did not turn out to be true, and Biden has taken an attitude that directly targets China from the moment he formed his government (Regilme 2023). We have witnessed the mutually aggressive rhetoric of China and the US on issues such as the trade wars, Xinjiang, the climate agenda, and most recently, the launching of the Build Back Better World (B3W) to counter the rising Chinese influences in the Global South. Details of the B3W have not yet been disclosed at the time of writing, but unlike the BRI, it is expected to focus on financial development assistance, not infrastructure. By doing so, the B3W would not compete with the BRI directly, but would offer financial aid to the countries allegedly debt-trapped by the BRI (Carrai and Yee 2022).

As for China, it has tried to seize the opportunity to present the rapid US withdrawal from Afghanistan and its failure to take any action to protect the people and staff of the Kabul government against the Taliban forces as another blow to the international legitimacy of the US, which has dwindled since the Trump era. The perceived decline of the US legitimacy, in Asia in particular, also puts the US allies in a difficult position. For example, India, despite all the efforts of the US, has been excluded from the negotiations for the future of Afghanistan with the cooperation of Pakistan, China, and Russia (Tiezzi 2021). US Vice President Harris even had to go to Vietnam and Singapore to reassure the US allies in Asia that what happened to Afghanistan would not happen to them (Rubin 2021).

Overall, the motivations of China's actions in the wake of the US withdrawal are consistent with its traditional foreign policy orientation of protecting its national security, both in terms of borders and public safety, as well as economic interests. However, the way China's actions are executed constitutes a major shift from its traditional foreign policy approach because China is now communicating with political actors (that is, the Taliban) other than the officially recognized government. The uncertainty about the political future of Afghanistan forces China to compromise its non-intervention policy.

Conclusion

While the US and China have been following a path of power politics and interventionism and a path of anti-imperialism and non-intervention, respectively, in terms of their policies toward the Middle East, there seems to be a "critical juncture" emerging as a result of the US withdrawal from Afghanistan. Back in the Cold War era, during the USSR occupation and US intervention in Afghanistan, China maintained its relations with the local political actors over there, albeit at a distance, in order to balance the power of these two rival superpowers in the region. After 9/11, the concern that international terrorism would affect the Xinjiang region pushed China to cooperate with the US and continue to be relatively less assertive. Today, it announces openly and publicly that it would diplomatically recognize any actor that will fully seize power, including the Taliban, as stabilizing Afghanistan is its top priority. The Taliban, on the other hand, has already declared China the main ally of the newly formed government. The possibility of China recognizing the Taliban as a legitimate political actor means that China's foreign policy toward the Middle East diverges from that of the US on yet another issue (Kaura 2022).

However, whether this development will lead to a significant hegemonic competition between the US and China in the Middle East remains to be seen. The multiple factions within the Taliban increase the likelihood of a civil war in Afghanistan even if the de facto Taliban government is officially recognized by China and the international society in general. Therefore, China's primary concern regarding Afghanistan is more about the former's national security in general and the safety of its nationals on the ground in particular, as opposed to challenging the US hegemonic position in the Middle East (Calabrese 2021). China is in a position to provide the infrastructure to connect Afghanistan by land and sea to international trade routes, and this could enable the long-term extraction of Afghanistan's underground resources by China. However, even if China decides to provide financial support to the Taliban government, the safety of Chinese diplomats and engineers must be guaranteed before infrastructure and energy investments can begin. The Taliban formally extends the guarantee for the safety of Chinese nationals but the factional fights within the Taliban prevent the government members to control fully the organization members. As a result, there was already a suicide attack against Chinese nationals in Afghanistan after the Taliban government's commitment to their safety (Jalil 2022).

China has yet to comment on when and under what conditions it will officially recognize the Taliban government. On the other hand, the Chinese Ministry of Foreign Affairs, on the day the cabinet was announced, guaranteed that it would provide more than US$30 million in health and food aid to Afghanistan. These two foreign policy actions confirm that China's ultimate goal is not to support the Taliban or replace the US as the regional hegemon, but to prevent the political and economic collapse of Afghanistan next to its borders. To conclude, Afghanistan remains a volatile locus for both China and the US. Therefore, while the US might become a little bit less interventionist in the Middle East as it shifts its major focus to the Indo-Pacific and China might become a little bit more interventionist as it tries to deal with the aftershocks of the power vacuum left by the US withdrawal from Afghanistan, the two countries still cannot afford a complete change of their "paths" in terms of their policies toward the Middle East. After all, the US has no interest in giving up its hegemonic position in the Middle East, and China still cares about its non-interventionist reputation over there. As a result, while the tension between the US and China in the Middle East might increase, whether there will be a significant hegemonic competition between the two in the region remains to be seen.

It is worth noting that, since the Taliban's takeover of Afghanistan in 2021, regional and global dynamics have changed further due to the Ukraine War. The redefinition of regional security alliances, interruptions to global supply chains, and, consequently, the reconsideration of regional investments by major economic powers have all occurred. International organizations are also struggling to maintain their normative order in such a tumultuous international environment. China and the US are going through a series of confrontations, but none have resulted in a total breakdown between these two superpowers, as there are eminent global issues that require the collective action of major international actors. The political and economic volatility in Afghanistan is potentially one of these issues that will test the US–China rivalry.

Note

[1] The part about China's policy toward the Middle East is adapted from the following article: Chen, Chien-Kai. 2021. "China in the Middle East: an Analysis from a Theoretical Perspective of 'Path Dependence'." *East Asia: An International Quarterly* 38(2): 105–121. We thank its publisher (Springer) for the permission to reuse the article.

References

Asian Society. 1997. "Speech by President Jiang Zemin of the People's Republic of China." October 30. https://asiasociety.org/speech-president-jiang-zemin-peoples-republic-china

BBC News. 2018. "Xi Jinping Says China Will Not Seek to Dominate." December 18. https://www.bbc.com/news/world-asia-china-46601175

Beijing Review. 2009. "Hu: China Would Never Seek Hegemony." April 21. http://www.bjreview.com/quotes/txt/2009-04/23/content_192517.htm

Birgbauer, P. 2022. "The US Pivot to Asia Was Dead on Arrival." *The Diplomat*. https://thediplomat.com/2022/03/the-us-pivot-to-asia-was-dead-on-arrival/

Calabrese, J. 2021. "China's Taliban Conundrum." *Middle East Institute*. https://www.mei.edu/publications/chinas-taliban-conundrum

Carrai, M.A. and Yee, W.Y. 2022. "B3W Might Not Be Able to Compete With BRI in Southeast Asia, But That's Okay." *The Diplomat*. https://thediplomat.com/2022/02/b3w-might-not-be-able-to-compete-with-bri-in-southeast-asia-but-thats-okay/

Chen, Y. 2012. "China's Relationship with Israel, Opportunities and Challenges, Perspectives from China." *Israel Studies* 17(3): 1–21.

Clarke, R. 2017. "Five Inauguration Days." *Middle East Journal* 71(1): 147–154.

Conduit, D. and Akbarzadeh, S. 2019. "Great Power-Middle Power Dynamics: The Case of China and Iran." *Journal of Contemporary China* 28(117): 468–481.

Duchatel, M. 2019. "China's Foreign Fighters Problem." *War on the Rocks*. https://warontherocks.com/2019/01/chinas-foreign-fighters-problem/

Ehteshami, A., Horesh, N. and Xu, R. 2018. "Chinese-Iranian Mutual Strategic Perceptions." *The China Journal* 79: 1–20.

Foreign Policy Association. 1988. "US and the Middle East: Dangerous Drift?" *Great Decisions '88*: 49–61.

Fuller, G. 1990. "The Middle East in US-Soviet Relations." *Middle East Journal* 44(3): 417–430.

Gendzier, I. 2002. "Invisible by Design: US Policy in the Middle East." *Diplomatic History* 26(4): 593–618.

Green, M. and Scheinmann, G. 2021. "How Biden Can Save His China Strategy After Afghanistan." *Foreign Policy*. https://foreignpolicy.com/2021/08/25/afghanistan-withdrawal-china-geopolitics-biden/

Greener, I. 2005. "The Potential of Path Dependence in Political Studies." *Politics* 25(1): 62–72.

Gutfeld, A. and Zumbrunnen, C. 2013. "From Nickel Grass to Desert Storm: The Transformation of US Intervention Capabilities in the Middle East." *Middle Eastern Studies* 49(4): 623–644.

Hubbell, S. 1998. "The Containment Myth: US Middle East Policy in Theory and Practice." *Middle East Report* 208: 8–11.

Ibrahim, A. 2019. "Muslim Leaders Are Betraying the Uighurs." *Foreign Policy*, July 8. https://foreignpolicy.com/2019/07/08/muslim-leaders-are-betraying-the-uighurs

Jalil, Z.A. 2022. "Pakistan Attack: China Condemns Killing of Tutors in Pakistan Blast." *BBC News*, April 27. https://www.bbc.com/news/world-asia-61225678

Johnson, I. 2021. "How Will China Deal With the Taliban?" *Council on Foreign Relations*. https://www.cfr.org/in-brief/china-afghanistan-deal-with-taliban

Kaura, V. 2022. "China Draws Closer to the Taliban as Regional Foreign Ministers Prepare to Meet in Beijing." *Middle East Institute*. https://www.mei.edu/publications/china-draws-closer-taliban-regional-foreign-ministers-prepare-meet-beijing

Khalili, J. 1970. "Communist China and the United Arab Republic." *Asian Survey* 10(4): 308–319.

Kuniholm, B. 1987. "Retrospect and Prospects: Forty Years of US Middle East Policy." *Middle East Journal* 41(1): 7–25.

Lai, H.H. 2007. "China's Oil Diplomacy: Is It a Global Security Threat?" *Third World Quarterly* 28(3): 519–537.

Leithner, A. and Libby, K. 2017. "Path Dependency in Foreign Policy." *Oxford Research Encyclopedia of Politics*, July 27, pp 1–28. https://oxfordre.com/politics/view/10.1093/acrefore/9780190228637.001.0001/acrefore-9780190228637-e-376

Lo, K. and Zhao, B. 2022. "China's Meetings with Middle East Ministers Sets the Scene for Beijing to Step Up in Region." *South China Morning Post*, January 12. https://www.scmp.com/news/china/diplomacy/article/3163143/chinas-meetings-middle-east-ministers-sets-scene-beijing-step

Marx, J. 2010. "Path Dependency and Change in International Relations: Institutional Dynamics in the Field of Intellectual Property Rights." *Historical Social Research* 35(3): 175–199.

Ministry of External Affairs, India. 1954. "Agreement on Trade and Intercourse with Tibet Region." April 29. https://www.mea.gov.in/bilateral-documents.htm?dtl/7807/Agreement+on+Trade+and+Intercourse+with+Tibet+Region

Ministry of Foreign Affairs, China. 2000a. "zhongguo changdao hepinggongchu wuxiang yuanze" [China Advocating the Five Principles of Peaceful Coexistence], November 7. https://www.fmprc.gov.cn/web/ziliao_674904/wjs_674919/2159_674923/t8987.shtml

Ministry of Foreign Affairs, China. 2000b. "zai hepinggongchu wuxiang yuanze de jichushang jianli guoji xinzhixu" [Building a New International Order on the Basis of the Five Principles of Peaceful Coexistence], November 7. https://www.fmprc.gov.cn/web/ziliao_674904/wjs_674919/2159_674923/t8981.shtml

Ministry of Foreign Affairs, China. 2016. "China's Arab Policy Paper." January 13. http://www.china.org.cn/world/2016-01/14/content_37573547.htm

Mohamedi, F. and Sadowski, Y. 2001. "The Decline (But Not Fall) of US Hegemony in the Middle East." *Middle East Report* 220: 12–22.

Mohan, G. and Power, M. 2008. "New African Choices? The Politics of Chinese Engagement." *Review of African Political Economy* 35(115): 23–42.

Office of the Historian, Department of State, US. nd. "Bandung Conference (Asian-African Conference), 1955." https://history.state.gov/milestones/1953-1960/bandung-conf

Regilme, S.S.F. 2023. "United States Foreign Aid and Multilateralism Under the Trump Presidency." *New Global Studies* 17(1): 45–69.

Roberts, S. 2020. *The War on the Uyghurs: China's Internal Campaign against a Muslim Minority*. Princeton: Princeton University Press.

Rosenthal, S. 2010. "The US Foreign Policy and the Middle East." *Policy Perspectives* 7(1): 11–14.

Rubin, J. 2021. "Why Kamala Harris's Trip to Asia was so Important." *The Washington Post*, August 31. https://www.washingtonpost.com/opinions/2021/08/31/why-kamala-harriss-trip-asia-was-so-important/

Shichor, Y. 2013. "Fundamentally Unacceptable yet Occasionally Unavoidable: China's Options on External Interference in the Middle East." *China Report* 49(1): 25–41.

Shichor, Y. 2017. "Maximising Output while Minimising Input: Change and Continuity in China's Middle East Policy." In H.T. Boon (ed) *Chinese Foreign Policy Under Xi*. New York: Routledge, pp 109–129.

Sjoberg, L. 2008. "Scaling IR Theory: Geography's Contribution to Where IR Takes Place." *International Studies Review* 10(3): 472–500.

State Council, China. 2019. "China and the World in the New Era." September 27. http://english.www.gov.cn/archive/whitepaper/201909/27/content_WS5d8d80f9c6d0bcf8c4c142ef.html

Sun, D. and Zoubir, Y. 2018. "China's Participation in Conflict Resolution in the Middle East and North Africa: A Case of Quasi-Meditation Diplomacy?" *Journal of Contemporary China* 27(110): 224–243.

Tiezzi, S. 2021. "China Snubs India, Backs Pakistan in Dueling Afghanistan Meetings." *The Diplomat*. https://thediplomat.com/2021/11/china-snubs-india-backs-pakistan-in-dueling-afghanistan-meetings/

Totten, M. 2013. "No Exit: Why the US Can't Leave the Middle East?" *World Affairs* 176(4): 8–14.

Wehrey, F., Kaye, D.D., Watkins, J., Martini, J. and Guffey, R. 2010. *The Iraq Effect: The Middle East After the Iraq War*. Santa Monica, CA: RAND Corporation.

Westcott, B. and Xiong, Y. 2018. "China Legalizes Xinjiang 'Re-education Camps' After Denying They Exist." *CNN*, October 11. https://www.cnn.com/2018/10/10/asia/xinjiang-china-reeducation-camps-intl/index.html

Wu, G. nd. "deng xiaoping chuxi lianheguo tebiehuiyi de taiqian muhou" [Backstage Stories about Deng's Attending the UN Special Meeting]. *News of the Communist Party of China*. http://cpc.people.com.cn/BIG5/85037/8534293.html

Zhang, F. 2022. "China's New Engagement with Afghanistan after the Withdrawal." *LSE Public Policy Review* 2(3): 1–13.

9

Arctic Interests: How China Is Challenging the US

Cameron Carlson and Linda Kiltz

Introduction

Over the past decade, the People's Republic of China (PRC) has continued to rise as a great power on global politics and to challenge the interests of the US. While security competition is not new to US–China relations, its nature is changing and evolving in a new direction with past differences becoming more acute, and new areas are emerging, such as the Arctic region, that are intensifying this security dilemma (Allison 2017; Medeiros 2019; Mearsheimer 2021). The rapidly changing climate of the Arctic has given rise to China's emergence as major influence within the region. Scholars have discussed the geopolitical ramifications of Arctic ice melt and accelerated prospects of an ice-free Arctic (Depledge 2021; Briggs 2013; Depledge 2021). As a rising global superpower, China has amassed incredible diplomatic, informational, military, and economic capabilities to influence and reshape the Arctic region (Briggs 2013; Connolly 2017). China was granted status as an observer to the Arctic Council in 2013, providing it a seat at the table with a new-found voice and ability to engage within the region. This engagement, primarily through economic and diplomatic means, has for many raised serious concerns regarding its long-term intentions considering its heavy-handed practices in other regions of the world (Miller 2019; Vitug 2018; Garlick 2019). China's efforts within the region are considered a threat to long-term regional stability, impacting the human, environmental, and national security objectives for several members of the Arctic Council, including the US, Canada, and Sweden (Cassotta et al 2015; Lackenbauer et al 2018; Doshi et al 2021). With regional resource, access, and longer-term interests at stake, Chinese investment and diplomatic overtures within the Arctic serve as a point of regional friction prompting numerous countries to take notice and address the competitive challenges posed by this evolving rivalry (Connolly 2017; Depledge 2021). While there have been many studies on the influence of China in the Arctic region, there has been little research on how abrupt climate change in combination with Chinese actions in the region could create unpredictable black swan events that undermine US and regional security (Zysk and Titley 2015; Valentine et al 2021). The Arctic can provide a useful illustration of how foresight of environmental conditions and knowledge of nonlinear effects of abrupt climate change can contribute to a better understanding of potential environmental, economic, social, and cultural impacts of Chinese actions and policies in the region.

Geography provides an ideal backdrop in which to view potential outcomes for international discourse for China within the Arctic. Arctic Council members, like the US, are legitimate Arctic actors, with a geographical presence, history, and long-standing relationships strategic interests to be safeguarded (Barry et al 2020; Rottem 2020). The Arctic has traditionally been governed by an eight-nation governing body called the Arctic Council. Those eight Arctic states—Sweden, Denmark, Finland, Norway, Iceland, Canada, Russia, and the US—each have sovereignty over the lands within the Arctic Circle and have had the sole deciding power over policies that govern the polar region located at the northernmost part of Earth (Abdulmuminov 2021). For China, which has declared itself as a "Near-Arctic State," though it is geographically separated from the region by nearly a thousand miles and has a limited history, the story is far different (Depledge 2021).

China sees the Arctic as a new strategic frontier with its seabed and space labeled as ungoverned or under-governed public spaces (Doshi et al 2021). Further, Chinese military texts note that "the great powers' will increasingly focus on the struggle over and control of "global public spaces" like the Arctic (Doshi et al 2021). While the Arctic Council does not address topics specific to security, a gap already exists for the PRC's exploitation with numerous other countries, including the US, similarly behind in addressing the increasing level of competition and impacts to the Arctic ecosystem.

With the invasion of Ukraine by Russia in early 2022, however, two areas of consideration may prove noteworthy in terms of the inner workings of the Arctic Council and the potential extended reach of the PRC within the region. In reaction to Russia's invasion of Ukraine, member nations of the Arctic Council, including the US, Canada, Finland, Iceland, Denmark, Norway, and Sweden, announced a suspension in their participation in the Arctic Council soon after the invasion took place (Arctic Portal 2022). While the longer-term implications are not fully understood, the invasion prompted both Finland and Norway to announce their intent to join NATO, a move which would leave Russia as the only non-NATO nation in the Arctic

(Northam 2022). The challenge for the PRC will be found in its ability to straddle both sides of the road simultaneously. While its relationship with Russia is important to access and energy, it will need to be calculated in its efforts to remain on good terms with Arctic countries while it works toward realizing its goals of creating a Polar Silk Road (Greenwood and Luo 2022).

As such, a primary purpose of this chapter is to describe the context of geography for the Arctic and how China has successfully leveraged economic, scientific, and diplomatic capabilities to gain access and legitimacy regionally. As Chinese engagement increases within the short term, their longer-term prospects set the stage for a black swan event to occur within the Arctic region. This would serve to radically alter the region, affecting the national, human, and environmental security dynamics for all the Arctic Council and its stakeholders. This chapter will first discuss the geographical context of the Arctic. Next, there will be an analysis of China's Arctic objectives using black swan and weak signal theories as well as the methodology of horizon scanning technique. Finally, there is a conclusion highlighting possible scenarios of the PRC's impact on the Arctic in the future. We conclude in the future that the Arctic will see an increase in Chinese activity to support their national and military strategic goals which will result in greater conflict with the US and other members of the Arctic Council; this activity could also lead to unpredictable black swan events as a result of the cascading effects of climate change on fragile Arctic ecosystems in combination with growing exploitation of resources and environmental degradation by Chinese economic and military activities in the region.

The geographical context of the Arctic (and *near* Arctic)

The Arctic as a polar region is perhaps best characterized by its cold temperatures resulting from the lack of solar radiation it receives as the northernmost region of the world. While solar radiation exposure during the winter months is almost nonexistent, during the summer it receives constant exposure, with much of the solar exposure being reflected into space by a near continuous cloud cover as well as the snow and ice which blankets both water and land surfaces (Murray et al 1998; Yu and Leng 2022). The *albedo* effect provided by this reflection of the solar radiation has served to be one of the most important cooling mechanisms for the planet and has historically served to keep the region relatively stable in terms of its temperatures (He et al 2019; Yu and Leng 2022). The land formations surrounding the Arctic, subdivided for the purpose of this chapter, include Europe (Norway, Sweden, Iceland, and Finland), Asia (Russia) and North America (US, Canada, and Greenland [Denmark] due to Greenland's proximity to the Canadian Archipelago). These three Arctics differ from one

Figure 9.1: Map of the three Arctics

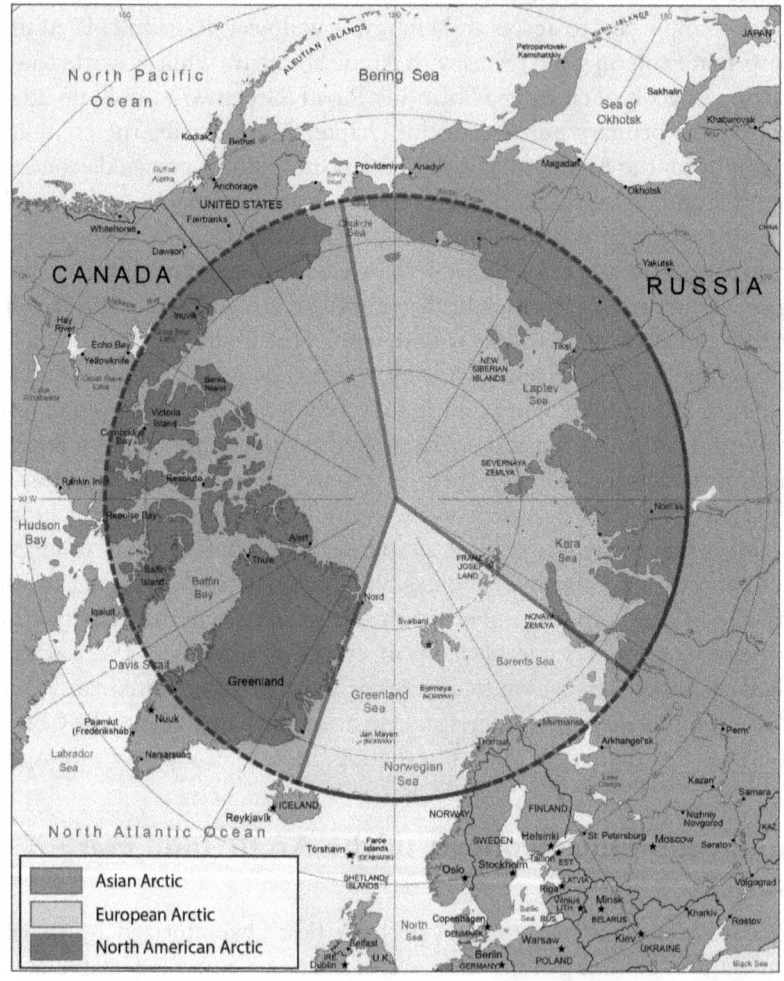

Source: Center for Arctic Security and Resilience, University of Alaska Fairbanks

another in numerous ways based upon factors to include terrain, climate, infrastructure, and population (Bader et al 2014; see Figure 9.1).

Environmental changes in the Arctic

The Arctic has undergone unprecedented change, as both the climate and geopolitical related circumstances have begun to shift interconnectedly at an ever-increasing pace (Djalante 2019; Depledge 2021). The most critical phenomenon that has occurred is Arctic amplification, where enhanced warming in the Arctic is twice or three times as fast as the rest of the planet due to the decreasing amount of sea ice extent and volume (Peng et al 2018; NSIDC 2020; Horvath et al 2021).

Other Arctic climate trends include rising river flows, declining snow cover, increasing precipitation, diminishing lake and river ice, melting glaciers, changes in ocean salinity, and thawing permafrost (Malcolm et al 2013). As the permafrost thaws, methane is released, adding to the total greenhouse gas emissions. Further, climatologists are predicting an estimated 2.5 million square miles of permafrost—40 percent of the world's total—could disappear by the end of the century, with enormous consequences (Struzik 2020). Permafrost thaw is a pervasive threat that impacts the wellbeing of Arctic communities, ecosystems, and economies as well as the health of the planet by releasing methane gas, damaging critical infrastructure, causing erosion and unprecedented flooding, and displacing communities (Melvin et al 2017; Bykova 2020). Despite these environmental challenges, China views the Arctic as a region of critical strategic importance because of its abundant resources and strategic location.

China's Arctic objectives

The Arctic region is in a state of change unlike any other time in its history because of climate change and the increased access and opportunity it has subsequently provided. The interests of both traditional and non-traditional Arctic actors such as China closely converge and diverge with the opening of the region and the long-term potential it provides. Such circumstances challenge many of the established norms for the region, and those between the US and China—which has declared itself a "Near-Arctic State" (State Council of the PRC 2018: 3). China's ascent to become a major influence in the Arctic has been fueled by the region's rapidly changing environment. As a developing global superpower, China has effectively cultivated immense diplomatic, informational, military, and economic tools of national power to pursue influence throughout the region. In 2013, China was awarded observer status to the Arctic Council, giving it key access to the top international forum for the region. Beyond this access, China signaled more than just a benign interest in the region, when in 2014, Xi Jinping, China's president, asserted that China was to become a "Great Polar Power" (Brady 2017). The stability of the Arctic region is increasingly being called into question because of a shift in the balance of power affecting alliances and international security dynamics (DDIS 2020). A Danish Defense Intelligence Service (DDIS) report noted that while the COVID-19 pandemic has made the shift more apparent, both China and Russia have become more assertive in their efforts to pursue interests in the Arctic (DDIS 2020). As the Arctic continues to transform as a result of changes to the climate, increased access facilitates growing influence and potential for China, where natural resources, shipping, and strategic military interests are at stake in its quest to surpass the US as a global superpower.

China's regional engagement, which has mostly been conducted through economic, diplomatic, and scientific means, has prompted serious concerns over the country's long-term intentions, given its practices in other parts of the world (Zysk and Titley 2015; Depledge 2021). As we face more abrupt climate change, we will likely see significant changes in commodity and energy prices, global maritime and transportation infrastructure, and environmental and governance policies (Valentine et al 2021). These changes will force governments to form new policies toward the Arctic region, as we have seen with China's 2018 White Paper that outlines its Arctic policy and plans to develop a Polar Silk Road (Lim 2018; Mariia 2019). Given these drastic changes, the Arctic has a higher potential for a black swan event (Zysk and Titley, 2015).

The black swan of the Arctic

A black swan event is described as unpredictable and highly improbable, with an impact that is extreme in nature (Taleb 2010). The three attributes of a black swan event include it being an outlier and beyond what would be expected; that its impact would be extreme; and, finally, that occurrence of the event—despite it being an outlier, its explanation would be accounted for *after* the fact (Taleb 2010). A black swan event within the Arctic has previously been a topic examined by others. The record low ice extents for both the Arctic and Antarctic in 2016 caused Scott (2016) to ask if "Black Swans are flocking to both poles?" Others have noted the potential of an Arctic black swan in relation to different causes and effects. Pincus (2015) questions our collective ability to adequately respond to a disaster within the Arctic, noting that it is a wicked problem which could lead to a black swan scenario. A black swan in the form of an environmental disaster in the Arctic is likewise predicted by Andreassen and Borch(2020). Shedov (2021) asserts the idea that China is a black swan in Arctic waters with it having become a great power within the region. In providing a narrative covering China's need for Arctic access and resources, he details their use of "soft power" to successfully insert itself into the midst of almost every Arctic Council country and transition from a minor to a major regional player within a ten-year period. Identification of early warning signs indicating that some type of "black swan" event is likely to occur in the future, and proactively managing the knowledge gained from these indicators, can help to lessen the drastic consequences of these events (Ansoff 1975; Hajikazemi et al 2016).

There is not a consensus among researchers on the level of predictability of a black swan event. Taleb (2010) believes that black swan events are unpredictable and highly improbable events which are inevitable in our world. In general, there are two types of perspectives toward black swan events. They are either managed through prediction or through dealing with their circumstances (Hajikazemi et al 2016). In the following sections we will shed light on another view of predicting black swan events by applying the early warning procedure called weak signal theory.

Analysis: weak signal theory

In the 1970s, research on the perception of early signals, also known as weak signals, began in the field of strategic planning (Ansoff 1975; Hajikazemi et al 2016). Weak signal theory is a concept in which, by perceiving and evaluating information that may be unusual or perhaps considered insignificant in the near term, may indicate a trend or significant change in the longer-term environment (Griol-Barres et al 2020). A weak signal itself is that indicator, which once perceived serves as evidence to discern subtle changes which will have a future impact on a given environment (Dufva 2020). Ansoff (1975) is a noted pioneer for his work on weak signal theory; he defined it as a concept and showed how the collection, interpretation and use of weak signals can be used to avoid "Strategic Surprises" and the ensuing strategic discontinuity. Nikander (2002) shows how weak signals theory can support numerous applications to military science, future studies, international security, and risk management. Heinonen et al (2017) apply the use of weak signals to identify future black swan events and discontinuity in relation to future studies. Their work integrates the use of weak signals to better discern the underlying processes which might give rise to discontinuity and black swans given the increasing complexity associated with our current environment (Heinonen et al 2017).

Strong signals likewise serve a function in the use of weak signal theory. A strong signal can be defined as evidence of change, such as reliable data or a concrete fact, or the aggregation and linkage of multiple weak signals (Boutout and Wahabi 2020). While weak signals are vulnerable to rejection and can prove to be more ambiguous and incomplete, strong signals are evident in their significance, and can consequently signal impending change or that change has already taken place (Boutout and Wahabi 2020).

While weak signal theory and its use became a more common approach within the field of strategic planning as a tool to prevent strategic surprise, it is not without criticism. As research has continued to focus on weak signals, numerous disciplines have conducted further research into the concept, and have done so in a siloed manner, fragmenting the terminology and concept itself. Van Veen and Ortt (2021) note that weak signal detection can be highly dependent upon the experience of the individual and their background. Further, some futurists and strategists note a limitation of weak signals to be the instrument used to probe the future; for example, "a scanning system meant to seek for financial weak signals will not detect political upheaval" (Boutout and Wahabi 2020: 127). A tool that can be used to identify and analyze possible weak signals is horizon scanning.

Horizon scanning as a tool for analysis

This chapter will utilize the horizon scanning technique in which to assess the PRC's potential future impact to the Arctic region. The use and practical application of horizon scanning has been reviewed by others (Schultz 2006; Bengston 2013; National Academies of Sciences, Engineering, and Medicine 2020) and validated by Habegger (2009) as a strategic tool that methodically accumulates a wide range of information regarding emerging challenges and trends in an organization's geopolitical, socioeconomic, social, technical, or environment. Utilizing country-specific case studies Habegger (2009) highlights the value and utility in the use of horizon scanning to obtain strategic insights to deal with an uncertain and complex future.

Our analysis uses a qualitative weight of evidence framework (Linkov et al 2009) to establish an organized process for filtering information from multiple sources to analyze evidence and locate weak signals of change. This framework provides the ability to better connect emerging insights as future challenges and extrapolate future risks and possibilities (Garnett et al 2016; see Figure 9.2).

The first step (Tier 1) in conducting this horizon scan is the selection of observation criteria which will serve as the evidence used to perceive emerging issues of significance (weak signals). The criteria used include observations in the form of:

1. Information, actions/activities in relation to PRC interest and access to the Arctic region. This information will be drawn from the PRC, US, Arctic Council members, and associated communications. The output of this step is a list of resources as documents which will support the second step.
2. The second step (Tier 2) involves an assessment of the information provided as an output from step one. Professional judgment will be performed to evaluate the strength of the evidence (information and actions/activities) with a short narrative of analysis to accompany the select output evaluated. The output of step two is a series of short narratives.
3. The third step (Tier 3) serves as the final stage where the evaluation of the step two products summarizes the potential likelihood and importance of future events. Step two narratives serve as the basis for this evaluation as the final output from the horizon scan.

The next section of the chapter will provide a discussion of the analysis that was conducted on these articles.

Figure 9.2: Weight of Evidence Framework to evaluate evidence from horizon scanning

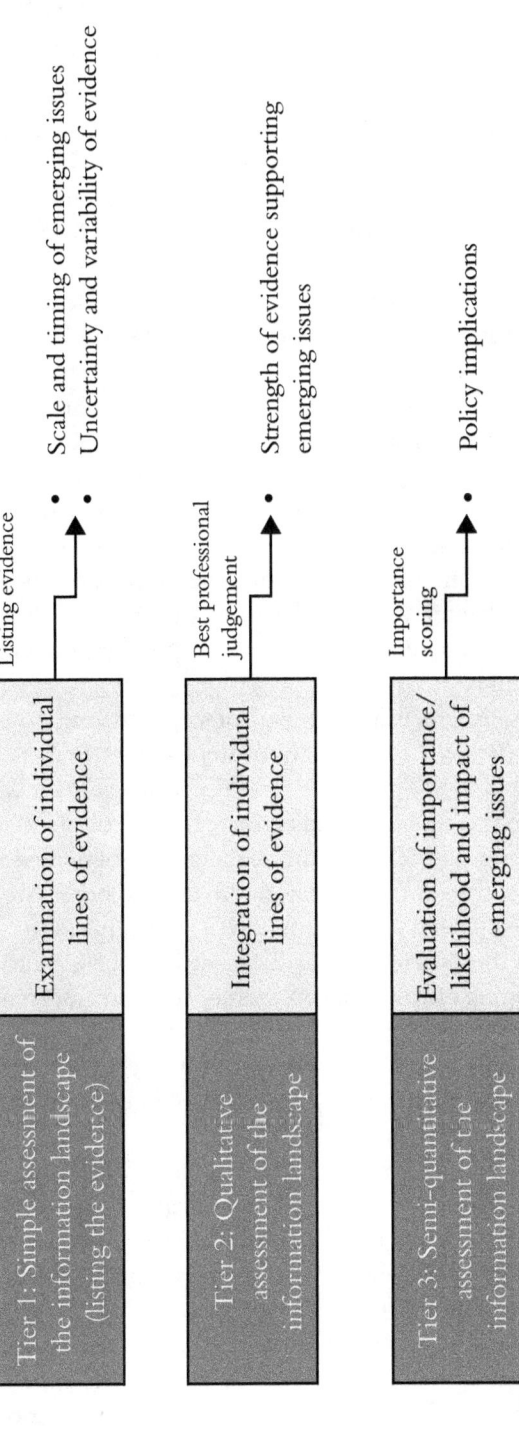

Source: Reprinted with permission from Springer Nature: *China in the Middle East: An Analysis from a Theoretical Perspective of "Path Dependence"* by Chien-Kai Chen © 2020

Discussion: analysis of the drivers for Arctic interest by the Chinese

This chapter is a synthesis of our research that pairs the narrative, perspective-driven reading of a broad range of literature with a structured meta-analysis focusing on peer-reviewed publications (Mosteller and Colditz 1996). Meta-analysis is a method of research synthesis that is useful for identifying and summarizing key actionable issues and evidence, whether weak or strong, from a body of literature (Mosteller and Colditz 1996; Cooper et al 2009). A strength of meta-analysis is that it enables researchers to explore answers to questions that are not or cannot be easily addressed by individual studies or a single discipline (Mosteller and Colditz 1996).

A total of 101 documents representing interdisciplinary scholarship were selected for screening as part of the first step. The documents selected were collected via Google Search and Google Scholar. We excluded results not related to the Arctic, conference papers, commentaries, newspapers, professional journals, and editorials in peer-reviewed journals. We selected articles based on our research questions, their timeliness and relevancy to the themes of the chapter. Many of the articles were from scholars representing the various Arctic states (Canada, Finland, Norway, Greenland), as well as scholars in China.

In screening the documents as part of step 2, declarations such as "great polar power" (Brady 2017) and "near-arctic-state" (Francis 2020) serve as a defined signal as to the intent for the PRC's engagement within the Arctic region. While the PRC has had an increasing level of engagement within the region for the past 30 years, the deliberate use of these descriptors served as an awareness trigger of which both the US and other Arctic nations have taken note (Doshi et al 2021). Sun (2020) noted that as the Arctic becomes a new front in the strategic competition between the US and China, that the obscure messaging of China has only served to create uncertainty as to its true intentions within the region. Doshi et al extend this insight providing that the PRC speaks with "two voices on the Arctic: an external one aimed at foreign audiences and a more cynical internal one emphasizing competition and Beijing's Arctic ambitions" (2021: 1).

A Lloyds Risk Insight Report noted that, while the opening of the region would continue to present significant challenges, opportunities, and uncertainty, the Arctic itself would attract increased investment and interest in the development of oil and gas, mining, fisheries, and shipping (Emmerson and Lahn 2012). The report additionally highlights risks which arise from this opening, to include those posed to the environment because of development as well as an inevitable geopolitical shift which will arise due to increased access to and through the region for food, mineral, and energy-based resources. Despite these risks, China is enhancing its presence in the Arctic because of its energy and mineral resource deposits, extensive fisheries, and new sea routes for global trade and transportation. By collecting data and information on Chinese economic, military, and political activity in the Arctic region over time we can better predict Chinese ambitions in the region. Economic activity can include energy and natural resource development activities and investments including in the areas of oil and natural gas, minerals, fishing, and maritime shipping.

Oil and gas

Considering that the Arctic contains some of the world's largest recoverable hydrocarbon reserves, the melting of the sea ice makes the area more and more economically attractive for future exploitation of the oil and gas fields. It is estimated that the Arctic concentrates 90 billion barrels of oil (16 percent of the global total) and nearly 30 percent of the world's undiscovered natural gas reserves (AGI 2018). Given the increased access to the Arctic region, the region will become a major oil and gas developer during the next two to three decades, and the major activity will take place both in Norway and Russia (Henderson and Loe 2014; Shedov 2021). China, as the world's second largest importer of liquid natural gas, has been a significant investor in Russian natural gas development on the Yamal peninsula (Tsafos 2019). China has provided nearly 60 percent of the funds for the Yamal LNG projects; in return, Chinese shipyards have been producing 80 percent of all necessary equipment (Dams et al 2020). Gas from Yamal can reach Chinese ports in two weeks, half the time required to ship gas from the Middle East via the Suez Canal (Dams et al 2020). Also, in 2019, Neftegazholding, a Russian company, signed a deal with China National Chemical Engineering Group to develop the Payakha oilfield; the Chinese company promised to invest US$5 billion over the four-year period (Dams et al 2020). As both Russia and China are motivated to find additional oil (and gas) to support their economies, longer-term development can be anticipated of Arctic oil and gas resources (Henderson and Loe 2014; Shedov 2021).

Other initiatives to gain additional access to natural resources within the region are relatively trivial in comparison to the investments made in Russia through the Yamal. Investment and extraction have become more problematic as either geopolitical wrangling or environmental concerns have developed to derail Chinese investment. Due to the complex and complicated climate conditions in the Arctic, actual development of these resources and critical infrastructure to support oil and gas extraction, processing, and transportation is still in the future for China and other Arctic nations (Shedov 2021). However, as nation states, like China, continue to exploit these natural resources, it is more likely that a catastrophic disaster will occur.

Minerals

As one of the remaining land regions with extensive areas of mineral exploration and extraction potential, the Arctic is of particular interest to extractive industries (Boyd et al 2016). The World Economic Forum Global Agenda Council on the Arctic estimates that total mining, oil, natural gas, and infrastructure investments will reach US$1 trillion by 2030 (Rosen 2016).

China is the world's largest consumer and producer of so-called rare earth elements (REEs) (Koivurova et al 2019). Although many countries have REE deposits, China has taken the lead in their mining and production (Koivurova et al 2019). The Arctic is a mineral rich environment providing a broad spectrum of minerals to include bauxite, copper, nickel, diamonds, and iron ore as well as numerous REEs, including cerium, europium, holmium, promethium, samarium, scandium, terbium, and even uranium. For industrialized economies, these minerals are tremendously important to manufacturing, ranging from some of the most basic of household items to the advanced circuitry required for satellites. Russia has the highest mineral concentrations, with approximately 20,000 mineral deposits having been discovered, and over 30 percent of them being mined (Jørgensen-Dahl 2010). In Russia, the Nornickel company sought Chinese investment in exploitation of rare-earth metals, vanadium, molybdenum, and wolframite in the Kola Peninsula, the Taimyr Peninsula, and in the Sakha Republic of Sakha (Koivurova et al 2019). Across Canada, many Canadian mining companies established relationships with Chinese companies, including State Sponsored Enterprises, ranging from sources of capital to long-term buyers or active operators (Lajeunesse and Lackenbauer 2016). One of China's first investments in Canadian commodities—a zinc mine in Yukon acquired by China's Jinduicheng Molybdenum Group (JDC) — ended disastrously with the mine losing $100 million (Doshi et al 2021). Moreover, JDC essentially refused to clean up the closed mine, leaving behind an environmental disaster that will cost more than $35 million in clean-up costs (Doshi et al 2021). An ongoing challenge with mining processes are the far-reaching impacts on natural landscapes that may also lead to the degradation of the surrounding environment in the form of mountain top removals, deposits of mine cuttings, release of chemicals in soil and bodies of water, and air pollution (Tolvanen et al 2019).

Greenland also has a wealth of natural resources, much undiscovered as it remains under a one-mile-thick sheet of ice (Northam 2019). What has been developed, however, is being initiated by a shared partnership between Chinese and other international investors, with the US simultaneously working to obtain access (Northam 2019). The General Nice Development has played a major role in Greenland having acquired the Isua Mine Site (iron ore) in 2014 as one of the first projects in the Arctic to come under the complete ownership of China (Wolfson et al 2022). Future extraction within the Arctic will be highly dependent on the development of technologies which will provide for the ability to locate and extract from yet to be found sources within the region (Turunen 2021).

Fisheries

China is not only a main seafood producer but also the largest seafood consuming country in the world (Einarsson and Óladóttir 2020). Further, China is expected to account for 38 percent of the global consumption of fish by 2030 (Kobayashi et al 2015). With a growing population, this means that food, such as fish, needs to be obtained from every possible source, including the Arctic. China reported an annual marine capture of 13 million tons in 2015, or 15 percent of the total world marine capture (Einarsson and Oladottir 2020). Distant water fisheries are important to China's marine capture, thus Chinese fishing vessels operate throughout the world including off the coasts of Africa, South America, and Antarctica (Shen and Heino 2014). There are concerns of the international community for China's distant water fisheries because the management of these is not as strict as in its domestic fisheries (Pauly et al 2014). In fact, there are no publicly accessible databases of access agreements between China and the countries in whose Exclusive Economic Zones Chinese fishing vessels operate (Pauly et al 2014). Therefore, the activities and catches of the Chinese distant-water fleets are almost completely undocumented and unreported, and thus may include all aspects implied by the 'IUU' (Illegal, Unreported and Unregulated) acronym (Pauly et al 2014). Some fishing vessels have multiple IUU fishing records yet have not been penalized accordingly (Shen and Heino 2014). This is alarming because with changing climate change, there is a tremendous potential for a future increase in fishing yields in the Arctic Sea, Barents Sea, and other fisheries (JOCI 2017; Stupachenko 2018; Tai et al 2018). Conversely, Tai et al (2018) notes that considerations for sustainability should be paramount to prevent broader adverse impacts to the marine environments. A common concern among scholars is the need to remain vigilant in the development of fishing resources in the Arctic considering the reliance on these fisheries by local and indigenous communities. While the PRC has highlighted its peaceful efforts in the region and willingness to work within the international framework to support international regulations against IUU fishing, it has not established effective fisheries management policies to prevent this with its distant water fleet (Pauly et al 2014; Chang and Khan 2021).

Maritime shipping

The recent accelerating melting of Arctic sea ice underscores the potential advent of Arctic sea routes that are geographically much shorter between the

Atlantic and the Pacific than traditional routes through Panama or Suez and Malacca (Guy and Lasserre 2016). The established Arctic maritime routes in definition under examination include the Northeast Passage (NEP), the Northwest Passage (NWP) and the Transpolar Sea Route (TSR). The NEP, as a shipping lane, extends from the Atlantic to the Pacific Oceans and runs along the northern coast of Asia and Europe.[1] In contrast, the NWP runs likewise from the Pacific to the Atlantic through the northern archipelago of Canada which has several routes for transit. The TSR represents a third potential route through the region if and when an ice-free Arctic should actually occur. The TSR, unlike either the NWP or NEP, would largely occur through international open seas, where shallow sea beds and sovereignty-related requirements are much less of a concern (see Figure 9.3).

Arctic sea routes are critical to China's expanding economy because gaining access to them will significantly decrease the time and money spent to transport cargo. For example, rerouting its trade routes via the Northern Sea Route (NSR) may allow China to save $60 billion to $120 billion per year (Shedov 2021). China aims at the diversification of its trade routes and linking itself with Arctic countries by a network of maritime corridors. Implementation of the Polar Silk Road initiative requires first and foremost improvement of navigation safety and passability of northern routes, primarily through the NSR (Tianming and Erokhin 2021). Transportation of oil, gas, and other goods is also key for China. China is committed to constructing a new megaport in Arkhangelsk, Russia, which will be used by China Ocean Shipping Company Limited as its base for Arctic shipping (Dams et al 2020). Because of the random but persistent presence of ice, navigation in Arctic waters requires an ice-strengthened hull, powerful night ice-spotting radars, an experienced crew, and equipment to cope with icing, and to protect cargo from frost, thus increasing costs (Guy and Lasserre 2016; Theocharis et al 2018).

Despite the challenges posed by maritime shipping in the Arctic, for the Chinese, the potential use of the Arctic as a part of the Belt and Road Initiative (BRI) looms large as access through the Arctic and the use of the numerous shipping routes is necessary. The BRI is one of the highest priorities of China as it attempts to develop an infrastructure network across the Asian landscape through and to Europe (Rolland 2017). In its "Vision for Maritime Cooperation" under the BRI, released in mid-June 2017, the PRC's National Development and Reform Commission and the State Oceanic Administration envision a "blue economic passage" linking China with Europe via the Arctic Ocean. The BRI is an ambitious development program through which China plans to build infrastructure connecting it to countries in Asia and Europe, thereby boosting trade and stimulating economic growth (Connolly 2017; Tillman et al 2018).

A Polar Silk Road could shorten shipping times between China and Europe substantially, while simultaneously sidestepping alternate and more

Figure 9.3: Arctic shipping routes

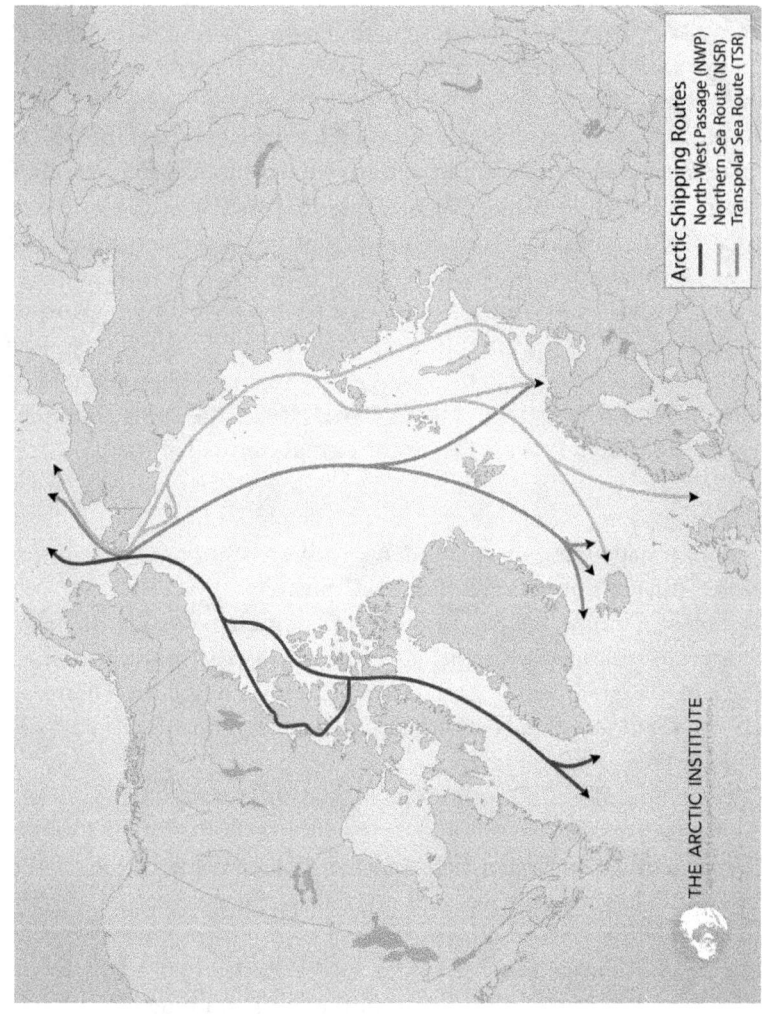

Source: Malte Humpbert, The Arctic Institute, https://www.thearcticinstitute.org/future-northern-sea-route-golden-waterway-niche/

increasingly crowded shipping routes through either the Suez or Malacca Straits (Lim 2018). An obvious benefit to the Polar Silk Route would be a cost savings in terms of time and general costs for shipping as well as the establishment of maritime shipping routes less prone to disruption. As part of the Polar Silk Road, China is collaborating with Russia to build maritime shipping infrastructure in the Russian Arctic.

China's strengthened cooperation with the Arctic region under the BRI is predominantly based on its relations with Russia. However, China continues to engage with other Arctic nations such as Iceland, Norway, and Finland to further a broader cooperation. In this way, "increased regional cooperation in the building of the Arctic Silk Road under the auspices of the BRI offers remarkable considerations in replacing a hegemonic, US-led, world order" (Hossain 2019: 1). Hossain (2019) argues that the BRI, and its extension into the Arctic, should be seen as an attempt by China to manifest itself as a major global actor.

Utilizing existing expertise via guided brainstorming session, the researchers identified the possible external drivers of change that could affect the international relations in the Arctic. Driving forces are understood here as the key trends and dynamics that will determine the course of the future in the Arctic. The following drivers of change were identified:

- The intensity of tensions between the US and China. This can be lower or higher depending on if presidential administrations choose to engage with China or counter growing PRC power.
- Extent of Chinese interest in the Arctic region as seen by high or low economic, political, scientific, and military interest in the region.
- Place of the Arctic in the great power strategic competition between the US and China as central or marginal as seen in national security objectives, trade policies, and foreign policies.
- Effectiveness of global institutions such as the Arctic Council to govern the Arctic region.
- Climate change impacts in the Arctic and their consequences and responses to them. These could have high impacts to low impacts.

The increased engagement of China in the Arctic could lead to several possible future scenarios depending on the level and type of activities and the drivers of change occurring over time.

Future scenarios

China as a hegemon in the Arctic would serve as a black swan event for the region. Left unchecked, its environmental (Spiegel 2021), human rights (Human Rights Watch 2021), and economic coercion (Glaser 2021) will continue to destabilize a region already undergoing profound changes due to climate change and undercut efforts of the US and other Arctic Council members with interests to provide stability. Weak signals, as observations of China's increased activities within the Arctic over the past decade, coupled to their continued actions in the mid and longer term will be critical in developing future scenarios for the PRC's association to the region. In order to capture the spectrum of uncertainty with regard to different trajectories that the international political situation can take in the Arctic, possible future scenarios and drivers of change can be identified as a mechanism to identify weak signals and gather evidence in horizon scanning. A scenario is not a single prediction, but a way of organizing many statements about the future. It is a plausible description of what might occur and how that could emerge from the present (Koivurova et al 2022).

NATO's *Regional Perspectives Report on the Arctic* (2021) provides several thought-provoking future's scenarios for a transforming Arctic region in 2040. The baseline scenario (best case) provides for an Arctic where cooperation remains of vital importance to the region's protection and sustainability; the Arctic Council continues to be the principal form of governance, but in a diminished capacity. Russian and Chinese cooperation continues on its current trajectory as the PRC leverages its access to energy and maritime shipping routes while the US and Canadian focus begins to turn toward environmental considerations. Each of the three successive alternative scenarios (going from bad to worse) depict an Arctic Council and governance structure that transitions from dysfunctional to fragmented, lacking the ability to influence activities within the region. Similarly, Russian and Chinese cooperation and alignment continue to strengthen alternative scenarios one and two, until in scenario three, China is seen as the major regional power, having become the major global superpower. In this final scenario (the very worst case), China, without restrictions and limits, disregards environmental consequences thus driving Russia toward NATO and the West as the PRC encroaches on Siberia and threatens Russian sovereignty. Each of the alternative scenarios depicted note an increasingly more significant degradation of the Arctic environment and status quo related to PRC involvement—suggesting the PRC to be the probable black swan event for the region.

Conclusion

The more rapid warming of the Arctic relative to the rest of the world is termed "Arctic amplification" and has been highlighted in each of the Intergovernmental Panel on Climate Change reports (IPCC 2014, 2018). As the extent of sea ice continues to diminish with the Arctic Ocean, and the accessibility to the region continues to increase, it is anticipated that the PRC will continue to place a tremendous amount of interest in the region based upon state objectives as outlined in its Arctic Policy of 2018 (Lim 2018; Mariia 2019). As outlined through the use of the horizon scan, weak signals do exist to demonstrate the PRC's ever increasing level of engagement within the region. In response, the US and other Arctic Council countries have taken notice, albeit slowly, and start to address concerns regarding their respective security, economic, and environmental interests.

In evaluation of the potential likelihood and importance of future events as part of step 3, the likelihood is that the PRC will continue to increase its presence within the Arctic region. The corresponding reaction of the US and initially some of the Arctic Council countries will be to resist these efforts through closer collaboration. Some Arctic countries such as Iceland may initially forego these collaborative efforts in favor of PRC economic overtures, but in time, that will likely change if they determine that the PRC ventures do not provide as favorable an outcome as anticipated.

What is certain, however, is that time is on the side of the PRC as climate research models have indicated a summer-ice-free Arctic as soon as the mid 2030s, with other models forecasting out to 2050 (Peng et al 2020). With this in mind, the PRC has a continued ability to influence and shape the Arctic to its favor should the US and other Arctic Council members fail to be proactive in accounting for the weak signals as to the PRC's long-term intentions. While China has outwardly expressed its intent and record of conduct in the region to be one of peace, cooperation, and win-win, it is likewise difficult not to infer that there exists the potential that its activities within the region will serve to further destabilize the sensitive climate and political processes.

Note

[1] Of note, the NEP is most often denoted as the Northern Sea Route (NSR). However, the NSR is specifically defined by Russian Federation law and represents only a portion of the NEP.

References

Abdulmuminov, E.A.A. 2021. *Who Matters in the Arctic? The Rise of Permanent Participants in the Arctic Council and International Affairs.* Seattle: University of Washington.

AGI (American Geoscience Institute). 2018. "Oil and Gas in the Arctic." https://www.americangeosciences.org/sites/default/files/AGI_PE_Arctic_web_final.pdf

Allison, G. 2017. "The Thucydides Trap." *Foreign Policy*: 3–9.

Andreassen, N. and Borch, O.J. (eds). 2020. *Crisis and Emergency Management in the Arctic: Navigating Complex Environments.* New York: Routledge.

Ansoff, H.I. 1975. "Managing Strategic Surprise by Response to Weak Signals." *California Management Review* 18(2): 21–33.

The Arctic Institute. 2020. "Russia." https://www.thearcticinstitute.org/countries/russia/

Arctic Portal. 2022. *Joint Statement by the Arctic 7 on the Limited Resumption of Arctic Council Cooperation – without Russia!* https://arcticportal.org/ap-library/news/2855-joint-statement-by-the-arctic-7-on-the-limited-resumption-of-arctic-council-cooperation-without-russia

Bader, H., Carlson, C. and Bouffard, T. 2014. "Tale of Two Arctics: Impact of Geography Affecting Security and Disaster Response Capabilities between North American and Europe." *Homeland Security Review* 8: 122–126.

Barry, T., Daviðsdóttir, B., Einarsson, N. and Young, O.R. 2020. "The Arctic Council: An Agent of Change?" *Global Environmental Change* 63(1): 102–120.

Bengston, D.N. 2013. "Horizon Scanning for Environmental Foresight: A Review of Issues and Approaches." *Gen. Tech. Rep. NRS-121*. Newtown Square: US Department of Agriculture, Forest Service, Northern Research Station.

Boutout, A. and Wahabi, R. 2020. "Weak Signals Interpretation to Prevent Strategic Surprises: A Literature Review. In *4th International Conference on Business, Management and Economics*. Berlin: icbmeconf.org, pp 120–130.

Boyd, R., Bjerkgård, T., Nordahl, B., and Schiellerup, H. 2016. *Mineral Resources in the Arctic: An Introduction*. Trondheim: Geological Survey of Norway.

Brady, A.-M. 2017. *China as a Polar Great Power*. Cambridge: Cambridge University Press.

Briggs, C.M. 2013. "Arctic Environmental Security and Abrupt Climate Change." *Environmental and Human Security in the Arctic* 1: 122–136.

Bykova, A.V. 2020. "Permafrost Thaw in a Warming World." *The Arctic Institute*, October 1. https://www.thearcticinstitute.org/permafrost-thaw-warming-world-arctic-institute-permafrost-series-fall-winter-2020/

Cassotta, S., Hossain, K., Ren, J., and Evan Goodsite, M. 2015. "Climate Change and China as a Global Emerging Regulatory Sea Power in the Arctic Ocean: Is China a Threat for Arctic Ocean Security?" *Beijing Law Review* 6: 195–204.

Chang, Y.-C. and Khan, M.I. 2021. "May China Fish in the Arctic Ocean?" *Sustainability* 13(21): 11875.

Conley, H.A. 2018. *China's Arctic Dream*. Washington, DC: Center for Strategic & International Studies.

Connolly, G.E. 2017. *NATO and Security in the Arctic*. Brussels, Belgium. NATO Parliamentary Assembly.

Cooper, H., Hedges, L., and Valentine, J. (eds). 2009. *The Handbook of Research Synthesis and Meta-analysis*, 2nd edn. New York: The Russell Sage Foundation.

Dams, T., Van Schaik, L., and Stoetman, A. 2020. *Presence before Power: China's Arctic Strategy in Iceland and Greenland*. The Hague, Netherlands, Clingendael Institute.

DDIS (Danish Defence Intelligence Service). 2020. "Intelligence Risk Assessment 2020." https://www.fe-ddis.dk/en/produkter/Risk_assessment/riskassessment/riskassessment2020/#

Depledge, D. 2021. "NATO and the Arctic: The Need for a New Approach." *The RUSI Journal* 165(5–6): 80–90.

Djalante, R. 2019. "Key Assessments from the IPCC Special Report on Global Warming of 1.5 C and the Implications for the Sendai Framework for Disaster Risk Reduction." *Progress in Disaster Science* 1: 1–20.

Doshi, R., Dale-Huang, A., and Zhang, G. 2021. "Northern Expedition: China's Arctic Activities and Ambitions." *The Brookings Institute.* Https://www.brookings.edu/research/northern-expedition-chinas-arctic-activities-and-ambitions/

Dufva, M. 2020. "What Is a Weak Signal?" *Sitra*, February 11. https://www.sitra.fi/en/articles/what-is-a-weak-signal/

Einarsson, Á. and Óladóttir, Á.D. 2020. *Fisheries and Aquaculture: The Food Security of the Future*. London:Academic Press.

Emmerson, C. and Lahn, G. 2012. "Arctic Opening: Opportunity and Risk in the High North." *Chatham House, Lloyds Rep.* https://www.chathamhouse.org/2012/04/arctic-opening-opportunity-and-risk-high-north

Francis, E. 2020. *Arctic Governance and China's Claim of Near Arctic State*. Middlebury Institute of International Studies. https://nps.edu/documents/114698888/121792798/Francis_Arctic_Governance_China_30_Dec_2020.pdf/4acb9f99-38d3-b96b-bdb1-aa98804e54d8?t=1609373841253

Garlick, J. 2019. *The Impact of China's Belt and Road Initiative: From Asia to Europe*. New York:Routledge.

Garnett, K., Lickorish, F.A., Rocks, S.A., Prpich, G., Rathe, A.A., and Pollard, S.J.T. 2016. "Integrating Horizon Scanning and Strategic Risk Prioritisation using a Weight of Evidence Framework to Inform Policy Decisions." *Science of the Total Environment* 560: 82–91.

Glaser, B. 2021. "Time for Collective Pushback against China's Economic Coercion." *Center for Strategic and International Studies*. https://www.csis.org/analysis/time-collective-pushback-against-chinas-economic-coercion

Greenwood, J. and Luo, S. 2022. "Could the Arctic Be a Wedge Between Russia and China?" *War on the Rocks*. https://warontherocks.com/2022/04/could-the-arctic-be-a-wedge-between-russia-and-china/

Griol-Barres, I., Milla, S., Cebrián, A., Fan, H., and Millet, J. 2020. "Detecting Weak Signals of the Future: A System Implementation Based on Text Mining and Natural Language Processing." *Sustainability* 12(19): 7848.

Guy, E. and Lasserre, F. 2016. "Commercial Shipping in the Arctic: New Perspectives, Challenges and Regulations." *Polar Record* 52(3): 294–304.

Habegger, B. 2009. *Horizon Scanning in Government: Concept, Country Experiences, and Models for Switzerland.* Zurich: Center for Security Studies.

Hajikazemi, S., Ekambaram, A., Andersen, B., and Zidane, Y.J.T. 2016. "The Black Swan–Knowing the Unknown in Projects." *Procedia-Social and Behavioral Sciences* 226(1): 184–192.

He, M., Hu, Y., Chen, N., Wang, D., Huang, J., and Stamnes, K. 2019. "High Cloud Coverage over Melted Areas Dominates the Impact of Clouds on the Albedo Feedback in the Arctic." *Scientific Reports* 9(1): 1–11.

Heinonen, S., Karjalainen, J., Ruotsalainen, J., and Steinmüller, K. 2017. "Surprise as the New Normal: Implications for Energy Security." *European Journal of Futures Research* 5(1): 1–13.

Henderson, J. and Loe, J. 2014. "The Prospects and Challenges for Arctic Oil Development." *The Oxford Institute for Energy Studies.*

Horvath, S., Stroeve, J., Rajagopalan, B., and Jahn, A. 2021. "Arctic Sea Ice Melt Onset Favored by an Atmospheric Pressure Pattern Reminiscent of the North American-Eurasian Arctic Pattern." *Climate Dynamics* 57(7): 1771–1787.

Hossain, K. 2019. "China's BRI Expansion and Great Power Ambition: The Silk Road on the Ice Connecting the Arctic." *Cambridge Journal of Eurasian Studies* 3: F3OSGP.

Human Rights Watch. 2021. "World Report 2021: Rights Trends in China." https://www.hrw.org/world-report/2021/country-chapters/china-and-tibet#

IPCC. 2014. "Mitigation of Climate Change." *Contribution of Working Group III to the Fifth Assessment Report of the Intergovernmental Panel on Climate Change* 1454: 147.

IPCC. 2018. *Special Report on Global Warming of 1.5°C (SR15).* Geneva: Intergovernmental Panel on Climate Change, World Meteorological Organization. https://www.ipcc.ch/sr15/

Joint Ocean Commission Initiative. 2017. "Remote Arctic Exploration Offers Promise for Fisheries." *Ocean Action Agenda.* https://oceanactionagenda.org/story/remote-arctic-exploration-offers-promise-fisheries/

Jørgensen-Dahl, A. 2010. *Arctic Mineral Resources.* ARCTIS. http://www.arctis-search.com/Arctic+Mineral+Resources

Kobayashi, M., Msangi, S., Batka, M., Vannuccini, S., Dey, M.M., and Anderson, J.L. 2015. "Fish to 2030: The Role and Opportunity for Aquaculture." *Aquaculture Economics & Management* 19(3): 282–300.

Koivurova, T., Kauppila, L., Kopra, S., Lanteigne, M., Shi, M., Smieszek, M., et al. 2019. "China in the Arctic; and the Opportunities and Challenges for Chinese-Finnish Arctic Co-operation." https://julkaisut.valtioneuvosto.fi/bitstream/handle/10024/161371/8-2019-China_Arctic_andFinland.pdf?sequence=1&isAllowed=y%20March%202019

Koivurova, T., Heikkilä, M., Ikävalko, J., Kirchner, S., Kopra, S., Mikkola, H., Pursiainen, R., Sepponen, S., Moisio, M., and Stepien, A. 2022. "Arctic Cooperation in a New Situation: Analysis on the Impacts of the Russian War of Aggression." https://julkaisut.valtioneuvosto.fi/handle/10024/164521

Lackenbauer, P.W., Lajeunesse, A., Manicom, J., and Lasserre, F. 2018. *China's Arctic Ambitions and What They Mean for Canada*. Calgary: University of Calgary Press.

Lajeunesse, A. and Lackenbauer, P. 2016. *Governing the North American Arctic*. New York: Palgrave-Macmillan.

Lim, K.S. 2018. "China's Arctic Policy and the Polar Silk Road Vision." *Arctic Yearbook* 2018: 420–432.

Linkov, I., Loney, D., Cormier, S., Satterstrom, F.K., and Bridges, T. 2009. "Weight-of-Evidence Evaluation in Environmental Assessment: Review of Qualitative and Quantitative Approaches." *Science of the Total Environment* 407(19): 5199–5205.

Malcolm, D., Gjørv, G.H., Bazely, D., Goloviznina, M., and Tanentzap, A. 2013. "Climate Change Impacts, Adaptation, and the Technology Interface." In *Environmental and Human Security in the Arctic*. London: Routledge, pp 113–127.

Mariia, K. 2019. "China's Arctic Policy: Present and Future." *The Polar Journal* 9(1): 94–112.

Mearsheimer, J.J. 2021. "The Inevitable Rivalry: America, China, and the Tragedy of Great-Power Politics." *Foreign Affairs* 100: 44–49.

Medeiros, E.S. 2019. "The Changing Fundamentals of US-China Relations." *The Washington Quarterly* 42(3): 93–119.

Melvin, A.M., Larsen, P., Boehlert, B., Neumann, J.E., Chinowsky, P., Espinet, X., et al. 2017. "Climate Change Damages to Alaska Public Infrastructure and the Economics of Proactive Adaptation." *Proceedings of the National Academy of Sciences* 114(2): E122–E131.

Miller, T. 2019. *China's Asian Dream: Empire Building Along the New Silk Road*. London: Bloomsbury Publishing.

Mosteller, F. and Colditz, G. 1996. "Understanding Research Synthesis (Meta-Analysis)." *Annual Review of Public Health* 17(1): 1–23.

Murray, J.L., Gregor, D.J. and Loeng, H. 1998. "Physical/Geographical Characteristics of the Artic." In *AMAP Assessment Report: Arctic Pollution Issues*. Arctic Environmental Assessment Programme (AMAP), pp 9–24.

National Academies of Sciences, Engineering, and Medicine. 2020. "Horizon Scanning and Foresight Methods." In *Safeguarding the Bioeconomy*. Washington DC: National Academies Press.

NATO Supreme Allied Command Transformation (SACT). 2021. *Regional Perspectives Report on the Arctic*. Strategic Plan and Policy Strategic Foresight Analysis Team.

Nikander, I.O. 2002. *Early Warnings: A Phenomenon in Project Management.* Helsinki: Helsinki University of Technology. https://aaltodoc.aalto.fi/bitstream/handle/123456789/2170/isbn9512258889.pdf?sequence=1&isAllowed=y

Northam, J. 2019. "Greenland is Not for Sale but it Has Rare Earth Minerals America Wants." *NPR*, November 24. https://www.npr.org/2019/11/24/781598549/greenland-is-not-for-sale-but-it-has-the-rare-earth-minerals-america-wants

Northam, J. 2022. "Russia May Become the Only Non-NATO Nation in the Arctic, Sparking Fears of Conflict." *NPR*, May 12. https://www.npr.org/2022/05/12/1098585422/russia-may-become-the-only-non-nato-nation-in-the-arctic-sparking-fears-of-confl

NSIDC (National Snow & Ice Data Center). 2020. "All About Arctic Climatology and Meteorology." *Climate Change in the Arctic.* https://nsidc.org/cryosphere/arctic-meteorology/climate_change.html

NSIDC (National Snow & Ice Data Center). 2021. "Arctic Sea Ice Has Reached Minimum Extent for 2021." https://nsidc.org/news/newsroom/arctic-sea-ice-has-reached-minimum-extent-2021

Pauly, D., Belhabib, D., Blomeyer, R., Cheung, W.W.L., Cisneros-Montemayor, A.M., Copeland, D., et al. 2014."China's Distant-Water Fisheries in the 21st Century." *Fish and Fisheries* 15(3): 474–488.

Peng, G., Steele, M., Bliss, A.C., Meier, W.N., and Dickinson, S. 2018. "Temporal Means and Variability of Arctic Sea Ice Melt and Freeze Season Climate Indicators using a Satellite Climate Data Record." *Remote Sensing* 10(9): 13–28.

Peng, G., Matthews, J.L., Wang, M., Vose, R., and Sun, L. 2020. "What Do Global Climate Models Tell Us About Future Arctic Sea Ice Coverage Changes?" *Climate* 8(1): 15–30.

Pincus, R. 2015. "Large-Scale Disaster Response in the Arctic: Are We Ready?" *Arctic Yearbook 2015*: 234–246.

Rolland, N. 2017. "China's 'Belt and Road Initiative': Underwhelming or Game-Changer?" *The Washington Quarterly* 40(1): 127–142.

Rosen, J. 2016. "Arctic Dreams: As it Pursues Independence, Greenland Seeks to Develop its Economy without Ruining One of Earth's Last Pristine Places." *Nature* 532(7599): 296–300.

Rottem, S.V. 2020. "The Arctic Council: Between Environmental Protection and Geopolitics." In *The Arctic Council.* Singapore: Palgrave Pivot, pp 91–95.

Schultz, W.L. 2006. "The Cultural Contradictions of Managing Change: Using Horizon Scanning in an Evidence-Based Policy Context." *Foresight* 8(4): 3–12.

Scott, M. 2016. "Global Sea Ice in November: Black Swans Flock to Both Poles." *NOAA*, December 14. https://www.climate.gov/news-features/features/global-sea-ice-november-black-swans-flock-both-poles

Shedov, Y. 2021. "A Black Swan in the Arctic Waters. Has China Become a Great Power in the Arctic?" *RIAC*, March 25. https://russiancouncil.ru/en/analytics-and-comments/columns/arctic-cooperation/a-black-swan-in-the-arctic-waters-has-china-become-a-great-power-in-the-arctic/

Shen, G. and Heino, M. 2014. "An Overview of Marine Fisheries Management in China." *Marine Policy* 44: 265–272.

Spiegel, J.E. 2021. "The Potential Climate Consequences of China's Belt and Roads Initiative." *Yale Climate Connections*. https://yaleclimateconnections.org/2020/02/the-potential-climate-consequences-of-chinas-belt-and-roads-initiative/

The State Council of the PRC. 2018. "Full Text: China's Arctic Policy." http://english.gov.cn/archive/white_paper/2018/01/26/content_281476026660336.htm

Struzik, E. 2020. "How Thawing Permafrost is Beginning to Transform the Arctic." *Yale Environment*: 358–369.

Stupachenko, I. 2018. "Can Russia's Arctic Deliver on Big Fishing Promises?" *SeafoodSource Official Media*, April 4. https://www.seafoodsource.com/features/can-russias-arctic-deliver-on-big-fishing-promises

Sun, Y. 2020. "Defining the Chinese Threat in the Arctic." *The Arctic Institute*. https://www.thearcticinstitute.org/defining-the-chinese-threat-in-the-arctic/

Tai, T.C., Steiner, N.S., Hoover, C., Cheung, W.W.L., and Sumaila, U.R. 2018. "Evaluating Present and Future Potential of Arctic Fisheries in Canada." *Marine Policy* 108: 103–119.

Taleb, N.N. 2010. *The Black Swan: The Impact of the Highly Improbable*. New York: Random House.

Theocharis, D., Pettit, S., Sanchez Rodrigues, V., and Haider, J. 2018. "Arctic Shipping: A Systematic Literature Review of Comparative Studies." *Journal of Transport Geography* 69: 112–128.

Tianming, G. and Erokhin, V. 2021. "China-Russia Collaboration in Shipping and Marine Engineering as One of the Key Factors of Secure Navigation along the NSR." *China's Arctic Engagement* 9: 234–263.

Tillman, H., Yang, J., and Nielsson, E.T. 2018. "The Polar Silk Road: China's New Frontier of International Cooperation." *China Quarterly of International Strategic Studies* 4(3): 345–362.

Tolvanen, A., Eilu, P., Juutinen, A., Kangas, K., Kivinen, M., Markovaara-Koivisto, M., et al. 2019. "Mining in the Arctic Environment: A Review from Ecological, Socioeconomic and Legal Perspectives." *Journal of Environmental Management* 233: 832–844.

Tsafos, N. 2019. *How Is China Securing Its LNG Needs?* Center for Strategic and International Studies.

Turunen, E. 2021. "Resources in the Arctic 2019." *Nordregio*, April 6. https://nordregio.org/maps/resources-in-the-arctic-2019/

Valentine, J., Moon, S., and Kliskey, A. 2021. "Asymmetric Competition in the Arctic." *Journal of Indo-Pacific Affairs* Winter: 1–28.

van Veen, B.L. and Ortt, J.R. 2021. "Unifying Weak Signals Definitions to Improve Construct Understanding." *Futures* 134: 102–110.

Vitug, M.D. 2018. *Rock Solid: How the Philippines Won Its Maritime Case against China.* Manila: Ateneo de Manila University Press.

Wolfson, R., Overfield, C., Rosen, M., DeThomas, B., and Tallis, J. 2022. *Arctic Prospecting: Measuring China's Arctic Economic Footprint.* Montreal, Canada.

Yu, L. and Leng, G. 2022. "Identifying the Paths and Contributions of Climate Impacts on the Variation in Land Surface Albedo over the Arctic." *Agricultural and Forest Meteorology* 313: 108–122.

Zysk, K. and Titley, D. 2015. "Signals, Noise, and Swans in Today's Arctic." *The SAIS Review of International Affairs* 35(1): 169–181.

10

Europe's Role in US–China Strategic Competition

Richard Maher and Till Schöfer

Introduction

This chapter examines how Europe is both a site of and participant in contemporary US–China geopolitical competition. As one of the richest and most technologically advanced regions in the world, the US and China compete for economic and political influence across the continent. At the same time, in everything from trade to investment to emerging technologies, US–China competition increasingly shapes Europe's policy choices and strategic priorities.

For Europe—defined here as the European Union (EU) and European members of NATO—US–China competition differs in many important respects from US–Soviet competition during the Cold War. During that period, Europe was the main site and prize of US–Soviet rivalry. The continent was divided economically, politically, militarily, and ideologically. An Iron Curtain had descended across Europe, "from Stettin in the Baltic to Trieste in the Adriatic." Both the US and the Soviet Union devoted enormous resources to secure and defend their respective parts of the continent (Hanhimäki 2012).

Europe today is neither the main site nor the main prize of US–China competition. The key flashpoints lie not in Europe but in East and Southeast Asia, including Taiwan and the South China Sea (Shambaugh 2021). Nevertheless, both the US and China view Europe as an important strategic partner, and the continent has become an increasingly active economic battleground between the two countries (Brandt and Taussig 2020).[1] In this new era of great power confrontation, therefore, "Europe has a comparable position to that of Japan before 1989: a reliable American ally, but one outside the main field of confrontation" (Krastev and Leonard 2021b).

This chapter analyzes Europe's role and place in US–China competition with a focus on Huawei's presence in Europe's fifth generation (5G) wireless networks. This case reveals three broader features of Europe's role in US–China competition. First, European countries' desire to expand and deepen their economic links with China while continuing to depend on the US for their defense represents the central challenge they face in this new strategic environment. Second, while US and European views on China have converged in recent years, they are not identical, and European countries are unlikely to take as firm a position toward China as countries in Western Europe did against the Soviet Union during the Cold War. Third, while internal divisions will prevent Europe from acting as a third power alongside the US and China in world politics, Europe will still be able to shape its regional environment, resist US and Chinese demands, and even influence US–China competition in various ways. Cumulatively, these trends mean that Europe is both a theater of and an actor in the US and China's ongoing strategic rivalry.

While the literature on EU–China relations has grown in recent years, there has been less attention devoted to analyzing how Europe both affects and is affected by US–China competition. At the same time, the advent of the US–China trade war, the global expansion of economic nationalism and deglobalization, and the growing securitization of trade and investment—particularly in the case of China—has increased the salience of US–China strategic competition for other regions. These global transformations, emanating from the growing geopolitical and economic clout of China—as well as the move away from trade liberalism under the Trump and Biden administrations—serve as a backdrop for recent European economic and security debates concerning digital infrastructure and inbound investments. This chapter thus contributes to our understanding of both how Europe is navigating this new strategic environment and how China and the US are competing for advantage and influence in Europe. It does so by focusing on Europe's role both as an intermediary and as an actor in its own right in a geopolitical environment increasingly shaped by the intensification of US–China competition.

This chapter proceeds as follows. It first clarifies China's, Europe's, and the US's main goals in their trilateral relations. It then discusses in turn how Europe is a site of and a participant in US–China geopolitical competition. Finally, it discusses the factors most likely to shape Europe's role and place in an era defined by US–China strategic competition.

China–Europe–US trilateral relations

US–China competition has become one of the defining features of contemporary international politics. The US increasingly views China as a great power rival and a threat to its economic, military, and technological supremacy (US Department of Defense 2018; Biden 2021). China sees the US as an obstacle to its continued economic and political rise and even a threat to its internal stability (Nathan and Scobell 2014).[2] While US–China competition is most intense in the Asia-Pacific, it has become increasingly globalized in recent years (Economy 2022).

The US has three broad aims in its trilateral relations with China and Europe: curb China's economic and political influence in Europe; restrict Beijing's access to advanced European technology; and enlist its European allies in its effort to manage China's rise (Small et al 2022).[3] The US views its European allies as crucial partners in its competition with China, and has urged them in recent years to take a firmer position against Beijing (White House 2021). In particular, the US has pressed European countries to avoid any actions that could help China in its military and technological competition with the US, such as lifting the arms embargo the European Community (EC), the EU's predecessor, imposed on China following the 1989 Tiananmen crackdown, or including Huawei equipment in their 5G wireless networks, which the US sees as an intelligence and security risk (Barkin 2020).

China's goals are to expand and deepen its economic presence and political influence in Europe, maintain access to European technology, and avoid a united US–European front designed to counter its economic and political rise (Kuchins 2021; Tatlow et al 2021).[4] China depends on trade with Europe to maintain its economic growth and development and to achieve its goal of becoming an economic, military, and technological great power by mid-century. The EU is China's top trade partner, and Europe remains an important source of advanced technology and know-how for China (Nouwens and Legarda 2018; Cliff 2022). China has also long desired Europe to emerge as a counterweight, at least some of the time and on issues that China cares deeply about, to the US, and has sought to weaken Western unity "both within Europe and across the Atlantic" (Benner and Wright 2018).[5] As relations with the US have deteriorated in recent years, China has sought to strengthen ties with Europe, which it sees as more pragmatic than the US (Chang and Pieke 2018).

Europe's aims are to preserve (and, if possible, enhance) its economic and technological sovereignty in the face of renewed great power competition, protect the liberal international order from becoming a victim of US–China competition, and avoid having to pick sides in this growing rivalry. While US and European views on China have converged in recent years, European leaders, unlike their US counterparts, have largely sought to avoid an overly confrontational approach toward China (see, for instance, Borrell 2020; Bermann 2021). Nonetheless, European countries have implemented various measures to avoid economic or technological dependence on non-European countries, namely China, by introducing a new investment-screening mechanism and restricting foreign suppliers' access to their next-generation wireless broadband networks (Wright 2021; Deni 2022). Europeans are also concerned that growing US–China competition could upset multilateralism and the liberal international order, of which Europe has been one of the main supporters and beneficiaries.[6]

Europe as a site of US–China geopolitical contestation

US–China competition in Europe is unlikely to take on the highly militarized or ideological character that defined US–Soviet rivalry in Europe during the Cold War. China is far from Europe, lacks any European allies, and has no territorial ambitions on the continent. Instead, this competition has mainly focused on trade and technology, and especially on what the US sees as the security risks of including Chinese suppliers in Europe's 5G network infrastructure.

US–China competition in Europe takes place within a political, historical, and social context that in many respects distinguishes it from other regions. The two sides of the Atlantic are connected economically, culturally, and militarily. Some of the US's longest and most capable alliance partners are in Europe (Gardner 2020; McKean and Szewczyk 2021). The US and its European allies have long shared a commitment to democracy and the liberal international order. While many European countries want to deepen their commercial and investment relationship with China, they continue to depend on the US for their defense (Odgaard 2020).[7]

European countries, however, do not share the US's assessment of China as a military threat (Krastev and Leonard 2021a). For Europe, China is far away and poses little danger to the continent's sovereignty or territorial integrity. Thus, the key structural factor that ensured a close relationship between the US and Western Europe during the Cold War—a common threat, embodied in the Soviet Union—is missing from contemporary US–China competition in Europe. Compared to the Cold War, therefore, European countries have greater freedom of movement to pursue policies toward China that may not fully align with those of the US (Walt 2021).

China and Europe today are much more economically interdependent than Western Europe and the Soviet Union were during the Cold War. Over the past two decades, China has steadily deepened and expanded its economic presence in Europe (Le Corre and Sepulchre 2016; Reilly 2021: chapters 3 and 4). The EU is China's top trade partner, and in 2020 China surpassed the US to become the EU's main trade partner. EU–China bilateral trade in goods approaches €1.5 billion per day. China's signature Belt and Road Initiative extends into Europe, and Chinese companies have invested in a wide range of European infrastructure, including ports, airports, and the energy sector (Casarini 2016; Le Corre 2018; Cristiani et al 2021). Between 2010 and 2020, Chinese investment in Europe totaled €170 billion (Kratz et al 2021: 9).[8] While China's top trade and investment partners in Europe are Germany, the UK, and France, it has also sought to deepen economic ties with countries in Central and Eastern Europe via the 17+1 format (Hillman 2020; Reilly 2021: chapter 4).

Perhaps in no other area has US–China competition in Europe played out more openly and intensely than over Huawei's inclusion in Europe's 5G wireless networks (Triolo et al 2018; Kaska et al 2019). The US pressed its European allies to exclude Huawei equipment from their next-generation wireless infrastructure, arguing that it posed an unacceptable security risk (Krach 2017). Trump administration officials even warned that the US might restrict military and intelligence cooperation with countries that included Huawei equipment in their networks (Pancevski and Germano 2019). In response, China threatened retaliation against any country that banned the company from its domestic market (see, for instance, Bennhold and Ewing 2020). Instead of a strictly economic or technical decision, therefore, the decision of who should build out European countries' 5G networks took on strategic importance.

US concerns over Huawei's presence in Europe's (and other allies' and partners') 5G network infrastructure were based on two main factors: risks inherent in the nature of the technology, and risks related to the nature of China's political system (Williams 2019).

5G represents a fundamental shift from earlier generations of wireless technology (Wheeler and Simpson 2019; Williams 2019). According to many projections, 5G will be the backbone of the next-generation economy and of critical infrastructure such as power grids, water supplies, and transport infrastructure. 5G will also enable many emerging technologies such as artificial intelligence (AI), advanced robotics, and autonomous vehicles (Wheeler and Simpson 2019). Unlike earlier generations of network technology, 5G's importance to both national economic competitiveness and national security makes it part of a state's critical infrastructure. Thus, who builds the network involves both technical and political considerations. Such debates were absent in previous upgrades to next-generation cellular technology.

Both China and the US believe that being at the forefront of 5G and other emerging technologies will provide economic as well as a strategic benefits in their competition for global leadership (Brown and Singh 2018; Triolo et al 2018; Hoffmann et al 2021). China aims to overtake the US to become the world's pre-eminent technological power by mid-century (Cheung 2022). The Made in China 2025 program, for instance, calls for China to become a world leader in areas such as robotics, information technology, aerospace, and telecommunications (Goldkorn et al 2018;

Xinhua 2018; Gewirtz 2019; Zenglein and Holzmann 2019). China also aims to become a "global innovation leader" in fields such as AI, quantum computing, and biotechnology (Fu 2015: part III). The competition over 5G is thus part of a broader US–China competition for global technological supremacy (Schneider-Petsinger et al 2019; Inkster 2020; Triolo 2020b; Allison et al 2021).

China's strategic intentions, the absence of reliable checks on government power, and the threat to human rights and liberal values posed by Chinese leadership in 5G provide additional elements of risk. From its actions in the East and South China Sea to the Taiwan Strait, China has become increasingly assertive in recent years. Under President Xi Jinping, China has also become more authoritarian, exemplified by the crackdown in Hong Kong and mass repression against the Uyghur minority in Xinjiang (Ang 2018). The Chinese Communist Party faces no domestic institutional opposition, and no Chinese company is fully beyond government control. Western intelligence and security officials have pointed to China's 2017 National Intelligence Law, which requires Chinese companies to cooperate with intelligence and security services, as evidence that Huawei and other Chinese telecom companies pose an inevitable national security threat (Sanger 2020: 116).

Huawei has been an important part of China's ambition to become a global technological powerhouse (Wen 2020). Founded in the late 1980s, by 2020 Huawei had become the world's biggest telecommunications equipment maker and one of the world's biggest technology companies. In 2019, it recorded revenue of $122 billion, making it roughly the size of Microsoft.[9] It had 180,000 employees and claimed to operate in 170 countries around the world (Johnson and Groll 2019).

The US has long viewed Huawei as a security threat (Sanger 2018: chapter 5; Kaska et al 2019). US officials have suspected the company of having links to the Chinese government and Communist Party. Huawei's founder, Ren Zhengfei, served in the People's Liberation Army for over a decade. The company's ownership structure is opaque, and it has received billions in government loans and other state subsidies.[10] Huawei has engaged in various kinds of misconduct, including bribery, corruption, and intellectual property theft (Zhong 2018). US officials have also accused the company of violating US sanctions against Iran (Sanger et al 2019a).

Over the past decade, the US has adopted an increasingly hard line against Huawei (Segal 2021).[11] It banned the company from the US market, pressed its allies and partners to exclude the company from their 5G networks, and imposed a range of restrictive measures against it. Starting in 2019, the US imposed a range of export controls against Huawei, which deprived the company of vital components and technology it needed for its products, putting the company's very future in doubt.

The US warned European countries that Huawei's inclusion in their 5G wireless networks could facilitate Chinese espionage or sabotage (Sanger et al 2019a). The Chinese government could use Huawei as a conduit to gain access to all communications flowing across its networks in Europe, including NATO and US military communications. US officials also argued that China could order the networks to be sabotaged in the event of a military conflict. Moreover, US officials worried about the growth and expansion of a Chinese company in a critical industry such as 5G. Huawei's inclusion in European 5G networks could help it cement a leading position in next-generation telecommunications equipment. US officials preferred Western suppliers rather than Chinese firms to be at the forefront of 5G technology (White House 2020). In response, the Trump administration introduced its "Clean Network" program, which aimed to counter what it called "long-term threats to data privacy, security and human rights posed to the free world from authoritarian malign actors, such as the Chinese Communist Party."[12]

In 2020, European countries began to roll out their 5G wireless networks. Initially, most countries announced that they would include Huawei equipment in their 5G network infrastructure. European telecom providers had used Huawei equipment in their networks for years, and Huawei was widely seen as a reliable, cost-effective supplier (Sanger and McCabe 2020).[13] Huawei put significant effort into growing its share of the European telecommunications equipment market, which became one of its most important markets outside China (Stevis-Gridneff 2019). The company launched a high-profile advertising campaign and sponsored a wide range of partnerships with European universities and spent large amounts of money on advertising and lobbying regulators (Stevis-Gridneff 2019).

At first the US campaign to convince its European allies to ban Huawei met with little success. European countries did not share US concerns over Huawei and were wary of antagonizing China (Sanger and McCabe 2020). Even the UK announced that it would not ban Huawei from its 5G network but would instead merely block its access to the core or sensitive parts of the network and limit its market share to 35 percent of the network. Other EU countries announced that they did not intend to impose a ban on Huawei (Barnes and Satariano 2019). The US campaign to convince its European allies to ban Huawei from their domestic markets stumbled in part due to distrust of the Trump administration. European governments believed that the US campaign against Huawei could simply be part of the broader trade war between the two countries. In a bid to win concessions from China, Trump could reverse course on Huawei, leaving European countries exposed to Chinese retribution (Barnes and Satariano 2019).

Europe was therefore the site for what may turn out to be one of the first battles between China and the US for global technological supremacy. European countries gradually adopted a firmer line against Huawei, illustrating that they are not just a site of US–China competition, but also a participant.

Europe as a participant in US–China geopolitical contestation

Two factors have complicated Europe's response to US–China competition. First, European countries disagree over which approach to take toward this new strategic environment. On relations with China, European countries have different interests, outlooks, and priorities. There is no consensus over whether to regard Beijing as primarily a partner, a competitor, or an adversary. Some countries stress the economic benefits of a closer relationship with China, while others see China as more of a long-term economic and political challenge (Godement and Vasselier 2017: 17–19).

Second, European countries disagree over how closely to cooperate with the US on China (Smith and Taussig 2019). European countries do not share all the US's concerns or priorities regarding China. They may be alarmed at some of China's actions, but they do not view China as a strategic or military threat the way the US does.[14] As then EU trade commissioner Cecilia Malmström said, "We expressly do not share Trump's approach. China is an economic rival for us, but not a political enemy" (quoted in Foot 2020: 71). Or as French Finance Minister Bruno Le Maire put it, "The United States wants to confront China. The European Union wants to engage China" (quoted in Alderman and Cohen 2021). For most countries in Europe, China is not a strategic priority. Some countries, such as France and Germany, are wary of adopting an overly confrontational approach toward Beijing. Other countries, such as Poland or the Baltic states, may broadly share US assessments of China, but see Russia as their main strategic concern.

Some analysts and former government officials in Europe argue that US and European interests on China do not automatically align (see, for example, Bermann 2021). Opinion polls show the degree to which publics on both sides of the Atlantic view the challenge posed by China's rise differently. While nearly two-thirds of European respondents in one recent poll thought that a new cold war was emerging between China and the US, majorities in each European country said that their own country was not in a cold war with China (Krastev and Leonard 2021a). A 2019 poll found that most European respondents would prefer to remain neutral in a conflict between the US and China or Russia (Dennison 2019: 10).[15] While Europe–China relations take place against the backdrop of growing US–China strategic competition, European leaders are seeking to chart their own path on relations with China rather than simply following the US (Godement 2020: 251). In December 2020, for instance, European leaders concluded the EU–China Comprehensive Agreement on Investment over objections from the incoming Biden administration.[16]

Nevertheless, European views of China are hardening (Small 2019; Smith and Taussig 2019; Brattberg 2022). There is growing consensus across Europe that the strategy of engagement with China has largely failed. Over the past two decades, freedom, democracy, and human rights have not improved in China.[17] Instead, as a 2019 European Commission "strategic outlook" on EU–China relations put it, China is as an "economic competitor in the pursuit of technological leadership, and a systemic rival promoting alternative models of governance" (European Commission 2019: 1).

Central to Europeans' shifting attitudes toward China is the belief that Beijing engages in unfair economic practices. EU–China economic relations lack reciprocity. Europe's market is largely open to Chinese firms, but China's domestic market remains heavily protected (Holslag 2015; Kratz and Oertel 2021). In addition to restricted market access for foreign companies, European countries are losing patience with many other Chinese economic practices, such as intellectual property theft, forced technology transfers and joint ventures, and state subsidies and other benefits for state-owned companies. Many Europeans view the Made in China 2025 plan, which aims to make China the world leader in advanced manufacturing, as a threat to Europe's economic competitiveness (Holslag 2017). Chinese takeovers of companies in Europe have led to growing concern, and European countries are wary of becoming overly dependent on China (Oertel 2020).[18]

The EU has taken various steps to counter China's influence in Europe, including restricting Chinese access to European technology, pressing for greater reciprocity, and introducing its own infrastructure financing initiative to balance the Chinese-led Belt and Road Initiative (Small 2019). At the same time, Europe recognizes that cooperation with China is necessary on global challenges important to Europe, such as climate change, pandemics, and nuclear proliferation (European Commission 2019).

In response to these new geopolitical dynamics, and to ensure that Europe will be able to formulate its own policy independent of the US or China, some European analysts have championed greater European strategic autonomy (Simón 2021; see also Biscop 2019). Advocates of European strategic autonomy argue that Europe should be less dependent on the US for its defense. French Minister Bruno Le Maire said that Europe's goal is to become "independent from the United States, able to defend its own interests, whether economic or strategic interests" (quoted in Alderman and Cohen 2021). While most EU governments agree in principle with the concept of strategic autonomy, there is no consensus over what it requires or entails. Differences have emerged over capabilities (how much and what kind), level of ambition, and institutional arrangements (Meijer and Brooks 2021; Retter et al 2021).

Nevertheless, the US and the EU have launched a new dialogue on China to better coordinate their policies. The EU–US Trade and Technology Council, launched in June 2021, aims to promote transatlantic coordination on issues such as investment screening, export controls, new technology standards, and supply chain security (European Commission 2021b). China occupied a bigger role in NATO's latest Strategic Concept, which was unveiled at the Madrid summit in June 2022.[19] Some analysts have even suggested that a transatlantic division of labor could emerge. Europe could enhance its capacity in the areas of crisis management and its ability to manage low-intensity conflicts, allowing the US to devote more attention to China (Tunsjø 2015). Or the US could recommit to European security in return for Europe doing more to help the US on China (Walt 2019).

Huawei's inclusion in Europe's 5G wireless technology illustrates how Europe is a participant and not just a site of US–China geopolitical competition. At various times, European countries were able to resist either US or Chinese pressure as they decided their 5G network policy. In fact, the level of attention both Washington and Beijing devoted to Europe's 5G future testifies to the region's importance in shaping the growing US–China tech rivalry.

Rather than one single market, the European telecoms market is fragmented into separate national markets. Each country typically has three or four network operators and is responsible for setting its own 5G security standards and regulatory policies (European Court of Auditors 2022). In light of this patchwork of national policies, the European Commission has tried to establish a common approach to 5G network security in the EU. In October 2019, it published a coordinated risk assessment on 5G network security (NIS Cooperation Group 2019). In January 2020, it published a toolbox of risk mitigation measures (NIS Cooperation Group 2020). The Commission recommended that members should limit high-risk 5G vendors, a category that included Huawei, in their 5G wireless networks. A non-European supplier, it warned, could be forced by its government to help infiltrate networks, putting private data, trade secrets, and national security at risk. Many smaller EU member states wanted a joint EU position on this issue, which they thought might shield them from Chinese retaliation.

On Huawei's inclusion in their 5G wireless networks, European countries broadly fit into one of three categories: those that have formally banned Huawei (the UK and Sweden); those that have not formally banned the company but have implemented restrictions that amount to a de facto ban (Germany, France, Italy, and most Central and Eastern European countries); and those that have welcomed Huawei in their 5G networks (Austria and Hungary).

In January 2020, the UK announced that it would permit Huawei equipment in its 5G wireless networks, going against US appeals to ban the company (Satariano 2020). The government stated, however, that it would limit Huawei to the non-core parts of the network and cap its presence at no more than 35 percent (Satariano 2020). In July 2020, the UK reversed this decision and announced that it would ban Huawei from its 5G networks and required telecom operators to remove all existing Huawei equipment from its networks by 2027.[20]

In October 2020, Sweden's telecoms regulator, the Post and Telecom Authority, banned the use of Huawei and ZTE equipment for telecom operators participating in the country's 5G auction (Milne 2020). It also announced that telecom operators supplying 5G would have until 2025 to remove Huawei and ZTE equipment from their networks and that no new equipment should be installed. The decision was made on the advice of the country's military and security services, which described China as "one of the biggest threats against Sweden" (Mukherjee and Soderpalm 2020; PTS 2020).

Other EU countries, including Germany and France, have not implemented formal bans on Huawei, but have announced restrictions that amount to a de facto ban. In Germany, former Chancellor Angela Merkel feared that alienating China over the issue of 5G would hurt trade relations (Oertel 2019). Many in her own party, however, advocated a tough stance against the company. Norbert Röttgen, for instance, chair of the Bundestag's foreign affairs committee, said that the question "was not whether we trust Huawei but whether we trust the Chinese Communist Party to which Huawei is clearly beholden" (quoted in Benner 2019).

Germany's IT Security Act 2.0, which parliament adopted in May 2021, gives the government power to veto procurement from an untrustworthy supplier (Chazan 2020). The law does not single out Huawei specifically, but requires companies involved in supplying critical infrastructure to guarantee that their equipment cannot be misused for illegal purposes, such as sabotage, espionage, or terrorism. Germany thus stopped short of an outright Huawei ban but raised the bar so high that the company would be effectively unable to enter Germany's 5G market (Hoppe and Koch 2020). As Christian Democratic Union parliamentarian Christoph Bernstiel said, "Companies that are under the control of authoritarian states are considered to be untrustworthy" (quoted in Noyan 2021b).

Like the UK, France reversed an earlier decision to allow Huawei equipment in its 5G networks. The head of the French National Cybersecurity Agency (ANSSI) initially said there would be no "total ban" on Huawei (Dèbes and Schmitt 2020). The agency reportedly told French telecom operators that Huawei equipment would be allowed in the rollout of 5G mobile networks, but it would be excluded from the networks' core (Rosemain and Barzic 2020a). Later, however, French regulators told telecom operators that it would not renew Huawei licenses when they expire in three to five years

(Rosemain and Barzic 2020b). ANSSI recommended network operators pursue contracts with Ericsson and Nokia instead of Huawei.

Italy has not banned Huawei outright (see Ghiretti 2020). However, the government can veto 5G supply deals that are deemed a threat to national security. In 2020, for instance, Italian authorities blocked a proposed deal between Fastweb, the Italian unit of Swisscom, and Huawei (Fonte and Pollina 2020). Many other countries, including most in Central and Eastern Europe, have imposed measures that effectively ban Huawei from their 5G networks.[21] Denmark, while not mentioning Huawei by name, announced that it would not allow equipment from countries that were not considered security allies (Reuters 2020).

While nearly all European countries have either banned or heavily restricted Huawei's presence in their 5G network infrastructure, Austria and Hungary have been more welcoming (Reuters 2019; Noyan 2021b). Leaders in both countries argued that there was no evidence that Huawei equipment would pose a security threat and announced that they intended to include Huawei in their 5G rollouts.

Conclusion

Europe is once again "between the superpowers."[22] US–China geopolitical competition has become globalized, with Europe forming one of the key battlegrounds. The clearest manifestation of this competition to date has been the struggle over Huawei's inclusion in Europe's 5G network infrastructure. The securitization of digital infrastructure has led this issue to serve as a microcosm of broader global transformations, centered on both the broadening of security concerns in the digital age and the role of Chinese companies in the provision of global information networks. The US–China rivalry thus plays out in a rapidly changing sphere of global economic activity with potential flashpoints emerging around specific private entities, such as China's Huawei.

As this chapter has shown, the battle over Huawei's role in Europe's 5G network infrastructure has revealed three broader features of how Europe is both a site of and participant in US–China geoeconomic competition and strategic rivalry. First, it has shown the complexities Europe faces in navigating this new geopolitical environment. Europe must decide how closely to align with the US and to what degree an independent approach toward China is viable. European countries have not simply copied US policies toward China, but they have taken steps to counter Chinese influence in Europe. While the political, historical, and cultural bonds linking the two sides of the Atlantic likely prevent Europe from attempting to take a middle path or one of equidistance between China and the US, this also depends in part on US actions. If the US displays more isolationist impulses and engages in more transactional rather than multilateral relations, Europe is more likely to view the benefits of an independent approach toward China as greater than the costs it may entail. In any event, China will be a more central reference point in transatlantic relations.

Second, European countries' strategies and approaches toward China do not always align. Countries disagree over a host of issues, including the risks associated with Chinese investment, how to respond to China's assertive behavior in Europe and other regions, and the presence of Chinese companies in 5G telecommunications networks. In response, China has at times been able to pursue an effective divide-and-rule strategy in Europe, taking advantage of differences between European countries to advance its economic or political interests. Chinese leaders "pay token respect to European integration," Godement says, "but they play upon the diverse interests of member states" (Godement 2020: 265). Collectively the EU would be better able to resist Chinese pressure, but underlying differences among European countries are likely to frustrate any common approach toward China for the foreseeable future.

Finally, European countries have been able to resist US and Chinese pressures to pursue their own strategies based on their own interests and preferences in this new strategic environment. While US–China competition may increasingly shape Europe's strategic choices, Europe's size and its central position in global networks and institutions guarantee that it will retain considerable room for maneuver. How Europe positions itself in this new strategic environment will hinge in part on how the US responds to its growing competition with China. If the US simply demands Europe to fall into line behind US leadership, Europe is likely to look for ways to find a balance between relations with Washington and Beijing. If, however, the US seeks to build a genuine partnership with Europe and take its interests and preferences into account, a transatlantic consensus on China is more likely to emerge.

Notes

[1] By "strategic partner," we mean an actor whose cooperation is perceived to be important or even essential for achieving key foreign policy and/or strategic goals.
[2] See also Digichina (2013).
[3] The 2017 US National Security Strategy argued, for instance, that "China is gaining a strategic foothold in Europe by expanding its unfair trade practices and investing in key industries, sensitive technologies, and infrastructure" (White House 2017: 47).
[4] See also Ministry of Foreign Affairs of the People's Republic of China (2018). China's economic strategy in Europe includes investments in strategic industries and funding infrastructure projects through its Belt and Road Initiative to establish transport corridors linking the two ends of the Eurasian landmass.
[5] Unlike Russia, however, China does not actively seek to undermine NATO or the EU.
[6] "The presence of strong international rules, norms, and institutions," one analyst explains, "help provide international stability and practicability, ensure free and open global commerce, and protect smaller countries from being coerced by their bigger neighbors"

7. Though the US military presence in Europe has declined significantly since the end of the Cold War, the US continues to station tens of thousands of active-duty military personnel across the continent. While the US military presence in Europe since the end of the Cold War has mainly been used for power projection into other regions, over the past decade it has become more focused on defense and deterrence in response to increasing Russian assertiveness, especially its February 2022 invasion of Ukraine.
8. Chinese investment in Europe has declined sharply since 2016, however.
9. Of this US$122 billion, Huawei's telecom equipment division recorded about US$42 billion in sales (Strumpf 2019).
10. A *Wall Street Journal* investigation found that "Huawei had access to as much as $75 billion in state support as it grew from a little-known vendor of phone switches to the world's largest telecom-equipment company" (Yap 2019).
11. Ren seems to have anticipated this outcome. "We have sacrificed ourselves and our families … for the sake of a dream, that we will stand on top of the world," he said. "For the sake of this dream, conflict with the United States is sooner or later inevitable" (quoted in Kania 2019).
12. US Department of State (nd).
13. Huawei had become the sole supplier of telecom equipment in some countries (Strand Consult 2020). On Huawei's operations in Europe before 2017, see Drahokoupil et al (2017).
14. Moreover, Europe's limited military capacity makes it unlikely that it will play a major military role in the Asia-Pacific. While in 2021 the European Commission unveiled an "Indo-Pacific" strategy, European countries have few concrete strategic interests in the Asia-Pacific and minimal military presence. Some countries, such as the UK and France, have announced their intention to increase their naval presence in the Indo-Pacific to support freedom of navigation. On the EU's Indo-Pacific strategy, see European Commission (2021a). On Europe's role in the Asia-Pacific region, see Meijer (2022) and Paul (2021).
15. At the same time, Europeans profess to feel a much stronger connection with the US than with China (see Bartsch and Laudien 2020).
16. In response to the imposition of Chinese sanctions against European academics, think tanks, and some of its own members, the European Parliament has refused to ratify the agreement.
17. On the limited impact of the EU's human rights dialogue with China, for instance, see Kinzelbach (2014).
18. On protecting Europe's "economic sovereignty," see Leonard et al (2019).
19. See NATO (2022). On how the alliance increasingly sees China as a global security challenge, see Heisbourg (2020). On the EU–US dialogue on China, see US Department of State (2021).
20. UK National Cyber Security Centre (2020).
21. The Trump administration signed bilateral agreements with several countries in Central and Eastern Europe, which pledged to restrict suppliers from untrustworthy countries (Pompeo 2020).
22. The phrase comes from DePorte (1979).

References

Alderman, L. and Cohen, R. 2021. "Clear Differences Remain Between France and U.S., French Minister Says." *New York Times*, October 11. https://www.nytimes.com/2021/10/11/world/europe/france-us-differences-bruno-le-maire.html

Allison, G., Klyman, K., Barbesino, K., and Yen, H. 2021. "The Great Tech Rivalry: China vs the U.S." Belfer Center for Science and International Affairs, Harvard Kennedy School, December. https://www.belfercenter.org/sites/default/files/GreatTechRivalry_ChinavsUS_211207.pdf

Ang, Y.Y. 2018. "Autocracy With Chinese Characteristics: Beijing's Behind-the-Scenes Reforms." *Foreign Affairs* 97(3): 39–46.

Barkin, N. 2020. "Export Controls and the US-China Tech War." Mercator Institute for China Studies, March 18. https://merics.org/en/report/export-controls-and-us-china-tech-war

Barnes, J.E. and Satariano, A. 2019. "U.S. Campaign to Ban Huawei Overseas Stumbles as Allies Resist." *New York Times*, March 17. https://www.nytimes.com/2019/03/17/us/politics/huawei-ban.html

Bartsch, B. and Laudien, A. 2020. "Survey: Europe's Views of China and the US-China Conflict." Bertelsmann Stiftung, January. https://www.bertelsmann-stiftung.de/fileadmin/files/user_upload/eupinions_China_DA_EN.pdf

Benner, T. 2019. "The Future of Huawei in Europe." *ChinaFile*, October 18. https://www.chinafile.com/conversation/future-of-huawei-europe

Benner, T. and Wright, T. 2018. "Testimony to U.S.-China Economic and Security Review Commission." Brookings, April 5. https://www.brookings.edu/wp-content/uploads/2018/04/wrightbennerchinatransatlanticrelations.pdf

Bennhold, K. and Ewing, J. 2020. "In Huawei Battle, China Threatens Germany 'Where It Hurts': Automakers." *New York Times*, January 16. https://www.nytimes.com/2020/01/16/world/europe/huawei-germany-china-5g-automakers.html

Bermann, S. 2021. "European Strategic Autonomy and the US–China Rivalry: Can the EU 'Prefer Not to Choose'?" Istituto Affari Internazionali, July. https://www.iai.it/sites/default/files/iaip2132.pdf

Biden, J.R. 2021. *Interim National Security Strategy Guidance*. March. https://www.whitehouse.gov/wp-content/uploads/2021/03/NSC-1v2.pdf

Biscop, S. 2019. *European Strategy in the 21st Century: New Future for Old Power*. Abingdon: Routledge.

Borrell, J. 2020. "The Sinatra Doctrine: How the EU Should Deal with the US-China Competition." Istituto Affari Internazionali, September. https://www.iai.it/sites/default/files/iaip2024.pdf

Brandt, J. and Taussig, T. 2020. "Europe's Authoritarian Challenge." *The Washington Quarterly* 42(4): 133–153.

Brattberg, E. 2021. "Middle Power Diplomacy in an Age of US–China Tensions." *The Washington Quarterly* 44(1): 219–238.

Brattberg, E. 2022. "Shifting European Attitudes toward China." In J.R. Deni (ed) *China, Europe, and the Pandemic Recession: Beijing's Investments and Transatlantic Security*. Carlisle, PA: US Army War College, pp 69–88. https://press.armywarcollege.edu/cgi/viewcontent.cgi?article=1945&context=monographs

Brown, M. and Singh, P. 2018. "China's Technology Transfer Strategy: How Chinese Investments in Emerging Technology Enable a Strategic Competitor to Access the Crown Jewels of U.S. Innovation." Defense Innovation Unit Experimental (DIUx), January. http://nationalsecurity.gmu.edu/wp-content/uploads/2020/02/DIUX-China-Tech-Transfer-Study-Selected-Readings.pdf

Casarini, N. 2016. "When All Roads Lead to Beijing. Assessing China's New Silk Road and Its Implications for Europe." *The International Spectator* 51(4): 95–108.

Chang, V.K.L. and Pieke, F.N. 2018. "Europe's Engagement with China: Shifting Chinese Views of the EU and the EU-China Relationship." *Asia Europe Journal* 16(4): 317–331.

Chazan, G. 2020, December 17. German IT law sets high bar for Huawei; Cyber security. *Financial Times*: 4.

Cheung, T.M. 2022. *Innovate to Dominate: The Rise of the Chinese Techno-Security State*. Ithaca, NY: Cornell University Press.

Cliff, R. 2022. "China's Strategy and Policy toward Europe Today." In J.R. Deni (ed) *China, Europe, and the Pandemic Recession: Beijing's Investments and Transatlantic Security*. Carlisle, PA: US Army War College, pp 27–68. https://press.armywarcollege.edu/cgi/viewcontent.cgi?article=1945&context=monographs

Cristiani, D., Ohlberg, M., Parello-Plesner, J., and Small, A. 2021. "The Security Implications of Chinese Infrastructure Investment in Europe." The German Marshall Fund of the United States, September. https://www.gmfus.org/sites/default/files/2021-09/Cristiani%20et%20al%20-%20report%20%281%29.pdf

Dèbes, F. and Schmitt, F. 2020. "'Il n'y aura pas un bannissement total de Huawei,' affirme le patron de l'Anssi." *Les Echos*, July 6. https://www.lesechos.fr/tech-medias/hightech/il-ny-aura-pas-un-bannissement-total-de-huawei-affirme-le-patron-de-lanssi-1221434

Deni, J.R. 2022. "Shifting European Poicies toward China." In J.R. Deni (ed) *China, Europe, and the Pandemic Recession: Beijing's Investments and Transatlantic Security*. Carlisle, PA: US Army War College, pp 89–116. https://press.armywarcollege.edu/cgi/viewcontent.cgi?article=1945&context=monographs

Dennison, S. 2019. "Give the People What They Want: Popular Demand for a Strong European Foreign Policy." European Council on Foreign Relations, September. https://ecfr.eu/archive/page/-/popular_demand_for_strong_european_foreign_policy_what_people_want.pdf

DePorte, A.W. 1979. *Europe between the Superpowers: The Enduring Balance*. New Haven: Yale University Press.

Digichina. 2013. "Communiqué on the Current State of the Ideological Sphere (Document No. 9)." Translated by R. Creemers, April 22. https://digichina.stanford.edu/work/communique-on-the-current-state-of-the-ideological-sphere-document-no-9/

Drahokoupil, J., McCaleb, A., Pawlicki, P., and Szunomár, Á. 2017. "Huawei in Europe: Strategic Integration of Local Capabilities in a Global Production Network." In J. Drahokoupil (ed) *Chinese Investment in Europe: Corporate Strategies and Labour Relations*. Brussels: European Trade Union Institute, pp 211–229.

Economy, E.C. 2022. *The World According to China*. Cambridge: Polity.

European Commission. 2019. "EU–China: A Strategic Outlook." JOIN(2019) 5 final. https://ec.europa.eu/info/sites/default/files/communication-eu-china-a-strategic-outlook.pdf

European Commission. 2021a. "The EU Strategy for Cooperation in the Indo-Pacific." JOIN(2021) 24 final, September 16. https://eeas.europa.eu/sites/default/files/jointcommunication_2021_24_1_en.pdf

European Commission. 2021b. "EU-US Trade and Technology Council Inaugural Joint Statement." September 29. https://ec.europa.eu/commission/presscorner/detail/en/STATEMENT_21_4951

European Court of Auditors. 2022. *5G Roll-Out in the EU: Delays in Deployment of Networks with Security Issues Remaining Unresolved*. Luxembourg: Publications Office of the European Union. https://www.eca.europa.eu/Lists/ECADocuments/SR22_03/SR_Security-5G-networks_EN.pdf

Fonte, G. and Pollina, E. 2020. "Italy Vetoes 5G Deal between Fastweb and China's Huawei." *Reuters*, October 23. https://www.reuters.com/article/us-huawei-italy-5g-idUSKBN2782A5

Foot, R. 2020. "US-China Relations in the Era of Xi and Trump: Implications for Europe." In R.S. Ross, Ø. Tunsjø, and W. Dong (eds) *US–China Foreign Relations Power Transition and its Implications for Europe and Asia*. London: Routledge, pp 63–74.

Fu, X. 2015. *China's Path to Innovation*. Cambridge: Cambridge University Press.

Gardner, A.L. 2020. *Stars with Stripes: The Essential Partnership between the European Union and the United States*. Basingstoke: Palgrave Macmillan.

Gewirtz, J.B. 2019. "China's Long March to Technological Supremacy: The Roots of Xi Jinping's Ambition to 'Catch Up and Surpass.'" *Foreign Affairs*, August 27. https://www.foreignaffairs.com/articles/china/2019-08-27/chinas-long-march-technological-supremacy

Ghiretti, F. 2020. "Europe's Manoeuvring on 5G Technology: The Case of Italy." *IAI Commentaries* 20(67): 1–6.

Godement, F. 2020. "China's Relations with Europe." In D. Shambaugh (ed) *China and the World*. New York: Oxford University Press, pp 251–269.

Godement, F. and Vasselier, A. 2017. *China at the Gates: A New Power Audit of EU-China Relations*. London: European Council on Foreign Relations. https://ecfr.eu/wp-content/uploads/China_Power_Audit.pdf

Goldkorn, J., et al. 2018. "Made in China 2025: The Domestic Tech Plan That Sparked an International Backlash." *SupChina*, June 28. https://supchina.com/2018/06/28/made-in-china-2025/

Hanhimäki, J.M. 2012. "Europe's Cold War." In D. Stone (ed) *The Oxford Handbook of Postwar European History*. Oxford: Oxford University Press, pp 283–298.

Heisbourg, F. 2020. "NATO 4.0: The Atlantic Alliance and the Rise of China." *Survival* 62(2): 83–102.

Hillman, J.E. 2020. *The Emperor's New Road: China and the Project of the Century*. New Haven: Yale University Press.

Hoffmann, S., Bradshaw, S., and Taylor, E. 2021. "Great Power Rivalries in 5G Technology Markets." In C.A. Crocker, F. Osler Hampson, and P. Aall (eds) *Diplomacy and the Future of World Order*. Washington, DC: Georgetown University Press, pp 241–271.

Holslag, J. 2015. "Explaining Economic Frictions Between China and the European Union." In V.K. Aggarwal and S.A. Newland (eds) *Responding to China's Rise: US and EU Strategies*. Cham: Springer, pp 131–150.

Holslag, J. 2017. "How China's New Silk Road Threatens European Trade." *The International Spectator* 52(1): 46–60.

Hoppe, T. and Koch, M. 2020, September 9. 5G: Hohe Hürden für Huawei. https://www.handelsblatt.com/politik/international/5g-mobilfunknetz-hohe-huerden-fuer-huawei-das-verfahren-kommt-einem-ausschluss-gleich/26229670.html

Inkster, N. 2020. *The Great Decoupling: China, America and the Struggle for Technological Supremacy*. London: Hurst.

Johnson, K. and Groll, E. 2019. "The Improbable Rise of Huawei." *Foreign Policy*, April 3. https://foreignpolicy.com/2019/04/03/the-improbable-rise-of-huawei-5g-global-network-china/

Kania, E.B. 2019. "The 5G Fight Is Bigger Than Huawei." *Foreign Policy*, May 22. https://foreignpolicy.com/2019/05/22/the-5g-fight-is-bigger-than-huawei/

Kaska, K., Beckvard, H., and Minárik, T. 2019. "Huawei, 5G and China as a Security Threat." NATO Cooperative Cyber Defence Centre of Excellence. https://ccdcoe.org/uploads/2019/03/CCDCOE-Huawei-2019-03-28-FINAL.pdf

Kinzelbach, K. 2014. *The EU's Human Rights Dialogue with China: Quiet Diplomacy and Its Limits*. London: Routledge.

Krach, K. 2017. "The Free World Must Unite Against Huawei." *The Daily Telegraph*, June 25. https://2017-2021.state.gov/The-free-world-must-unite-against-Huawei/index.html

Krastev, I. and Leonard, M. 2021a. "What Europeans Think about the US–China Cold War." European Council on Foreign Relations, September. https://ecfr.eu/wp-content/uploads/What-Europeans-think-about-the-US-China-Cold-War-2.pdf

Krastev, I. and Leonard, M. 2021b. "Europeans Want to Stay Out of the New Cold War." *Foreign Policy*, September 22. https://foreignpolicy.com/2021/09/22/europeans-want-to-stay-out-of-the-new-cold-war/

Kratz, A. and Oertel, J. 2021. "Home Advantage: How China's Protected Market Threatens Europe's Economic Power." European Council on Foreign Relations, April. https://ecfr.eu/wp-content/uploads/Home-advantage-How-Chinas-protected-market-threatens-Europes-economic-power.pdf

Kratz, A., Zenglein, M.J., and Sebastian, G. 2021. "Chinese Investment in Europe: 2020 Update." Rhodium Group and the Mercator Institute for China Studies (MERICS), June. https://merics.org/sites/default/files/2021-06/MERICSRhodium%20GroupCOFDIUpdate2021.pdf

Kuchins, A.C. 2021. "China's Policy toward Russia and Europe: The Eurasian Hookup." In D.B.H. Denoon (ed) *China's Grand Strategy: A Roadmap to Global Power?* New York: New York University Press, pp 191–211.

Le Corre, P. 2018. "Chinese Investments in European Countries: Experiences and Lessons for the 'Belt and Road' Initiative." In M. Mayer (ed) *Rethinking the Silk Road: China's Belt and Road Initiative and Emerging Eurasian Relations*. Singapore: Palgrave Macmillan, pp 161–175.

Le Corre, P. and Sepulchre, A. 2016. *China's Offensive in Europe*. Washington, DC: Brookings Institution Press.

Leonard, M., Pisani-Ferry, J., Ribakova, E., Shapiro, J., and Wolff, G. 2019. "Securing Europe's Economic Sovereignty." *Survival* 61(5): 75–98.

McKean, D. and Szewczyk, B.M.J. 2021. *Partners of First Resort: America, Europe, and the Future of the West*. Washington, DC: Brookings Institution Press.

Meijer, H. 2022. *Awakening to China's Rise: European Foreign and Security Policies toward the People's Republic of China*. Oxford: Oxford University Press.

Meijer, H. and Brooks, S.G. 2021. "Illusions of Autonomy: Why Europe Cannot Provide for Its Security If the United States Pulls Back." *International Security* 45(4): 7–43.

Milne, R. 2020. "Sweden Bans Huawei and ZTE from 5G Telecoms Networks." *Financial Times*, October 20. https://www.ft.com/content/3933d9f9-b466-4d1e-8067-ef3c7a8b01f4

Ministry of Foreign Affairs of the People's Republic of China. 2018. "China's Policy Paper on the European Union." December 18. https://www.fmprc.gov.cn/mfa_eng/wjdt_665385/2649_665393/201812/t20181218_679556.html

Mukherjee, S. and Soderpalm, H. 2020. "Sweden Bans Huawei, ZTE from Upcoming 5G Networks." *Reuters*, October 20. https://www.reuters.com/article/sweden-huawei-int/sweden-bans-huawei-zte-from-upcoming-5g-networks-idUSKBN2750WA

Nathan, A.J. and Scobell, A. 2014. *China's Search for Security*. New York: Columbia University Press.

NATO. 2022. *NATO 2022 Strategic Concept*. June 29. https://www.nato.int/nato_static_fl2014/assets/pdf/2022/6/pdf/290622-strategic-concept.pdf

NIS Cooperation Group. 2019. "EU Coordinated Risk Assessment of the Cybersecurity of 5G Networks." https://ec.europa.eu/commission/presscorner/detail/en/IP_19_6049

NIS Cooperation Group. 2020. "Cybersecurity of 5G Networks: EU Toolbox of Risk Mitigating Measures." https://ccdcoe.org/uploads/2020/01/EU-200129-Cybersecurity-of-5G-networks-EU-Toolbox-of-risk-mitigating-measures.pdf

Nouwens, M. and Legarda, H. 2018. "China's Pursuit of Advanced Dual-Use Technologies." International Institute for Strategic Studies, December 18. https://www.iiss.org/blogs/research-paper/2018/12/emerging-technology-dominance

Noyan, O. 2021a. "Austria to Also Rely on Huawei in 5G Rollout." *Euractiv*, October 29. https://www.euractiv.com/section/5g/news/austria-to-also-rely-on-huawei-in-5g-rollout/

Noyan, O. 2021b. "EU Countries Keep Different Approaches to Huawei on 5G Rollout." *Euractiv*, May 19. https://www.euractiv.com/section/digital/news/eu-countries-keep-different-approaches-to-huawei-on-5g-rollout/

Odgaard, L. 2020. "Europe's Place in Sino-U.S. Competition." In A.J. Tellis, A. Szalwinski, and M. Wills (eds) *Strategic Asia 2020: U.S.–China Competition for Global Influence*. Seattle: The National Bureau of Asian Research, pp 247–274.

Oertel, J. 2019. "Germany Chooses China Over the West." *Foreign Policy*, October 21. https://foreignpolicy.com/2019/10/21/germany-merkel-chooses-china-over-united-states-eu-huawei/

Oertel, J. 2020. "The New China Consensus: How Europe Is Growing Wary of Beijing." European Council on Foreign Relations, September. https://ecfr.eu/wp-content/uploads/the_new_china_consensus_how_europe_is_growing_wary_of_beijing.pdf

Pancevski, B. and Germano, S. 2019. "Drop Huawei or See Intelligence Sharing Pared Back, U.S. Tells Germany." *Wall Street Journal*, March 11. https://www.wsj.com/articles/drop-huawei-or-see-intelligence-sharing-pared-back-u-s-tells-germany-11552314827

Paul, M. 2021. "Europe and the South China Sea: Challenges, Constraints and Options." In S. Biba and R. Wolf (eds) *Europe in an Era of Growing Sino-American Competition: Coping with an Unstable Triangle*. London: Routledge, pp 92–106.

Pompeo, M.R. 2020. "The Tide Is Turning Toward Trusted 5G Vendors." June 24. https://2017-2021.state.gov/the-tide-is-turning-toward-trusted-5g-vendors/index.html

PTS. 2020. "Four Companies Approved for Participation in the 3.5 GHz and 2.3 GHz auctions." October 10. https://www.pts.se/en/news/press-releases/2020/four-companies-approved-for-participation-in-the-3.5-ghz-and-2.3-ghz-auctions

Reilly, J. 2021. *Orchestration: China's Economic Statecraft Across Asia and Europe*. Oxford: Oxford University Press.

Retter, L., Pezard, S., Flanagan, S., Germanovich, G., Grand Clement, S., and Paille, P. 2021. *European Strategic Autonomy in Defense: Transatlantic Visions and Implications for NATO, US and EU Relations*. Santa Monica: RAND Corporation. https://www.rand.org/pubs/research_reports/RRA1319-1.html

Reuters. 2019. "Hungarian Minister Opens Door to Huawei for 5G Network Rollout." November 5. https://www.reuters.com/article/us-hungary-telecoms-huawei/hungarian-minister-opens-door-to-huawei-for-5g-network-rollout-idUSKBN1XF12U

Reuters. 2020. "Denmark Wants 5G Suppliers from Closely Allied Countries, Says Defence Minister." June 8. https://www.reuters.com/article/us-telecoms-5g-denmark-idUSKBN23F1IT

Rosemain, M. and Barzic, G. 2020a. "France to Allow Some Huawei Gear in Its 5G Network." *Reuters*, March 12. https://www.reuters.com/article/us-france-huawei-5g-exclusive/exclusive-france-to-allow-some-huawei-gear-in-its-5g-network-sources-idUSKBN20Z3JR

Rosemain, M. and Barzic, G. 2020b. "French Limits on Huawei 5G Equipment Amount to De Facto Ban by 2028." *Reuters*, July 22. https://www.reuters.com/article/us-france-huawei-5g-security-exclusive/exclusive-french-limits-on-huawei-5g-equipment-amount-to-de-facto-ban-by-2028-sources-idUSKCN24N26R

Sanger, D.E. 2018. *The Perfect Weapon: War, Sabotage, and Fear in the Cyber Age*. New York: Crown.

Sanger, D.E. 2020. "Managing the Fifth Generation: America, China, and the Struggle for Technological Dominance." In L. Bitounis and J. Price (eds) *The Struggle for Power: U.S.–China Relations in the 21st Century*. Washington, DC: The Aspen Institute, pp 113–121.

Sanger, D.E. and McCabe, D. 2020. "Huawei Is Winning the Argument in Europe, as the U.S. Fumbles to Develop Alternatives." *New York Times*, February 17. https://www.nytimes.com/2020/02/17/us/politics/us-huawei-5g.html

Sanger, D.E., Benner, K., and Goldstein, M. 2019a. "Huawei and Top Executive Face Criminal Charges in the U.S." *New York Times*, January 28. https://www.nytimes.com/2019/01/28/us/politics/meng-wanzhou-huawei-iran.html

Sanger, D.E., Barnes, J.E., Zhong, R., and Santora, M. 2019b. "In 5G Race With China, U.S. Pushes Allies to Fight Huawei." *New York Times*, January 26. https://www.nytimes.com/2019/01/26/us/politics/huawei-china-us-5g-technology.html

Satariano, A. 2020. "Britain Defies Trump Plea to Ban Huawei From 5G Network." *New York Times*, January 28. https://www.nytimes.com/2020/01/28/technology/britain-huawei-5G.html

Schneider-Petsinger, M., Wang, J., Jie, Y., and Crabtree, J. 2019. "US–China Strategic Competition: The Quest for Global Technological Leadership." Chatham House, November. https://www.chathamhouse.org/sites/default/files/publications/research/CHHJ7480-US-China-Competition-RP-WEB.pdf

Segal, A. 2021. "Huawei, 5G, and Weaponized Interdependence." In D.W. Drezner, H. Farrell, and A.L. Newman (eds) *The Uses and Abuses of Weaponized Interdependence*. Washington, DC: Brookings Institution Press, pp 149–166.

Shambaugh, D. 2021. *Where Great Powers Meet: America and China in Southeast Asia*. Oxford: Oxford University Press.

Simón, L. 2021. "Subject and Object: Europe in Sino-American Competition." Robert Schuman Centre Policy Brief, European University Institute, September. https://cadmus.eui.eu/bitstream/handle/1814/72602/QM-AX-21-042-EN-N.pdf?sequence=1&isAllowed=y

Small, A. 2019. "Why Europe Is Getting Tough on China: And What It Means for Washington." *Foreign Affairs*, April 3. https://www.foreignaffairs.com/articles/china/2019-04-03/why-europe-getting-tough-china

Small, A., Glaser, B.S., and Mohan, G. 2022. "US-European Cooperation on China and the Indo-Pacific." The German Marshall Fund of the United States, February 2. https://www.gmfus.org/news/us-european-cooperation-china-and-indo-pacific

Smith, J. and Taussig, T. 2019. "The Old World and the Middle Kingdom: Europe Wakes Up to China's Rise." *Foreign Affairs* 98(5): 112–124.

Stevis-Gridneff, M. 2019. "Blocked in U.S., Huawei Touts 'Shared Values' to Compete in Europe." *New York Times*, December 27. https://www.nytimes.com/2019/12/27/world/europe/huawei-EU-5G-Europe.html

Strand Consult. 2020. "Understanding the Market for 4G RAN in Europe: Share of Chinese and Non-Chinese Vendors in 102 Mobile Networks." https://strandconsult.dk/understanding-the-market-for-4g-ran-in-europe-share-of-chinese-and-non-chinese-vendors-in-102-mobile-networks/

Strumpf, D. 2019. "Huawei's Revenue Hits Record $122 Billion in 2019 Despite U.S. Campaign." *Wall Street Journal*, December 30. https://www.wsj.com/articles/huaweis-revenue-hits-record-122-billion-in-2019-despite-u-s-campaign-11577754021

Szewczyk, B.M.J. 2019. "Europe and the Liberal Order." *Survival* 61(2): 33–52.

Tatlow, D.K., Feldwisch-Drentrup, H., and Fedasiuk, R. 2021. "Europe: A Technology Transfer Mosaic." In W.C. Hannas and D.K. Tatlow (eds) *China's Quest for Foreign Technology: Beyond Espionage*. London: Routledge, pp 113–129.

Triolo, P. 2020a. "China's 5G Strategy: Be First Out of the Gate and Ready to Innovate." In S. Kennedy (ed) *China's Uneven High-Tech Drive: Implications for the United States*. Washington, DC: Center for Strategic and International Studies, pp 21–28.

Triolo, P. 2020b. *The Telecommunications Industry in US–China Context: Evolving toward Near-Complete Bifurcation*. Baltimore: Johns Hopkins Applied Physics Laboratory. https://www.jhuapl.edu/Content/documents/Triolo-Telecomms.pdf

Triolo, P., Allison, K., and Brown, C. 2018. "The Geopolitics of 5G." Eurasia Group White Paper, November 15. https://www.eurasiagroup.net/siteFiles/Media/files/1811-14%205G%20special%20report%20public(1).pdf

Tunsjø, O. 2015. "China's Rise: Towards a Division of Labor in Transatlantic Relations." In V.K. Aggarwal and S.A. Newland (eds) *Responding to China's Rise: US and EU Strategies*. Cham: Springer, pp 151–174.

UK National Cyber Security Centre. 2020. "Huawei to Be Removed from UK 5G Networks by 2027." July 14. https://www.gov.uk/government/news/huawei-to-be-removed-from-uk-5g-networks-by-2027

US Department of Defense. 2018. *Summary of the National Defense Strategy of the United States of America: Sharpening the American Military's Competitive Edge*. Washington, DC: Office of the Secretary of Defense. https://dod.defense.gov/Portals/1/Documents/pubs/2018-National-Defense-Strategy-Summary.pdf

US Department of State. 2021. "U.S.–EU: Joint Press Release by the EEAS and Department of State on the Second High-Level Meeting of the U.S.-EU Dialogue on China." December 2. https://www.state.gov/u-s-eu-joint-press-release-by-the-eeas-and-department-of-state-on-the-second-high-level-meeting-of-the-u-s-eu-dialogue-on-china/

US Department of State. nd. "The Clean Network." https://2017-2021.state.gov/the-clean-network/index.html

Walt, S.M. 2019. "Europe's Future Is as China's Enemy." *Foreign Policy*, January 22. https://foreignpolicy.com/2019/01/22/europes-future-is-as-chinas-enemy/

Walt, S.M. 2021. "Will Europe Ever Really Confront China?" *Foreign Policy*, October 15. https://foreignpolicy.com/2021/10/15/will-europe-ever-really-confront-china/

Wen, Y. 2020. *The Huawei Model: The Rise of China's Technology Giant*. Champaign: University of Illinois Press.

Wheeler, T. and Simpson, D. 2019. "Why 5G Requires New Approaches to Cybersecurity." Brookings Institution, September 3. https://www.brookings.edu/research/why-5g-requires-new-approaches-to-cybersecurity/

White House. 2017. *National Security Strategy of the United States of America*. December. https://trumpwhitehouse.archives.gov/wp-content/uploads/2017/12/NSS-Final-12-18-2017-0905.pdf

White House. 2020. *National Strategy to Secure 5G of the United States of America*. March. https://trumpwhitehouse.archives.gov/wp-content/uploads/2020/03/National-Strategy-5G-Final.pdf

White House. 2021. "Remarks by President Biden at the 2021 Virtual Munich Security Conference." February 19. https://www.whitehouse.gov/briefing-room/speeches-remarks/2021/02/19/remarks-by-president-biden-at-the-2021-virtual-munich-security-conference/

Williams, R. 2019. "Securing 5G Networks: Challenges and Recommendations." Council on Foreign Relations, July 15. https://www.cfr.org/report/securing-5g-networks

Wright, T. 2021. "Europe Changes Its Mind on China." In T. Chhabra, R. Doshi, R. Haas, and E. Kimball (eds) *Global China: Assessing China's Growing Role in the World*. Washington, DC: Brookings Institution Press, pp 140–148.

Xinhua. 2018. "Xi Calls for Developing China into World Science and Technology Leader." May 29. http://english.www.gov.cn/news/top_news/2018/05/28/content_281476163679658.htm

Yap, C.-W. 2019. "State Support Helped Fuel Huawei's Global Rise." *Wall Street Journal*, December 25. https://www.wsj.com/articles/state-support-helped-fuel-huaweis-global-rise-11577280736

Zenglein, M.J. and Holzmann, A. 2019. "Evolving Made in China 2025: China's Industrial Policy in the Quest for Global Tech Leadership." Mercator Institute for China Studies, July. https://merics.org/sites/default/files/2020-04/MPOC_8_MadeinChina_2025_final_3.pdf

Zhong, R. 2018. "Huawei's 'Wolf Culture' Helped It Grow, and Got It Into Trouble." *New York Times*, December 18. https://www.nytimes.com/2018/12/18/technology/huawei-workers-iran-sanctions.html

PART III
Conclusions

11

Conclusions: Reframing the Puzzle of US–China Rivalry

Salvador Santino F. Regilme Jr

At the start of the 21st century, the international system underwent at least three major critical junctures: the 9/11 terror attacks that paved the way for the US-led global war on terror and its consequent human rights abuses (Acharya 2007; Christie 2008; Foot 2008; Herman 2011; Shafiq 2013; Sanders 2017; Regilme 2018a, 2018b, 2021a); the 2007/2008 global financial crisis (Aydın 2011; Helleiner 2011; Drezner 2013; Kiely 2018; Ansell and Bartenberger 2019); and the COVID-19 pandemic (May and Daly 2020; Regilme 2020; Theidon 2020; Greer et al 2021). The most recent critical juncture—the COVID-19 pandemic—killed at least 6.6 million people since 2020 until October 2022. That pandemic, however, is not merely a global health crisis. Rather, it emerged as a powerful vector of other transnational challenges of catastrophic proportions, whereas some of these challenges may not be directly attributable to the pandemic itself, while others may have been reinforced after the start of the pandemic: the widespread inflation crisis in many parts of the globe (Aharon and Qadan 2022); democratic backsliding and widespread human rights abuses (Greer et al 2020; Pleyers 2020; Thomson and Ip 2020; Lundgren et al 2021; Passos and Acácio 2021; Regilme 2021b); climate catastrophes and extreme weather conditions (Bergquist et al 2022; Ford et al 2022); food insecurity (Kumar and Ayedee 2021; Sacks et al 2021; Bergquist et al 2022); energy insecurity (Ghilès 2022); and, the looming probability that Russian militarized aggression in Ukraine could spill over to other Central and Western European countries, which in turn, could trigger intensified military conflict elsewhere (deLisle 2022; Wu 2022).

Consequently, an apparent consensus seems to be emerging, perhaps regardless of one's political ideologies: the world is in deep, multidimensional crisis (Ndlovu-Gatsheni 2020; Regilme 2020; Steger 2021). What this crisis means could differ depending on your positionality in this deeply hierarchical and differentiated world-system (Anthias 2008; Sakai 2012; Koinova 2017; McIntosh 2020; Soedirgo and Glas 2020). For a white, super-rich man living in the affluent quarters of New York, London, or Zurich, the crisis is likely triggered by a growing popular resistance against capitalism and extreme socioeconomic inequalities, while invoking that their private property rights are violated by state policy actions that redirect wealth to the most marginalized (Hammond 2016; Regilme 2019a; Whyte 2019). For a financially struggling, Black, Muslim woman living in a small Bavarian town in Germany, the terms socioeconomic equality and crisis have life-and-death consequences. Of course, while the systematic persecution from the Chinese state has started even before the pandemic, Uyghur families in the Xinjiang region struggle to escape from the daily realities of imprisonment in government-sponsored concentration camps, enslaved labor, forced sterilization, and many other horrendous abuses that do not only threaten individual Uyghurs but the future of their collective existence (Roberts 2020; Alpermann 2022). Although systemic violence and domination have persisted for most of human history, the aforementioned challenges seem to suggest that the global order legitimized through the discourse of liberal democracy and underwritten by Western militarism is in deep crisis. Whereas it is difficult to ascertain if the 21st-century challenges are extreme or more severe than in previous generations since the age of global interdependence, Walden Bello (2022: 3), nonetheless paints the similarities between climate change crisis and the sociopolitical crises of humanity:

> So you see, extreme events are taking place not only in the physical climate. They too take place in the political climate. January 6, 2021, the storming of the Capitol in the US, was another such event. The return of the Marcoses, Trump's incitement to rebellion, Modi's ethnonationalist regime in India, Bolsonaro's fastcistoid government in Brazil, and just in the last few days, the electoral triumphs of the far right in traditionally Social Democratic Sweden and, horror of horrors, in the birthplace of fascism itself, Italy—all of these are extreme events, and they are, in turn, symptoms of a much larger extreme event: the deepening crisis of liberal democracy. (Bello 2022)

Amidst this crisis-ridden global system, the US and China have emerged as the two most powerful state actors, despite all the optimism that was invigorated about the so-called 'emerging powers' during the last two decades (Regilme and Parisot 2017, 2020). Notably, political analysts and commentators have overestimated the potential of other re-emerging powers and actors of the post-Cold War global order. In Europe, although not a unitary state actor on its own, the EU—and its most powerful member states such as Germany and France—is facing a complex crisis that shows the union's structural vulnerabilities, which in turn, undermine its capacities as a credible partner—if not competitor or challenger—to US dominance in world politics. Once considered as a re-emerging power a few years back, Russia did not live up to its promise as showcased by its horrendous war of aggression against Ukraine, where the tactical and strategic weaknesses of the Russian military became more evident. As the EU's biggest economy, Germany is facing its most severe economic crisis since the Second World War—a situation directly triggered by the extreme shortages in energy supply due to the country's enduring dependence on Russia. As the EU and the US imposed sanctions on Russia due to Moscow's militaristic aggression against Ukraine, Europe's energy insecurity transformed into a severe existential problem for many households, who have been battling against inflation, unemployment, and job insecurity—many of which were reinforced after the COVID-19 pandemic (Osička and Černoch 2022). Germany is not alone in that predicament; France, Italy, Spain, and others in Western Europe also face the same fate as Germany. It is difficult to imagine the future of a supposed re-emerging power with a severe energy supply problem, which in turn does not only undermine its military security but more so its population's basic economic and existential security. In South America, Brazil was once touted as the rising power of the region, with staggering economic growth and increased optimism for the future—and that was in the first decade of the new millennium (Sotero 2010; Dauvergne and Farias 2012). Yet, the rise of far-right populism and the horrendous policies of the Bolsonaro government backtracked all the social and economic progress of the preceding government: widespread human rights abuses, severe public security crisis, widespread disinformation, proliferation of extreme poverty and hunger, as well as unprecedented environmental devastation (Hunter and Power 2019). In the Indo-Pacific region, other key regional players such as India and Indonesia have persistently focused on their domestic challenges that are primarily aggravated during this pandemic; in doing so, they have fell short in demonstrating that their influence could transcend their own regions and in ways that either US or China do (Nilsen 2021; Warburton 2022). Despite their severe domestic economic and political challenges, the US and China seem to have the unique capabilities to project their economic, cultural, political, and social influence far beyond their immediate regional neighborhood—at least in comparison to Western European powers (UK, France, and Germany) and other so-called re-emerging or emerging powers.

In the emerging post-COVID-19 global order, scholars, public intellectuals, and influential political commentators frame the question of global transformation as a question of competing states (Ndlovu-Gatsheni 2020). In 2022, the most anticipated books concerning US–China rivalry, as written by some high-profile public commentators, problematize the nature of that bilateral relation simply as just that: two nations battling for world dominance (Doshi 2021; Bergsten 2022; Economy 2022; Friedberg 2022; Rudd 2022). As we should have learned during this pandemic, framing serious global challenges as purely an inter-state matter is indeed a widespread but avoidable mistake. The failure of many states to cooperate in ways that could have made medical supplies and effective vaccines more accessible to all countries—all perhaps in the name of nationalistic state interests buttressed by corporate interests holding proprietary rights over vaccine patents—suggests that global challenges should be framed as shared problems of humanity, regardless of one's nationality (Guttry 2020; Mittelman 2021; Idris et al 2022; Jecker 2022).

For scholars, however, it is high time to reformulate the puzzle concerning global transformation. It is likely the case that, regardless whether it is China or the US that emerges as the most powerful state actor a decade from now, the world's human population suffering from extreme material poverty will continue to grow (Oxfam 2020; Cousin and Chauvin 2021). On the one hand, China's blatantly authoritarian political culture, with its economy governed by neoliberal capitalist logic, generated widespread physical integrity rights abuses, blatant dehumanizing and genocidal practices of historically minoritized populations, as well as severe curtailment of dissenting views in the civil society sphere (Roberts 2020; Alpermann 2022). On the other hand, several decades of the US-dominant world order have shown what systemic hypocrisy looks like in global governance. US elites could preach about human rights, justice, and democracy both at home and abroad; yet, those same normatively appealing discourses, among many other lofty ideals, are blatantly disregarded whenever it is convenient for the ruling capitalist class (Acharya 2007; Moyn 2017; Regilme 2019b, 2022).

As such, the puzzle of global transformation should entail an interrogation of what such an inter-state rivalry could mean across various regions and to the less powerful and marginalized sectors of the human population. Those analytic perspectives are unfortunately missing, and that is why this book aimed to provide an alternative space for rethinking US–China rivalry. In all cases, the chapter contributors in this anthology stepped back and interrogated rivalry from the positionality of the region where they specialize as researchers and, perhaps in many cases, are geographically located. The chapters in this volume did so in several notable ways.

First, the need to accumulate capital and crucial resources for continued economic growth are crucial factors in shaping the trajectory of the rivalry, although the precise conditions of such a need depends on *where* this economic conflict occurs. For instance, the chapter by Parisot and Lin focuses on global capitalism as an abstracted space of rivalry, whereby China is described as an authoritarian capitalism, while the US tends to have a more liberal capitalist system. Nonetheless, Parisot and Lin highlight the problem of capitalist state-centrism that generated uneven and combined development, thereby sharpening material inequalities and bolstering conflict. Similarly, in my analysis of the South China Sea dispute, I highlight the economic motives of all small claimant states, China, and the US. The militarization of the maritime dispute coincided with the rapid economic growth of China, and the naval control of the disputed region has tremendous consequences on which states are most likely to benefit from the so-called "freedom of navigation" rights therein as well as the supposed natural resources of the area. In the aforementioned maritime dispute, I urge claimant states as well as the US to ensure that any conflict resolution framework should ensure that economic gains and resources should benefit the claimant states' most marginalized populations, whose livelihood, wellbeing, and social identity are intricately imbricated in the South China Sea. Focusing on Europe as another site of US–China competition, Richard Maher and Till Schöfer examine the motivation of European countries in increasing their economic growth through productive trade and financial relations with China, as shown by the case of China's 5G telecommunications network investments in the continent. Yet, that motivation coincides with the enduring need for Europe to depend on the US for its defense needs, and balancing those two desires constitutes a key challenge as Beijing and Washington DC have conflicting visions of the global order. While admitting that the Asia-Pacific remains the key flashpoint of US–China rivalry, Maher and Schöfer note that not all European countries have converging views on China, and that fragmentation is most likely to prevent Europe from functioning as a coherent third actor in US–China rivalry. Yet, the authors infer that Europe remains in a good position to influence its immediate regional neighborhood, as the continent functions as an important node in global financial networks and global governance institutions, thereby rendering European countries some leverage in shaping how and under which conditions US–China rivalry could impact regional security.

Second, intersubjective interpretations about physical geography and social relations play an important role in the trajectory of great power relations, yet those elements are often sidelined in mainstream scholarly analysis in favor of military- and economic-oriented factors. In the chapter focusing on Northeast Asia, Jing Sun argues that physical geography functions as a malleable social construct that is relevant for weaponizing Chinese national identity as well as a security concept that could be shaped by political elites for what they view as crucial state interest. As such, the influential Chinese concept of *"tianxia"* (All under Heaven) serves as a spatial-positioning discursive device, in which various political actors interpret it in ways that could mean accommodation to domination—and those specific interpretations explain the shift from a policy preference focusing on Chinese dominance in land or to the high seas. Similarly, in the chapter focusing on Africa, Lina Benabdallah investigates how the Chinese state targets political elites in various African states through what she calls as "party-to-party" diplomacy. In such a mode of diplomacy, the focus is on fostering strong and positive intersubjective views between Chinese and African elites, thereby enhancing trust among participant countries. Whereas so much of the literature on Chinese relations in the Global South focus on concrete material investments such as physical infrastructures and loan agreements, understanding the non-material aspects of international relations such as social platforms through professional training programs could provide another way of enhancing our view of power mediated across national boundaries.

Third, understanding how intersubjective meanings about physical geography change over *time* provides important insights in the analysis of US–China rivalry. As such, spatialization as an analytic tool becomes more useful when geographic space is juxtaposed with temporal conditions, particularly in analyzing great power conflict. In the chapter focusing on the Middle East, Chien-Kai Chen and Ceren Ergenc use the notion of *path dependence* to demonstrate that the contemporary actions of key political actors from the US, China, and the Middle East are shaped by previous policy outcomes. Although they acknowledge that China might emerge as a bit more interventionist in the region due to the instability and political vacuum directly caused by the sudden US withdrawal in Afghanistan, both authors emphasized that the non-interventionist image of Beijing among Middle Eastern states has persisted over time and will most likely remain in the foreseeable future. In the chapter focusing on the Southeast Asian region, I emphasized that the disputed maritime space of the South China Sea has persisted for several decades, yet China's rapid economic growth and the domestic political struggles in Beijing paved the way for intensified militarization and regional insecurity. As such, long-standing territorial disputes could escalate through intensified military build-up by conflicting parties when certain structural conditions are met. Meanwhile, Cameron Carlson and Linda Kiltz underscore that the rapid warming of the Arctic means the fast disappearance of sea ice, thereby increasing the accessibility to the region. That unprecedented physical transformation of the Arctic region triggers the expectation that China will become more assertive in expressing its interest despite the fact that Beijing has historically been a non-participant in the Artic Council. Carlson and Kiltz warn that time is likely to favor China, considering that climate research models suggest an ice-free Arctic region during the summer season, and it is very likely that Beijing could increase its presence therein, especially if the US and other Arctic Council members fail to ascertain and counter the long-term strategy of China. Those three chapters show that physical geography only makes sense in political analysis when one analyzes how intersubjective views about it change over time, or across temporal dimensions.

Fourth, the manifestations of how physical geography emerges as the locus of contestation between great power could be investigated through the developments in institutional structures. Juan Serrano-Moreno focuses on the institutionalization of the Belt and Road Initiative (BRI) and the participation of Latin American and Caribbean (LAC) countries. Accordingly, the BRI emerged as an institutional response of China to the decreasing US presence in South America, which has been a supposed traditional sphere of influence for Washington DC. For Serrano-Moreno, the BRI appears as an ambiguous yet malleable form of institutional platform for generating financial investments, trade deals, and public infrastructure projects that are quite difficult to ascertain whether they are beneficial to LAC countries—although China appears as the biggest winner due to the diplomatic gains accrued through the BRI. As a transnational institution, the BRI functions as a discursive tool that allows LAC governments to discern their preferred degree of involvement, while discursively depicting China as the mobilizer of connectivity and innovation within the region.

Fifth, the chapters herein show the promising explanatory potential of transcending the limits of state-centric analysis in International Relations (IR). Deepshikha Shahi, in her chapter on South Asia, adopts a non-dualistic "Global IR" approach, particularly the Indian philosophical perspective of Advaita as an analytic lens. In doing so, Shahi evaluates India's foreign policy responses to the ongoing US–China contestations in South Asia by highlighting the notion of "single hidden connectedness" that makes all the actors within and beyond the South Asian region interdependent, thereby making them stakeholders and participants in US–China contestations, albeit to varying degrees. Whereas Western-style IR thinking is fixated on dualistic logics such as enmity/friendship, the Advaita philosophy aids our understanding of US–China conflict in South Asia by acknowledging the complex interactions not only of state leaders but also by other key actors *and* over historical time. Similarly, in the chapter on Southeast Asia, I explained the unprecedented militarization of the South China Sea by espousing analytic eclecticism, whereby domestic and transnational political factors are teased out in order to build a coherent causal story of recently intensified US–China rivalry. In the chapter on Africa, Benabdallah examines China's power projection in Africa through a "relational power" framework that underscores the processes of party-to-party diplomacy between African and Chinese political elites. Consequently, Benabdallah distinguishes Chinese power mechanisms in Africa from American foreign policy strategies in the African continent.

This book began with the puzzle on how great power rivalry and cooperation are created and transformed across various territorial spaces.

The chapters here contribute to ongoing scholarly and policy debates concerning the seemingly unprecedented challenges of the post-COVID-19 world order. Specifically, the contributors demonstrate that the formations and transformations of US–China rivalry ultimately depend on one's positionality in a highly interdependent global order: across various world-regions, temporal conditions, and socioeconomic backgrounds. While discussions in the corridors of power and in the academic ivory-tower focus so much on which next great power will emerge at a time in what appears to be a critical juncture of global politics, it is high time that we realize that global politics—for many of those in other parts of the world—is not about great power rivalry. Rather, global politics is a struggle for power, justice, and survival amidst a system that is entrenched by logics of hierarchies, stratification, differentiation, and domination. In realizing that is the case, the question of global transformation should shift from inter-state rivalry to explaining why such perverse logics of oppression persist and to what extent they could be undermined and, in doing so, how global justice could emerge.

References

Acharya, A. 2007. "State Sovereignty After 9/11: Disorganised Hypocrisy." *Political Studies* 55(2): 274–296.

Aharon, D.Y. and Qadan, M. 2022. "Infection, Invasion, and Inflation: Recent Lessons." *Finance Research Letters* 50: 103307.

Alpermann, B. 2022. "The War on the Uyghurs: China's Internal Campaign against a Muslim Minority." *Politics, Religion & Ideology* 23(2): 243–244.

Ansell, C. and Bartenberger, M. 2019. *Pragmatism and Political Crisis Management*. Cheltenham: Edward Elgar.

Anthias, F. 2008. "Thinking through the Lens of Translocational Positionality: An Intersectionality Frame for Understanding Identity and Belonging." *Translocations* 4(1): 5–20.

Aydın, N. 2011. "The 2008 Financial Crisis: A Moral Crisis of Capitalism." *African Journal of Business Management* 5(22): 8697–8706.

Bello, W. 2022. "Extreme Events Are the New Normal, and Not Just in the Weather." *Transnational Institute*. https://www.tni.org/en/article/extreme-events-are-the-new-normal-and-not-just-in-the-weather

Bergquist, P., De Roche, G., Lachapelle, E., Mildenberger, M. and Harrison, K. 2023. "The Politics of Intersecting Crises: The Effect of the COVID-19 Pandemic on Climate Policy Preferences." *British Journal of Political Science* 53(2): 707–716.

Bergsten, C.F. 2022. *The United States vs. China: The Quest for Global Economic Leadership*. London: Polity Press.

Christie, K. 2008. *America's War on Terrorism: The Revival of the Nation-State Versus Universal Human Rights*. New York: Edwin Mellen Press.

Cousin, B. and Chauvin, S. 2021. "Is There a Global Super-bourgeoisie?" *Sociology Compass*. https://doi.org/10.1111/soc4.12883

Dauvergne, P. and Farias, D.B.L. 2012. "The Rise of Brazil as a Global Development Power." *Third World Quarterly* 33(5): 903–917.

deLisle, J. 2022. "China's Russia/Ukraine Problem, and Why It's Bad for Almost Everyone Else Too." *Orbis* 66(3): 402–423.

Doshi, R. 2021. *The Long Game: China's Grand Strategy to Displace American Order*. Oxford and New York: Oxford University Press.

Drezner, D.W. 2013. "The System Worked: Global Economic Governance during the Great Recession." *World Politics* 66(1): 123–164.

Economy, E. 2022. *The World According to China*. London: Polity Press.

Foot, R. 2008. "Exceptionalism Again: The Bush Administration, the 'Global War on Terror' and Human Rights." *Law and History Review* 26(3): 707–725.

Ford, J.D, Zavaleta-Cortijo, C., Ainembabazi, T., Anza-Ramirez, C., Arotoma-Rojas, I., Bezerra, J., et al. 2022. "Interactions between Climate and COVID-19." *The Lancet. Planetary Health* 6(10): e825–833.

Friedberg, A. 2022. *Getting China Wrong*. London: Polity Press.

Ghilès, F. 2022. "War in Ukraine and the Gas Crisis Force a Rethink of EU Foreign Policy." *Notes Internacionals CIDOB* (268): 1–5.

Greer, S.L., King, E.J., Massard da Fonseca, E., and Peralta-Santos, A. 2020. "The Comparative Politics of COVID-19: The Need to Understand Government Responses." *Global Public Health* 15(9): 1413–1416.

Greer, S.L., King, E.J. Massard da Fonseca, E., and Peralta-Santos, A. 2021. "Introduction: Explaining Pandemic Response." In S.L. Greer, E.J. King, E. Massard da Fonseca, and A. Peralta-Santos (eds) *Coronavirus Politics: The Comparative Politics and Policy of COVID-19*. Ann Arbor: University of Michigan Press, pp 3–33.

Guttry, A. 2020. "Is the International Community Ready for the Next Pandemic Wave? A Legal Analysis of the Preparedness Rules Codified in Universal Instruments and of Their Impact in the Light of the COVID-19 Experience." *Global Jurist* 20(3): 20200038.

Hammond, C. 2016. "Despising the Poor." *The British Psychological Society*. https://www.bps.org.uk/psychologist/despising-poor

Helleiner, E. 2011. "Understanding the 2007–2008 Global Financial Crisis: Lessons for Scholars of International Political Economy." *Annual Review of Political Science* 14(1): 67–87.

Herman, S. 2011. *The War on Terror and the Erosion of American Democracy*. Oxford: Oxford University Press.

Hunter, W. and Power, T.J. 2019. "Bolsonaro and Brazil's Illiberal Backlash." *Journal of Democracy* 30(1): 68–82.

Idris, I.O., Omoniyi Ayeni, G., and Adebayo Adebisi, Y. 2022. "Why Many African Countries May Not Achieve the 2022 COVID-19 Vaccination Coverage Target." *Tropical Medicine and Health* 50(15): 1–3.

Jecker, N.S. 2022. "Global Sharing of COVID-19 Vaccines: A Duty of Justice, Not Charity." *Developing World Bioethics* 23(1): 5–14.

Kiely, R. 2018. *Neoliberalism and the 2008 Financial Crisis*. Cheltenham: Edward Elgar.

Koinova, M. 2017. "Beyond Statist Paradigms: Sociospatial Positionality and Diaspora Mobilization in International Relations." *International Studies Review* 19(4): 597–621.

Kumar, A. and Ayedee, N. 2021. "An Interconnection between COVID-19 and Climate Change Problem." *Journal of Statistics and Management Systems* 24(2): 281–300.

Lundgren, M., Klamberg, M., Sundström, K., and Dahlqvist, J. 2021. "Emergency Powers in Response to COVID-19: Policy Diffusion, Democracy, and Preparedness." *Nordic Journal of Human Rights* 38(4): 305–318.

May, J.R. and Daly, E. 2020. "Dignity Rights for a Pandemic." *Law, Culture and the Humanities*: 1743872120944351.

McIntosh, C. 2020. "Writing Quantum Entanglement into International Relations: Temporality, Positionality, and the Ontology of War." *Millennium: Journal of International Studies* 49(1): 162–174.

Mittelman, J.H. 2021. "Global Transitioning: Beyond the Covid-19 Pandemic." *Globalizations* 19(3): 439–449.

Moyn, S. 2017. "Beyond Liberal Internationalism." *Dissent* 64(1): 116–122.

Ndlovu-Gatsheni, S.J. 2020. "Geopolitics of Power and Knowledge in the COVID-19 Pandemic: Decolonial Reflections on a Global Crisis." *Journal of Developing Societies* 36(4): 366–389.

Nilsen, A.G. 2021. "India's Pandemic: Spectacle, Social Murder and Authoritarian Politics in a Lockdown Nation." *Globalizations* 19(3): 466–486.

Osička, J. and Černoch, F. 2022. "European Energy Politics after Ukraine: The Road Ahead." *Energy Research & Social Science* 91: 102757.

Oxfam. 2020. *Time to Care: Unpaid and Underpaid Care Work and the Global Inequality Crisis*. Oxford: Oxfam International. https://oxfamilibrary.ope nrepository.com/bitstream/handle/10546/620928/bp-time-to-care-ine quality-200120-en.pdf

Passos, A.M. and Acácio, I. 2021. "The Militarization of Responses to COVID-19 in Democratic Latin America." *Revista de Administração Pública* 55(1): 261–272.

Pleyers, G. 2020. "The Pandemic is a Battlefield. Social Movements in the COVID-19 Lockdown." *Journal of Civil Society* 16(4): 1–18.

Regilme, S.S.F. 2018a. "A Human Rights Tragedy: Strategic Localization of US Foreign Policy in Colombia." *International Relations* 32(3): 343–365.

Regilme, S.S.F. 2018b. "Does US Foreign Aid Undermine Human Rights? The 'Thaksinification' of the War on Terror Discourses and the Human Rights Crisis in Thailand, 2001 to 2006." *Human Rights Review* 19(1): 73–95.

Regilme, S.S.F. 2019a. "Constitutional Order in Oligarchic Democracies: Neoliberal Rights versus Socio-Economic Rights." *Law, Culture and the Humanities*: 14–18.

Regilme, S.S.F. 2019b. "The Decline of American Power and Donald Trump: Reflections on Human Rights, Neoliberalism, and the World Order." *Geoforum* 102: 157–166.

Regilme, S.S.F. 2020. "COVID-19: Human Dignity under Siege amidst Multiple Crises." *E-International Relations*. https://www.e-ir.info/pdf/85067

Regilme, S.S.F. 2021a. *Aid Imperium: United States Foreign Policy and Human Rights in Post-Cold War Southeast Asia*. Ann Arbor: University of Michigan Press.

Regilme, S.S.F. 2021b. "Contested Spaces of Illiberal and Authoritarian Politics: Human Rights and Democracy in Crisis." *Political Geography* 89: 102427.

Regilme, S.S.F. 2022. "United States Foreign Aid and Multilateralism Under the Trump Presidency." *New Global Studies* 17(1): 45–69.

Regilme, S.S.F. and Parisot, J. 2017. "Introduction: American Hegemony – Global Cooperation and Conflict." In J. Parisot and S.S.F. Regilme (eds) *American Hegemony and the Rise of Emerging Powers*. London: Routledge, pp 3–18.

Regilme, S.S.F. and Parisot, J. 2020. "Contested American Dominance: Global Order in an Era of Rising Powers." In S.A.H. Hosseini, J. Goodman, S.C. Motta, and B.K. Gills (eds) *The Routledge Handbook of Transformative Global Studies*. London: Routledge, pp 181–193.

Roberts, S.R. 2020. *The War on the Uyghurs: China's Internal Campaign Against a Muslim Minority*. Manchester: Manchester University Press.

Rudd, K. 2022. *The Avoidable War: The Dangers of a Catastrophic Conflict between the US and Xi Jinping's China*. New York City: Public Affairs.

Sacks, E., Yangchen, S., and Marten, R. 2021. "COVID-19, Climate Change, and Communities." *The Lancet. Planetary Health* 5(10): e663–664.

Sakai, N. 2012. "Positions and Positionalities: After Two Decades." *positions: asia critique* 20(1): 67–94.

Sanders, R. 2017. "Human Rights Abuses at the Limits of the Law: Legal Instabilities and Vulnerabilities in the 'Global War on Terror'." *Review of International Studies* 44(1): 1–22.

Shafiq, A. 2013. "The War on Terror and the Enforced Disappearances in Pakistan." *Human Rights Review* 14(4): 387–404.

Soedirgo, J. and Glas, A. 2020. "Toward Active Reflexivity: Positionality and Practice in the Production of Knowledge." *PS: Political Science & Politics* 53(3): 527–531.

Sotero, P. 2010. "Brazil's Rising Ambition in a Shifting Global Balance of Power." *Politics* 30(1): 71–81.

Steger, M.B. 2021. "The State of Globality in a (Post)-COVID World." *New Global Studies* 15(2–3): 117–143.

Theidon, K. 2020. "A Forecasted Failure: Intersectionality, COVID-19, and the Perfect Storm." *Journal of Human Rights* 19(5): 528–536.

Thomson, S. and Ip, E.C. 2020. "COVID-19 Emergency Measures and the Impending Authoritarian Pandemic." *Journal of Law and the Biosciences* 7(1): 1–33.

Warburton, E. 2022. "Indonesia in 2021." *Asian Survey* 62(1): 93–104.

Whyte, J. 2019. *The Morals of the Market: Human Rights and the Rise of Neoliberalism*. London: Verso.

Wu, A. 2022. "What a Cold War Crisis over Taiwan Could Tell Us about China-Russia Relations Today." *Bulletin of the Atomic Scientists* 78(5): 261–267.

Index

A

Advaita 13, 73–91
Afghanistan 165–166, 171–177
Africa 10, 12, 15, 81, 103–104, 116–134
aircraft carriers 4, 103, 107
albedo effect 183
All under Heaven 14, 97–98, 100–102, 107–108, 111, 237
American Enterprise Institute 146
Arab-Israeli conflict 164, 174
Arc of Freedom and Prosperity 109
Arctic Council 16–17, 181–183, 186, 188, 196–199
Argentina 139–140, 142, 146–149, 151, 153
arms race 73, 79
ASEAN–China Declaration on Conduct of Parties in the South China Sea 59
Asian Development Bank 4
Asian Infrastructure Investment Bank (AIIB) 140, 147–151
Association of South East Asian Nations (ASEAN) 52–53, 55–56, 59–60, 62, 65
AUKUS Agreement 4
Australia 4, 50, 52, 58, 63, 107, 120, 149, 160
Austria 215, 217
authoritarian capitalism 34, 236

B

Bachelet, Michelle 141, 149
Bandung Conference 121, 168–169
Bangladesh 74–75, 77, 89
Belt and Road Initiative 3, 37, 81, 127, 138–153, 194, 209, 214, 218, 239
Biden, Joseph 5, 7, 13, 49, 63, 102, 110, 119, 133, 174, 207–208, 214
billionaires 34
Bolivarian Alliance for the Peoples of Our America (ALBA) 149
Brazil 6, 81, 139, 140, 146–151, 153, 155, 234, 235, 241
Brunei 4, 13, 47, 62

C

Canada 16, 142, 182, 183, 190, 192, 194
capitalism 8, 26–41, 234, 236
Caribbean Network on China 146
Cayman Islands 147
CCTV 110, 112
Central Treaty Organization (CENTO) 76
Chile 139
Chimerica 38
China–Africa Cooperation (FOCAC) 116, 130
China Daily 116, 151
China Ocean Shipping Company Limited (COSCO) 194
Chinese Communist Party (CCP) 34, 53, 56, 101, 114, 125, 135, 141, 211, 212, 216
Chinese Dream 14, 98, 101–103, 109, 111, 112
climate change 5, 39, 182, 183, 185, 186, 193, 214, 234
Clinton, Hillary 38, 53, 62
Clinton, Bill 73
Colombia 138, 148–151, 153
Communist Party of China (CPC) 57, 64, 116, 120
constructivism 9, 27, 90
copper 139, 146
Costa Rica 148, 149
COVID-19 3, 5, 6, 8, 11, 18, 50, 63, 81, 88, 89, 103, 110, 112, 119, 126, 128, 130, 142, 145, 151, 185, 233, 235, 240
critical juncture 16, 53, 161, 162, 171, 174, 175, 233, 240
Cuba 31, 139, 148

D

Danish Defense Intelligence Service 185
Democratic Party of Japan 109
Deng Xiaoping 34, 35, 53, 103, 106, 113, 169, 180
Denmark 16, 182, 184, 217
Duque Márquez, Ivan 150
Duterte, Rodrigo 7, 55, 58, 61, 62

E

economic growth 6, 8, 13, 14, 52, 55, 64, 65, 71, 77, 85, 118, 124, 155, 194, 208, 235–238
Ecuador 139, 140, 148, 149
El Salvador 149, 153, 157
elite capture 15, 117, 121
emerging powers 6, 11, 22, 33, 48, 70, 234
Enhanced Defense Cooperation Agreement 57
European Union (EU) 79, 206, 213

F

fifth generation (5G) 17, 207
Financial crisis 5, 20, 38, 48, 144, 146, 147, 233, 240
Finland 16, 182–183, 190, 196
fisheries 190, 191, 193
Five Principles of Peaceful Coexistence 168–171
Forum of China–Africa Cooperation (FOCAC) 116, 130, 131, 134
France 57, 58, 79, 213, 215, 216, 219, 235

G

Gandhi, Mahatma 76, 77, 83, 84
gas 162, 185, 190–192
geographic space 8, 11, 12, 17, 47, 238
Germany 27, 58, 210, 213, 215, 216, 235
global IR 9, 10, 13, 19, 73, 74, 82–90, 239
Global South 5, 8, 11, 12, 22, 37, 119, 123, 126, 127, 133, 152, 167, 170, 171, 174, 238
Greenland 183, 190, 192
Guam 4, 31
Guanxi 15, 54, 123, 125, 131
Gulf War 107, 165

H

Han Dynasty 99, 104
Harvey, David 32
Hawaii 31
Health Silk Road 145
hedging 48, 49, 61, 62, 65
hegemony 5, 7, 11, 13, 23, 33, 37, 48, 50, 60, 63, 65, 77, 89, 102, 144, 163, 164, 168, 169, 172, 173
historical institutionalism 163
Hong Kong 35, 39, 103, 105, 110, 112, 127, 128, 146, 211
Horizon Scanning 183, 188, 189, 197
Huawei 17, 39, 150, 207–219
human rights 5, 8, 38, 39, 103, 112, 119, 124, 128, 196, 211, 212, 214, 219, 235, 236
Hungary 215, 217
hydrocarbon 191

I

Iceland 16, 182, 184, 196, 198
India 6, 11, 13, 48, 68, 73–91, 140, 143, 160, 168, 175, 234, 235, 239, 242

Indian Ocean 48, 74, 79, 88, 108
Indonesia 4, 13, 35, 47, 50, 51, 58, 59, 62, 63, 140, 168, 235
Indo-Pacific 6, 11, 14, 18, 50, 81, 98, 108, 109, 112, 172, 174, 176, 219, 235
Iraq 5, 107, 161, 162, 165, 166
Israel 162, 164, 166, 174
Italy 215, 217, 234, 235

J

Japan 4, 7, 31, 36, 50–52, 58, 59, 61, 63, 79, 102, 104, 105, 109, 149, 157, 160, 206

K

Kashmir 73, 77, 78, 80, 81, 84

L

Latin America 138–160
liberalism 9, 27, 32, 33, 49, 90, 207

M

Malaysia 7, 13, 35, 47, 50, 51, 59, 62, 104
Mao Zedong 34
Marxism 26
Mexico 39, 146–152
Middle East 160–180
Middle Kingdom 97–99, 104, 105, 111
militarization 7, 13, 15, 47–65, 98, 237–239
minerals 191, 192
Monroe Doctrine 140

N

National People's Congress (China) 36
navy ships 4
Near-Arctic State 16, 182, 185, 190
Nehru, Jawaharlal 75, 76, 84
network-building 15, 117, 123, 125, 127, 130, 134
neutrality 74, 75, 81, 83
New Neighborhood Policy 174
New Zealand 63
newly industrialized countries (NICs) 36
nonalignment 75, 76
North Atlantic Treaty Organization (NATO) 182, 197, 206, 212, 215, 218, 219, 239
Northern Sea Route 194, 198
Norway 16, 182, 183, 191, 196

O

Obama, Barack 39, 59, 108, 109, 114, 132, 133, 173, 174
oil 16, 51, 59, 66, 87, 162, 166, 190–194
One-China policy 139, 149

P

Pakistan 14, 73, 74, 76–90, 143, 161, 173
party-to-party diplomacy 15, 118–124, 238–239

INDEX

path dependence 16, 161–171, 238
Peking University 116
People's Liberation Army 53, 64, 211
Philippines, the 7, 13, 31, 47, 50, 51, 55, 57–64
Piñera, Sebastian 141, 149
Polar Silk Road 183, 186, 194, 196
polarization 5, 8, 63
Pompeo, Mike 110, 150
Puerto Rico 31

Q

Qing Empire 99
Quadrilateral Security Dialogue 81, 160

R

rare earths 4
realism 9, 13, 27, 49, 73, 82, 84, 88–90
relational approach 15, 117
rivalry 3, 7, 9–17, 26, 37–38, 41, 50, 60, 61, 73, 75, 79, 88, 90, 138, 139, 150, 153, 160, 161, 177, 182, 207, 209, 215, 217, 236–240
Rosenberg, Justin 26, 27
Russia 4, 6, 11, 16, 28, 34, 63, 65, 73, 79, 81, 82, 87, 99, 109, 133, 161, 175, 182, 183, 191, 192, 194, 196–198, 213, 218

S

Shanghai Cooperation Organization 173
Singapore 4, 7, 35, 47, 51, 53, 63, 175
social capital 15, 17, 117
South Asia 13, 14, 73–91, 161, 172, 239
South Asian Association for Regional Organization (SAARC) 77
South China Sea 47–72, 98, 206, 211, 237–239
South Korea 4, 7, 36, 50, 59, 63, 109
Southeast Asia 47–72, 11, 13, 91, 104, 108, 109, 238, 239
South-East Asia Treaty Organization (SEATO) 76
Soviet Union 38, 75, 76, 121, 172, 206–209
soybeans 139
spatialization 9, 12, 13, 17
strategic partner 7, 17, 58, 59, 61, 134, 143, 206, 218
submarines 4, 107
Sweden 16, 182, 183, 215, 216

T

Taiwan 4, 7, 11, 13, 35, 47, 51, 54, 58. 63, 64, 103–107, 109, 110, 112, 127, 139, 149, 168, 170, 206, 211
Taliban 73, 77, 79, 81, 87, 165, 173–176
Thailand 7, 11
Tianxia 14, 97, 98–102, 111, 237
Tibet 54, 76, 168, 170
Trans-Pacific Partnership (TPP) 108, 173
Trotsky 28–32
Trump, Donald 5, 39, 62, 103, 108, 117, 126, 133, 139, 174, 175, 207, 210, 212, 213, 219

U

Ukraine 7, 49, 58, 63, 65, 79, 81, 87, 133, 176, 182, 219, 233, 235
uneven and combined development (U&CD) 26–46, 237
United Front Work Department (UFWD) 120
United Kingdom 79
United Nations Convention on Law of the Sea (UNCLOS) 55, 58
Uruguay 139, 148, 149
Uyghur 39, 170, 171, 174, 211, 234

V

Venezuela 39, 140, 147–149
Virgin Islands 146

W

Wang Yi 90, 110, 142
War on Terror 5, 38, 233
White House 14, 63, 208, 212, 218
working class 28, 33–35, 38, 40
World Bank 3, 4, 5, 37, 77, 124, 144
World Economic Forum 103, 192

X

Xi Jinping 13, 15, 34, 36, 48, 51–56, 60, 98, 101, 111, 118–120, 123, 145, 170, 185, 211
Xinjiang 37, 38, 103, 110, 112, 145, 170–175, 234

Y

Yuan Dynasty 99

Z

Zhongguo 98, 99, 110, 111

www.ingramcontent.com/pod-product-compliance
Lightning Source LLC
Chambersburg PA
CBHW051535020426
42333CB00016B/1939